# DIALECTICAL ANATOMY OF THE EUCHARIST

# DIALECTICAL ANATOMY OF THE EUCHARIST

## An Étude in Phenomenology

*Donald Wallenfang, OCDS*

FOREWORD BY *Jean-Luc Marion*

CASCADE *Books* • Eugene, Oregon

DIALECTICAL ANATOMY OF THE EUCHARIST
An Étude in Phenomenology



Cascade Books
An Imprint of Wipf and Stock Publishers
199 W. 8th Ave., Suite 3
Eugene, OR 97401

www.wipfandstock.com

PAPERBACK ISBN: 978-1-4982-9339-6
HARDCOVER ISBN: 978-1-4982-9341-9
EBOOK ISBN: 978-1-4982-9340-2

*Cataloguing-in-Publication data:*

Names: Wallenfang, Donald, author. | Marion, Jean-Luc, 1946–, foreword.

Title: Dialectical anatomy of the Eucharist : an étude in phenomenology / Donald Wallenfang ; foreword by Jean-Luc Marion.

Description: Eugene, OR : Cascade Books, 2017 | Includes bibliographical references and index.

Identifiers: ISBN 978-1-4982-9339-6 (paperback) | ISBN 978-1-4982-9341-9 (hardcover) | ISBN 978-1-4982-9340-2 (ebook)

Subjects: LCSH: Sacraments—Catholic Church. | Phenomenology.

Classification: BX2200 .W35 2017 (print) | BX2200 .W35 (ebook)

Manufactured in the U.S.A. MAY 22, 2017

To Megan Joanna Wallenfang

"How beautiful is your love,
my sister, my bride . . .
Such is my lover, and such my friend!"
Song of Songs 4:10, 5:16b (NABRE)

And to Ellen Agnes, Aubin Augustine, Tobias Xavier,
Callum Ignatius, Simeon Irenaeus, and Oliver Isidore

"Certainly children are a gift from the LORD,
the fruit of the womb, a reward.
Like arrows in the hand of a warrior
are the children born in one's youth.
Blessed is the man who has filled his quiver with them."
Psalm 127:3–5a (NABRE)

That which was from the beginning, which we have heard, which we have seen with our eyes, which we have looked upon and touched with our hands, concerning the word of life—the life was made manifest, and we saw it, and testify to it, and proclaim to you the eternal life which was with the Father and was made manifest to us—that which we have seen and heard we proclaim also to you, so that you may have fellowship with us; and our fellowship is with the Father and with his Son Jesus Christ. And we are writing this that our joy may be complete.

—1 JOHN 1:1–4 (RSV)

# Contents

# Acknowledgments

It is a difficult yet necessary task to name all those friends who helped make this book a reality. I am overwhelmed with gratitude at the host of teachers, colleagues, and collaborators who have had a part in forming my soul and have inspired me to write such a book. For all those named and left unnamed, how can I ever thank you enough for your influence and fellowship?

First, I thank my biological mother for loving me to birth and through the process of adoption. Though I have not met you since I departed from your trembling arms in that hospital room years ago, I hope our paths will cross along the threshold of eternity. To John and Linda Wallenfang, my adoptive parents who loved me through my good days and bad, may this book be a token of joy from this side of forever. To Michael Wallenfang, my lone sibling and faithful brother, may we continue to "entertain angels" as responsible husbands, fathers, and followers of Christ. To Jim, Julie, and Natalie Nelson, thank you for welcoming me as son and brother and for your steadfast companionship on the journey of life. To the Muldoons, thank you for your constant support year in and year out, and Jim, may this book be the beginning of a sure response to your trainer's battle cry to me years ago: "Give 'em hell, Donald!" My hope is that the following pages may serve as the transcendent fruit of many miles run and many weights lifted. To the Sundarams, thank you for your friendship, incessant intellectual engagement, and harmonious hospitality. To the Higman Park community of Benton Harbor, Michigan, thank you for being a wonderful place to grow up. To the Lake Michigan Catholic community of St. Joseph, Michigan, thank you for sharpening my intellect and discipleship from kindergarten onward. To Niles Road Community Church (now Road to Life Church), thank you for being a haven of faith and the study of Scripture during my final years of secondary school.

To the learning community of Albion College, Michigan, thank you for leading me to the summit of Victory Hill and beyond. To the learning community of Western Michigan University, thank you for teaching me how to "sharpen my ax" and to sing through the music. To the parish communities of St. Augustine Cathedral in Kalamazoo, Michigan (1999–2001), St. Joseph Catholic Church in St. Joseph, Michigan (2001–3), St. Peter the Fisherman Catholic Church in Two Rivers, Wisconsin (2004–6), and Holy Spirit Catholic Community in Naperville, Illinois (2006–10), thank you for inviting me into ministry and for teaching me theological lessons that are only possible to learn through experience. A special thank you to Dick Bennett for being a great cheerleader, supporter, and visionary for mission-driven ministry and for affirming the complementarity between pastoral ministry and academic studies in theology. To the teens and young adults with whom I had the privilege of ministering, especially in LifeTeen, The Wharf, The Edge, Afterburn, Koinonia, and Dry Bones, you taught me more than you'll ever know and you all remain in my prayers. To Jim Morris, thank you for your pastoral guidance over the years and for the courage to risk new ideas in ministry. To Jake and Tina Wagner and family, thank you for your constant friendship, encouragement and love. To the theology faculty and staff at St. Norbert College in De Pere, Wisconsin, thank you for welcoming me into your outstanding MA program in theology and for quenching my thirst for theological investigation, while at the same time making that thirst grow stronger. In particular, thank you to Howard Ebert, Tom Reynolds, Tom Bolin, Paul Wadell, Darin Davis, and John Bostwick.

To the theology faculty, staff, and fellow students at Loyola University Chicago, thank you for moments of intellectual sparring, for times of theological breakthrough, and for entrusting me with the legacy of Jesuit spirituality and education. *Ad majorem Dei gloriam*. In particular, thank you to John McCarthy, Mark Bosco, Dennis Martin, Bob DiVito, Mark McIntosh, Catherine Wolf, and Marianne Wolfe. Mark B., thank you for introducing me to Louis-Marie Chauvet and the fruitful intersection of pastoral ministry and theology. Dennis, thank you for taking me under your wing and keeping me close to the lives of the saints. Bob, thank you for your vote of confidence in me at the eleventh hour, taking a risk in admitting me—a nobody from nowhere—into the doctoral program at Loyola. Mark M., thank you for raking me over the coals with blue books and gobs of reading in your History of Christian Theology class. It undoubtedly was the "Organic Chemistry" course of the program. Catherine and Marianne, thank you for putting up with my shenanigans, precociousness, and suitcase-on-wheels full of books. I will cherish the support, generosity, and wisdom of the faculty and staff at Loyola University Chicago for all my days. In particular, to John McCarthy, thank you for your invaluable guidance through my coursework and dissertation project. Your mentorship and countless hours of conversation have formed my hermeneutical sensibilities tremendously. May my work contribute to the legacy of the "Chicago School"—that astute hermeneutical tradition of Mircea Eliade, Paul Tillich, Paul Ricoeur, David Tracy, Jean-Luc Marion, yourself, and others.

To the University of Chicago, thank you for the opportunity to study with today's Master of phenomenology, Jean-Luc Marion. To Jean-Luc, thank you for taking such a beginner under your tutelage and putting up with my lists of questions during office hours. You have been for me a beacon of intellectual life and have set forth a most convincing rational assurance for belief. To Judy Lawrence, thank you for your wisdom and for helping me stay in touch with the Master. To David Tracy, thank you for teaching me to be on the lookout always for dialectical relationships, specificity in method, and truth as revealed through the play of conversation. To John Cavadini, thank you for your undying encouragement in my vocation as a college professor and as a theologian. May you continue to model the spirituality of St. Joseph through the way you mentor young scholars and pursue truth with passion. To the learning community of Walsh University, thank you for welcoming me to teach, to write, and to serve within such a wonderful context imbued with the mission of the Brothers of Christian Instruction: "to make Jesus Christ known and loved." *Sed Deus dat incrementum*. Colleagues, students, and acquaintances are too numerous to name, but the following deserve special mention: Richard and Terie Jusseaume—your love and generosity cannot be outdone, Laurence Bove, Doug Palmer, Dave Baxter, Chris Petrosino, Ute Lahaie, Tom Cebula, Anselm Zupka, Walter Moss, Patrick Manning, Chad Gerber, Chris Seeman, Andrew Kim, Joe Torma, John Spitzer, John Trapani, Brad Beach, Leslie Whetstine, Joe Vincenzo, Dan Suvak, Heidi Beke-Harrigan, Frank McKnight, Dan Rogich, Amber Mueser Vaught, Steve Dyer, Glenn Siniscalchi, Joe Surmitis, Benson Okpara, and Debbie Phillips. A special thank you to all of the students involved in my seminars on the work of Marion, Stein, and Levinas: Matt Humerickhouse, Samantha VanAtta, Dominic Colucy, Jen Harig, A. J. Hoy, Zach Laughlin, Brenton Kiser, and Christina Kustec. Thank you to all of my students, who are too many to name.

Thank you to the additional parish communities who have welcomed and nurtured my family over the years, in addition to those mentioned above: Ss. John & Bernard Catholic Church in Benton Harbor, Michigan; St. Teresa of Avila Catholic Church in Chicago, Illinois; St. Anthony/All Saints Catholic Church in Canton, Ohio; and Pastor Leo Wehrlin and Little Flower Catholic Church in North Canton, Ohio. Special thanks to the Catechesis of the Good Shepherd community, which remains a model for evangelization, catechesis and contemplation, attuned to the religious potential of the child.

To the Order of Secular Discalced Carmelites, Community of the Holy Family (Akron/Cleveland), thank you for welcoming my family and me into the fold of contemplative prayer and the charism of Carmel. We have found a new home in you, in which to live and to die. Thank you to the following popes, cardinals, and bishops who have provided much spiritual guidance over the years: John Paul II, Benedict XVI, Francis, Donald Wuerl, Allen Vigneron, Francis George, Charles Chaput, Francis Arinze, Robert Barron, George Murry, David Zubik, James Murray, William Lori, Seán O'Malley, Justin Rigali, Theodore McCarrick, Timothy Dolan, and Peter Sartain.

As this book emerged from its long-suffering incubation period—no less than five years—following the composition of my dissertation, "Trilectic of Testimony: A Phenomenological Construal of the Eucharist as Manifestation-Proclamation-Attestation" (2011), once again I thank the members of my dissertation committee: John P. McCarthy, Mark Bosco, and Jean-Luc Marion. Their guidance helped these ideas rise off the ground and none of this work would have come together apart from their remarkable insights and ongoing evaluation and critique. Over the past few years, several other scholars have had direct and indirect influence on the evolution of the manuscript, especially Merold Westphal, Crina Gschwandtner, Cyril O'Regan, and Stephen Lewis. In addition, I thank the many wonderful scholars involved in the March 2015 conference at King's University College in London, Ontario, "Breached Horizons: The Work of Jean-Luc Marion," in particular: Antonio Calcagno, Stephen Lofts, Jeffrey Kosky, Ryan Coyne, Shane Mackinlay, Stephanie Rumpza, Kevin Hart, Jennifer Rosato, Claudio Tarditi, Peter Joseph Fritz, Kadir Filiz, Cassandra Falke, Carole Baker, and Levi Checketts. As all scholars know, oftentimes the best part of an academic conference is the table fellowship—in this case, upon the conclusion of the conference at the Sakata Bar & Grill, surrounded by food, laughter, and intellectual life.

On the Levinas side of the coin, I thank the many tremendous scholars of the North American Levinas Society and the Société Internationale de Recherche Emmanuel Levinas, most especially: Georges and Simone (Levinas) Hansel, David and Joëlle Hansel, Sandor Goodhart, Sol Neely, Erik Garrett, Katherine Kirby, Jonathan Weidenbaum, David Seltzer, Ann Astell, Dorothy Chang, Abigail Doukhan, Timothy J. Golden, Leila Shooshani, Jennifer Wang, Rebecca Nicholson-Weir, Jim Hatley, Brian Bergen-Aurand, Drew Dalton, Nathan Nun, J. Aaron Simmons, David Banach, Luis Rubén Díaz Cepeda, Cristina Bucur, Merridawn Duckler, Octavian Gabor, Yves Sobel, Hugh Miller, Leah Kalmanson, Roger Burggraeve, Monica Osborne, Claire Katz, Robert Bernasconi, Adriaan Peperzak, Lisa Guenther, Steven

Shankman, Jae-Seong Lee, Alphonso Lingis, Hanoch Ben-Pazi, Jojo Joseph, and Paula Schwebel.

Thank you to my friends and colleagues at Wipf and Stock, especially Charlie Collier, Conor Cunningham, Eric Austin Lee, Matt Wimer, Jacob Martin, Chris Graham, Brian Palmer, and Heather Carraher. Thank you, again, for welcoming my book for publication with Cascade Books and for your expert skills in honing the book to its present form. To the seven outside readers involved in giving feedback on the text, most of whom are anonymous, thank you for your careful and generous engagement with the text. Thank you especially to Conor Sweeney for your very close reading and encouraging remarks.

Thank you to the following publishers for granting permission to reprint excerpts from following texts:

> Some material from chapter 1 appeared previously as "Figures and Forms of Ultimacy: Manifestation and Proclamation as Paradigms of the Sacred," *The International Journal of Religion in Spirituality and Society* 1:3 (2011) 109–14.
>
> Some material from chapter 2 appeared previously as "Sacramental Givenness: The Notion of Givenness and its Import for Interpreting the Phenomenality of the Eucharist," *Philosophy and Theology* 22:1–2 (2011) 131–54, and as "Aperture of Absence: Jean-Luc Marion on the God Who 'Is Not,'" in *Models of God and Alternative Ultimate Realities*, edited by Jeanine Diller and Asa Kasher (Dordrecht: Springer, 2013) 861–73.

Finally, with greatest love and gratitude I thank my wife, Megan Joanna, and our six children: Ellen Agnes, Aubin Augustine, Tobias Xavier, Callum Ignatius, Simeon Irenaeus, and Oliver Isidore. You have breathed life into every word spoken and unspoken of this text and witness to the abundant fruits of divine love incarnate. I love you!

# Ouverture

Ce qui rend si originale et innovatrice l'étude de Donald Wallenfang tient à la conjonction entre sa méthode, la phénoménologie, et son intention, l'Eucharistie. J'avais moi-même tenté une première approche dans ce style en 1982, dans *Dieu sans l'être.* Mais à l'époque, outre que je ne disposais pas encore d'une pratique suffisante de la phénoménologie dans son ensemble, j'avais centré mon effort sur une question d'importance certes, mais trop partielle—la question de la présence réelle. Il ne s'agissait donc pas de l'entreprise, autrement raisonnée et ambitieuse, que le lecteur découvrira ici: considérer en fait toute la sacramentalité dans l'une de ses expressions les plus décisives, avec le baptême, l'eucharistie, du point de vue de sa phénoménalité. Car enfin tout sacrement, signe visible d'une réalité invisible comme le définit exactement la théologie classique, constitue un cas—particulier, paradoxal sans doute, étrange si l'on veut—un cas indiscutable de manifestation et de visibilité, la visibilité de l'invisible. En comprendre la phénoménalité n'a donc rien d'optionnel, et la théologie, surtout la théologie entée sur sa pragmatique et sa performance liturgique, ne peut pas se dispenser d'en appeler à toutes les ressources de la rationalité pour y discerner la correcte articulation du visible et de l'invisible. Nous avons depuis tenté de progresser dans cette direction,[1] mais Donald Wallenfang fait ici un pas décisif en concentrant tout son effort sur la seule phénoménalité de l'Eucharistie et en demandant: dans *cette* croisée du visible, comment les espèces consacrées manifestent-elles l'invisible présence du Christ ressuscité?

Dans une étude très rigoureusement construite, précise, informée et élégante, Donald Wallenfang, ayant, au chapitre 1, construit la question (c'est-à-dire établi la légitimité de conjoindre ainsi la théologie de l'Eucharistie avec la ou les méthodes de la phénoménologie), suit trois voix différentes, mais en principes non exclusives les unes des autres. D'abord

1. Et d'abord demandant, "Qu'attend la théologie de la phénoménologie?," in *Nous avons vu sa gloire: Pour une phénoménologie du Credo*, ed. Nicolas Bauquet, Xavier d'Arodes de Peyriargue, Paul Gilbert (Brussels: Lessius, 2012) (voir n. 143).

la voie de la manifestation (chapitre 2), qui reprend nos concepts fondamentaux: donation, saturation, icône. Ici la manifestation paradoxale de la *res* dans le *sacramentum* se fait, icôniquement, à partir de la présence eucharistique elle-même, en direction (centrifuge) du croyant priant (adoration eucharistique, dans le style catholique). L'adoration joue ici le rôle de la réception du don par l'adonné, que précède et provoque la manifestation à partir d'elle-même du don.

Les deux étapes suivantes (chapitre 3) obéïssent à une démarche inversées. L'approche de Ricoeur se fait selon la logique de la vérité comme ce dont témoigne le sujet humain, d'un témoignage actif parce qu'il met en oeuvre le travail herméneutique. L'approche de Lévinas se fait, elle selon la voix qui ne montre pas, et manifeste même en ne montrant rien à voir, mais faisant *entendre* la gloire. Plus particulièrement, en distribuant des traces de l'infini, sous la figure transférée du visage qui, lui non plus, ne montre rien, mais se signale en ce qu'il parle silencieusement. Le lecteur ne manquera pas de remarquer que la mise en ligne des ces trois auteurs repose sur une ambiguïté, voire masque une différence essentielle: seul le premier (Marion) s'attaque à l'Eucharistie au sens strict, puisque ni Lévinas (juif), ni Ricoeur (évangélique) n'admettent ni donc ne font l'épreuve et l'expérience de la *res* eucharistique (la présence en personne du Réssuscité), quoi qu'ils puissent éventuellement et à des degrés différents en considérer le *sacramentum* (le texte et le visage, sinon le pain et le vin). C'est pourquoi les deux dernières démarches s'articulent à partir de celui qui en parle (le témoin et l'interprète), de manière centripète, et non de ce qui se manifeste, l'icône eucharistique, de manière centrifuge.

Telle nous semble la signification, au moins tacite, du rebondissement de la seconde partie du travail (chapitres 4–6): il reste en effet, en combinant, autant que faire se peut, les trois itinéraires déjà repérés (chapitre 4), à trouver le lieu et le style propres de l'Eucharistie. C'est ici que Donald Wallenfang atteint le meilleur de son effort, en proposant un ensemble de concepts dont la conjonction lui est, à tout le moins, propre. En particulier, apparaissent décisifs les deux mouvements de reprise du phénomène eucharistique selon d'abord ce que nous nommons le phénomène érotique, ensuite selon la poétique de la réponse (en fait le discours de louange). Et c'est précisément cette double repris qui permet, ce que nous n'aurions pas osé tenter, de rapprocher la manifestation (phénoménologie) de la vérité (théorétique, sinon métaphysique). Ainsi retrouve-t-on la question initiale: lorsque l'on caractérise le sacrement de l'eucharistie par la *présence réelle*, qu'entend-on par *présence* et par *chose* (*res, réalité*)? On ne saurait, bien entendu, penser la chose (la grâce du don du Christ) comme la présence (*parousia*), où un étant subsistant (*ousia* comme *substantia*) s'obstinerait à persévérer dans son être (*conatus*). Comment donc penser une présence qui se prolonge sur le mode d'un don, au lieu de s'imposer sur le mode d'une possession (par soi)? Il faudrait penser cette endurance sur le mode d'un don, de la fidélité d'un don sans cesse donné et redonné, de pardon en pardon; le don ainsi redoublé sans fin, comme le pardon re-donné soixante dix sept fois sept fois, ne peut se concevoir que dans le temps eschatologique, le temps donné à partir de la fin, le temps de la fidélité du don donné de toute éternité, avant le commencement du don. C'est peut-être vers cela que la magnifique étude qui suit conduira le lecteur, maintenant ou plus tard.

Jean-Luc Marion
de l'Académie française
Professeur à l'université de Chicago

# Foreword

WHAT MAKES DONALD WALLENFANG'S study so original and innovative lies in the conjunction between its method, phenomenology, and its intention, the Eucharist. I myself had attempted an initial approach in this style back in 1982, in *Dieu sans l'être* (*God without Being*). But at that time, besides the fact that I had not yet gained sufficient practice in phenomenology in its fullness, I had centered my effort on a question that was indeed of importance, but too partial: the question of the real presence. Thus, despite being reasoned and ambitious, it didn't have to do with what the reader will discover here: consideration of the whole of sacramentality in one of its most decisive expressions—alongside baptism, the Eucharist—from the point of view of its phenomenality. For in the end every sacrament—as defined by classic theology, the visible sign of an invisible reality—constitutes a case (particular, probably paradoxical, strange if you like) that is unquestionably one of manifestation and of visibility, the visibility of the invisible. Understanding its phenomenality is therefore in no way optional, and theology, especially theology centered on its liturgical pragmatics and performance, must call on all of rationality's resources when seeking to discern in the sacrament the correct connection between the visible and the invisible. I have subsequently tried to make progress in this direction,[1] but Donald Wallenfang here takes a decisive step by concentrating all his effort on the phenomenality of the Eucharist, and by asking: in *this* crossing of the visible, how does the consecrated species manifest the invisible presence of the resurrected Christ?

In a very rigorously constructed, precise, informed and elegant study, Donald Wallenfang, having in the first chapter constructed the question (that is to say, having established the legitimacy of conjoining the theology

1. By asking first of all, "Qu'attend la théologie de la phénoménologie?," in *Nous avons vu sa gloire: Pour une phénoménologie du Credo*, ed. Nicolas Bauquet, Xavier d'Arodes de Peyriargue, and Paul Gilbert (Brussels: Lessius, 2012) (see note 143).

of the Eucharist with the method or methods of phenomenology), follows three paths that are different but in principle nonexclusive of one another. First, the path of manifestation (chapter 2), which takes up my fundamental concepts: givenness, saturation, icon. Here the paradoxical manifestation of the *res* in the *sacramentum* happens on the basis of the eucharistic presence itself, in the (centrifugal) direction of the praying believer (eucharistic adoration in the Catholic style). Here adoration plays the role of the reception of the gift by the gifted (*l'adonné*), which the manifestation, on the basis of itself, of the gift, precedes and provokes.

The two following stages (chapter 3) pursue an opposite way of reasoning. Ricoeur's approach takes place according to the logic of the truth as that which the human subject testifies to, with an active testimony because he puts the hermeneutic work into operation. The approach of Levinas takes place according to the voice that does not *show*, and manifests even by showing nothing to see, instead only making glory *heard*; or more precisely, by distributing traces of the infinite, under the transferred figure of the face which, likewise, shows nothing, but signals itself by speaking silently. The reader will not fail to note that the lining up of these three authors rests on an ambiguity, or even masks an essential difference between them: only the first (Marion) tackles the Eucharist in the strict sense, since neither Levinas (a Jew) nor Ricoeur (an Evangelical) accepts and therefore tests and experiences the eucharistic *res* (the in-person presence of the Resurrected One), although they might, to different degrees, consider the Eucharist as *sacramentum* (the text and the face, if not the bread and the wine). This is why the latter two approaches are articulated on the basis of the one who speaks (the witness and the interpreter), in a centripetal manner, and not on the basis of that which manifests itself, the eucharistic icon, in a centrifugal manner.

This seems to me to be the at least tacit meaning of the new development in the second part of the book (chapters 4–6): after combining as much as possible the three itineraries already presented (chapter 4), we nevertheless still need to find the Eucharist's proper site and style. This is where Donald Wallenfang achieves the promise of his effort, proposing a set of concepts whose conjunction is decidedly his own. In particular, there is a decisiveness to the two movements in which he takes up the eucharistic phenomenon first according to what I have named the erotic phenomenon, and then according to the poetics of response (in fact, the discourse of praise). And it is precisely this double approach that allows a bringing together—something that I myself would not have dared to attempt—of (phenomenological) manifestation with (theoretical, if not metaphysical) truth. Thus we return to the initial question: when we characterize the sacrament of the Eucharist by *real presence*, what do we mean by the words *presence* and *thing* (*res, reality*)? We of course cannot conceive the thing (the grace of the gift of Christ) as the presence (*parousia*), where a substantive being (*ousia* as *substantia*) would persist in persevering in its own being (*conatus*). How then do we think of a presence that prolongs itself in the mode of a gift, instead of imposing itself in the mode of a possession (of itself)? It would be necessary to think this endurance in the mode of a gift, in the mode of the fidelity of a gift unceasingly given and re-given, from forgiveness to forgiveness. The gift thus endlessly repeated, like forgiveness re-given seventy times seven times, can be conceived only in eschatological time, time given on the basis of the end, the time of the fidelity of the gift given from eternity, before the beginning of the gift. Perhaps it is towards this that the magnificent study that follows will lead the reader, sooner or later.

Jean-Luc Marion
of the Académie française
Professor, The University of Chicago

[Translated by Stephen E. Lewis]

# Prelude

Upon surveying the global landscape of religion and culture today, it is difficult to find one's bearings. A rich panoply of religious traditions are coming into contact with one another like never before: Hinduism and Buddhism; Judaism, Islam, and Christianity; Shintoism, Taoism, and Confucianism; atheism, agnosticism, and many more besides.[1] Despite the crass attempts to exile religion to the margins of critical thought—whether according to ideological and political programs, or according to the false dichotomy set up between religion and science—religion is not going away anytime soon. From its Latin root, *religare* ("to bind together again"), religion is one of the defining characteristics of being human, even when one's so-called religion denounces the term and becomes antireligious. For religion refers to that which one holds to be of greatest value, most meaningful and true, even for one who self-identifies as atheist or agnostic—in a word, God/s, even if in the form of its negation, no God/s. Religion signifies the act of binding together one's perception of reality into a coherent, intelligible, and meaningful whole. It also signifies the fundamental experience of being bound to something transcendent, what Friedrich Schleiermacher called "the feeling of absolute dependence."[2] The human being is the religious being. To be human is to ask the God-question and to grapple with it. Moreover, closely related to the term religion is that of theology. From its Greek roots, *theos* ("God") and *logos* ("science, meaning, rationality"),

1. While it may seem strange to list atheism and agnosticism alongside other long-standing religious traditions, I do so nevertheless to make the point that these two growing traditions are religions in the form of the negative. Similar to the denominational term, "nondenominational," within Christianity, atheism and agnosticism could be considered religious denominations with respect to the religious traditions that they deny religiously. Atheism denies a particular concept (or concepts) of God/s, while agnosticism denies the possibility of sure knowledge of God/s. See Wardley, *Praying to a French God*, 1: "Once it seemed that 'the presence of divinities' was obvious, but now the gesture of faith makes 'no difference'; atheism is just as valid a point of departure."

2. See Schleiermacher, *Christian Faith*, 5–18.

theology pursues the question of God and everything meant by the term "God" (kataphatic) and everything not meant by it (apophatic), whether in a philosophical sense or in reference to any particular religious tradition. Human beings innately ask the question of God, and it is arguably the most decisive question we ask. Our response to this question determines what we do and why we do it. Whatever we consider ultimate inevitably will be our dominant motivation. Our confrontation with the God-question and our daily response to it define our personal and communal religion. It is the express task of theology to investigate religion and everything meant by the term God/s and its denial.

Nevertheless, two foul temptations lurk beneath the twilight of the postmodern world: nihilism and fundamentalism. Amidst the surge of the Information Age, the either/or of meaning confronts the mind shaken by vertigo. Either there is really no meaning after all (nihilism) or meaning is regarded as a frozen and static anchor for my radically vulnerable existence (fundamentalism). While nihilism gives up hope on any lasting meaning for one's personal life, for humanity or for the universe, fundamentalism contends that there is fundamentally only one meaning to be had, and it is mine. Both conclusions lend themselves to violence toward oneself and toward others because both imply destruction. On the one hand, nihilism proposes to destroy all claims to meaning—even that of the goodness of life—and on the other hand, fundamentalism opts to eradicate all other meanings—and all those associated with these other meanings—besides its own myopic point of view. Nihilism and fundamentalism taken together are an example of where extremes meet. Each implies a breakdown in communication and in respect for otherness. Each signifies a totality achieved precisely through a reduction of the whole, confusing a single aspect of reality for the whole. With respect to nihilism: yes, sometimes meaning unravels, especially in the face of those limit-situations in life in which we find ourselves helpless and overcome with . . . With respect to fundamentalism: yes, there must be a singularity to truth but perhaps not to be recognized in only one verbal or symbolic articulation of it. How to avoid the extremes of nihilism and fundamentalism? That is exactly what this book is about.

Unity and diversity, not unity or diversity. This book is all about dialectics. Not the dialectical materialism of Marx and Engels, not the dialectical idealism of Hegel, not the dialectical crisis theology of Barth, but certainly in some way related to all of the above. Instead of ending up with a reduction to one thing alone by confusing a part for the whole, it is necessary to prevent the dialectic from collapsing. Dialectic implies more than one because it suggests conversation, and conversation requires more than one to go on. Marx and Engels reduced the whole of reality to the economics of matter alone and denied the possibility of spiritual being and transcendence. Hegel reduced the whole of reality to unity alone through a sublation of diversity and otherness. In the end, Hegel leaves no room for the other and, thereby, commences a closure of conversation in which the end is just a static synthesis rather than a new dynamic beginning. Barth reduced theology to the content of divine revelation alone without taking adequate account of its rational uptake by the human subject. In his polemic with natural theology, he affirmed that God indeed speaks but meanwhile put human speech on mute. As the title of this book intimates, dialectics are necessary not only for philosophy and theology, but for every academic discipline and intellectual pursuit.

The dialectical philosophy and theology proposed in this book is inspired, above all, by Paul Ricoeur and Emmanuel Levinas. What these phenomenologists recognized was the basic structure of being and phenomena: both/and. Talmudic rationality lives according to its inherent conflict of interpretations. Both unity and diversity underpin the very coherence of the cosmos. There is a unity of existence and a diversity of existents. Unity itself implies difference and more than one, while diversity likewise alludes to a unified order of relation. To begin with the end in mind, an end that becomes a new beginning, the main point of this book is to refuse the collapse of the dialectic in every application of the term. Yes, this book is a project in phenomenology and sacramental theology, but it is more. It boldly claims that at the root of every act of destructive violence, at the root of every fundamentalism, at the root of every reductionism, at the root of every forgetfulness of mystery is a breakdown of the dialectic. Communication breakdown is a closure of the dialectic. World wars are the result of a closure of the dialectic. Eugenics and genocide are the result of a closure of the dialectic. Callused ideologies are formed by a closure of the dialectic. Ignorance is a refusal of the dialectic. On the other hand, the dialectic is the key to understanding the relationships between liberal and conservative, between male and female, between positive and negative charges of atomic particles, between body and soul, between material being and spiritual being, between God and humanity, between the three divine Persons of the triune Godhead as revealed by the *Logos* become flesh, between vision and voice, between universality and particularity, between the diversity of cultures and religious traditions around the world and the one human family. Unlike Hegel, the dialectical method proposed in this book does not include a synthesis but rather an anti-sublation that checks every attempt to reduce the other to more of the same.

So what is meant by "dialectic"? Derived from the Greek noun *dialektikos*, dialectic infers debate, conversation, and dialogue. Further derived from the Greek verbs *dialegesthai* ("to converse") and *legein* ("to speak"), dialectic indicates a unified coherence of discourse carried on by more than one conversation partner. The Greek prefix *dia-* means "through, across, consisting of . . ." Dialectic refers to the pursuit of truth through the course of conversation. This book's use of the term is influenced by the trajectory running from Plato to present-day thinkers such as Ricoeur, Levinas, Stein, Gadamer, Lonergan, Tillich, Tracy, and Chauvet. The dialectical method presented here is on the lookout at all times for hasty reductionisms and the collapse of the dialectic, that is, a breakdown of conversation. As human beings, we can do none other than communicate, even if in the form of a refusal to communicate or in the forms of violence or cold silence. Communication is the essence of our existence as interpersonal beings, and without it we die. It is the conviction of this book that without the dialectic, we die. More precisely, without the dialectic, we inevitably kill ourselves and one another. Without sustaining the dialectic, we destroy one another by tearing apart the fabric of our interpersonal relationships.

Dialectical philosophy and theology, as proposed by this book, is not another triumphalism because it does not set up a win/lose dichotomy in a zero-sum game. It is not another thought-system or totality to fuel a new totalitarianism of the happenstance victors. To the contrary, it offers a script in which the so-called losers are the true prophets and paragons of authentic personhood. David Tracy says as much in his book *The Analogical Imagination* when he writes that "the experience of the uncanny awaits us everywhere in the situation."[3] The uncanny prevents the closure of the dialectic. The dance between dialectical poles is sustained to the extent that the uncanny continues to reemerge on the scene, to speak and to manifest itself. As this book will show, dialectical logic is the logic of paradox. It is the logic of surprise and wonder. It is the logic of call and response, of crisis and responsibility. A religious phenomenon has been chosen to demonstrate this logic because it lives at the limen between ordinary and extraordinary, between natural and supernatural, between immanence and transcendence, between excess and lack. The Eucharist, as a phenomenon from the Judeo-Christian trajectory of religious experience, will serve as a case study in dialectical phenomenology. In particular, the overarching

3. Tracy, *Analogical Imagination*, 357. Similarly, see Schrijvers's account of Jean-Yves Lacoste's "phenomenology of the fool" in Schrijvers, *Introduction to Jean-Yves Lacoste*, 97–113, for example, 97: "For Lacoste, the religious fool is able, precisely because of his unsettling otherness, to make others restless (EA 214/177; 222/185). Hence, the phenomenological task of the fool is to make the liturgical transgression of the world visible to all others . . . for it is precisely such a visibility which allows the other to truly see what is hidden through the masks one likes to wear."

metaphor of sexuality will be employed to understand best the nature of the dialectic and the possibility of divine love and redemption. Examining the truth and meaning of human sexuality will act as a translucent optic through which to view the sacramental phenomenon of the Eucharist.

What does the Eucharist have to do with sex? Everything. Similar to the terms "God" and "love," the word "sex" is one of the most ambiguous and misconstrued vocables in the English language today. Derived from the Latin noun *sexus*, itself stemming from the Latin verb *secare* ("to cut"), the word "sex" conjures up a host of connotations to the modern ear. Yet as its Latin etymology suggests, the word "sex" implies distinction and plurality. There is more than one. Certainly we are referring to the respective anatomic configurations of male and female that constitute the sine qua non natural condition for the possibility of offspring. Yet even further, the distinction and plurality connoted by the term "sex" refer to alterity—and from a human perspective, the specific alterity of individuated persons. Alterity, or otherness, is the prevenient condition for both justice and love. Even more, alterity is the preamble to fertility, for that which is generated comprises an unquestionable other in relation to those from whom it originates. As will be argued in this study, the Eucharist is a phenomenon of alterity—a phenomenon that is sacramental, embodied, interpersonal, fruitful, and indeed, sexual.

This book attempts to hold together two general areas that are not found often to be in meaningful conversation because of their specificity of language sets and conceptual constructs: (1) phenomenology and (2) sacramental theology. Phenomenology consists of a vast span of growing literature that is highly technical and oftentimes mentally nauseating. It aims at the utmost scientific precision through rigorous procedures of constant revision and clarification, like any good science would do. Similar to the various layers of Earth's crust, phenomenology contains the accretions of a philosophical tradition that has leveled the grand touché to the reductionisms of the so-called natural sciences and their perennial scorn for the *Geisteswissenshaften*, or the humanities. Serving as defense attorney for possibility, phenomenology has done its homework and has illuminated the scientific method by exposing its unwarranted presuppositions about "the real world out there." Asking questions not only about sense data, objectivity, numerical calculations and causality, phenomenology poses questions about meaning and even about the meaning of meaning. After all, are not questions about meaning those which we humans find most meaningful? Are not these questions those around which we live and breathe, around which we orient our daily lives? However, to take meaning seriously opens up an exorbitant can of worms. One quickly realizes that, of questioning and meaning, there is no end.[4]

Sacramental theology, on the other hand, sets for itself a delimited field of inquiry: the sacrament. Couched in liturgical repertoires and doctrines, sacramental theology tends to be a matter of window dressing. In particular, from a Catholic perspective on the Eucharist, what is theologically interesting to say beyond the doctrine of transubstantiation as authoritatively defined by the Ecumenical Council of Trent in the sixteenth century? Yet as Thomas insists, "The believer's act [of faith] does not terminate in the propositions, but in the realities [which they express]."[5] The task of the theologian, then, is to aid in making the doctrines of sacramental theology relevant for contemporary contexts. Doctrines must continue to be unpacked in new ways in order for them to serve their illuminating purpose. Finding ourselves within a post-Enlightenment context today, this suggests that reason must apply itself to its limits and, in the end, exhaust itself in pursuing the meaning of the sacrament. Reason must take the sacrament seriously if reason is to take itself seriously. The folly of reason lies in its pretensive premonitions and claims as to what is factual before it finishes taking stock of the facts. If reason is true to itself, it must admit that it is never finished with its speculation. As all science is ever partial and provisional, reason, too, bears the weight of ambiguity and therefore should be humbled before the infinite possibilities that escape its overbearing yet limited trajectory. Hoping against the hope of reason's self-sufficiency, the present project proposes to exercise reason fully even if running aground due to its finitude and frailty. The sacrament is a formidable phenomenon that demands the loftiest possibilities of intellectual rigor in order to explore its breadth and depth.

Yet this book is not the first time phenomenology has been applied to the topic of Catholic sacramental theology. Several studies have been conducted already in this vein. Most notably, the works of Robert Sokolowski (1934–), Louis-Marie Chauvet (1942–), Jean-Luc Marion (1946–), Jean-Yves Lacoste (1953–), and Emmanuel Falque (1963–) comprise the growing

4. See Eccl 1:18; 12:11–12: "For in much wisdom there is much sorrow; whoever increases knowledge increases grief . . . The sayings of the wise are like goads; like fixed spikes are the collected sayings given by one shepherd. As to more than these, my son, beware. Of the making of many books there is no end, and in much study there is weariness for the flesh" (NABRE).

5. Aquinas, *Summa theologiae*, IIa IIae, 1, 2. Cf. *Catechism of the Catholic Church*, 170: "We do not believe in formulas, but in those realities they express, which faith allows us to touch . . . All the same, we do approach these realities with the help of formulations of the faith which permit us to express the faith and to hand it on, to celebrate it in community, to assimilate and live on it more and more."

canon of compelling attempts at using phenomenology to understand better sacramental phenomena, especially that of the Eucharist. It is important to note that among these five scholars, only Chauvet is a theologian, properly so-called, while the rest are philosophers. Even though the intersection of philosophy and theology is the same, philosophers doing theology is not the same as theologians doing philosophy. The respective points of emphasis are different for obvious reasons. *Dialectical Anatomy of the Eucharist* is the product of a theologian doing philosophy with all the feebleness and risk this entails. While being informed by each one of the aforementioned authors, this book is influenced above all by the work of Chauvet and Marion. The dialectical structure of the analysis is inspired by that of Chauvet—for example, his pairing of terms such as objective-subjective, word-sacrament, and excess-lack. Chauvet's triumvirate of Sacrament-Scripture-Ethics especially has induced the attunement to dialectical relationships in the area of liturgy and sacraments found in this book. Along with John P. McCarthy and Mark Bosco, Marion helped supervise my dissertation work from which this book is a substantial outgrowth. McCarthy, who studied with Paul Ricoeur and David Tracy, taught me hermeneutics. Bosco taught me Chauvet. And Marion taught me Husserl, Heidegger, and, well, Marion. Before entering the thick of the argument set forth in *Dialectical Anatomy of the Eucharist*, let us say a general word about each of the above authors in order to delineate the restricted parameters of this book.

An established expert in the phenomenology of Husserl and also a Roman Catholic priest, Sokolowski has written extensively on phenomenology applied within theology.[6] One of his signature motifs is what he calls a "theology of disclosure."[7] Understood according to the primary rubric of disclosure-concealment, Sokolowski's phenomenological theology places its attention on appearances and instances of manifestation. He writes that "the theology of disclosure takes advantage of resources found in the thought of Edmund Husserl, who broke through the axioms of modernity and was not restricted by them."[8] In other words, phenomenology takes seriously the intellectual milieu of a post-Kantian world but nevertheless

6. For helpful introductions to Sokolowski's work on the whole, see Drummond and Hart, *The Truthful and the Good*, and Mansini and Hart, *Ethics and Theological Disclosures*.

7. For more on Sokolowski's theology of disclosure, see Sokolowski, *Eucharistic Presence*, 173–208; Sokolowski, *God of Faith and Reason*, 88–103; and Sokolowski's "Exploring the Identity of the Bishop through the Theology of Disclosure," in Boguslawski and Fastiggi, *Called to Holiness and Communion*, 129–45. See Lacoste's similar proclivity for categories of disclosure (*aperité/Erschlossenheit*) in Lacoste, *Experience and the Absolute*, 10–11, 40–41, 106–9.

8. Sokolowski, *Eucharistic Presence*, 181.

demonstrates how religious phenomena cannot be dismissed so casually. This quote from Sokolowski's *Eucharistic Presence* reveals the exclusively Husserlian character of the method of phenomenology he has in mind. By retrieving the power of phenomenal appearance through phenomenology, Sokolowski shows how religious phenomena, such as the sacrament, can be brought to life once again. He considers the human person as the "agent of truth" vis-à-vis the givenness of phenomena. If truth (*alétheia*) is essentially a removal of the veil of manifestation, then seeking theological truth is a process of disclosure, or unveiling.

Chauvet, also an ordained Roman Catholic priest, has applied the phenomenology of Martin Heidegger, in particular, to his exploration of liturgy and sacraments in his books *Symbol and Sacrament* and *The Sacraments*.[9] In addition to his ontological return to the question of being within phenomenology, Heidegger is known for his hermeneutical turn toward language, text and interpretation. It is this latter turn that Chauvet employs in order to expose the objectivist view of the sacrament that has dominated Catholic sacramental theology over the centuries. Chauvet proposes a post-conciliar approach to the sacrament that brings the objectivist model into conversation with the (predominantly Protestant) subjectivist model. He traces the relational dynamism between Sacrament, Scripture, and Ethics in order to account for the full phenomenality and potential of the liturgical event. Though he does not speak explicitly of a dialectical relationship between manifestation and proclamation, his intentional pairing of Sacrament and Scripture suggests as much. One of the delightful fruits of Chauvet's work is his application of the insights gained through a phenomenology of the sacraments to pastoral ministry.[10]

As a seasoned scholar on the philosophy of René Descartes, Marion has pioneered some of the most significant advances in the method of phenomenology today. From his groundbreaking study on Husserl and Heidegger, *Reduction and Givenness*, in which he proposes the new phenomenological axiom "so much reduction, so much givenness," to his systematic study of givenness, *Being Given*, Marion has developed an entirely new version of phenomenology compared with that of Husserl and Heidegger.[11] He claims to have advanced the phenomenological reduction one step further than that of his predecessors, thereby unlocking the fullness of givenness in all of

9. For helpful introductions to the work of Chauvet on the whole, see Ambrose, *The Theology of Louis-Marie Chauvet*; Bordeyne and Morrill, *Sacraments*; Willis, "Language as the Sanctuary of Being."

10. See Chauvet, *Sacraments*, 173–200.

11. For a helpful introduction to the work of Marion on the whole, especially concerning its theological applications, see Horner, *Jean-Luc Marion*.

its potential dimensions. Rather than limit givenness to the domain of the transcendental ego or its ontological foray, Marion recognizes the oftentimes saturating power of givenness over human subjectivity. Informed by the primacy of the other in the work of Emmanuel Levinas, Marion yields to the primacy of givenness in all of its force. While most of Marion's more recent work is devoted to the methodological implications of a phenomenology of givenness, at times he has turned his attention to religious phenomena as prime instances of saturation—for example, divine revelation, the icon, and the Eucharist. His most sustained analysis of the Eucharist appears in *God without Being*. Because Marion represents the canonical trajectory of phenomenology, running through Husserl and Heidegger, his work was chosen to represent the entire school of what I call a phenomenology of manifestation in *Dialectical Anatomy of the Eucharist*.

Lacoste, like Chauvet, has applied the phenomenology of Heidegger, in particular, to the sacramental phenomenon.[12] However, instead of focusing on the hermeneutical aspects of Heidegger's phenomenology (as does Chauvet), Lacoste attends to the ontological dimensions of the experience of being within liturgy. Lacoste, also a trained and ordained Roman Catholic priest, performs his phenomenology of liturgy from firsthand experience. Influenced by Heideggerian tropes such as "being-in-the-world" and "being-toward-death," Lacoste generates a Heideggerian matrix for perceiving liturgical events. For example, he coins terms such as "being-in-peace," "being-in-alliance," "being-before-God," "being-in-the-Church," and the "nocturnal non-experience" and the "non-place" of liturgy. Just as Being (*Sein*) maintains a non-aperture of concealed-ness before *Dasein*, so God maintains a non-advent of hiddenness and incomprehensibility before the liturgical subject, even if in and through sacramental advent. Implicitly influenced by, and indebted to, the work of John of the Cross (1542–91) and Dietrich Bonhoeffer (1906–45), Lacoste recognizes the hidden excess of non-phenomenality alongside every given phenomenon, especially those of liturgy. Overall, Lacoste's phenomenology operates under the aegis of manifestation with a proclivity toward understanding phenomena in terms of vision and revelation.

Finally, the most recent work to apply phenomenology within the context of liturgy, in particular eucharistic liturgy, is Emmanuel Falque's *Les*

12. For helpful introductions to the work of Lacoste on the whole, see Schrijvers, "Jean-Yves Lacoste: A Phenomenology of Liturgy"; Schrijvers, "Phenomenology, Liturgy, and Metaphysics"; Schrijvers, *Introduction to Jean-Yves Lacoste*; Bloechl, "Introduction: Eschatology, Liturgy, and the Task of Thinking," in Lacoste, *From Theology to Theological Thinking*, vii–xxviii; Wardley, *Praying to a French God*; and Gschwandtner, "The Vigil as Exemplary Liturgical Experience."

*noces de l'agneau: Essai philosophique sur le corps et l'eucharistie.*[13] As the third part of a triptych on the paschal mystery of Christ, in addition to *Passeur de Gethsémani* and *Métamorphose de la finitude*, *Les noces de l'agneau* is within the same genus as *Dialectical Anatomy of the Eucharist*. While not yet published in English translation, Falque's *Les noces de l'agneau* is a significant musing on the Eucharist through the lens of phenomenology. Concentrating on the nuptial meanings of the Lord's Supper, the title indicates the book's focus: the wedding feast of the Lamb. Meditating on the conversion of what he calls the "animality" of human, incarnate and sacramental being, Falque attempts to spell out the concrete in-the-flesh ramifications of eucharistic meaning. Having studied with Marion at the Sorbonne, Falque is attentive to the erotic phenomenality of the Eucharist as a phenomenon occurring between incarnate P/persons, human and divine. In conversation with figures such as Bernard of Clairvaux and Ignatius of Antioch, reflecting on the fact that the Catholic rite of marriage is celebrated ordinarily during the course of the Mass, Falque writes that "*'this is my conjugal body' finds its source and its accomplishment in 'this is my eucharistic body,'* even when the former (conjugality) sometimes happens, even often, without the latter (the eucharistic act). The spousal erotic not only elucidates and expresses the Sunday Eucharist, but it incorporates and reveals it as metamorphosis."[14] Just as husband and wife form a one-flesh union (Gen 2:24) in the sacramental bond of marriage, so does God initiate a covenantal union of P/persons—namely, Christ, the Bridegroom, and the Church, the Bride—through eucharistic liturgy. A veritable metamorphosis of flesh takes place through the course of a sacramental itinerary aimed at intimate spousal union with God. More recently, Falque has taken into consideration hermeneutics within his phenomenological theology in *Passer le Rubicon*. In this work, he carries out a similar comparative analysis to that of *Dialectical Anatomy of the Eucharist*, namely, a comparison of Jewish, Protestant, and Catholic hermeneutic approaches. Like *Dialectical Anatomy of the Eucharist*, he elucidates the work of Ricoeur and Levinas in comparison as a way to examine the hermeneutical aspects of religious experience, especially in approaching Scripture.[15] Falque describes Protestant hermeneutics (via Ricoeur) as "le sens du texte" ("the meaning of the text"), Jewish hermeneutics (via Levinas) as "le corps de la lettre" ("the body of the letter"), and Catholic hermeneutics (via Claudel, Chrétien, Merleau-Ponty, Falque) as "le texte du

13. For helpful introductions to Falque's work on the whole, see Hackett's "Translator's Foreword," in Falque, *God, the Flesh, and the Other*, ix–xviii; and Gilbert, "Écriture phénoménologique et méthode patristique."

14. Falque, *Les noces de l'agneau*, 229 (translation my own).

15. See Falque, *Passer le Rubicon*, 27–85.

corps" ("the text of the body").[16] Finally, later on in the work, Falque refers to the Eucharist as "le corps de la voix" ("the body of the voice").[17] Similar to Falque, *Dialectical Anatomy of the Eucharist* intuits the complementarity between Jewish, Protestant, and Catholic hermeneutics, situating these respective approaches according to the manifestation-proclamation dialectic. However, instead of reemphasizing a hermeneutic of manifestation as does Falque in the end, *Dialectical Anatomy of the Eucharist* proposes a sustained dialectic between a hermeneutic of manifestation (Catholic/Orthodox) and a hermeneutic of proclamation (Jewish/Protestant).

With all of the rich insights to be elucidated from the work of Sokolowski, Chauvet, Lacoste, and Falque, why does *Dialectical Anatomy of the Eucharist* confine itself primarily to the work of Marion as representative of the Catholic voice, especially given the fact that Marion references the other four authors virtually not at all? Moreover, it must be observed that there has not seemed to be much cross-pollination among any of these five authors. Let us recall that Sokolowski is working out of a Husserlian framework, Chauvet and Lacoste are working out of a Heideggerian framework (in different ways), and Falque, a former student of Marion, can be placed likewise within the Husserl-Heidegger framework with concentrated reference to Patristic texts. *Dialectical Anatomy of the Eucharist*, though similar in many respects to all of the above, aims at a quite different target. It is a bit more ambitious (perhaps to its detriment) in its scope. It attempts to think phenomenology beyond Husserl, Heidegger, and even Marion by putting this trajectory of givenness in conversation with the hermeneutical phenomenology of Ricoeur and Levinas. It must be admitted that the method of phenomenology did not cease to evolve with Husserl and his disciples, including Heidegger. Its toolbox has continued to grow and I argue that one can no longer conduct an adequate phenomenology today without resolute attention to the ethical turn in Levinas, let alone the hermeneutical turn in Ricoeur. In a post-Holocaust world, one never can return to a carefree phenomenology of appearances before or beyond ethics.

In anticipation, *Dialectical Anatomy of the Eucharist* offers five distinct and original propositions:

1. A new version of phenomenology: dialectical phenomenology accomplished by the dialectical reduction(s)
2. A demonstration of dialectical phenomenology as applied to the Eucharist, based on the dialectic between manifestation and proclamation

16. Ibid., 42–54 (translation my own).
17. Ibid., 83–84 (translation my own).

3. A redefinition of gift as dialectic and conversation
4. A transposition from prosaic discourse to poetic discourse in the face of the personal religious phenomenon
5. An argument proposing the truth of the Eucharist, suggesting the methodological dialectic between phenomenology and metaphysics

The first point is made in chapter 1. The second point is made in chapters 2–4. The third point is made in chapters 4–5. The fourth point is made in chapters 5–6, and the fifth point is made in chapter 6. Throughout the book, Sokolowski, Chauvet, Lacoste, and Falque will reemerge from time to time in the conversation, but the book is focused ultimately on the work of Marion, Ricoeur, and Levinas for the reasons alluded to above and which will become more evident with each passing page of the text. Not only does *Dialectical Anatomy of the Eucharist* intend to advance the phenomenological method and to augment contemporary Catholic understanding of the Eucharist, it also proposes its dialectical method as instructional for the tasks of interfaith and interreligious dialogue. By inviting three voices from three distinct confessional contexts—Levinas (Jewish), Ricoeur (Reformed Christian), and Marion (Roman Catholic)—the fruits of dialectical phenomenology are borne out along the way.

This book most likely will aggravate its elect readers due to its precarious attempt at negotiating between phenomenology and sacramental theology. For those interested in its phenomenological analyses, it may read as overly personal, poetic, and theological. For the sacramental theologians, on the other hand, the book will read more like Leviticus than the Gospels. Yet the most brilliant Christian theologians will concede that the better one understands Leviticus, the better one understands the Gospels. Moreover, these same theologians will admit that there is some rather interesting content in Leviticus. This book must be read through in its entirety to get it. Each of the chapters makes sense only in light of the others. It is a taxing read, indeed, but well worth the while. Rumination on the text is necessary. Those already conversant in the work of Levinas, Marion, and Ricoeur, as well as in theological concerns, will be the most likely candidates to read through the entire book. However, even for those not familiar with phenomenology and its plethora of accoutrements, the book offers an entrée into the genius of these respective thinkers in addition to applying their thought to the question of the Eucharist. As lively incentive, keep in mind that the climax of the book occurs in chapter 5, with chapters 1 through 4 serving as rising action, and chapter 6 providing the falling action. It is not that the Eucharist will be sexualized, for it is already the most sexual of phenomena.

Donald Lee Wallenfang, OCDS / Emmanuel Mary of the Cross
Memorial of Saint Teresa Benedicta of the Cross, Virgin & Martyr
August 9, 2016

# *chapter 1*

# The Eucharist and Phenomenology

The point of departure most often decides the point of arrival, for the target depends on the aim and the aim on the sight and the angle of the shot. The exercise of thought makes no exception to this rule; it even makes it all the more imperative, since, in this case more than any other, nobody can turn back once out of the gate or take back the shot once fired. And, for that matter, there is no second chance at a first beginning.

—JEAN-LUC MARION, *IN THE SELF'S PLACE*

HOCUS-POCUS. THIS IS HOW the postmodern world typically views the religious phenomenon of the Eucharist, and virtually all religious phenomena in general. Magic, trickery, bullshit. Yet the irony is that this phrase—hocus-pocus—is derived directly from the Latin words of consecration in Roman Catholic liturgy: *Hoc est corpus meum* ("This is my body"). Why do religious phenomena, such as the Eucharist, meet with such scorn, contempt and indifference according to the natural attitude of the public sector? Is there a way for religious phenomena to be considered seriously as to their intelligibility, plausibility and even truth? If the answer to this question is yes, then phenomenology is the method that holds the most promise for exploring religious phenomena in a serious intellectual and public manner for today. Phenomenology is the method that justifies all scientific inquiry and claims, inasmuch as all perceptible data—that is, givens—emerge from a human subject's interaction with given phenomena. Phenomenology carefully examines the most basic and fundamental processes of conscious perception and meaning-making that form the very heart of every human experience. This book aims at considering the religious phenomenon of the Eucharist according to the most stringent demands of rationality possible. It will attempt to probe the meaning and truth of the Eucharist by using the phenomenological method, especially as developed by French phenomenologists Jean-Luc Marion (1946–), Emmanuel Levinas (1906–95), and Paul Ricoeur (1913–2005). The primary question to be asked is this: How does the Eucharist say and/or give itself? Phenomenology will be called upon to best detect this "how." Ultimately this study will be situated within a Roman Catholic theological context, though significantly informed and enhanced by Jewish and Protestant theologies. Before diving into the heart of the matter, let us submit a warrant for using phenomenology within the discipline of theology.

## I. Phenomenology as a Method for Theology

Can theology be justified in employing phenomenology as a central method of investigation? The argument of the pages to follow hinges on the affirmative response to this hotly contested topic of recent debate.[1] To be in agreement with Emmanuel Falque, "in contrast to the 'liberation of philosophy by theology' (Balthasar), a 'liberation of theology by philosophy' will take place today."[2] Not only is theology justified in sequestering phenomenology from the field of philosophy alone, it is enhanced and set free by its incisive methodology. If the science of phenomenology operates according to the aperture of the exacted reduction (*epoché*), by definition one cannot predetermine that which may or may not give or say itself to human perception to the measure that the reduction is deployed effectively. The genius of the phenomenological method is that it seeks to extricate and set aside all

1. For other affirmative responses to this question, see Janicaud, *Phenomenology and the "Theological Turn"*; Marion, *Visible and the Revealed*; Lacoste, *Experience and the Absolute*; Lacoste, *La phénoménalité de Dieu*; and Lacoste, *From Theology to Theological Thinking*. On the difference between theological discourse in comparison with philosophical discourse, see Lacoste, "More Haste, Less Speed in Theology."

2. Falque, *God, the Flesh, and the Other*, 281. And further on 282: "But, in fact, the true grandeur of theology is totally different. In the act of his kenosis, God becomes the proper object of theology and makes the choice not to be satisfied in himself. He who could demonstrate anything by himself (the absolute power of theology) nevertheless leaves to be shown and revealed by another that which it does not and ought not to exhibit all alone (the conditional power of phenomenology)."

biases, pre-understandings and presuppositions (or what Husserl has called the "natural attitude") from its purgative procedure of examination.[3] Instead of beginning with so-called first principles, schemas of causality, predetermined configurations of reality, definitive laws of nature, metaphysical constructs, or frozen avatars of the transcendental ego, phenomenology proves itself to be a purely descriptive method of analysis. If this is truly the case with phenomenology, why could it not serve as a productive method for theology and the investigation of theological phenomena?

## A. Phenomenology and Religious Traditions

Some may argue that theology implies a tacit acceptance of actual divine reality at first blush. Indeed, this is a valid objection as phenomenology would demand that any predetermination of God and divine revelation be held at bay according to the exigencies of the phenomenological reduction. Phenomenology cannot begin its method with an explicit or implicit assent to the truth status of a particular content of alleged divine revelation if it is to proceed with openness and intellectual integrity in describing phenomena as they give or say themselves in the course of human experience. Rather, the phenomenologist must bracket not the question of God but only any ready-made answers to this question. It would be intellectually dishonest to bracket out any question of possibility prior to the start of exploration. All questioning must remain open just as all possibilities must remain open if

3. This being said, one must agree with Michel Henry that "as all research, phenomenology is implicated in presuppositions. But the particular presuppositions in phenomenology present a distinctive trait. In ordinary research, the presuppositions which command reasoning are chosen by thought and, as such, they can modify being . . . The distinction of presuppositions of phenomenology is that they are phenomenological, and that in a radical sense: it is a question of the appearance by which they come to speech, of pure phenomenality. It is that which must guide the analysis of phenomena in a phenomenological sense, that is to say one is to consider the manner in which they give themselves to us, the 'How' of their appearance" (*Incarnation*, 39–40, translation my own). In other words, the presuppositions (faith!) at work in phenomenology include an attention to the self-givenness of phenomena, their modes and manners of appearing, and the confidence (that is, presupposition) that phenomena do indeed appear as such. In aiming merely to describe that which gives itself, phenomenology claims to bracket the "natural attitude" that would assume a definitive totality of the state of affairs of reality prior to investigation and thereby limit the possibilities of what in fact may give itself. For more on the transition from the natural attitude to the phenomenological attitude, see Husserl, *Ideas Pertaining to a Pure Phenomenology and to a Phenomenological Philosophy: First Book* (hereafter *Ideas I*), 51–62 (§§27–32), and Lacoste's essay "The Appearing and the Irreducible," in Benson and Wirzba, *Words of Life*, 42–67.

phenomenology is to succeed in its proposal and method. As a field of study, theology bears within itself its antithesis: a-theology, that is, the possibility that its object of study does not give or say itself—in a word, atheism. Moreover, the possibility of atheism is a necessary condition for any assertion of theological faith whatsoever. What, after all, is faith if not the overcoming of doubt? Faith is precisely the risk one takes in assenting to a proposition that may not be true after all. Joseph Ratzinger has put it this way:

> No one can lay God and his Kingdom on the table before another man; even the believer cannot do it for himself . . . Both the believer and the unbeliever share, each in his own way, doubt *and* belief, if they do not hide from themselves and from the truth of their being. Neither can quite escape either doubt or belief; for the one, faith is present *against* doubt; for the other, *through* doubt and in the *form* of doubt. It is the basic pattern of man's destiny only to be allowed to find the finality of his existence in this unceasing rivalry between doubt and belief, temptation and certainty.[4]

Ratzinger correctly notes that the phenomenon of faith is operative both in the affirmative and the negative responses to a proposition. Faith is that riskful stake a person puts in a given testimony, whether for or against a proposed state of affairs. The human act of faith, for instance, is a phenomenon that cannot be bracketed out of phenomenological inquiry for the simple reason that to commence the method of phenomenological analysis in the first place, one must put faith in the very method of phenomenology! Faith turns out to be a sine qua non of asking a question insofar as asking a question is to trust implicitly that an answer may be found and that the question itself is meaningful.

To recapitulate, the field of theology does not necessarily imply a ready-made answer to the question of God. Yet theology does imply asking the question of God vis-à-vis various religious traditions and their constitutive testimonies, including the tradition that proclaims that no God as such gives and/or says Godself—or in more common parlance, the tradition of atheism that holds that "there is" (*es gibt*) no God/s. Employing phenomenology as a helpful method within theology is to allow phenomenology to serve as a hermeneutic for diverse religious traditions and the question of God. Phenomenology thus comes as a welcome method for the expanding context of religious pluralism. A method of investigation is needed for today that allows all religious traditions to be put at arm's reach—a method that levels the playing field of truth-claims and alleged instances of divine

4. Ratzinger, *Introduction to Christianity*, 46–47.

revelation. Phenomenology, as a method that claims to ask questions of universal proportion, permits so-called religious phenomena to be described while temporarily suspending the determination of the absolute truth status of such phenomena.[5] The logic and rational coherence of religious phenomena can be examined while, at the same time, postponing the adjudication (that is, judgment) of their absolute veracity. In the end, phenomenology could be described as a method of observation and listening—or, more precisely, a method of attunement—whereby the human subject intentionally attempts to recognize the most precise intuitive data of phenomena as they say or give themselves prior to perception.[6]

## B. What Is Phenomenology?

Before attempting to apply the method of phenomenology within the discipline of theology, it is necessary to define the primary steps of the method. Phenomenology is a distinct method within philosophy begun explicitly by Edmund Husserl (1859–1938) at the beginning of the twentieth century.[7] Trained as a mathematician, Husserl eventually turned his attention to logic and philosophy. His primary concern was to develop a philosophical method that would escape the vortex of relativism, or what was called in his day, "psychologism." Since the turn to subjectivity, especially as inaugurated by Descartes, philosophy and psychology commonly fell prey to relativistic conclusions. Objectivity became a distant memory of Scholastic naïveté and all that was left was an assortment of indeterminate points of view. Was it possible to make contact with objective truth in a post-Cartesian world? Husserl wondered if objectivity and universal data were still possible and he sought to prove that they were. Beginning with his *Logical Investigations*

5. Cf. Paden, *Interpreting the Sacred*, 73–74, on the possibility and plausibility of suspending judgment while investigating religious phenomena. While it is possible to suspend judgment of truth-claims in phenomenology, it is nevertheless possible to describe the phenomenality of truth, or at least its possibility.

6. See Nancy, *Listening*.

7. For a succinct introduction to the basic principles of Husserl's phenomenology, see Husserl, *The Idea of Phenomenology*. For a concise history of twentieth-century phenomenology, with emphasis on the front end of the century, see Sokolowski's essay "Phenomenology in the Last Hundred Years," in Shanley, *One Hundred Years of Philosophy*, 202–15. Regarding phenomenology's reception in the United States, Sokolowski observantly writes, "In the North American philosophical world, phenomenology has always been something like Apple Computer in the world of electronics: it enjoys a durable presence, but is restricted to a relatively small (though enthusiastic) market share in comparison with the huge numbers of those who follow the philosophical analogue of IBM and DOS, viz. analytic philosophy and its various clones."

of 1900–1901, Husserl began to develop what would come to be known as "phenomenology." Derived from the Greek words *phainómeno* ("that which appears" or "shows itself") and *logos* ("meaning, word, science"), phenomenology is the science of phenomena, or more specifically, the science of meaning, of that which gives, shows, or says itself. Phenomenology is concerned with getting "to the things themselves" as precisely as possible. It investigates how meanings or essences are given to consciousness through the interplay of intentionality and intuition. Phenomenology involves the human subject, what gives or says itself to the human subject, and the interaction between the two. Husserl would disciple many students, such as Edith Stein (1891–1942) and Martin Heidegger (1889–1976), who would take the method to new stages in its development. A host of others would continue to extend the tradition into the twenty-first century, including Emmanuel Levinas, Maurice Merleau-Ponty (1908–61), Hans-Georg Gadamer (1900–2002), Michel Henry (1922–2002), Jacques Derrida (1930–2004), Paul Ricoeur, and Jean-Luc Marion. Phenomenology has come a long way since the work of Husserl, so much so that it cannot be confined to the work of Husserl alone. In fact, I suggest that there are two distinct strands within the tradition that have developed since Husserl, according to the following genealogy:

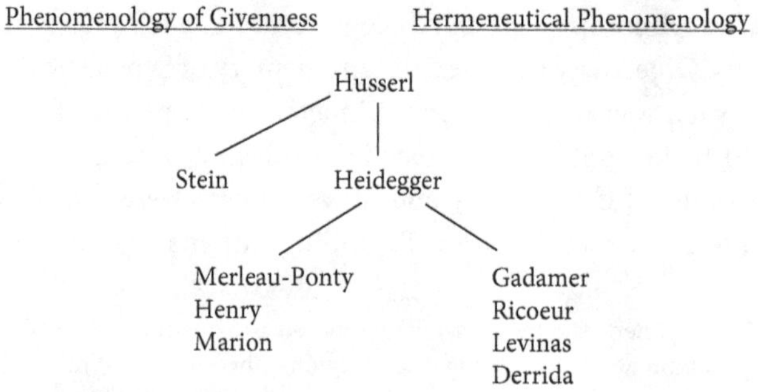


According to this diagram, the two schools of phenomenology that have evolved are (1) phenomenology of givenness and (2) hermeneutical phenomenology. Stein is placed in her own category because of her Thomistic (re)turn to metaphysics along with a phenomenology of givenness. The two schools branch off in the wake of Heidegger because he encompassed both schools in his work retrospectively, although a phenomenology of givenness tended to dominate his thinking. Phenomenology of givenness, as represented by Merleau-Ponty, Henry, and Marion, also could be called a "phenomenology of manifestation" because of how all given phenomena are interpreted according to the optic of manifestation, inherently turning to the contemplative possibilities of human experience.[8] It is a visual phenomenology. According to the optic of manifestation, phenomena give themselves to perception. Most scholars working in phenomenology could be placed in the phenomenology of givenness category, including those who have applied phenomenology to theological themes, for example, Chrétien, Henry, Lacoste, Falque, et al. Chauvet may be the exception here as one who oscillates between phenomenology of givenness and hermeneutical phenomenology. Hermeneutical phenomenology, in contrast to phenomenology of givenness, as represented by Gadamer, Ricoeur, Levinas and Derrida, also could be called a "phenomenology of proclamation" because of how all phenomena are interpreted according to the structures of proclamation, of verbal call, response and interpretation.[9] It is an aural and textual phenomenology, inherently turning to the ethical character of human experience. According to the structures of proclamation, phenomena speak themselves to perception, especially the most acute phenomenon: the call of the other. While both strands in the tradition have much in common, they are distinct enough to justify reference to their noticeable divergence. Many other names could be added to the genealogy, depending on whose work a particular scholar has concentrated his or her studies. However, the lineage depicted here attests to the general contours of the two peculiar emergent schools of phenomenology as they have evolved over the past century.

All this is to say that phenomenology, like many other methods in philosophy, is not a homogeneous method. It has as much variety as it has individual proponents. As Jean-Luc Marion once said to me, "Phenomenology is not a doctrine; it is a toolbox." To my knowledge, there is no systematic textbook of phenomenology. Rather, it is a method represented by countless texts that attempt to "do phenomenology" in one shape or another. If phenomenology is indeed a toolbox, I would suggest that every bona fide project in phenomenology contains the following three steps:

1. Perform the phenomenological reduction
2. Describe what gives or says itself in experience

8. For a systematic presentation of a phenomenology of manifestation, see Marion, *Being Given*.

9. For a somewhat systematic presentation of a phenomenology of proclamation (although it is not its nature to be systematic), in an intensified form, see Levinas's two *magnum opera*: *Totality and Infinity* and *Otherwise than Being or Beyond Essence*. For a more succinct introduction, see "Philosophy and Awakening," in Levinas, *Entre Nous*, 77–90.

3. Compare various descriptions of phenomena

Before describing each individual step of the phenomenological method, let us recall the steps of the universal scientific method in order to show how the two methods are similar and different:

1. Ask a question and form a hypothesis
2. Develop an experiment to test hypothesis
3. Perform experiment many times
4. Make observations and gather aggregate data
5. Interpret data
6. Test hypothesis in light of interpreted data and form provisional conclusion
7. Reformulate hypothesis, if necessary, and begin the process again[10]

What do the phenomenological method and the scientific method have in common? Both pursue data, that is, that which gives itself to perception. Both methods are, in this sense, scientific and aim at knowledge of data and processes involving those data. Both methods, similarly, begin with inquiry and continue with investigation. Both involve observation from an intended neutral point of view and conclude by examining interpreted data, only to begin the process all over again. Two key differences between the two methods involve the terms "hypothesis" and "experiment." For the scientific method, developing hypotheses is necessary in order to fashion better informed theories about the sensory world. Preliminary hypotheses are revised to become provisional scientific theories, ever open to revision and reformulation based on new data and new interpretations of data. Phenomenology, on the other hand, is not in the business of developing and testing hypotheses. Rather, it simply describes phenomena. It is on guard against various theses, theories and doctrines because they can obstruct its purely descriptive methodology. Moreover, the term "experiment" is not found typically within phenomenology's lexicon because it, too, implies a limitation of the conditions of possibility in which a phenomenon may give or say itself. For example, not all phenomena are measurable according to numeric graduation or even external sense observation. Phenomena such as joy, hope, love, intersubjectivity, ethical exigency, eidetic objects of abstract thought, meaning, etc., cannot be manipulated and measured in an external

10. Although the universal scientific method, since its codification with Francis Bacon (1561–1626), is formulated in a variety of ways, these seven steps refer to the general progression of the method as it is commonly understood.

laboratory of external sense observation. Yes, there is an external world of experience, but there is also an internal and interior world of consciousness that constantly abstracts from matter and the world of external objects. It is this internal world of intelligibility and deciphering upon which all meaningful external sense observation is based. In fact, it is this interior world of meaning, motivation, value—in a word, spiritual life—from which all genuine science stems. Therefore, phenomenology rightly can be called the science of science.

By giving an account of the universal structures and data of consciousness and the intrinsic structures of intersubjectivity, phenomenology reveals the foundational components upon which every scientific enterprise is built: human subjectivity and its interaction with any and all phenomena. Phenomenology, in addition to being the science of science, is the science of meaning and meaningfulness. Its concern is not so much with external phenomena of sense perception, but with internal phenomena of meaning and signification. It works to "peel back the onion" of every experience, arriving at the interior core of meaning-making within conscious perception. Let us return to the proposed three-step method of phenomenology to find out how this works:

1. Perform the phenomenological reduction
2. Describe what gives or says itself in experience
3. Compare various descriptions of phenomena

The first step of phenomenology is to perform the phenomenological reduction. Without this crucial step, the method is unable to work its "magic" and access raw phenomenal givenness, hermeneutics, and ethical imperatives. By reduction is meant an intentional bracketing of the so-called "natural attitude" in order to open perception to unconditional receptivity to phenomena.[11] The natural attitude assumes many forms and figures

11. See Husserl, *Ideas I*, 7, 46–47, 57, 59–60, 148: "Natural cognition begins with experience and remains *within* experience. In the theoretical attitude which we call the '*natural*' <*theoretical attitude*> the collective horizon of possible investigations is therefore designated with *one* word: It is the *world*. Accordingly, the sciences of this original attitude are, in their entirety, sciences of the world; and, as long as it is the exclusively dominant <theoretical attitude,> the concepts 'true being,' 'actual being,' that is, real being and—since everything real joins together to make up the unity of the world—'being in the world' coincide . . . Scientific investigators of Nature thus *speak skeptically* of mathematics and of everything eidetic; but they *proceed dogmatically* in their eidetic method . . . turned toward things, unconcerned with epistemological or skeptical problems. *Instead of remaining in this attitude, we propose to alter it radically . . . refraining from judgment which is compatible with the unshaken conviction of truth* . . . phenomenology, by virtue of its essence, must claim to be 'first' philosophy and to

depending on social, cultural and political context, but it always implies assumed limits to possibility. David Hume, for example, exercised a frank natural attitude when he questioned the religious appeal to miracles.[12] For him, natural science had uncovered the inviolable laws of nature, and if a miracle claimed to have transgressed these laws, it simply could not occur by definition. It just was not possible. Hume contributed to the growing attitude of skepticism that pervades most of the postmodern world today.

In addition to skepticism, the natural attitude tends to close in on itself by the influence of ideology (whether liberal or conservative), education (typically deprived of studies in philosophy and theology), notions of common sense, the pretense of self-sufficiency, concupiscence, overriding economic concerns, religious fundamentalism, technological distraction (video games, apps, and the like), and the promises of progress in limited terms (for example, technocracy). The natural attitude always implies some reductionism and delimitation of possibility. For postmodernity, the natural attitude has been influenced by the historical trajectory running through the following events and more recent paradigmatic personas: the scientific revolution, the Western Enlightenment, the Industrial Revolution, Ludwig Feuerbach (1804–72; religion as anthropology), John Stuart Mill (1806–73; utilitarianism), Charles Darwin (1809–82; evolutionary biology), Karl Marx (1818–83; dialectical materialism), Friedrich Nietzsche (1844–1900; will to power), Sigmund Freud (1856–1939; libido principle), John Dewey (1859–1952; pragmatism), Bertrand Russell (1872–1970; analytic [atheistic] philosophy), Gianni Vattimo (1936–; nihilism), and the sexual revolution. Altogether, this historical trajectory has come to shape the transcultural postmodern Weltanschauung, tending toward material reductionism—that is, reducing the whole of reality to "matter in motion" alone—and relativism in how it understands "the world as we know it." Phenomenology deliberately brackets and sets aside the natural attitude in order to open the floodgates of intuition to possibility. Good science never closes the door on possibility, but is ever open to data and how they may give or say themselves. Similar to the Christian concept of *metanoia*, or conversion, the natural attitude must be converted to receive phenomena with a disposition of complete passivity. The self is called to surrender to the phenomenon in its unique and unrepeatable giving or saying.

The second step of phenomenology is to describe what gives or says itself in experience. Phenomenology describes rather than merely observes

---

offer the means for carrying out every possible critique of reason; therefore it demands the most perfect freedom from presuppositions and, concerning itself, an absolute reflective insight."

12. See Hume, "Of Miracles," in *Enquiry Concerning Human Understanding*, 96–116.

because the process of observation, too, demands description. Phenomenology seeks to call a thing what it is. More precisely, it seeks to relate how phenomena give and say themselves in the most accurate ways possible. It describes by taking stock of the various meanings and significations unleashed in the human subject's experience of this or that phenomenon. Since the natural attitude has been bracketed, perception is free to experience phenomena in their purity. No shadow is cast over possibility, as if possibility could be informed of its own boundaries. Instead, the method of pure description indexes an unlimited plethora of meanings and significations for consideration. Phenomenology looks with wide eyes and listens with big ears. Phenomenology raises the senses and conscious awareness to their most heightened capacities. An astute phenomenologist is attuned to the cosmos in its diversity of perceptible givens and utterances. Above all, a phenomenologist listens closely and carefully. Just as the observer within the scientific method must interpret the data of observation, phenomenological description implies interpretation in its method as well. However, for phenomenology, interpretation is tethered always to the phenomenological reduction, and this makes all the difference. It becomes a peculiar method of interpretation that demands interpretation of interpretation and the constant process of de-interpretation. Interpretation must be deconstructed and reconstructed at every turn in order that it not dominate what gives or says itself. Humility is the cardinal virtue for phenomenological interpretation.

The third step of phenomenology is to compare various descriptions of phenomena. Once phenomena have been described to a degree of relative adequacy, the distinct descriptions can be put in conversation with one another. All the while suspending judgment on the truth status of this or that phenomenon, the final step of the method is able to make distinctions between the variety of patterns, characters, configurations, paradigms, and meaning structures of diverse phenomena. Phenomenology effectively unmasks the array of language games involved in naming what gives or says itself. For example, given the experience of drinking a cup of lemon and ginger tea, phenomenology takes account of the host of meanings lighting up within consciousness. While drinking a cup of tea is a form of hydration, phenomenology demonstrates that it is much more than that. The experience is charged with meaning: custom, culture, break in the day, enjoyment, desire, relaxation, respite, warmth, nourishment, the elemental, memories associated with this particular kind of tea, interpersonal relationships, alterity, empathy, etc. These are just some of the experiential vectors phenomenology would follow, given a quite common and mundane experience such as that of drinking a cup of tea. One of the ingenious traits of phenomenology is that it tends to find the wondrous in the most ordinary experiences of life. Upon such discoveries, phenomenology naturally opens onto contemplation and ethics.

To sum up the method of phenomenology according to these three basic steps assists in forming a preliminary understanding of its intention and scope. Admittedly, phenomenology is much more complicated than these three basic steps. One of its most significant complications is the multiple versions of the phenomenological reduction. In fact, four different reductions can be identified from Husserl to today. Let us proceed to restate the meaning of the reduction and sketch its four distinct forms.

## C. The Phenomenological Reduction

As mentioned above, the method of phenomenology begins by executing the reduction (*epoché*) and, therefore, it is absolutely necessary to understand how the reduction works and its various modifications since Husserl introduced it at the turn of the century. Among the most helpful pages that illuminate the meaning of "phenomenological reduction" and its evolution since its incipient usage by Husserl are those at the end of Marion's book, *Reduction and Givenness*.[13] Marion concludes his magisterial study of the phenomenology of Husserl and Heidegger by summarizing what he sees to be their respective versions of the phenomenological reduction and by adding his own original revision of the reduction. It is clear that Marion sees his own work in phenomenology in direct continuity with Husserl and Heidegger specifically. In order to examine the distinct reductions in force in the work of Husserl, Heidegger and Marion, one first must recall the meaning and purpose of the reduction for the method of phenomenology: to describe phenomena as they give or say themselves in human experience ("experience" as *Erlebnis* rather than as *Erfahrung*).[14]

In order to go beyond the "natural attitude" that predetermines phenomena before they are experienced (and therefore sets fixed boundaries within which a phenomenon may give itself), a reduction must be enacted that explicitly names and sets aside all predeterminations that may in effect

13. See Marion, *Reduction and Givenness*, 203–5.

14. For the precise distinction between "experience" as *Erlebnis* and as *Erfahrung*, see Horner, *Jean-Luc Marion*, 27. *Erfahrung* (connoting the sense of a "traversal" or "finding out") refers to the experience of one having the "natural attitude," regarding reality as a totality of objects that can be known through natural science alone. *Erlebnis* refers to the experience of the phenomenologist, who remains open to the adventure of possibility—in particular the lived inner experiences of that which is immanent to consciousness (Husserl), and all possible meanings thereof.

distort the originality and integrity of a phenomenon and curtail possibility. In other words, not to come clean with pre-given worldviews and presumed restrictions of "the possible" is to perceive according to a set of assumptions that altogether may not, after all, be the case. The reduction conscientiously identifies any a priori barriers to possibility and then brackets them—that is to say, the reduction pierces through the temptation of a premature act of judgment and opens to any and all phenomenal saying or giving. In essence, the reduction permits phenomenologists to ask sincerely, "What gives or says?" Phenomenological description then must proceed with great caution so as not to fall too quickly back into preset judgments of what is the case, that is, what has been actualized already. Phenomenology is open always to possibility—confined neither to a subjunctive outlook (for example, "if, that, were, would, should, could, ought, must, let, may . . .") nor to a conditional outlook (for example, "if, were, would, could, will, might . . ."). Rather, phenomenology outstrips the limitations of linguistic, social, historical and cultural convention in order to render the phenomenon its due, that is, the phenomenon's right to give or say itself rather than only under the arbitrary conditions we may permit it to give or say itself. Phenomenology's power is in its openness, honesty and willful naïveté in asking, "What says or gives?" Its weakness is in its recognition of the immense (im)possibilities (that is, infinity) of the task it sets before itself. For phenomenology, the beginning is the end and the end is the beginning.[15]

## *1. Husserl's Transcendental Reduction and Heidegger's Existential/Ontological Reduction*

The first version of the phenomenological reduction specified by Marion is that of Husserl, namely, the transcendental reduction. Marion describes Husserl's reduction as amounting to "a constitution of objects."[16] It is called

15. See Tracy, *Dialogue with the Other*, 17: "We are driven to perfect our creations, our language. We are driven, wherever we begin, to god-terms. The basic necessity for the symbolic animal is to speak, to learn negatives, to create and *not* stop. Perfection is our *telos*—which seems to mean, paradoxically, that end *is* origin"; and Marion, *In the Self's Place*, 229: "Running does not have as its goal attaining what precedes, so as to nullify the advance, but to put me too in the advance itself. To run, I must in effect constantly put myself in a disequilibrium, put myself into the advance itself. And the happiness of running the race consists in remaining permanently in the unbalanced advance, perfectly and continually free from the permanence and stability, which is illusory anyway, of a *nunc stans*. If God inspires the desire in me, it is not first to fulfill it by satisfying it, but to fulfill it by hollowing it with achievements that become so many new beginnings."

16. Marion, *Reduction and Givenness*, 204.

a "transcendental" reduction because, in reference to the transcendental "I," "it is deployed for the intentional and constituting *I* [and] gives to the *I* constituted objects."[17] Yet the deficiency of the transcendental reduction is that it "excludes from givenness everything that does not let itself be led back to objectivity."[18] In other words, the transcendental reduction does not open effectively to all possible forms of givenness as well as it could, for example, those forms of givenness that are not objects as such but nonetheless give themselves, such as consciousness itself, the world, time, etc. The second version of the reduction indicated by Marion is that of Heidegger, which Marion refers to as the existential and/or ontological reduction. It is existential "in that it sets itself into operation through the existing being" (*Dasein*), and it is ontological "in that it works the question of Being" (*Seinsfrage*/*Seinssinn*).[19] The existential/ontological reduction is deficient in that it excludes from possibility "that which does not have to be, in particular the preliminary conditions of the 'phenomenon of Being.'"[20] Like the restrictions of Husserl's objectivity, ontology is not open entirely to possibility either, nor does it get at the most anterior aspect of phenomenality. For Marion's analysis, there is a more originary and absolute layer of phenomenality beyond Being and the ways it is disclosed, namely, givenness (*Gegebenheit*). Before the self-reflexive pre-apprehension of Being as such, it gives.

## 2. *Marion's Donative Reduction*

Marion, for his part, proposes a third phenomenological reduction that we may designate as the donative reduction.[21] This is a reduction to givenness or "the pure form of the call," recognizing the givenness of the appealing phenomenon to be absolute and thus rendering the human subject "as an auditor preceded and instituted by the call."[22] The reduction brings to recognition "the absolutely unconditional call and the absolutely unconstrained response."[23] Marion views the call of givenness "as originarily

17. Ibid.

18. Ibid.

19. Ibid.

20. Ibid.

21. Though Marion does not call the absolute reduction to givenness the "donative reduction," I am taking liberty here to do so for the sake of categorizing it in relation to those distinct reductions of Husserl, Heidegger, and Levinas.

22. Marion, *Reduction and Givenness*, 204.

23. Ibid.

unconditional."[24] For Marion there is no further layer to be peeled back, for, in fact, according to the donative reduction, it is precisely the phenomenon that constitutes the human subject as such (*l'interloqué*), and this counter-constitution occurs through the various modes of givenness. Even though Marion refers to givenness as "the pure form of the call" in *Reduction and Givenness*, chapter 2 of this book will prove that Marion understands givenness primarily in terms of visibility—for example, showing, appearance, apparition, manifestation, etc.—rather than in terms of audibility.

## 3. *Levinas's Vocative Reduction*

While it is clear that Marion's third reduction is influenced significantly by the notion of "the call" in Levinas, a fourth reduction can be identified specifically with Levinas: the vocative reduction.[25] Influenced by Husserl's "intersubjective reduction" as outlined in his 1925 summer lectures, published as *Phenomenological Psychology*, Levinas exacts the most reduced reduction possible: a reduction to the proximate yet transcendent intersubjective relationship, the call of the other at its heart.[26] The call of the other precedes any and all appearing and itself cannot be reduced further to any modality of givenness. Levinas identifies the most original call as the call of the personal other, rather than that of givenness. The ethical exigence imposed by the other on the self, constitutes the basic structure of human perception. Before I have time to reflect, I am responsible for the other. According to the vocative reduction, the transcendental ego is recognized as being disturbed into wakefulness by the other before consciousness even comes to the fore: "the subjectivity of the subject shows itself in the traumatism of wakefulness"—a wakefulness provoked by the call of the other.[27] For Levinas "the other" is

24. Ibid., 205.

25. The term "vocative reduction" is my own designation of Levinas's unique revision of the phenomenological reduction. It highlights the call of the other as the essential and core element of all phenomenality. Also, see Carlson, *Indiscretion*, 203: "Following within a rich tradition of reflection on 'the call,' Marion's third phenomenological reduction, a 'donative' reduction, is also fundamentally vocative: reduction to unconditional givenness is a reduction to the unconditional givenness of the call or the claim exercised over me by the phenomenon as such." Even though Carlson describes Marion's reduction as both donative and vocative, I reserve the specification "vocative" for the peculiar character of Levinas's reduction, wherein the call of the other is not just another form of givenness. For Levinas, the call of the other is not an instance of manifestation but of proclamation, and this makes all the difference.

26. See Husserl, *Phenomenological Psychology*, and Levinas, "Philosophy and Awakening," in *Entre Nous*, 77–90.

27. Levinas, *Entre Nous*, 86.

not just any other, not just any form of givenness, but the personal human other (*l'autrui*) who transcends the category of givenness as a witness to otherwise than givenness. It is with Levinas that phenomenology undergoes its most radical inversion: when the reduction is exacted to the nth degree, what says itself is infinity as a trace in the summons of the other person to me to become responsible for him. The reduction inverts the interiority of subjectivity by recognizing the exteriority and anteriority of alterity. Levinas even goes so far as to describe the product of the reduction as an "inversion of intentionality" and "counterconsciousness": "Proximity is not a consciousness of proximity. It is an obsession that is not an overenlarged consciousness, but counterconsciousness, reversing consciousness."[28] According to Levinas, upon carefully performing the phenomenological reduction, the primordial phenomenon is heard ethically before it appears cognitively: the call of the other, indicting me and summoning me to responsibility for her. The call is heard precisely in the responsorial issuing from my own lips, or a lack thereof (in which case the call is denied). To utter "Here I am!" is the inauguration of consciousness, for what consciousness can be believed which does not respond affirmatively to the clarion call of the other? What consciousness gives or says itself in the form of a "no" rather than a "yes"? Would not the rejection of the call of the other amount to unconsciousness—amnesia—perpetual comatose? The beginning is the end, the end is the beginning. To respond affirmatively to the call of the other means life, to respond negatively means death.

An inherent tension can be felt between the donative reduction of Marion and the vocative reduction of Levinas.[29] Though the two reductions

28. Ibid., 58, and further, "It is an event that strips consciousness of its initiative, that undoes me and puts me before an Other in a state of guilt; an event that puts me in accusation—a persecuting indictment, for it is prior to all wrongdoing—and that leads me to the *self*, to the accusative that is not preceded by any nominative." Cf. Levinas, *Otherwise than Being*, 47, 53.

29. This tension is palpable in Marion's essay on Levinas, "The Voice without Name: Homage to Levinas," in Bloechl, *Face of the Other*, 224–42; Marion, "From the Other to the Individual," in Schwartz, *Transcendence*, 43–60; and Marion, *In Excess*, 104–27. Cf. Marion, *Being Given*, for example, 282–308 (§§28–29), 320–24 (conclusion), and endnotes 23 (331) and 73 (374), for example, 294: "The pertinent question is not deciding if the gifted is first responsible toward the Other (Levinas) or rather in debt to itself (Heidegger), but understanding that these two modes of responsibility flow from its originary function of having to respond in the face of the phenomenon as such, that is to say, such as it gives itself"; Marion, *Visible and the Revealed*, 41: "Such saturation of a horizon by a single saturated phenomenon presents a danger that cannot be underestimated, since it is born from the absolutely real, in no way illusory, experience of totality, with neither door nor window, with neither other [*autre*] nor Other [*autrui*]." It is clear that in this last quotation Marion is invoking the bifurcated notion of the other in Levinas, only to overtake it with the unconditioned primacy of saturating givenness.

seem virtually identical at first glance, they prove to be radically different. Marion argues that the call of the other can be reduced to a mode of givenness, while Levinas insists that the call of the other is irreducible and most originary. For Levinas, the call of the other is precisely that which awakens consciousness even to begin to speak of categories of givenness and their meaning. Not only does "the ethical exigency to be responsible for the other (undermine) the ontological primacy of the meaning of being," it also undermines the absolute status of givenness as primordial.[30] Whereas for Marion the call of the other is simply one of many manifestations of givenness, for Levinas the perpetual summons of the other, and my immediate exposure to her, proclaim a command for my consciousness to come alive.[31] The question that asks what is most originary, while being a question of chronological sequence, is a fortiori a question of hermeneutic precision. If givenness is asserted as most primary, ethics follows as secondary; if ethics is asserted as most original, givenness follows as a witness to the fundamental ethical configuration of interpersonal relationships. The unresolvable tension between Marion's and Levinas's claims to phenomenal primacy is the very tension this book desires to highlight in its attempt to think the Eucharist phenomenologically. This book, in the end, will argue that it is exactly the irreducible tension between these two claims to the unconditioned (givenness and ethical injunction, respectively) that unlocks the most adequate rendering of eucharistic phenomenality, and any phenomenality for that matter. It will continue to ask if a paradoxical relationship between givenness and ethics is possible in which both come in first place as complementary contenders for the reduction's prized fruit.

## *4. Marion's Erotic Reduction and Back to Levinas*

To complicate matters further, Marion introduces yet another distinct reduction in his 2003 publication, *The Erotic Phenomenon*, namely, the erotic reduction.[32] The main point of this work is to call into question the entire

30. This quote is taken from Levinas's response in an interview with Richard Kearney in Cohen, *Face to Face with Levinas*, 23.

31. Similar to Marion's "fold of givenness," comprised of (1) the given and (2) the giving, we could speak of a "fold of ethical injunction" in terms of (1) the call of the other and (2) the ethical exigency to be responsible for the other. Altogether this fold is witnessed in the ethical reduction of Levinas.

32. See Horner's analysis of Marion's erotic reduction in *Jean-Luc Marion*, 135–46. While Horner provides an insightful analysis of the nuances of Marion's erotic reduction, we will try to simplify these admitted nuances for the sake of brevity and clarity within the present study.

aim and history of philosophy—not only to call it into question, but to chastise it for failing to concern itself with love most of all. The very genre of *The Erotic Phenomenon* sends a message. There is no mention of Husserl, Heidegger, or any other phenomenologists by name. The only philosopher named is René Descartes at the very outset of the book, only to subvert his obsession with epistemological certainty. Marion admits in the preface that this book was a long time in the making—twenty-five years, to be exact. The tonality of the book is more akin to *Prolegomena to Charity* rather than to his more rigorous phenomenological treatments in *Reduction and Givenness*, *Being Given*, and *In Excess*. Yet the closing words of *Being Given* point to the coming fulfillment of *The Erotic Phenomenon*'s epiphany, indicating Marion's ongoing struggle with the radical implications of Levinas's vocative reduction and its unshrinkable demands:

> This situation, still unspoiled by exploration, not only allows and requires reconsidering the thematic of ethics—of respect and the face, obligation and substitution—and confirming its phenomenological legitimacy. It would also perhaps authorize broaching what ethics cannot attain: the individuation of the Other. For I neither want nor should only face up to him as the universal and abstract pole of counter-intentionality where each and every one can take on the face of the face. I instead reach him in his unsubstitutable particularity, where he shows himself like no other Other can. This individuation has a name: love. But we have for a long time now been without the concept that would do it justice, and this name remains the most prostituted of words. Nonetheless, phenomenology claims to make it its privileged theme—"Love, as basic *motive* for phenomenological understanding" (Heidegger). Could the phenomenology of givenness finally restore to it the dignity of a concept?[33]

33. Marion, *Being Given*, 324. Levinas, too, wrestles with the dialectical relationship between love and justice, for example, see *Entre Nous*, 108: "Justice comes from love. That definitely doesn't mean to say that the rigor of justice can't be turned against love understood in terms of responsibility. Politics, left to itself, has its own determinism. Love must always watch over justice . . . Love is originary. I'm not speaking theologically at all; I myself don't use it too much, the word love, it is a worn-out and ambiguous word . . . Responsibility is an individuation, a principle of individuation. On the famous problem: 'Is man individuated by matter, or individuated by form,' I support individuation by responsibility for the other." The tension is palpable between Marion and Levinas, between the notions of love and responsibility, the dialectical difference between *eros* and *agape*, the contrast between manifestation and proclamation. See also Levinas's discussion of the relationship between *eros* and *agape* in *Entre Nous*, 113: "I am definitely not a Freudian; consequently I don't think that Agape comes from Eros . . . I think in any case that Eros is definitely not Agape, that Agape is neither a derivative nor the extinction of love-Eros. Before Eros there was the Face; Eros itself is possible

This is the most incisive critique Marion issues to Levinas's phenomenology of alterity. Marion charges Levinas with being guilty of the same fault of which Levinas accuses Heidegger: that of a reduction to stale and insipid anonymity. This is a situation in which the particular is dimmed to the point of extinction by the refulgence of the universal. Marion argues that the anonymous other is no better than anonymous being, or the *il y a*, and that a reduction to the anonymous other amounts to a reduction to a kind of Kantian categorical imperative that is highly impersonal and artificial. Marion instead proposes that Levinas take his reduction even further: "put ethics in second place, substituting the term 'love.'"[34] Essentially, Marion is arguing for a reduction to the urgency of love—an ethos of love more anterior than the ethics of the face. For Marion this ethos of love shows itself primordially as givenness, but even more decisively as the individuated call of the specific other—for example, Megan, Kadir, Edith, Man-to, etc.—a recognition of individuation that itself proceeds from the urgency of the question, "Does anyone love me?" Here is where Marion and Levinas diverge. For Levinas, the ethical exigency—the weight of responsibility for the other—is issued in a call from outside of the self—a call to become responsible for all people. For Marion, the givenness of love, in its erotic tonality, is given as a void within the depths of the human subject who yearns to receive the corresponding gift of genuine love from another—a call that individuates both self and personally named others.[35] The waiting time for the arrival of

only between Faces. The problem of Eros is philosophical and concerns otherness . . . In *Totalité et Infini* [*Totality and Infinity*], there is a chapter on Eros, which is described as love that becomes enjoyment, whereas I have a grave view of Agape in terms of responsibility for the other." Further, see Gschwandtner, "Ethics, Eros, or Caritas?"

34. Marion, "From the Other to the Individual," in Schwartz, *Transcendence*, 54. As a phenomenologist of manifestation, Lacoste similarly critiques the radicality of Levinas's notion of "ethics as first philosophy" in *Experience and the Abosolute*, 70–75, for example, 72: "Amoralism does not govern our being-in-the-world. But nor is morality imposed on us in the way that the existence of the world is. And even though, from the dawn of experience, the human faces we meet with can be those of brothers to whom we are completely indebted, this possibility exceeds the facticity of our co-being-there; it is a free and charitable overdetermination of it. Yet the mute call that renders me 'hostage' to others places no obligation on me that would emanate solely from the a priori conditions of my presence in the world." Instead, Lacoste insists that the (non-)eschatological non-place of liturgy is necessary to awaken one to ethics, for example, 73: "But the world from which liturgy diverts us is not a world over which goodwill reigns, and, at bottom, it is this world from which we must take leave, in a meantime, so as to discover our responsibilities in the world." Because of his alliance with Heideggerian philosophy, Lacoste cannot accompany Levinas all the way to his vocative reduction.

35. Cf. Augustine, *Confessions* 1.1.1 (3): "You stir man to take pleasure in praising you, because you have made us for yourself, and our heart is restless until it rests in you."

this incomparable gift of love is anguish for the human subject, and upon this gift the entire universe depends.[36] All else is boredom and nothing but a "chase after wind."[37] Marion claims a reduction that surpasses the reduction to the ethical injunction in Levinas: a reduction to love.[38] While recalling the respective reductions of Husserl and Heidegger in passing (but without mentioning names), and implicitly claiming to go beyond Levinas's ethical reduction, Marion proposes the most radical reduction of all by beginning with the question, "Does anyone out there love me?"[39] Instead of groping for certainty (as in Descartes, "Am I?"), Marion's quest is one for assurance ("Am I loved?"). Marion argues that phenomenology only matters if it relates directly to our most fundamental yearning to be loved. Contra Levinas, Marion insists that love can be commanded (by the other) because it has first been given (by the other).[40] In the final analysis, one may conclude that the erotic reduction is simply a derivative of the donative reduction. It is the originary givenness of love to which all else pales in comparison; it is because of the givenness of love that we ask any question at all. A dialectic

36. See Marion, *Prolegomena to Charity*, 1–30, on the temptation to suicide as a means to break the cycle of vengeance, and Marion, *Erotic Phenomenon*, 54–55, on the experience of self-hatred in the complete absence of love's affirmation from outside of oneself.

37. See Marion's reflections on boredom in *Reduction and Givenness*, 169–205; cf. Marion, *Prolegomena to Charity*, 1: "In the experience of evil, what, in a sense, hurts the most (*fait le plus mal*) results from the indisputable rigor iniquity deploys. Iniquity is not characterized by any absurdity, any incoherence, nor even by any 'injustice' (in the everyday sense of an unfair wage, or an effect disproportionate to its cause). Rather, it is characterized only by an immutable logic that reproduces its rigor without end or flaw, to the point of nausea, according to an insurmountable boredom. But one dies of boredom, too, especially of boredom"; and Ecclesiastes, for example, 1:14: "I have seen all things that are done under the sun, and behold, all is vanity and a chase after wind" (NAB).

38. See Marion, "From the Other to the Individual," in Schwartz, *Transcendence*, 43–59, for example, 55, where Marion proposes to go beyond Levinasian ethics as first philosophy: "The face addresses itself to me, and to me alone, only if it individualizes me and thus individualizes itself. This double concentration, which renders us unsubstitutable, one for the other, is not accomplished in the ethical relation, but in the meeting of love."

39. See Marion, *Erotic Reduction*, 21–22.

40. Cf. 1 John 4:19: "We love because he first loved us" (NAB); Benedict XVI, *Deus caritas est*, 14: "Love can be 'commanded' because it has first been given"; Rosenzweig, *Star of Redemption*, 176: "Thou shalt love—what a paradox this embraces! Can love then be commanded? . . . Yes of course, love cannot be commanded. No third party can command it or extort it. No third party can, but the One can. The commandment to love can only proceed from the mouth of the lover. Only the lover can and does say: love me!—and he really does so. In his mouth the commandment to love is not a strange commandment; it is none other than the voice of love itself."

obtains between the divergent claims of Marion and Levinas: the donative/erotic reduction, the vocative/ethical reduction, or both? Is it possible to exercise both at the same time, in the form of a paradoxical reduction? This we will explore throughout the remainder of our study.

## D. Toward a Phenomenology of the Eucharist

Having submitted now a preliminary description of the phenomenological reduction in its varied apertures, we are able to proceed onward to our more specific inquiry into the phenomenality of the sacrament. To this point we have demonstrated that there is no unequivocal meaning of the phenomenological reduction, but that there are multiple reductions that take place inside one another, much like a Russian Matryoshka doll in which multiple dolls dwell one inside the other. In other words, the transcendental reduction of Husserl is followed by the existential/ontological reduction of Heidegger, which in turn is followed by the donative/erotic reduction of Marion, followed by the vocative/ethical reduction of Levinas.[41] In delving into the phenomenality of the Eucharist, these divergent reductions must be kept in mind in order not to proceed too quickly in the analysis. It is important first to come to terms with our intended methodology if we are to perform effectively the proposed analysis of the Eucharist. At this point we hope at least to have made a persuasive case and warrant for taking the liberty to utilize phenomenology as a most helpful method for theological inquiry. In effect, the phenomenological reduction disqualifies no phenomenon beforehand as out-of-bounds for investigation. All is fair game when the reduction is executed accurately and without prejudice.

This study purports to interrogate intellectually the Eucharist in order to trace the phenomenological contours of its logic, form and meaning. As sacrament par excellence, the specificity of the Eucharist will throw light on the more general notion of sacrament per se. While the Eucharist is a religious phenomenon within the Christian tradition, it will be demonstrated that this phenomenon functions differently within diverse communal contexts. The peculiarities between Protestant versus Catholic settings will be accentuated in particular, however, the overall hermeneutic of this study will assume a Roman Catholic tenor in terms of doctrine and tradition. The

41. It might seem that the reductions of Marion and Levinas are historically out of sequence here, and in one sense this is true as Marion certainly relied on the insights of Levinas's vocative reduction in order to develop his donative/erotic reduction. However, I will argue further that Marion overlooked some vital features of the vocative reduction, which allows for Levinas's reduction to resume place of primacy (anteriority), even if by way of conciliation, in the sequence of reductions.

terms "doctrine" and "tradition" are not mutually exclusive in relation to the method of phenomenology. Rather, doctrine and tradition signify a world of text and context within which one is able to raise the question of sacrament—and in particular, Eucharist—at all.

It is precisely doctrine and tradition that supply the language and lens for pursuing such an inquiry. The status of the truth-claims of the particular doctrine and tradition can be suspended all the while describing the phenomenality of the sacrament within its doctrinal and liturgical context. Indeed, doctrines involve an affirmative judgment of truth-claims on the part of those who worked to formulate the doctrines to serve as testimony to others. Yet to explore the veracity of any religious phenomenon, the doctrinal matrix in which the phenomenon is enmeshed is essential to accessing the phenomenon in the fullness of its scope and meaning. Phenomenology can, in effect, bracket the proposed truth-claims embodied in doctrinal formulations while tracing the logic, contours, and coherence of meaning of the religious phenomenon . . . at least at the outset of description. Phenomenology allows investigators to describe scientifically a religious phenomenon while suspending judgment of the transcendental truth-claims of the phenomenon. This is to say that truth-claims that would involve a transcendent character of assent—that is, an assent in relation to the "absolute" (Jean Nabert) or to a proposal of "ultimate concern" (Paul Tillich)—are able to be held in suspense throughout the course of phenomenological investigation. This is not to conjoin phenomenology with a breed of atheism, for that too would involve a transcendent assent in favor of the God who does not (could not) exist. Such an atheistic phenomenology would operate under the sway of its own "natural attitude," setting up for itself rigid borders, only inside of which the play of phenomenality is permitted to take place. In contrast, for phenomenology to carry out its task of describing what gives or says and how it gives or says, perception must remain open to that which gives and says and all possibilities as to what may give or say itself.

The pages to follow will demonstrate that by employing the phenomenological method, the sacramental phenomenon will be shown to be none other than a truth proposal that never could be determined absolutely as a manipulatable sense datum wherein God would be circumscribed conceptually and empirically, reduced to an object among objects, thereby corrupting the very idea of God that, by definition, repels all circumscription and manipulation. In the language of Marion, if God gives phenomenologically, the (im)possibility of God could be restricted neither to "common-law phenomena" nor to "poor phenomena."[42] By definition, the concept

42. Marion, *Being Given*, 221–28; cf. Steinbock's essay "The Poor Phenomenon," in

of God is enigmatic and the very (im)possibility of God suggests a saturation of phenomenality, even if in the form of a shortage of visibility and comprehension. As Augustine of Hippo has noted, "If, in fact, about what one speaks, if understood, it is not God," or again, "For if you understand it, it is not God."[43] Yet for this reason it would be naïve to sideline God as merely a Kantian postulate of pure reason—solely a limit-concept that cannot thereby enter into phenomenality. To the contrary, there remains the possibility that the incomprehensible reveal itself in the comprehensible, all the while remaining absolutely incomprehensible. There remains the possibility that that which is experienced cannot be comprehended fully or contained in the form of concept, matter, or sensation of the external alone. To deny this possibility would be to deny the very possibility of possibility. To agree with Lacoste, "phenomenality, of course, is not uniform," yet even if "the existence of God is essentially irreducible," assessing the possibility of experiencing a reception of divine revelation within the network of that which is reducible remains an open task while exercising the phenomenological reduction with integrity.[44]

In sum, I argue that phenomenology is an entirely appropriate method for theological inquiry, compromising neither the rigors of phenomenology nor the particularities of theological content. Moreover, phenomenology bears the promise of allowing the credibility and significance of theology to be considered in a public, rather than an exclusively confessional, way. Phenomenology may serve very well as a bridge between the polemically charged diversity of scientific disciplines, perhaps even inviting theology to test the seriousness of its logic within its traditionally esteemed persona as "queen of all sciences." The potential for biology, theology, physics, philosophy, mathematics, linguistics, psychology, geology, philosophy, sociology, chemistry, etc., to say something meaningful to one another hinges on the coherence of logic that underpins and makes meaningful every discipline of study.[45] After all, is it not possible that phenomenology provides a kind

Benson and Wirzba, *Words of Life*, 120–31, for a discussion on the notion of "poor phenomena" vis-à-vis Christian theological notions such as "grace" and "poverty of spirit."

43. Augustine, *Sermo* 52, 6, 16 and *Sermo* 117, 3, 5 (translations my own; PL 38:360, 38:663, respectively).

44. Lacoste, "The Appearing and the Irreducible," in Benson and Wirzba, *Words of Life*, 49 and 65, respectively.

45. It is unacceptable for any subdiscipline of science to "not think." It is dishonest for sciences to limit themselves to conditional frontiers of inquiry alone, especially those horizons conditioned and prefabricated by the inquirer. See Kearney's interview with Levinas in Cohen, *Face to Face with Levinas*, 22: "The greatest virtue of philosophy is that it can put itself in question, try to deconstruct what it has constructed, and unsay what it has said. Science, on the contrary, does not try to unsay itself, does not

of universal language and methodology through which various disciplines may communicate intelligibly with one another without succumbing to their inbuilt tendencies to reductionism? We answer this question in the affirmative.

## II. Prolegomena to Contemporary Sacramental Theology

What is a sacrament? Neither the classic and oft-quipped *Baltimore Catechism* definition, "an outward sign instituted by Christ to give grace," nor the tidy Calvinian definition, "a testimony of the divine favor toward us, confirmed by an external sign, with a corresponding attestation of our faith towards Him," will suffice to answer this question today.[46] The questions that search into the content, meaning and truth of the religious phenomenon called "sacrament" demand a method and language suited to the state of theology and philosophy at the dawn of the twenty-first century. A metaphorically charged language of faith will not do; neither will a metaphysically loaded language of "matter and form," "substance and accidents," "being and presence." Postmodern critique is not satisfied with ages-old descriptions and definitions that situate religious phenomena at a safe distance from scientific investigation. Neither "transubstantiation" nor "promise of God" supply a sufficient answer to the critical interrogation of the sacramental phenomenon of the Eucharist, though they may offer helpful places to begin.

---

interrogate or challenge its own concepts, terms, or foundations; it forges ahead, progresses. In this respect, science attempts to ignore language by constructing its own abstract nonlanguage of calculable symbols and formulae. But science is merely a secondary bracketing of philosophical language, from which it is ultimately derived; it can never have the last word. Heidegger summed this up admirably when he declared that science *calculates* but does not *think*. Now what I am interested in is precisely this ability of philosophy to think, to question itself, and ultimately to unsay itself. And I wonder if this capacity for interrogation and for unsaying (*dédire*) is not itself derived from the preontological interhuman relationship with the other." Cf. Marion, *Visible and the Revealed*, 150: "We know very clearly that the common rationality of objects knows nothing and can do nothing about what is closest to us. In *this* sense, Heidegger could legitimately say that 'science does not think.' He should have added that it has claimed this as its privilege: science does not think; it measures and orders in the form of modeling, of parameter, and of objectivation. Technology produces what is understood in this way and vice versa. By contrast, only the flesh reaches nonobjective phenomena, those where an excess of intuition saturates the limits of the concept already known and always foreseen."

46. Third Council of Baltimore, *Baltimore Catechism of 1891*, 35; Calvin, *Institutes of the Christian Religion*, 492.

Just as John XXIII found it necessary to convene the Second Vatican Council, signaled by the provocative call, *aggiornamento* (that is, "bring up-to-date"), so philosophers and theologians recently have found it necessary to issue the same call in response to a waning human attentiveness toward the Eucharist and the question of its meaning and truth. Three such notable efforts on the part of philosophers and theologians have been (1) the theological congress "Gesù Cristo unico Salvatore del mondo. Pane per la nuova vita," held April 27–28, 2000, organized by the Faculty of Theology and the Pastoral Institute Redemptor Hominis of the Pontifical Lateran University in Rome in collaboration with the local Committee in preparation for the 47th International Eucharistic Congress; (2) the two-day Colloquium on Eucharist held in Melbourne in February 2001, jointly sponsored by the Blessed Sacrament Congregation's Centre Eucharistia and the Faculty of Theology at the Australian Catholic University; and (3) the Second Biannual Congress of the Leuven Encounters in Systematic Theology (LEST II), November 3–6, 1999, dedicated to the question of the sacrament in a postmodern context.[47] The former of these events featured presentations made by Jean-Luc Marion, Michel Henry, et al., and should be recognized as a sui generis event within the Roman Catholic Church by officially endorsing phenomenology as a legitimate method through which to probe the sacramental phenomenon.[48] The Melbourne colloquium featured presentations of Robyn Horner, Kevin Hart, et al., and its express aim was to bring together "people engaged in research and renewal in disciplines related to the Eucharist, especially liturgy, theology and spirituality, in a collaborative, interdisciplinary and ecumenical spirit, with particular attention to developments in culture."[49] LEST II included a group of around 250 scholars and was devoted to the following questions: "Where can we think God appearing in a so-called postmodern setting, in which no foundation seems given? In what way is it possible to signify reflexively the presence of God, which is confessed to in faith? Moreover, how can we understand sacramental presence after the (supposed) end of metaphysics, the traditional philosophical tool for sacramental theological thinking?"[50] These three events serve as emblematic instances of intentional and public discourse on the meaning

47. See Reali, *Il mondo del sacramento*; Knowles, *Eucharist*; and Boeve and Leijssen, *Sacramental Presence in a Postmodern Context*, respectively, for conference proceedings.

48. Marion's contribution to this conference appears in *Il mondo del sacramento* under the title, "La fenomenalità del sacramento: Essere e donazione," 134–54; also published as "La phénoménalité du sacrement" and as "The Phenomenality of the Sacrament—Being and Givenness," in Benson and Wirzba, *Words of Life*, 89–102.

49. Knowles, *Eucharist*, vii.

50. Boeve and Leijssen, *Sacramental Presence*, vii.

and truth of the Eucharist in a postmodern context, with special consideration of phenomenology as a valid method within the broader field of theology.

This project proposes to situate itself in the vein of such recent attempts to examine critically the Eucharist in a postmodern context. It ultimately seeks to recuperate Catholic doctrine on the Eucharist by problematizing it and putting it into conversation with Evangelical/Protestant thinking on this elusive phenomenon of Christian belief. More specifically, this project employs the most recent developments in phenomenology in order to assess the logic, content and meaning of the Eucharist. The works of Jean-Luc Marion, Paul Ricoeur, and Emmanuel Levinas—three French phenomenologists of three different faith traditions—are brought into confrontation with the aim of submitting a careful and meticulous interpretation of the sacramental phenomenon called "Eucharist." Why the choice of Marion, Ricoeur, and Levinas specifically? Assuredly other triumvirates could have been chosen instead: Husserl, Heidegger, Merleau-Ponty; or Scheler, Stein, Henry; or Gadamer, Chrétien, Derrida; or Sokolowski, Lacoste, Falque; or any other combination of these phenomenologists mentioned and more besides. The choice of Marion, Ricoeur, and Levinas is highly intentional, for all three thinkers share something in common: phenomenology and openness to theological considerations in the name of genuine phenomenology. In addition, Marion, Ricoeur, and Levinas are among the most recent contributors to the development of the phenomenological method. Further still, these three thinkers line up nicely with the dialectical heuristic that will be tested throughout this study: manifestation ↔ proclamation.[51] Marion is placed on the side of manifestation, while Ricoeur and Levinas are aligned with the side of proclamation. Chapters 2 and 3 of this book will seek to substantiate this claim and its meaning for investigating the phenomenality of the Eucharist. Finally, as representative of diverse traditions of faith—Marion (Roman Catholicism), Ricoeur (Reformed Christianity), Levinas (Judaism)—the work of these three phenomenologists in conversation and conflict will reinforce the ability of the phenomenological method to reach across diverse faith traditions and worldviews in open inquiry.

## III. Manifestation and Proclamation

So as not to reinvent the wheel, in approaching the Eucharist as a religious phenomenon, it is necessary to begin with phenomenological insights that

51. The insertion of the symbol, ↔, between the terms "manifestation" and "proclamation" will be used to signal the meaning of the irreducible dialectical relationship that obtains between these terms.

have been proffered already by others engaged in phenomenology of things religious. Our point of departure, as previously mentioned, will be the manifestation ↔ proclamation dialectic as identified by both Paul Ricoeur and David Tracy (1939–).[52] While the logic of the manifestation ↔ proclamation dialectic will be expounded in chapter 4 of the present study, may it suffice for now to offer a foreword concerning the notions of manifestation and proclamation, and their integral yet contentious relationship.

In the fifth chapter of *The Analogical Imagination*, David Tracy introduces two forms of intensification of particularity by which the event of truth happens in religious expression: manifestation and proclamation.[53] According to this schema, the revelation of truth occurs precisely through an intensification of particularity, wherein the universal ("the whole") is disclosed veritably by appeal and force in and through the generative intensification of particularity. Religious phenomena purport to be a disclosure of the whole, or the universal, in and through the particular—a revelation of the infinite in the finite. Thus Gotthold Lessing's (1729–81) "ugly, broad (historical) ditch" is said to be surmounted by an intensification of particularity whether in the form of manifestation or in the form of proclamation.[54] As an astute adherent of the Western Enlightenment, Lessing viewed an unbridgeable chasm between the universal truths of reason and the historical particularities of alleged instances of divine revelation in space and time. He simply could not subscribe to any particularity that claimed universality for itself. Instead, Lessing insisted that "*accidental truths of history can never become the proof of necessary truths of reason*."[55] Yet the school of phenomenology opens the possibility of examining particular phenomena as they give or say themselves without precluding the possibility that the universal be disclosed in the particular, that is to say, the possibility of the paradox. According to Tracy, the paradox of the universal disclosed in and through the particular happens in two primary forms: manifestation and proclamation. Even though Tracy's analysis is aimed specifically at religious phenomena as such, the operation of manifestation and proclamation as rubrics within

52. Similar to Ricoeur's and Tracy's phenomenological distinction between manifestation and proclamation is Sokolowski's distinction between image and word. See Sokolowski, *Christian Faith and Human Understanding*, 77–85.

53. Tracy's insights into the manifestation ↔ proclamation dialectic were prefigured in and inspired by Ricoeur's article "Manifestation and Proclamation," in Ricoeur, *Figuring the Sacred*, 48–67. Tracy acknowledges his consultation with this article (as well as others) in endnote 26 of chapter 5 of *Analogical Imagination*, 221.

54. See Lessing, *Lessing's Theological Writings*, 55. Likewise, see Lacoste's response to such a dilemma in Lacoste, *Note sur le temps*.

55. Lessing, *Lessing's Theological Writings*, 53.

phenomenology can be described in even broader contours in terms of the distinction between givenness (manifestation) and hermeneutics/ethics (proclamation). This is, at the same time, the distinction between Marion's donative/erotic reduction (manifestation) and Levinas's vocative/ethical reduction (proclamation).

Manifestation is a rubric that includes terms such as event, disclosure, epiphany, revelation, gift, unconcealment (*alétheia*), appearance, apparition, visibility, presence and showing. It likewise connotes the metaphysical language of substance, being, essence, form, energy and light. It is primarily a rubric of vision, even if interpretation is to follow the original viewing of the given phenomenon. As indicated above, the word "phenomenon" itself is fraught with manifestation as derived from the Greek verb, *phaínesthai*, meaning "to show itself," and likewise the verb *phaíno*, meaning "to bring to light."[56] Manifestation is the privileged hermeneutic of phenomenology since its introduction by Husserl as a distinct method of philosophy. Further, the privileged place of consciousness throughout the history of phenomenology has tended to be viewed as a consciousness (*noesis*) of manifestations (*noema*). The English word "manifestation" is derived from the Latin word *manifestus*, in turn derived from the Latin words *manus* ("hand") and *-festus* ("struck, assailed, able to be seized"). Therefore the connotation of "manifestation" is the ability to seize something with one's hand, in a word, to manipulate. This is why phenomenology can claim to be in the same league as other sciences such as biology, chemistry, mathematics and physics, because it, too, manipulates sense data in the stock of manifestation. Phenomenology, as ruled by the rubric of manifestation, amounts to a gathering up of manifestations. Phenomenologists who easily fall into the camp of a manifestation driven phenomenology, in addition to Marion, include Husserl, Heidegger (at least in his predominant notion of unconcealment), Stein, Merleau-Ponty, Henry, Chrétien, and Sokolowski (with his notion of a theology of disclosure). These phenomenologists follow the ancient Greek notion of manifestation (*phaíno*) *simpliciter*. That is, manifestation in the nominative, manifestation as such. What gives itself is the primary objective term of the phenomenal process. To whom the phenomenon is given is arbitrary and of minor importance. What is essential is that which gives itself by itself, irregardless of who takes notice of the giving. The central phenomenological notions of givenness and *es gibt* ("it gives") are concentrated terms of manifestation. The verb, "to give," simply relates the movement of manifestation: from concealment to revelation for conscious perception. Manifestation is naturally hostile to the process

56. Cf. Heidegger, *Being and Time*, 51–55 (§7).

of interpretation, as interpreting a manifest phenomenon would seem to diminish its power, force and purity. Likewise, ethics takes a backseat to the preponderant prerogatives of manifestation since to prioritize the interpersonal ethical relationship over and above manifestation would seem to posit a datum for study that cannot be manipulated in the laboratory of an intellectual vision of presence. It may very well be that the dirty little secret of phenomenology is that it has been operating historically under the unspoken dogmatism of manifestation, limiting itself according to the parameters of manifestation.

One might ask then if there is an alternative rubric to that of manifestation for phenomenology. Yes, and it goes by the name "proclamation." Proclamation, in contrast to manifestation, signifies the phenomenality of language, speech, text, law, rhetoric, history, interpretation, hermeneutics, prophecy, testimony and ethics. It includes terms such as word, voice, said, saying, conversation, dialogue, call, response, witness, meaning, news, message and kerygma. Proclamation recognizes the hermeneutic interstices between that which is said and that which is heard. Even more, proclamation claims to proclaim a word prior to manifestation: the ethical exigency of responsibility for the other in the form of a call that is spoken, not given.[57] Rather than seizing or manipulating a given phenomenon in an ocular way, proclamation lets the phenomenon speak itself. According to proclamation, phenomenality is primarily a matter of hearing—of attunement. Proclamation, derived from the Latin word *proclamare* ("to cry out/call before"), contests the autonomy and primacy of manifestation. In its extreme comportment, proclamation declares war on manifestation for being idolatrous. Proclamation accuses manifestation of playing the phenomenological tyrant, forcing all to pay homage to its visual radiance when it in fact is dependent on the verbal and hermeneutic pathway of recognition. Phenomenologists who can be categorized as proclamation driven, in addition to Ricoeur and Levinas, include Heidegger (in part, with his attention to hermeneutics), Gadamer, and Derrida. These phenomenologists understand manifestation to have a dative component, without which manifestation would never come into view. A phenomenon must manifest itself through the various channels of interpretation aided by the peculiar hermeneutic aperture of a particular human subject and cultural context. Where and to whom the phenomenon gives itself shapes the very identity of its appearance. Moreover, subjectivity is included in the definition of phenomenon. In other words, the phenomenon is not something on the side of

57. Even the expression "I give you my word" suggests that a word first must be spoken before it can be given.

subjectivity, but is constituted in and through subjectivity. Or one could say that subjectivity constitutes the phenomenon in large part. If one goes as far as Kant, an irreducible caesura separates the phenomenon (that which appears in conscious intuition) and the noumenon (that which gives itself outside the subject). The aforementioned phenomenologists of proclamation follow Kant on his distinction between noumenon and phenomenon to varying degrees, yet all affirm at least the equality between the objective self-manifestation of the phenomenon and the subjective reception of the phenomenon through the manifold filters of interpretation. Proclamation contends with manifestation over the question of anteriority and primacy. While traditionally relegated to a subordinate position in relation to manifestation, proclamation insists that the ethical injunction antedates any and all appearing and itself makes possible the playing field of manifestation for an individual consciousness. According to Levinas's rendition of the vocative reduction, the counterconsciousness of the other's call awakens consciousness in the first place. The ethical vocation is most originary and absolute, more anterior than even the apparition of the other's visible figure and features.

To return to Tracy's analysis, the manifestation ↔ proclamation dialectic is crucial for understanding religious phenomena today, especially those that present themselves in Jewish, Catholic, Orthodox, and Protestant Christian contexts, to which the scope of this study will limit itself. Tracy suggests that for Catholic and Orthodox communities, manifestation trumps proclamation, whereas in Protestant congregations, proclamation wins the day. I group Judaism along with Protestant Christianity due to its predilection for text and interpretation, especially as instantiated within Torah and Talmud. Tracy begins his analysis with the phenomenon of "the classic." For Tracy, "the classic" refers to any text, event, image, ritual, symbol or person in which "we recognize nothing less than the disclosure of a reality we cannot but name truth."[58] Classics are those most persuasive paragons in culture and society that inspire people in an ultimate manner since they are regarded as having the power to reveal the most meaningful truths communicable. Tracy posits the classic (whether a religious classic or otherwise) as a form of testimony: "Every classic is a sign, a testimony scattered in the cultural world, calling for a reader who will render an interpretation faithful to the testimony itself."[59] He identifies the form of manifestation as a "disclosure of the whole by the power of the whole," a religious expression that bears an event-character and results in a dialectic of disclosure-con-

58. Tracy, *Analogical Imagination*, 108.

59. Ibid., 195.

cealment: a disclosure-concealment of and by the whole, and a letting-go on the part of the human subject in her reception of the classic.[60] For Tracy, if the religious expression assumes the form of manifestation, participation predominates in the experience; if the religious expression takes the form of proclamation, nonparticipation commands the experience. The sacrament is the prime religious expression of manifestation, with a "mystical-priestly-metaphysical-aesthetic emphasis," while word (especially in the form of the biblical text) is the foremost religious expression of proclamation, with a "prophetic-ethical-historical emphasis."[61] Furthermore, Tracy identifies the form of manifestation with the work of the Eastern Orthodox philosopher of religion, Mircea Eliade, while the form of proclamation is evident in the work of Protestant theologians Karl Barth, Dietrich Bonhoeffer, and Jürgen Moltmann. He argues that consistent hermeneutic patterns are observable throughout the history of Christian theology that can be categorized under the main headings of manifestation and proclamation.

How does Tracy's analysis play out in Catholic, Orthodox and Protestant contexts today? First, Tracy aligns both Catholicism and Eastern Orthodoxy with manifestation, while linking Protestantism with proclamation. When describing the respective forms of Christian worship, Tracy's diagnosis is confirmed. Attending either Catholic or Orthodox liturgy, an attentive observer notes the emphasis on sacrament over and against word or preaching. Incense, liturgical costuming, vessels made of precious metals, statuary, iconography, stained glass windows, gestures of reverence, material elements (for example, bread, wine, water, oil), candles, tabernacles, altars, ornate artwork, sacred music. All such liturgical components serve the phenomenality of manifestation. Likewise does Catholic and Orthodox doctrine on liturgy and sacramental theology. Language of "mystery, presence, transubstantiation, elements, species, synaxis, Eucharist, gift" permeates the theological ethos of manifestation. According to manifestation, the Eucharist is conceived in terms of its appearance and presence. In Catholic and Orthodox thought, the sacrament is primarily a thing of the sacred that

60. Even though Tracy aims at an equitable rendering of the dialectical relationship between manifestation and proclamation, he explicitly admits that his analysis may be interpreted as overemphasizing the manifestation side of the dialectic due to its rather Catholic tonality. See Tracy, *Analogical Imagination*, 221 (endnote 26): "This paradigm is developed in Paul Ricoeur's suggestive article 'Manifestation and Proclamation,' *The Journal of the Blaisdell Institute* 12 (Winter 1978). Readers of Ricoeur's article will note that in my use of his paradigm, I change the analysis considerably (on both manifestation and proclamation) in my own readings, partly the same, partly different, of these two classic possibilities of classic religious expression. For myself, Ricoeur's emphasis is classically Reformed. I suspect that he might find mine classically Catholic."

61. Ibid., 203.

is hallowed and set apart from the secular and profane. The Eucharist, in particular, is presented as the "real presence" of Christ—Christ's very body, blood, soul and divinity substantiated in the eucharistic species.[62] These species are meticulously distributed to the faithful via vessels of precious metal and leftovers are reserved with utmost care and reverence, to be worshipped and adored as the very incarnate divinity of Christ. Sacred spaces are demarcated clearly from the profane and commonplace, demanding the proper rituals—for example, contact with holy water and genuflection—to draw near reverently to the numinous presence of God under the disguise of bread and wine. In the domain of manifestation, there is a hypersensitivity to the sacred as that which is to be removed and distinguished totally from the profane. While there is a spectrum running between the extreme forms of manifestation and proclamation, what are the distinctive characteristics of Protestant worship?

The extreme form of proclamation can be witnessed especially in those Christian sects who claim to be nondenominational. In fact, the self-understanding of nondenominational itself attests to the character of proclamation. For proclamation is that which resists all preponderance of manifestation, even as enacted through denominating. When attending a nondenominational worship service, the observer perceives a radically different configuration of meaning than that which is observed in Catholic or Orthodox liturgies. Instead of "smells and bells," there is a near complete absence of the sense of sacred space. There is no demarcation between sacred and profane, there is no "holy of holies," there is no obsession with material elements, artwork or gestures of reverence. Rather, there is a preponderance for the idol-smashing power of the Word of God—not so much in the form of a person as in the form of speech and text. Call and response, exasperated rhetoric, polemical confrontation, exuberant preaching, words of promise and witness, spontaneous vocal prayer, appeals to the authority of the Bible. These are among the distinctive traits of Protestant worship that secularize the religious to the point of demonizing religion per se.[63] In the Protestant context, salvation is not a matter of ritual but a matter of personal relationship (communication) . . . or at least verbally so. In Catholic and Orthodox contexts, salvation is not so much a matter of personal relationship as a matter of the power of the numinous . . . or at least visibly

62. For a post-Heideggerian analysis of the notion of "presence" in relation to the sacrament, see Sweeney, *Sacramental Presence after Heidegger.*

63. Note the polemical YouTube video by Jefferson Bethke entitled, "Why I Hate Religion but Love Jesus" (posted January 10, 2012), which underscores this point of demonizing religion, and has tallied more than thirty million online views to date: http://www.youtube.com/watch?v=1IAhDGYlpqY (accessed February 26, 2016).

so.[64] Protestant theology understands the Eucharist primarily in terms of proclamation, that is, in terms of word, promise and testimony. This paradigm can be traced back to the writings of Martin Luther and John Calvin, as they sought to emphasize the potency of God's word over against the idolatrous configurations of the sacred.[65] In effect, proclamation exercises a desacralizing function to the degree that it succeeds in subverting the exaltation of the sacred in the name of God's in-breaking word that smashes all pretentious idols in its path. The Eucharist in the Protestant sector is more often called "communion" and can be observed in some instances to be in the form of mini-crackers and grape juice in plastic cups. The emphasis of Protestant liturgies, or worship services, is the preaching of God's word, not the adoration of the eucharistic species. In addition, Judaism can be paired with Protestantism as exhibiting a proclivity for proclamation over against manifestation.[66] Justification for this pairing can be found in the Jewish

64. See Otto's *Idea of the Holy* for the origin and meaning of the term "numinous." In summary, Otto coins the neologism "numinous" (from the Latin word *numen*, that is, "divine power/majesty") to signify the *mysterium fascinans et tremendum* ("fascinating and terrible mystery") of religious experience—that overplus of meaning and overpoweringness of divine mystery.

65. Cf. two such relevant instances in Martin Luther's "Pagan Servitude of the Church," in Dillenberger, *Martin Luther*, 272–79: "The mass or sacrament is Christ's testament which He bequeathed to be distributed after his death, among those who believed on him . . . what we call the mass is a promise made by God for the remission of our sins . . . God by His promises, is the author of our salvation . . . the mass, in essence, is solely and simply the words of Christ just quoted, viz., 'Take and eat,' etc. . . . during mass, nothing else should be done with greater zeal, indeed with all our zeal, than to give all our attention to these words, these promises of Christ, for they truly constitute the mass itself . . . more power resides in a testament than in a sacrament . . . [Peter Lombard in his *Sentences*] come[s] to the profundities, and talk[s] trumpery stuff about transubstantiation, and other metaphysical nonsense without end"; and Calvin's *Institutes of the Christian Religion*, 558–64: "Pious souls can derive great confidence and delight from this sacrament, as being a testimony that they form one body with Christ . . . To all these things we have a complete attestation in this sacrament . . . it sends us to the cross of Christ, where that promise was performed and fulfilled in all its parts . . . He is offered by the promises, not that we may stop short at the sight or mere knowledge of him, but that we may enjoy true communion with him . . . I now come to the hyperbolical mixtures which superstition has introduced. Here Satan has employed all his wiles, withdrawing the minds of men from heaven, and imbuing them with the perverse error that Christ is annexed to the element of bread. And, first, we are not to dream of such a presence of Christ in the sacrament as the artificers of the Romish court have imagined, as if the body of Christ, locally present, were to be taken into the hand, and chewed by the teeth, and swallowed by the throat."

66. Cf. Ricoeur, *Figuring the Sacred*, 56: "I will say first of all that with the Hebraic faith the word outweighs the numinous. Of course, the numinous is not absent from, say, the burning bush or the revelation at Sinai. But the numinous is just the underlying canvas from which the word detaches itself. This emergence of the word from the

emphasis of Torah, that is, "teaching, law, instruction," and prophecy. In Jewish thought, the prophetic word calls for the destruction of idols. Psalm 119 encapsulates the vocation to ruminate on the life-giving words of Torah—words that are to be consumed figuratively, for their taste is "sweeter than honey." To summarize the Christian sacramental dialectic, for Catholicism and Eastern Orthodoxy, manifestation is the saturating dynamism of the Eucharist, whereas for Protestantism, kerygma deflects any potentially idolatrous apparition.

The paradigms of manifestation and proclamation are hostile to one another according to their very nature. Given the oppositional and absolute tendencies of these poles of the dialectic, violence often precipitates. One need think only of such historical events as the iconoclasm controversies of the eighth and ninth centuries, the Crusades of the eleventh, twelfth and thirteenth centuries, and the Reformation iconoclasm of the sixteenth century. Iconoclasm indicates the destruction of sacred images by the power of proclamation's prophetic zeal. At the other extreme, the Crusades were an effort to reclaim and defend sacred space by force. Sacred space is sought after to the degree that manifestation attains to the primary dynamism of the religious. In Tracy's schema, manifestation attempts to eradicate proclamation and proclamation attempts to destroy manifestation. They are opposed, one to the other. Their difference is no mere dualism, but rather two irreducible sides of the same coin. Manifestation can lead to a hyper-sense of the sacred set apart from the profane, while proclamation tends toward desacralization, which is simultaneously "world-shattering and world-affirming."[67] Tracy claims that "Christianity lives in and by the paradigmatic power of both manifestation and proclamation," forming a "Christian ethos rooted in the dialectics of an enveloping always-already manifestation constantly transformed by a de-familiarizing, often shattering, not-yet proclamation."[68] Precisely according to this manifestation ↔ proclamation dialectic does Christian faith subsist wherein Christ is at once Word and Sacrament. Yet a tension persists between the historical/proleptic (always-already) and

---

numinous is, in my opinion, the primordial trait that rules all the other differences between the two poles of the religious . . . within the Hebraic domain . . . the instruction through the Torah overcomes any manifestation of an idol. A theology of the Name is opposed to any hierophany of an idol."

67. Tracy, *Analogical Imagination*, 211; cf. Ricoeur, *Figuring the Sacred*, 62–63: "Kerygmatic religion is virtually antisacral . . . Christianity's response to desacralization therefore is not to submit to it as an unavoidable destiny but to carry it out as a task of faith. Or to put it another way, faith and religion must be separated, and we need to go so far as to conceive of an a-religious Christianity such as that spoken of by Dietrich Bonhoeffer in his later writings."

68. Tracy, *Analogical Imagination*, 214, 218.

eschatological (not-yet) dimensions of the dialectic. Manifestation points to a disclosive totality in the present, while the trajectory of proclamation extends to a rendezvous of vindication ever beyond the horizon of the present, expressed by the particularities of speech and text in the form of attested promise. Manifestation and proclamation are by nature at war with one another, regarding themselves to be mutually exclusive. When reduced to their extreme forms, manifestation becomes idolatry and proclamation becomes a breed of textual fundamentalism. Nevertheless, Tracy recognizes the paradoxical relationship between manifestation and proclamation that is at once polar and complementary.

In addition to Tracy's analysis, Ricoeur's earlier assessment in his article, "Manifestation and Proclamation," contributes additional insights to this essential dialectical paradigm for understanding the religious phenomenon. Ricoeur, like Tracy, refers to Eliade's work as emphasizing the form of manifestation in his notion of "hierophany"—an appearance or epiphany of the holy. Ricoeur notes the preverbal, nonlinguistic and saturating character of manifestation, and even goes so far as to identify manifestation as the phenomenological side of the dialectic.[69] On the other side is the "hermeneutic of proclamation"—the "emergence of the word from the numinous," a saying in the form of poetic language that aims at "intensification" through the employment of paradox and hyperbole—a kerygmatic "language game of the eschatological saying" that mediates the meaning of manifestation.[70] The eschatological saying can be expressed through various forms of disorienting discourse (for example, proverbs, parables, narratives) that in effect tear the listener from his indigenous matrix of reality only to reorient him toward a trajectory extending into the *eschaton*: met by the voice of the eschatological saying, "every literal temporal scheme capable of providing a framework to read the signs of the kingdom collapses."[71] In

69. Cf. Ricoeur, *Interpretation Theory*, 60–62, reflecting on the symbolism of the Sacred in the work of Mircea Eliade and Rudolf Otto: "We are warned from the very beginning that we are here crossing the threshold of an experience that does not allow itself to be completely inscribed within the categories of *logos* or proclamation and its transmission or interpretation. The numinous element is not first a question of language, if it ever really becomes one, for to speak of power is to speak of something other than speech even if it implies the power of speaking. This power as efficacy *par excellence* is what does not pass over completely into the articulation of meaning," yet "it is always by means of discourse that this logic manifests itself for if no myth narrated how things came to be or if there were no rituals which re-enacted this process, the Sacred would remain unmanifested."

70. Ricoeur, *Figuring the Sacred*, 56–59; cf. ibid., 65: "There would be no hermeneutic if there were no proclamation."

71. Ibid., 59.

Christian proclamation, the kingdom of God "is among you" yet it "is not here."[72] Proclamation ultimately levels the attempts of manifestation at erecting temporal idols of totality. In other words, proclamation ensures the priority of a hermeneutics of future hope over and against a totality of the present. Ricoeur concedes that while manifestation precedes proclamation, manifestation would remain entirely concealed if it were not articulated meaningfully in the form of symbols and language. The intensification and excess of the religious phenomenon is communicated verbally, especially through apocalyptic, prophetic and poetic discourse. It is the poem or hymn that clothes with words the most saturating occasions of manifestation, even while demanding a divestment (*dépouillement*) of self-consciousness in its finitude and limitations.[73] Poetic discourse, as we will hear in chapters 5

72. Cf. Luke 17:20–21: "Asked by the Pharisees when the kingdom of God would come, he said in reply, 'The coming of the kingdom of God cannot be observed, and no one will announce, "Look, here it is," or "There it is." For behold, the kingdom of God is among you'" (NAB); and John 18:36: "Jesus answered [Pilate], 'My kingdom does not belong to this world. If my kingdom did belong to this world, my attendants [would] be fighting to keep me from being handed over to the Jews. But as it is, my kingdom is not here'" (NAB).

73. See Ricoeur's essay "The Hermeneutics of Interpretation," in Ricoeur, *Essays on Biblical Interpretation*, 119–54, for example, 147–49: "There is no unitary intuition, no absolute knowledge, in which consciousness would grasp both consciousness of the absolute and consciousness of itself . . . It is, in effect, a fact of finitude that original affirmation cannot appropriate itself in a totally intuitive reflection but that it must make a detour through an interpretation of the contingent signs that the absolute gives of itself in history . . . That self-consciousness is held in abeyance by whatever decision, by whatever choice, or whatever trial where it is made to answer a summons—even that which is the appearance of the absolute—does not express the feebleness of the proof of testimony, as in Aristotle, but the finitude of the consciousness to which absolute knowledge is refused." In other words, Ricoeur claims that one cannot perform the original affirmation of the absolute—that is, a personal judgment of ultimacy that relies exclusively on the testimony of/to the absolute in consciousness but which consciousness is not able to procure for itself through a perfect and absolute knowledge—without at the same time relinquishing the pretensions of self-consciousness to omniscience. The act of faith wherein self-consciousness is divested of its imperial prerogatives is evidenced in the writings of several Christian mystics. Cf. Pseudo-Dionysius, *The Mystical Theology*, in *Complete Works*, 135: "For this I pray; and, Timothy, my friend, my advice to you as you look for a sight of the mysterious things, is to leave behind you everything perceived and understood, everything perceptible and understandable, all that is not and all that is, and, with your understanding laid aside, to strive upward as much as you can toward union with him who is beyond all being and knowledge. By an undivided and absolute abandonment of yourself and everything, shedding all and freed from all, you will be uplifted to the ray of the divine shadow which is above everything that is"; Nicholas of Cusa, *Vision of God*, 78, 100: "I behold Thee, O Lord my God, in a kind of mental trace, for if sight be not sated with seeing, nor the ear with hearing, then much less is the intellect with understanding . . . So in Thee, Jesu, Master of masters, I see that the absolute idea of all things, and with it what resembles it in species, are united

and 6 of this book, has the potential to harness the generative power of polar difference between manifestation and proclamation inasmuch as it serves as manifestation proclaimed. Thus for Ricoeur, the manifestation ↔ proclamation dialectic can be characterized as a nonlinguistic ↔ linguistic dialectic, as a preverbal ↔ verbal dialectic, as an event ↔ meaning dialectic, as a phenomenology ↔ hermeneutics dialectic. Such a pattern reinforces Tracy's rubric formulation of the dialectic: sacrament ↔ word; or in Ricoeur's language: sacraments ↔ preaching. Through both Tracy's and Ricoeur's insights into the manifestation ↔ proclamation dialectic, the beginning of a phenomenological description of the Eucharist is underway. Yet one additional element is necessary to add to a phenomenological hermeneutic of the Eucharist, in close relation to manifestation and proclamation: testimony.

## IV. Testimony, Truth, and Knowledge

As Tracy has noted, "every classic is a sign, a testimony scattered in the cultural world, calling for a reader who will render an interpretation faithful to the testimony itself."[74] If every religious classic can be considered as a form of testimony, this is to suggest that testimony is operative in both the manifestation and the proclamation sides of the dialectic. The English word "testimony" is derived from the Latin word *testis*, which means "witness."[75]

---

in the highest degree"; Ignatius of Loyola's famous *Suscipe* prayer, as quoted in *Spiritual Exercises and Selected Works*, 177: "Take, Lord, and receive all my liberty, my memory, my understanding, and all my will—all that I have and possess. You, Lord, have given all that to me. I now give it back to you, O Lord. All of it is yours. Dispose of it according to your will. Give me your love and your grace, for that is enough for me"; Teresa of Avila, *Interior Castle*, 388: "The Lord joins the soul to himself. But he does so by making it blind and deaf, as was St. Paul in his conversion, and by taking away perception of the nature and kind of favor enjoyed, for the great delight the soul then feels is to see itself near God. Yet when he joins it to himself, it doesn't understand anything, for all the faculties are lost"; John of the Cross, "The Ascent of Mount Carmel," in *Collected Works*, 177: "We can gather from what has been said that to be prepared for this divine union the intellect must be cleansed and emptied of everything relating to sense, divested and liberated of everything clearly intelligible, inwardly pacified and silenced, and supported by faith alone, which is the only proximate and proportionate means to union with God"; and Thérèse of Lisieux, *Story of a Soul*, 194: "But just as Mary Magdalene found what she was seeking by stooping down and looking into the empty tomb, so I, abasing myself to the very depths of my nothingness, raised myself so high that I was able to attain my end" (Manuscript B).

74. Tracy, *Analogical Imagination*, 195.

75. Further, the English word "testicle" is also derived from the Latin word *testis* as to suggest that specific anatomical form of the male body that attests to his maleness, as distinct from femaleness.

The etymology of "witness" (for example, "wit") in turn signifies "knowing." Yet we may then proceed to ask the perennial epistemological question, "What is it to know?" It is with this question that we begin to formulate an understanding of what is meant by "testimony." Here we shall argue that "to know" is to believe in a given testimony, that is, to believe that such and such is the case based on the testimony of a personal witness to a given state of affairs. "To know" is thereby equivalent with "to believe" or even "to have faith that . . ." In addition, Tracy argues that (1) "We can never possess absolute certainty," (2) "With science we interpret the world. We do not simply find it out there. Reality is what we name our best interpretation. Truth is the reality we know through our best interpretations," and (3) "What we know, we know with relative adequacy, and we know it is bounded by the realities of language, society, and history. On any particular issue, we can know when we have no further relevant questions. It is possible, therefore, to know when we know enough."[76] Tracy's argument is helpful in that it highlights the role of interpretation in the limited acts of giving and receiving testimony. Knowledge is limited to degrees of relative adequacy achieved in particular social, historical and cultural contexts. Tracy's assertions further indicate the organic relationship between that which is known, the knower, and the many layers of interpretation that comprise knowledge as such. To demonstrate the relationship between the terms truth, testimony, interpretation, faith and knowledge, the following diagram may be helpful:

76. Tracy, *Plurality and Ambiguity*, 22, 48, and 61, respectively. It is vital to note here that we can speak of truth and the process of knowing truth phenomenologically while simultaneously suspending judgment as to what definitively is true and false. To make any assertion is to lay claim implicitly to the veracity of the assertion without forcing the addressee to assent to the assertion. Therefore the phenomenological method can be performed by making allegedly veracious descriptive assertions, for example, "Earth is spherical and appears to orbit around the sun," while suspending judgment in the form of absolute assertions, for example, "Earth and sun were created by God." Both assertions issue truth-claims, the former in a provisional sense (as one of many possible descriptive configurations) and the latter in an absolute sense (as one decidedly closed configuration of possibility).

Knowledge of Truth Schema

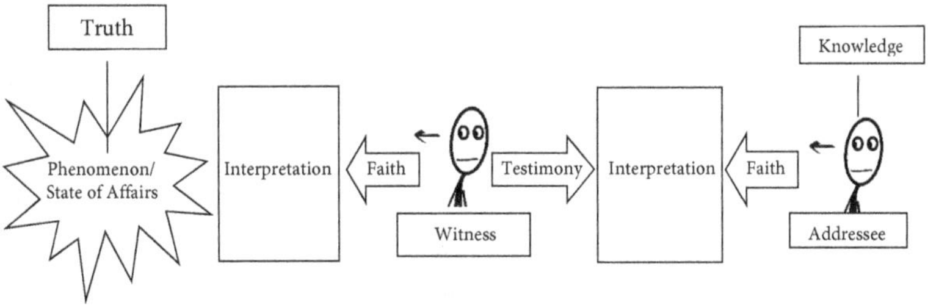


According to this schema, that which is held by knowledge to be true must pass through three layers of communication and meaning: testimony, interpretation and faith. This is to say that (1) any and every truth-claim must be communicated through a particular testimony, which implies a reliance on devices of meaning-making, whether language, symbol or otherwise; and (2) involved in every testimony is (*a*) an act of faith on the part of the witness who testifies, believing that such and such is indeed the case, (*b*) an interpretation of that which is held to be the case by the witness who testifies, (*c*) an interpretation of the testimony of the witness by the addressee, and (*d*) an act of faith on the part of the addressee in the doubly interpreted testimony of the witness. According to this schema, it is clear that knowledge is contingent on testimony, interpretation and faith. In some cases, one person alone can claim to prove the veracity of a given testimony by the accumulation of evidence obtained through the scientific method of experimentation and observation. Yet in most cases one relies on the testimonies of others in claiming to know what is true, what is the case.[77] For example, an automobile accident occurred that involved two vehicles. Four people witnessed the accident occur who were not in either vehicle. In this example the original phenomenon is the event of the automobile accident. The event was interpreted subsequently by four outside witnesses who each put faith in his or her personal perception of the accident. When each of the four witnesses gives his or her testimony to an addressee, the addressee then will have to interpret the testimony of the witnesses and ultimately put faith in that testimony if it is to be regarded as truthful. From a phenomenological standpoint, the task of the witness simply is to describe the event of the

77. On this point, René Descartes is rather transparent in Part Six of his *Discourse on Method*, 40–42, as he writes, "It is true that, with respect to experiments that can help here, one man alone cannot suffice to perform them all . . . I saw more and more every day the delay that the plan I have of self-instruction is suffering because of an infinity of experiments of which I have need and which it is impossible for me to perform without the help of others."

accident as he or she perceived it. Phenomenology is not concerned with the judgment of the witness as to which driver (if any) was at fault for the accident. Judgment is to be suspended in this regard in the context of the phenomenological method. An addressee knows the truth about the event of the accident only in relation to the trustworthy testimony of the witness to the accident and by putting faith in this testimony. "To know" is to put one's faith in a given testimony that such and such is the case, through the layers of interpretation involved in both the act of testifying and the act of assenting to the testimony. Truth makes its way to knowledge by way of interpretation, faith, and testimony.

This careful lineage between truth and knowledge is directly relevant for our study inasmuch as it levels the playing field for all phenomena, whether religious or otherwise. The veracity of phenomenological description is distinct from an act of judgment regarding the truth-claim issued by the religious phenomenon as such.[78] In other words, we are able to describe a religious phenomenon all the while interpreting it, though suspending judgment as to whether or not the truth that it proposes to say or give is indeed true or not. The space between knowledge and truth is traversed in the freedom of faith, interpretation and testimony. To witness a phenomenon is to have knowledge of the phenomenon's truth as it gives or says itself. The distance between knowledge and truth is a hollowed-out hiatus that opens for the sake of the freedom of faith and judgment. If there was not this riskful expanse between knowledge and truth, human beings would be robots essentially, mechanical automatons for which no meaning says or gives itself outside of the self. A closure of the breadth between knowledge and truth would amount to a closure of meaning, a cessation of creativity, an end to freedom and to the quest for happiness. The interstices that provide the terrain for the passage of meaning and truth are safeguarded by the possibilities of testimony.[79] Testimony is the certain and inevasible channel through which truth and knowledge kiss.

78. The difference between the act of faith involved in accurate phenomenological description (that is, the belief in the possibility of actually describing a phenomenon accurately) and the act of faith involved in assenting to the truth-claim of a phenomenon (in particular a religious phenomenon) is akin to the classic distinction between *fides quae* and *fides qua*. *Fides quae* ("faith that . . .") refers to believing in a particular cognitive content given to consciousness, for example, the *noema* ("the cognitive content") as provided to the *noesis* ("the act of cognition"). *Fides qua* ("faith in . . .") concerns the act of faith itself in the fullness of voluntary capacity, that is, that which involves a full act of the will in assenting and personally committing oneself to a given testimony, for better or for worse.

79. Yet these interstices between truth and knowledge also allow for the play of the lie or falsehood, that is, false testimony. Levinas acknowledges this in his 1934

Extending from the word "testimony" is the closely associated word "attestation." As key terms for this study, it is important to indicate the similarity and difference between "testimony" and "attestation." While "testimony" refers to the content proclaimed by the witness who testifies, "attestation" refers to the very act of bearing witness to . . . To attest is to testify. The nominal form "attestation" connotes an emphasis on the otherness between the testimony and the witness (that is, the one who testifies), according to its etymological roots: *ad-* ("to/toward") and *testari* ("to be a witness"). "Attestation," in effect, means to be a witness to . . . The ellipsis here signifies bearing witness to whatever, for example, an event, a person, a message, an object, an observation, a state of affairs, etc. It is essential to understand that "attestation" refers to a movement of meaning beginning with that which gives or says itself to be known. No given or said is known without passing through the layers of interpretation between the given or said and the knower, or without an act of faith on the part of the witness and on the part of the knower. Perception does not communicate automatic and certain knowledge, but rather interprets that which is said or given, thereby maintaining a character of openness and possibility. One's perceptions are ever open to clarification and revision. This is not to deny the possibility of objective truth—that is, truth given or said as such and not open to alteration in itself—but to describe carefully the process by which truth as such is known with degrees of relative adequacy. "Attestation" is the term used to indicate this process, emphasizing the precise role of testimony at the core of the process.

Given these preliminary considerations of "testimony" and "attestation," an integral relationship can be posited between manifestation, proclamation and attestation (which includes within itself the term "testimony"). Manifestation regards the given phenomenon as that which gives itself to a perception of visibility. Proclamation considers the said phenomenon as that which announces itself to a perception of audibility. Attestation refers to the phenomenality of both manifestation and proclamation inasmuch as both hermeneutic matrices depend on the pathway of attestation for recognition to occur. No phenomenon is recognized as manifest that does not supply a self-disclosure of testimony. All manifest phenomena testify on their own behalf in the precise ways in which they reveal themselves. No phenomenon is recognized as proclaimed that does not supply an intelligible language of testimony. All proclaimed phenomena, while not depending on the visual

essay, "Some Thoughts on the Philosophy of Hitlerism," in Levinas, *Unforeseen History*, 13–21, for example, 19: "This freedom intrinsic to the dignity of thought also harbors the danger. In the interval that separates man from the idea slips the lie."

display of manifestation, are recognized to the degree that they are heard via speech and language. Attestation is distinct from manifestation and proclamation, though it is at work in each pole of the dialectic. As will be demonstrated, attestation serves as a third party witness to the fervent and fruitful dialectic between manifestation and proclamation. It is precisely this tripartite configuration of manifestation, proclamation and attestation that phenomenalizes truth as such, especially in the religious context. Knowledge of truth proceeds along the passageway of faith, interpretation and testimony.

## V. Trilectic of Testimony

Before returning to the manifestation ↔ proclamation dialectic as perceived in the Eucharist, a methodological excurses is necessary to set up a heuristic device whereby the relationship between manifestation, proclamation and testimony can be analyzed further. The heuristic will be called the "trilectic of testimony," implying the threefold matrix of testimony: (1) self-testimony of that which is given (manifestation), (2) hermeneutical testimony that interprets and brings to recognition that which is given (proclamation), and (3) testimony of the third party witness to the manifestation ↔ proclamation dialectic. The logic of the trilectic is based on the more primitive logic of the dialectic. The form of dialectic in mind is not exclusively that of Plato or that of Hegel, but nonetheless related to each. The dialectical model proposed here is that of Paul Ricoeur:

> My inclination is to see the universe of discourse as a universe kept in motion by an interplay of attractions and repulsions that ceaselessly promote the interaction and intersection of domains whose organizing nuclei are off-centered in relation to one another; and still this interplay never comes to rest in an absolute knowledge that would subsume the tensions.[80]

Instead of a Platonic dialectic that would resolve itself through rational discourse, or a Hegelian dialectic in which a sublation (*Aufhebung*) would resolve all polarity, Ricoeur's proposed dialectic remains unresolved and open to further possibilities. For Ricoeur, the "universe of discourse" is constituted by the perpetual play of polarities between questions, assertions and meanings—in a word, communicative wonder. Much like the interplay of atoms in the material realm, the generation of meaning depends upon

80. Ricoeur, *Rule of Metaphor*, 357.

difference in proximate play. The form of the Ricoeurian dialectic is an ellipsis, with two foci of equivalence and proximity:[81]

Ellipsis

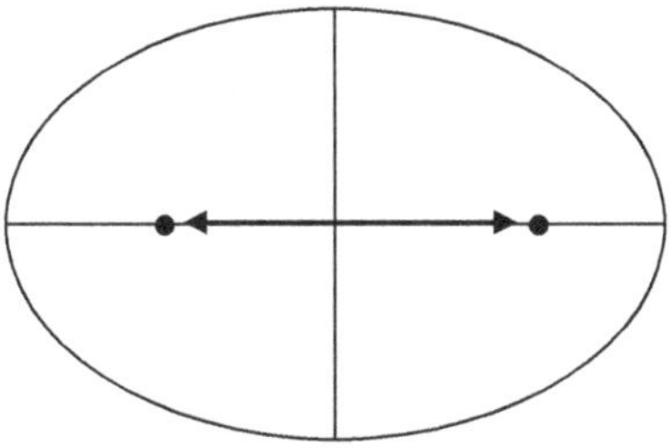

The elliptical form depends on two, and not only one, of the foci. Dialogue (Plato) is the impetus of this form, but likewise is Hegel's counterposing of positive and negative (tragic) assertions. However, rather than following Hegel's notion of *Aufhebung*, a sublative thrust toward absolute knowledge, the interaction between two different components resists reduction, conflation or synthesis. The law is unity in diversity rather than unity in sameness. There is wholeness yet not a totality. Such is Gregory of Nazianzus's conception of God as Trinity: "The one God, one in diversity, diverse in unity, wherein is a marvel," a "unity, having from all eternity arrived by motion at duality, [finds] its rest in trinity."[82] The suspicion is confirmed that this project rests on a hypothetical theology of God as Trinity, as well it should according to the context of Christian theological investigation. However, not only is the project inspired by Trinitarian theology, but the hermeneutic of the unity-in-diversity dialectic also finds its raison d'être in descriptive phenomenology. We live in a diverse world, and yet the world is one world. Unity presupposes the condition of diversity; unity depends on difference.[83] Unity in sameness is a static tautology, while unity in diversity

81. The polysemy of the word "ellipsis" is significant for the discussion at hand. Ellipsis can refer to the figure of an ellipse (illustrated here) or to omissions in a text that are signified with . . . or *** or [ ] or something similar, or may not appear with any textual marking at all. For instance, the elliptical statement "Kant disagreed as expected" implies "Kant disagreed as had been expected." The elliptical phenomenon is similar to the relationship between assertion and testimony. Testimony is implied in every assertion, whether or not the notion of "testimony" is rendered explicit in the process of making assertions, or acknowledged as the productive force behind the efficacy of the assertions.

82. Gregory of Nazianzus, *Second Theological Oration* 1, and *Third Theological Oration* 2, in Hardy, *Christology of the Later Fathers*, 136 and 161, respectively.

83. The notion of "difference" submitted here contests Deleuze's teleology of

expresses the paradoxical logic of generation, that is, not only one but also many. *Non solum . . . , sed etiam . . .* ("not only . . . , but also . . .").[84] Without genuine diversity, authentic unity is not possible. Throughout the course of this book it will be argued that a diverse unity between manifestation and proclamation—a rapprochement between the respective geniuses of Catholic/Orthodox and Protestant/Jewish thought—harnesses the generative potencies of the inherent polarity within the Eucharist.

Following the rule of the dialectic is the rule of the trilectic, namely, the trilectic of testimony. While this notion will be developed in the pages to follow, it is appropriate to introduce the concept at the start. Trilectic of testimony refers to the latent dynamism of the dialectic operative in all claims to meaning, truth and identity. As demonstrated above, meaning begins with that which gives or says itself to be interpreted, recognizable through the vectors of testimony that transmit the original given or said phenomenon. For example, the moon gives itself to be perceived. It is left to the various branches of science (phenomenology included) to interpret the moon as such. One could inquire into the molecular composition of the moon, the manner by which it appears to give light, the changes in its appearance (crescent, full, etc.), its specific relation to earth and to other celestial bodies. One also could inquire into its meaning, for example, why does the moon give itself and what symbolic potencies does the moon lend to meaning-making? Several testimonies can be developed that convey the givenness and symbolic call of the moon. Yet we can identify plainly a

---

difference as hostility and aggression, for example, see Deleuze, *Difference and Repetition*, xx: "The beautiful soul says: we are different, but not opposed . . . The *notion of a problem*, which we see linked to that of difference, also seems to nurture the sentiments of the beautiful soul: only problems and questions matter . . . Nevertheless, we believe that when these problems attain their proper degree of *positivity*, and when difference becomes the object of a corresponding *affirmation*, they release a power of aggression and selection which destroys the beautiful soul by depriving it of its very identity and breaking its good will . . . every thought becomes an aggression." Instead of hostility and aggression, we contend (peacefully, respectfully and dialogically) that difference bears the potency of unity and conciliation. The beautiful soul is sustained by hope, nourished by faith, and vindicated by love. For love and hospitality thrive on difference.

84. This Latin phrase—*non solum, sed etiam*—signifies what could be called the genius of Catholic theology, especially as on display in the work of Thomas Aquinas. He frequently uses this grammatical coupling to maintain the "both/and" testimony of/to truth. For example, see *Summa theologiae* I.1.10: "*Respondeo dicendum quod auctor sacrae Scripturae est Deus, in cuius potestate est ut non solum voces ad significandum accommodet (quod etiam homo facere potest), sed etiam res ipsas*" ("I respond that the author of sacred Scripture is God, in whose power it is to not only signify meanings by spoken words (which man is also able to do), but also by things themselves"; translation my own). The notion of *non solum, sed etiam* will be augmented by the phenomenon of paradox, addressed in chapter 2 of this study.

dialectical relationship between that which originally manifests itself (the moon as *such*) and the various testimonies that proclaim what manifests itself (the moon *as* such). In both the mode of manifestation and the mode of proclamation, testimony is operative as the primary agent of recognition between the phenomenon and the human subject who perceives the phenomenon. Transforming the linear and rather static form of the dialectic, the trilectic of testimony acknowledges the prominent and active role of testimony within the dialectic—testimony as that which makes the dialectic generative, dynamic, cohesive and unified.[85]

This schema will be analyzed further in chapter 4, but proposing a heuristic description at this point helps to orient the reader from the start. A pairing of key thinkers assigned to each pole of the dialectic also will be submitted: Marion as a thinker of manifestation and Ricoeur and Levinas as thinkers of proclamation and attestation. The linkage of these modern-day phenomenologists to the respective sides of the dialectic will allow the hermeneutic to "take on flesh" by comparing the work of diverse (yet similar) thinkers according to the proposed schema. Without such a critical comparison, the theory would remain in the abstract and perhaps be, in the end, inaccessible and irrelevant. Instead, inviting an amorous collision between the thought of Marion, Ricoeur and Levinas will tap into the potential of the proposed trilectic whereby alternative testimonies enter into dialogue and become generative by virtue of their unitive intercourse.

In the way of a primer, let us briefly consider the general contrast between Marion, Ricoeur and Levinas in terms of manifestation, proclamation and attestation. For his part, Marion exegetes the general notion of manifestation by positing a more fundamental notion of givenness (*Gegebenheit*), heeding Husserl's admonition: "to the things themselves!" Givenness is a way to recognize the ways in which phenomena give themselves by themselves. Implicitly influenced by the novel notion of difference in the work of his former teacher, Gilles Deleuze (1925–95), Marion posits givenness as that absolute modality that seeks to liberate phenomena from the shackles of subjectivity and the principle of sufficient reason.[86] Givenness

85. See the Appendix for a diagrammatic illustration of the trilectic of testimony.

86. While there are virtually no significant comparative studies between the work of Marion and Deleuze to date, Marion's influence by Deleuze can be surmised by the fact that he studied with Deleuze, coupled with their similar tasks of inverting traditional metaphysical paradigms about reality. Likewise, two minor texts suggest at least a remote influence of Deleuze on Marion: (1) Marion's testimony in his own words in Caputo and Scanlon, *God, the Gift, and Postmodernism*, 68: "The event is unique and cannot be repeated . . . For instance, if I give my word, I have to repeat it and go on; but I cannot repeat it as an identical act; the repetition is never identical (just refer

even transcends historical particularity in favor of a universal dynamic of manifestation, employing the language of *es gibt* ("it gives"). As applied to the Eucharist, a hermeneutic of givenness—givenness as the manifestation of manifestation—will help yield the expansive field of vision disclosed by the Eucharist, a vision allegedly "outside of the text" (*hors-texte*). Marion's extensive discourse on the Eucharist in *God without Being* will prove especially advantageous in considering how the Eucharist manifests itself as *such*. Helpful as this will be, we must at the same time admit that the givenness of phenomena remains imperceptible and unintelligible without passing through the various filters of consciousness—the manifold semantic, metaphorical and analogical filters that allow a phenomenon to appear *as* such.

Paul Ricoeur, for his part, recognizes the inherent and unresolvable tension between the idea of the absolute and the individual, particular experience of the absolute in consciousness.[87] He points to the necessary media-

---

to Kierkegaard, Heidegger, or even Deleuze)"; and (2) Cyril O'Regan's observation in his essay "Jean-Luc Marion: Crossing Hegel," in Hart, *Counter-Experiences*, 96: "And Marion rather easily allows himself to be read as presupposing the specifically French coda of Lévinas and Derrida, and maybe Deleuze, in which the imperialism and violence of *Geist* has been exposed, and what remains is thinking otherwise than metaphysics, whether ethically as in the case of Lévinas, grammatologically or semiotically as in the case of Derrida, and plurally in the case of Deleuze." The plurality of Marion's thinking givenness is to be found precisely in his notion of "the fold of givenness"; see Marion, *Being Given*, 64–68. "The fold of givenness" is the indivisible fold ("unity yet distinction") between (1) the given that gives itself uniquely (that is, "the gift"), and (2) the process of advent and unfolding through which the given gives itself (that is, "the giving"). No two enactments of givenness are ever the same.

87. Cf. Ricoeur's essay "The Hermeneutics of Testimony," in Ricoeur, *Essays on Biblical Interpretation*, 119–54. The idea of "the absolute" refers to the notion of an unconditioned and originary given or said in the depths of consciousness to which virtually all meaningful human action is tethered. The idea of the absolute also goes by such names as "the infinite, the Requisite, God, love, the call, the ultimate, conscience," etc. As in the work of Ricoeur and Levinas, this idea of the absolute is perceived not in and of itself but through the testimony of the witness to its idea. For Ricoeur, this testimony takes the form of an originary affirmation of the absolute embodied in the human will and action. For Levinas, testimony to the infinite is recognizable in the affirmative response of "me"—the "here I am"—to the call of the other. An absolute command demands an absolute response. The English word "absolute" is derived from the past participle of the Latin verb *absolvere*, which means "to set free/absolve." In turn, the Latin etymology of "absolve," *ab-solve*, means "to be loosened/released from." This etymological meaning is quite significant for understanding the weight and magnitude of the term "absolute": the idea of the absolute gives itself as the very impetus of liberation and salvation. Recall Augustine's distinction between *signa* ("signs") and *res* ("reality") in *De doctrina christiana*. For Augustine, there is only one indivisible and legitimate *res*, namely, God, the Absolute. All created and finite existents are *signa* in relation to the one *res*.

tion that allows the idea of the absolute to be assimilated in consciousness by way of testimony to the absolute. In a similar manner, the sacramental givenness of manifestation is mediated by testimony in the form of proclamation: *es gibt* ("it gives") becomes *es gibt als* . . . ("it gives as . . ."), and even further, *es gibt nach* . . . ("it gives according to . . ."). This modification of *es gibt* indicates that meaning proceeds from both the self-attested givenness of the phenomenon "in its own flesh" and the testimonial construction and construal of meaning by the witness. The sacramental givenness of manifestation depends upon the auto-attestation of manifestation as well as the alterity-attestation of proclamation for its transferal from the realm of obscurity and opacity to that of conscious recognition and reception, bearing the trace of an "originary affirmation."[88] Likewise, testimony depends upon the anterior "happening" of givenenss in order to have something about which to testify.

Levinas, for his part, submits ethics as first philosophy, recognizing the call of the other as the primordial phenomenon that precedes all others and awakens phenomenality itself. The call of the other, the proclaimed awakening, predates any manifest givenness, and is described symbolically and figuratively, in relation to its literal meaning, as the face of the other—a face that appears to the degree that it speaks. Levinas, in particular, accentuates the role of testimony as expressed in the affirmative response of the unique *moi* ("me"), called to responsibility for the unique other (*l'autrui*). The affirmative "Here I am!" attests to the proclaimed summons of the other who calls me to rise to responsibility for him. For Levinas, the call of the other outruns all other inquiry and reflection; the call of the other is most anterior and originary.[89] Because of the acuteness of this call, which gives rise to the operations of consciousness in the first place, the ethics of intersubjectivity speaks the first word of phenomenality. That is to say, we are awakened consciously by the call of the other. All recognition of intuitional essences, embodiedness, textuality, and even givenness are ancillary in relation to the call of the other that exhibits a phenomenal velocity surpassing even the speed of light. We might inquire, moreover, whether the call of the other is not only the beginning of the recognition of meaning but also its terminus. After all, is not the beginning the end, is not the end the beginning?[90] The

88. More will be said on the notion of "originary affirmation" in chapter 3 of this study.

89. See Levinas, *Otherwise than Being*, 150: "In approaching the other I am always late for the meeting."

90. The typical *Weltanschauungen* of the natural sciences today preclude the possibility of inquiring into final causality and concern themselves exclusively with a presumedly closed field of efficient and material causality. For a very helpful diagnosis of

overarching argument of this project will offer a generous corrective to the tendency in phenomenology to reduce a person's encounter with a phenomenon to a one-sided degree of distortion, whether in the form of givenness alone or subjective construction alone.

## VI. From Meaning to Truth: Assessing the Truth Status of the Eucharist

Even though the majority of this work will be a phenomenological analysis of the Eucharist according to the trilectic of testimony hermeneutic, the final chapter will be devoted to asking the question about the truth proposal of the Eucharist. This concluding question will move beyond phenomenology alone, setting up yet another dialectical relationship, that between phenomenology and transcendental reflection (metaphysics). Phenomenology is a method that describes, while transcendental reflection is a method that personally reflects and passes judgment on that which has been described. This dialectical pairing is inspired by David Tracy's revisionist model for contemporary theology as set forth in *Blessed Rage for Order*.[91] For our purposes, phenomenology will aim at describing the various meaningful dimensions of the Eucharist by applying the trilectic of testimony hermeneutic. Transcendental reflection, in turn, will seek to determine the truth status of the results of the phenomenological investigation by "(investigating) the cognitive claims of those religious and theistic meanings," searching for the conditions of possibility for any and all life experiences, and asking,

---

modern-day scientific worldviews and their relation to phenomenology, see Richard A. Cohen's foreword to the second edition of Levinas's *Theory of Intuition in Husserl's Phenomenology*, ix–xxxi. Cohen demonstrates how phenomenology once again opens the possibility of inquiring into the teleology of phenomenal meaning, challenging the post-Cartesian claim that final causality is a fallacy after all. For instance, Cohen describes the outlook of contemporary science in this way: "In the name of truth, the value of values is devalued; values become bankrupt. To know is to know prior rather than posterior causes, departures rather than destinations, grounds rather than goals, desires rather than the desirable. Efficient causality, sufficient reason, no more, no less. Religion and science henceforth part company, with science holding the monopoly on truth. Religion would thus become mortal enemy to science, and not only religion." One need only call to mind the contemporary obsession with the big-bang theory to validate the plausibility of Cohen's argument. This is to say that many people today seem to be content with theorizing the beginning of the universe as one colossal explosion from point zero without considering that which necessarily gave rise to such an event "in the beginning." What caused such an explosion and whence came the energy and matter involved in the blast? All questioning leads to the idea of infinity, the idea of the absolute, from whence the beginning is the end and to whither the end is the beginning.

91. See especially Tracy, *Blessed Rage for Order*, 43–56 (chapter 3).

"Why does any of this matter and is it true?"[92] Phenomenological descriptive analysis reaches adequacy insofar as it withholds judgment and investigates a phenomenon in an accurate manner. Transcendental reflective analysis succeeds insofar as it begs the question of truth, given the various meanings unearthed by phenomenology. Without transcendental reflective analysis, a phenomenological descriptive analysis may tell all about the what, where, who, when and how, but never arrive at the why. On the other hand, without a phenomenological descriptive analysis, a transcendental reflective analysis may issue a claim as to the why with little to no warrants, backing or rational evidence for its claim. In the end, the phenomenological ↔ transcendental/metaphysical dialectic will render the proposed trilectic of testimony meaningful, truthful and ultimately praxiological. To the chagrin of contemporary "post-metaphysical" phenomenologists, we will insist that metaphysics is necessary as a final step for making a truth-claim.[93] One

92. Ibid., 56.

93. To reinforce my claim about the necessity of metaphysics in relation to phenomenology, see John Paul II, *Fides et ratio*, 55, 82–83: "Surveying the situation today, we see that the problems of other times have returned, but in a new key. It is no longer a matter of questions of interest only to certain individuals and groups, but convictions so widespread that they have become to some extent the common mind. An example of this is the deep-seated distrust of reason which has surfaced in the most recent developments of much of philosophical research, to the point where there is talk at times of 'the end of metaphysics.' Philosophy is expected to rest content with more modest tasks such as the simple interpretation of facts or an enquiry into restricted fields of human knowing or its structures . . . A radically phenomenalist or relativist philosophy would be ill-adapted to help in the deeper exploration of the riches found in the word of God . . . We face a great challenge at the end of this millennium to move from *phenomenon* to *foundation*, a step as necessary as it is urgent. We cannot stop short at experience alone; even if experience does reveal the human being's interiority and spirituality, speculative thinking must penetrate to the spiritual core and the ground from which it rises. Therefore, a philosophy which shuns metaphysics would be radically unsuited to the task of mediation in the understanding of Revelation . . . Metaphysics thus plays an essential role of mediation in theological research. A theology without a metaphysical horizon could not move beyond an analysis of religious experience, nor would it allow the *intellectus fidei* to give a coherent account of the universal and transcendent value of revealed truth. If I insist so strongly on the metaphysical element, it is because I am convinced that it is the path to be taken in order to move beyond the crisis pervading large sectors of philosophy at the moment, and thus to correct certain mistaken modes of behavior now widespread in our society"; and Wojtyła, *Über die Möglichkeit*, 97, 109, 115, 196: "Despite its objectivist tendencies, Scheler's ethical system is not suitable for interpreting an ethics that has an objective character as Christian Ethics does. There is no doubt that Scheler's insufficient objectivism springs from his phenomenological principles. Because of these principles the ethical value always remains in an intentional and—despite everything—subjective position. In order to grasp ethical value in its real and objective position, one would have to proceed from different epistemological premises, namely, meta-phenomenological and even meta-physical premises

of the ironic realizations within a "post-metaphysical" world is that metaphysics can never be left behind.[94] To claim to do so definitively requires recourse to the self-evident first principles of metaphysics, such as that of the principle of non-contradiction.

All this is to say that phenomenology can take thought and meaning only so far. Phenomenology ultimately provides an endless hermeneutic to furnish descriptive interpretations of phenomena for consideration. Yet why would one wish to engage in the phenomenological method if not for a greater cause, namely, truth? Since phenomenology is bound to a suspension of judgment regarding the truth status of a phenomenon, an additional method must be used in order to make a sound judgment. Religious phenomena, in particular, demand a judgment from their witnesses, for that is their point: to provoke a judgment for or against their respective truth proposals. Religious phenomena do not give or say themselves merely as ancient museum artifacts, but rather call for an all-or-nothing decision of ultimacy—a personal response of conviction by the addressee: Yes or No. At some point each one of us must hazard a commitment as to what we consider to be the truth—what we hold to be Absolute, whether God/s or Otherwise. It is with this sense of doubly hopeful risk that this book opens onto new vistas for thinking the Eucharist.

---

. . . Due to its phenomenological principles, Scheler's system cannot directly grasp and express that the human person in its acts is the origin of moral good and evil. The whole difficulty is the result of the phenomenological premises of the system and we must assign the blame to these principles . . . [The theologian] should not forego the great advantages which the phenomenological method offers his work. It impresses the stamp of experience on works of ethics and nourishes them with the life-knowledge of concrete man by allowing an investigation of moral life from the side of its appearance. Yet, in all this, the phenomenological method plays only a secondary assisting role . . . At the same time, the investigations convince us that the Christian thinker, especially the theologian, who makes use of phenomenological experience in his work, cannot be a Phenomenologist." Quoted by Michael Waldstein in his introduction to John Paul II, *Man and Woman He Created Them*, 70, 71, 75, respectively.

94. Falque makes a similar claim in his pairing of medieval philosophy/theology and phenomenology in what he calls a "phenomenological practice of medieval philosophy." Even more, he recognizes the fruitful tension between the two distinct subdisciplines of philosophy and also the inherent (positive) tension between Greek metaphysics and theology, or the field of divine revelation. See his introduction, "*Fons Signatus*: The Sealed Source," and chapter 1 on Augustine, "Metaphysics and Theology in Tension (Augustine)," in Falque, *God, the Flesh, and the Other*, 3–46. For example, Falque writes that "the 'metaphysical restoration' faults phenomenology for having wanted to cut ties with every form of transcendence, while its 'overcoming' has never in reality signified a de-valorization of the divine, but only another manner of approaching it and of speaking about it. Briefly, if onto-theo-logy can now consider itself dead as a concept, it has however not yet admitted its end as 'prism'—that is, as 'filter' which enlightens by a 'new light' the 'spectrum' [*spectre*] of the scheme of thought" (23).

# chapter 2

# Jean-Luc Marion: Thinker of Manifestation and Adoration

## I. *Entreé* to the Paradox of the Saturated Phenomenon

In the hermeneutical matrix of Jean-Luc Marion, the Eucharist is a phenomenon of auto-manifestation to a saturating degree. Divine glory gives itself in the Eucharist as it is emptied of all speech and text, unfettered from all subjective appendages. For Marion, the Eucharist is the religious phenomenon par excellence that gives itself as the supreme instance of manifestation extending from the incarnation of Jesus of Nazareth, the Word made flesh (*Verbum-Caro*).[1] The Word of God is communicated veraciously to humanity to the extent that it is divested of all words and interpretive constructs. In fact, this Word interprets itself for the addressee, for the Word receives no testimony from human beings that would add to its glory and truth.[2] The proper and natural response of human beings in the face of di-

1. See von Balthasar, *Mysterium Paschale*, 221–80. At times our discussion of the Eucharist (especially in Marionian terms) will appear to have left phenomenology and moved into the realm of thetic judgment, that is, running in a language of actuality rather than possibility. While conceding that this may appear to be the case, I hold to the claim that this descriptive analysis remains phenomenology inasmuch as it operates under the allowances of Heidegger's phenomenological "as." Cf. Heidegger, *Being and Time*, 188–95 (§32). The Eucharist will be described as it gives itself within the context of Roman Catholic doctrinal and liturgical tradition. Thetic judgment nevertheless can be suspended all the while describing the Eucharist under the provisory brackets of the "as if," which essentially implies open possibility rather than predetermined actuality.

2. See John 5:33–34: "You sent emissaries to John, and he testified to the truth. I do not accept testimony from a human being, but I say this so that you may be saved"; and

vine glory is speechlessness. When human beings try to speak the saturating intuition of divine revelation, we stammer, babble and utter gibberish.[3] We cannot speak God adequately, for "only God can speak well of God."[4] Marion insists that "theology can reach its authentically *theo*logical status only if it does not cease to break with all theo*logy*."[5] For Marion, *theo*logy refers to the manifest self-attestation of the incarnate Word, whereas theo*logy* implies the priority of human interpretation of God's self-communication. This difference between *theo*logy and theo*logy* is precisely the dialectical relationship we seek to highlight between manifestation (*theo*logy) and proclamation (theo*logy*) throughout this book. In order to draw the sharp contrast between Marion as a proponent of manifestation, and Ricoeur and Levinas as advocates of proclamation, we first will devote this chapter to unpacking the specific brand of phenomenology in force for Marion.

Marion is, above all, a champion of the paradox.[6] His thought is found hovering over the chasm between the possibilities of human reason and divine revelation. For Marion, "paradox" is not synonymous with "contra-

---

1 John 5:9–11: "If we accept human testimony, the testimony of God is surely greater. Now the testimony of God is this, that he has testified on behalf of his Son. Whoever believes in the Son of God has this testimony within himself. Whoever does not believe God has made him a liar by not believing in the testimony God has given about his Son. And this is the testimony: God gave us eternal life, and this life is in his Son" (NAB). Cf. Marion, *God without Being*, 140, 144: "He says *himself*—the Word! . . . Better, he does not even have anything to say in order to say everything, since he incarnates the dict in saying it: no sooner said than done . . . The text does not at all coincide with the event."

3. Marion, *God without Being*, 142: "The Word says itself, it therefore becomes unspeakable to us; labile inhabitant of our babble, it inhabits our babble nevertheless as referent."

4. See ibid., 139, where Marion inserts the following quotation from Pascal. Cf. Pascal, *Pensées*, 296 (799): "An artisan who speaks well of riches, an attorney who speaks well of war, of royalty, etc.; but the rich speak well of riches, the king speaks coolly of a great gift for which he sends, and God speaks well of God" (translation my own).

5. Marion, *God without Being*, 139.

6. The Greek etymology of "paradox" is telling: *para*- ("beside/alongside" and/or "beyond/outside of") *doxa* ("opinion" and/or "glory"). Marion defines paradox in this way: "Paradox means what happens counter to (*para*-) received opinion, as well as to appearance, according to the two obvious meanings of *doxa*. But it also means what happens counter to expectation—'praeter expectationem offertur'—what arrives against all that representation or intention, in short the concept, would expect" (*Being Given*, 225–26). The paradoxical phenomenon is unleashed in the term "paradox" itself. It indicates a unity in diversity of meaning, a dialectic of difference. Ultimately for Marion, the meaning of paradox is the glory of saturation that bedazzles common opinion and expectation. In his above definition of paradox, Marion references Goclenius's (R. Göckel's) classic definition of paradox: "The paradox is inauspicious and strange, set apart from what opinion and expectation offer" (cf. *Being Given*, endnote 82, 366 [translation my own]).

diction," but remains possible inasmuch as any phenomenon remains possible.[7] In this regard, Marion takes, as his point of departure, the observation of a paradoxical phenomenon made by Alexius Meinong: "'it gives' objects, of which it is valid to say, 'it gives' not objects as such" (*es gibt Gegenstände, von denen gilt, es dergleichen Gegenstände nicht gibt*).[8] Such phenomena that simultaneously give and do not give objects per se would include a "golden mountain," "clouds of silk" in the sky, a "tree of pearls," the equation 3 = 1, any metaphor such as "a sea of misery." While these phenomena have not been found (to my knowledge) to appear literally as such in nature, or reach adequation in a certain static concept alone, they nevertheless give themselves to consciousness insofar as they can be received intuitionally, even by way of imagination, with a concomitant surplus of meaning.[9] They unfold meanings according to their paradoxical potencies and to the multiple horizons of interpretation they generate. For ". . . all that is knowable is given—precisely to the act of knowing. And to the extent to which all objects are knowable, givenness (*Gegebenheit*) can be attributed to them as a universal property, to all without exception, no matter that they are or are not."[10] This is to say that all phenomena that give themselves to consciousness need not be restricted to conceptual adequation or objective appearance "in nature"

7. Cf. Marion, *Prolegomena to Charity*, x: "In fact, love does not lack rationality. But its rationality unfolds in paradoxes, which elude the most quotidian rationality, the calculations and measurements of technology that are sufficient for constituting the world's objects . . . In order to enter into the tautology of love, we must risk following several paradoxes. But paradoxes do not put reason to question; on the contrary, they secure for reason its most unshakable supports." Cf. Marion, *Being Given*, 221–28. For Marion there are three categories of phenomena: (1) phenomena poor in intuition, that is, those phenomena that give themselves completely in their concept alone, for example, "a formal intuition in mathematics or a categorical intuition in logic"; (2) common-law phenomena, that is, those phenomena preceded by an intention of expectation and at best met with an expected intuition, for example, "the objects of physics and the natural sciences"; and (3) saturated phenomena, that is, those phenomena "in which intuition always submerges the expectation of intention," for example, the paradox, in which "the intuition sets forth a surplus that the concept cannot organize, therefore that the intention cannot foresee."

8. Meinong, "Über Gegenstandstheorie," 9 (translation my own).

9. It may be objected here that these examples are merely misplacements, or imaginative transpositions, of common-law phenomena that do occur as objects as such. However, this is precisely the point: two *doxa* (that is, two simultaneous positions/opinions) that hypostatically merge in a single instance, namely, a paradox. Meinong's point is that paradoxes are rationally demonstrable. In addition, the Greek term *doxa* can also mean "glory, splendor, grandeur, brightness, brilliance" or even "God." Therefore the term "paradox" will be very helpful for understanding the manifestation ↔ proclamation dialectic as it connotes both the sense of presence (manifestation) and that of absence (proclamation).

10. From Meinong's "Über Gegenstandstheorie," as quoted in Marion, *In Excess*, 22.

according to the presupposed "immutable laws of nature" and presumed properties of being or is-ness. Givenness is not limited to ontological (or ontic for that matter) forms of phenomenological giving. Further, this is to say that a phenomenon can be given that "is not," that is, one that cannot be circumscribed by metaphysical or ontological categories of being, essence, causality, substance, presence, etc. Meinong's rational paradox opens an avenue beyond being—beyond a notion of being confined to the world of poor or common-law phenomena, as well as beyond a phenomenality that is limited to the scope of being and its limited manifestations. Instead, the paradox gives itself to a degree surpassing any ready-made concept or noetic intention: the paradox saturates intentionality with an intuitive givenness that no intention can govern. Marion calls such phenomena "saturated phenomena."

The idea of the saturated phenomenon, *le phénomène saturé*, is one of Marion's most original contributions to phenomenology. It has been described in detail by both Marion and commentators on his work.[11] A basic question concerning the saturated phenomenon is, "How is the saturated phenomenon different from typical phenomena?" As previously indicated, a saturated phenomenon is that in which intuition is given to a degree that always outruns intentionality. The saturated phenomenon gives too excessively for consciousness to codify it with premade concepts and categories.[12] A saturated phenomenon gives itself with overwhelming magnitude, not merely in measurable terms, but in terms that nullify the egocentric attempt to measure it. According to Marion, saturated phenomena transgress the fourfold Kantian categories of the understanding: quantity, quality, relation and modality.[13] "The saturated phenomenon exceeds the categories and the principles of understanding—it will therefore be invisable according to quantity, unbearable according to quality, absolute according to relation, and

11. See Marion, *Being Given*, especially 225–47; Marion, *In Excess*; Marion, *Visible and the Revealed*; Horner, *Rethinking God as Gift*; Gschwandtner, *Reading Jean-Luc Marion*; Hart, *Counter-Experiences*; Leask and Cassidy, *Givenness and God*; Horner, *Jean-Luc Marion*; Mackinlay, *Interpreting Excess*; Jones, *Genealogy of Marion's Philosophy of Religion*; Schrijvers, *Ontotheological Turnings?*

12. See Marion, "Introduction: What Do We Mean by 'Mystic'?," in Kessler and Sheppard, *Mystics*, 5: "Saturated phenomena should not be constituted at all, and what we experience with them is precisely an intuition overwhelming any possible concept. This is not because the saturated phenomenon is irrational but because we are unable to be rational enough to produce concepts matching the intuition that is nevertheless in fact given . . . Thus in front of the saturated phenomenon, we must admit our lack of concepts, that is, of rationality."

13. Cf. Kant, *Critique of Pure Reason*, 229–302 [A 159–235; B 159–294]. More will be said on the transgression of these categories below.

incapable of being looked at according to modality."[14] In terms of space and time, "in space, the saturated phenomenon engulfs it with its intuitive flood; in time, it precedes it through an interpellation that is always already there."[15] Kantian judgment (both analytic and synthetic) is repelled in the face of the saturated phenomenon.[16] Cognition is unable to pin determinate predicates on saturation. In other words, because saturation incessantly gives, it cannot be met with an adequate concept that would describe it completely in its (over)fullness. Marion uses the language of "bedazzlement"—éblouissement—to denote that which the intentional gaze cannot bear, the instance "when perception passes beyond its subjective maximum," the excess of finite perception.[17] Though in all phenomena that give themselves can be recognized an unlimited abundance of meaning and givenness, saturated phenomena are those which give themselves in the pattern and posture of paradox. These phenomena can be called "counter-experiences" insofar as they reconfigure and invert intentionality so that the human subject is constituted, in effect, by the world of givenness rather than the other way around. The human subject does not so much come to bear on that which gives itself, as the given phenomenon determines the ego according to its peculiar freight. As a "fait accompli" (that is, "accomplished fact"), the saturated phenomenon cannot be tamed, manipulated, or possessed by the ego.

Marion provides five specific examples of the saturated phenomenon in his magisterial work on the phenomenology of givenness, *Being Given*: the event, the idol, the flesh, the icon, and the possibility of divine revelation. The event is characterized as saturating due to its unrepeatability, unforeseeability, and to the unlimited horizons of its interpretation left in the wake of its passing. The idol, as in the case of a visual work of art, "cannot be constituted but can still be looked at," that is, the idol gives an excess of content

14. Marion, *Visible and the Revealed*, 34. Marion intentionally uses the neologism *invisable* to indicate that which cannot be aimed at, meant, or intended. Cf. ibid., endnotes 27 and 33 (160–61).

15. Ibid., 44. Note the language of manifestation as described by Tracy in chapter 1 of this study: "always already there."

16. See Kant, *Critique of Pure Reason*, "Introduction to the Second Edition," 43–68 [A 1–16; B 1–30].

17. Marion, *Visible and the Revealed*, 36–37. It is significant to note the pervasiveness of éblouissement in twentieth-century French avant-garde art, for example, in the musical innovation of Olivier Messiaen. Cf. Robert Sholl's essay "Olivier Messiaen and the Avant-Garde Poetics," in Shenton, *Messiaen the Theologian*, 199–222; Sander van Maas's essay "Forms of Love: Messiaen's Aesthetics of Éblouissement," in Sholl, *Messiaen Studies*, 78–100; and van Maas, *The Reinvention of Religious Music*.

and meaning in a limited visual field.[18] The flesh, in its immanence and auto-affectivity, saturates itself by giving itself to itself, thereby saturating the category of relation to its maximum threshold of absence. The flesh, in essence, breaks all ties with exteriority in its solipsism: "[the flesh] remains by definition mine, unsubstitutable—nobody can enjoy or suffer for me (even if he can do so in my place)."[19] Examples of how the flesh auto-affects itself include "agony, suffering, and grief . . . desire, feeling, or orgasm."[20] The icon saturates through its counter-gaze wherein the invisible gaze portrayed in the icon gazes upon me and weighs upon me in such a way that I cannot prevent it, stop it, or contain it. The gaze of the iconic persona never ceases to look upon me with love. Closely related to the icon, Marion specifically instances the possibility of theophany (another term for divine revelation) as the maximum height of the saturated phenomenon "where the excess of intuition leads to the paradox that an invisible gaze visibly envisages me and loves me."[21] Theophany refers to the (im)possibility that an actual divine persona invisibly gazes upon me out of love, remaining invisible in order to spare and sustain my life. For the untempered saturation of the infinite over the finite would in effect obliterate the finite.[22] This is why the tempered saturation of the infinite over the finite can be described as love. Infinite *eros*

18. Marion, *Being Given*, 47. Marion's description of the idol and the icon as saturated phenomena (in *Being Given* and in *Visible and the Revealed*) is different than the contrast he draws between the two terms in *Idol and Distance* and in *God without Being*. In the latter works, Marion establishes a contrast between the idol and the icon in order to liberate philosophy and theology to think God in terms other than being, substance, *causa sui*, etc. For Marion, the brandishing of such metaphysical ways of thinking God has run ashore, amounting to a spoiled chest of conceptual idols that, in effect, obstruct the infinite givenness of God's glory. Marion in turn uses the term icon to steer thinking toward uncharted seas of divine mystery, recuperating the idea of God from the Nietzschean deathblows of modernity. More will be said on this latter distinction below.

19. Marion, *Being Given*, 232.

20. Ibid., 231.

21. Marion, *Visible and the Revealed*, 47–48.

22. Certainly we experience the obliterating power of the infinite in the vertigo of merely entertaining the idea of the infinite in our thoughts, let alone other forms of perception vis-à-vis the utter magnitude of infinite saturation. See Exod 33:18–23: "Then Moses said, 'Do let me see your glory!' He answered, 'I will make all my beauty pass before you, and in your presence I will pronounce my name, 'LORD'; I who show favors to whom I will, I who grant mercy to whom I will. But my face you cannot see, for no man sees me and still lives. Here,' continued the LORD, 'is a place near me where you shall station yourself on the rock. When my glory passes I will set you in the hollow of the rock and will cover you with my hand until I have passed by. Then I will remove my hand, so that you may see my back; but my face is not to be seen'" (NAB); John 1:18: "No one has ever seen God. The only Son, God, who is at the Father's side, has revealed him" (NAB); Matt 5:8: "Blessed are the pure in heart, for they shall see God" (RSV).

is at once infinite *agape*—a love that is as tender, composed and collected as it is passionate.[23] Such instances of the saturated phenomenon—the event, the idol, the flesh, the icon, and divine revelation—demonstrate the generous force of manifestation, all designated by Marion under the rubric of givenness.

While Marion has not considered specifically the Eucharist (or even God) as a saturated phenomenon per se in his writings, there is much warrant to define it as such. First, as sacrament the Eucharist is an instance of divine revelation par excellence. It is a sacramental extension of the manifest presence of the incarnate Son of God, offered for the many. It is bread become body, wine become blood, by the power of the Holy Spirit—the creative Spirit of God (as the very possibility of pure actuality) that raises up existents from nothing and transforms existents from one figure into another. The Eucharist is a sublime paradox that proposes to give veritably that which it does not appear to give, and what is more: it gives that which is presumed to be impossible to give, namely, the eternal Son of God under the material vestiges of bread and wine. Proposed by eucharistic giving is body under the appearance of bread, blood under the appearance of wine—most fundamentally, God under the appearance of human, Jesus—the God-man—under the appearances of bread and wine. The Eucharist purports to be a surplus of divine revelation in a manifest form of self-giving to the point of abandonment.

Second, the eucharistic phenomenon can be described therefore as an event, an icon, and a counter-experience of the flesh, ever immemorial, ever new. In the Eucharist, the end is the beginning.[24] As a pure event, the Eucharist "offer(s) a type of saturated phenomenon that is historical, and thus communal and in principle communicable."[25] It takes place in a communal context and lends itself to an "infinite hermeneutic" according to the

23. Cf. Pseudo-Dionysius, *The Divine Names*, in *Complete Works*, 79–83, for example, 82: "So they call him the beloved and the yearned-for since he is beautiful and good, and, again, they call him yearning [*eros*] and love [*agape*] because he is the power moving and lifting all things up to himself, for in the end what is he if not Beauty and Goodness, the One who of himself reveals himself, the good procession of his own transcendent unity?"; Benedict XVI, *Deus caritas est*, Part I.

24. See Rev 1:8: "'I am the Alpha and the Omega,' says the Lord God, 'the one who is and who was and who is to come, the almighty'" (NAB); Heb 13:8: "Jesus Christ is the same yesterday and today and forever" (RSV); Jas 1:16–17: "Do not be deceived, my beloved brethren. Every good endowment and every perfect gift is from above, coming down from the Father of lights with whom there is no variation or shadow due to change" (RSV).

25. Marion, *Visible and the Revealed*, 47.

"proliferation of [interpretive] horizons."[26] As an icon, the Eucharist takes its own initiative in giving itself. The Eucharist, as a phenomenon, cannot be conjured up arbitrarily but rather appears according to the prescribed rules and rites for its appearing, specifically, its liturgical inauguration and memorial institution by Christ at the Last Supper. No one indiscriminately can make the Eucharist happen. Instead the Eucharist is made according to its own terms and authority, historically stipulated and indexed in the form of doctrinal pronouncements, liturgical rubrics, canon law, and under the auspices of ecclesial authority and the Sacrament of Holy Orders. In effect, the Eucharist exercises a counter-gaze vis-à-vis the human spectator, disallowing any gaze that would master it.[27] Its sacred ministers, too, fall under its auto-intentional gaze. Even the human senses cannot master perceptibly eucharistic givenness; they cannot perceive fully all that the Eucharist gives because it has given to the point of abandonment, without residue or remainder. "For to define the phenomenality of the sacrament, it would be necessary to imagine that in it the invisible is translated, surrendering itself and abandoning itself in the visible to the point of appearing insofar as the invisible remains."[28] The invisible Deity, the eternal Son of God, gives himself without reservation in the visible sacrament, while not ceasing to give himself invisibly in the sacrament. Both senses and intellect short-circuit in the face of such radical saturating givenness. As a phenomenon that involves flesh at several levels, the Eucharist gives itself as a counter-experience to human flesh. The Eucharist, as the flesh of Christ, cannot be conflated into the recipient's flesh. Even though the recipient consumes the Eucharist and digests it within her own flesh, the Eucharist remains entirely other, as does the recipient. The Eucharist enters into a person only to vanish sacramentally therein upon complete digestion, that is, once the eucharistic species cease to subsist as such.[29] Auto-affection occurs for both the

26. Marion, *Being Given*, 211, 229.

27. Similarly, see Lacoste, *Experience and the Absolute*, 152: "[Liturgy is] a transgression of every capacity for experience that consciousness can avail itself of."

28. Marion, "La phénoménalité du sacrement," 59–75, 66 (translation my own here and below). For a similar article on the phenomenality of the sacrament, see Lacoste, "Phénoménologie de l'Esprit à la Montée du Carmel." Lacoste underscores the dispossession of human rationality by divine wisdom and the revelation of divine humility through the humiliation of humanity, especially vicariously in Christ. Lacoste presents the "folly of Christ and the cross" as the locus of divine revelation. It is the very logic underpinning the phenomenality of the sacrament.

29. See *Catechism of the Catholic Church*, 1377: "The Eucharistic presence of Christ begins at the moment of consecration and endures as long as the Eucharistic species subsist." This is to say that through the process of digestion, once the eucharistic species cease to subsist *in specie*, the "real presence" of Christ given in the sacramental

flesh of Jesus (inasmuch as the Eucharist is the very flesh and blood of Jesus) and the flesh of the recipient. The saturating auto-affectivity of human flesh cannot be measured or regulated.[30] It cannot be monitored or evaluated by any third party. The auto-affection of the recipient's flesh is sui generis as it breaks off all categories of immediate perceptible relation between distinct individuated bodies.

Third, the Eucharist saturates intentionality through its paradoxical self-giving. It cannot be constituted by intentionality nor can it be met with a prefabricated concept. It overtakes finite conceptual frameworks because it is a giving from the infinite, the gift that never ceases to give, a givenness from eternity.[31] The eternal givenness of God's very self outstrips human

---

subsistence converts to a given absence upon the termination of sacramental subsistence. This is also to say that the presence of Christ cannot be assimilated as such into the presence of the individual recipient of the Eucharist, so that the two individual, personal presences would merge into a singular, indistinguishable presence or person. If this were the case, there would be no need to receive Christ in the Eucharist over and over again, nor would there be need to adore Christ in the reserved Eucharist, since the recipient would have in effect become Christ irrevocably. As it is, we adore Christ in the reserved Eucharist and receive the Eucharist day after day because we admit the non-identity of Christ and ourselves. Indeed, we are "one body in Christ," but a body composed of many diverse members (cf. 1 Cor 12). A unity and communion of persons obtains, but precisely a union in difference. Here I am anticipating the effect of the proclamation side of the dialectic on manifestation. I am tugging at Marion's assertion: "that this fleshly body [of Christ] disappears and leaves place for the eucharistic body of bread that one eats, that one assimilates to oneself, and which, in this unique case, assimilates to itself those who assimilate it (Augustine), means: Christ becomes present, not to the senses (which cannot receive him, or even see him), but to the heart, burning from now on, and the mind, from hereafter understanding. The sensible disappearance allows the blessing to give the presence of Christ still more intimately, radically: the presence becomes still more of a gift, since it makes itself a gift communicable to the point of assimilation" (Marion, *Prolegomena to Charity*, 136). It is necessary for Marion to eat the dish he cooked: the unsubstitutable particularity of individuation is not to be sublated into a totality neither without unique face nor reduced to a homogenized pseudo-alterity (see Marion, *Being Given*, 324). "Assimilation" is the word for the event whereupon manifestation collapses onto itself—for example, Hegel's dream (or perhaps nightmare?) of the grand synthesis of thought and being, Plotinus's eternal return to the One (and only One), Alexandria's monophysite Christ who would amount to no savior of humanity at all, Narcissus's suicidal captivation of his own idolatrous image. Proclamation prevents manifestation from reducing the other to the same. Cf. *Catechism of the Catholic Church*, 1373–81; Ecumenical Council of Trent, Session XIII, *Decretum de sanctissimus Eucharistia*, in Denzinger and Schönmetzer, *Enchiridion symbolorum*, 1635–61.

30. Recall instances of involuntary auto-affection in the lives of saints, manifest in the phenomena of ecstasy and levitation. For example, see Teresa of Avila, *Las Moradas*, and *Relaciones Espirituales*.

31. For an extensive scholarly treatment of Marion's hermeneutics of gift in relation to the sacramental phenomenon, see Madathummuriyil, *Sacrament as Gift*, especially 236–308.

expectation, common opinion, and presumed parameters for appearing, in a word, the natural attitude. As paradox of paradoxes, as saturation of saturation, the Eucharist redoubles saturation by not only saturating once, but twice. The redoubling of saturation in the phenomenon of revelation is based on the general contours of creation followed by redemption. The act of creation is immensely saturating, only to be followed by a saturation of saturation, namely, the redemption of creation in Christ. In this saturation of saturation, reaching its apogee in Christ crucified, divine mercy and love overwhelm justice: "God's passionate love for his people—for humanity—is at the same time a forgiving love. It is so great that it turns God against himself, his love against his justice . . . (Jesus's) death on the Cross is the culmination of that turning of God against himself in which he gives himself in order to raise man up and save him. This is love in its most radical form."[32] God's love is revealed as not only gratuitously generous and giving through the act of creation, it is doubly revealed as forgiving through the act of redemption. Love is redoubled only by turning against itself and outdoing itself in the form of a shortage: "Not to be encompassed by the greatest, but to let oneself be encompassed by the smallest—that is divine."[33] On display in forgiveness is the doubly paradoxical logic of *kenosis* and sacrifice: "Only this giving of self—*kenosis* as abandonment that commits without return or retreat—immediately accomplishes in effect the authority, which qualifies water and blood as more than everyday utensils, but as the substance of the sacraments of the Spirit."[34] The double givenness of forgiveness irrevocably saturates to the second degree not as a coercive force of grandeur, but as the glorious splendor of the silent, still and hidden invitation to love and reconciliation.[35] The redemption accomplished by Christ's sacrifice on the cross commences the holy reversal whereby the *conatus essendi* ("struggle of being / struggle to be") and the primacy of presence give way to the radiance

32. Benedict XVI, *Deus caritas est*, 10, 12.

33. Quote taken from J. C. F. Hölderlin's preface to his novel *Hyperion* (as quoted in Ratzinger, *Introduction to Christianity*, 146). The original Latin text reads, "*Non coerceri maximo, contineri tamen a minimo, divinum est*," and also goes by the name "epitaph on Loyola." See footnote 3 in Ratzinger, *Introduction to Christianity*, 147. Cf. Marion's essay "The Withdrawal of the Divine and the Face of the Father: Hölderlin," in *Idol and Distance*, 81–136.

34. Marion, "La phénoménalité du sacrement," 74.

35. See Marion, *God without Being*, 107: "The silence that is suitable to the G×d who reveals himself as agape in Christ consists in remaining silent through and for agape: to conceive that if G×d gives, to say G×d requires receiving the gift and—since the gift occurs only in distance—returning it."

of absence manifest in the invisibility of spirit.[36] Let us now take a step back from the question of the Eucharist and turn in a more concentrated way to the notion of givenness as employed by Marion to help better understand his pervasive hermeneutic of manifestation.

## II. The Trajectory of Givenness

The idea of givenness in the work of Marion is a philosophical term that evolved in usage and meaning over time. It can be detected as early as in Kant, but was especially developed by Husserl, Heidegger and Marion.[37] Why, for Marion, does givenness serve as such a key and indispensable lens through which to view phenomena? The reason is that "givenness alone is absolute, free and without condition, precisely because it gives."[38] Given-

36. Cf. John 19:30: "When Jesus had taken the wine, he said, 'It is finished.' And bowing his head, he handed over the spirit" (NAB); John 20:22–23: "And when [Jesus] had said this, he breathed on them and said to them, 'Receive the holy Spirit. Whose sins you forgive are forgiven them, and whose sins you retain are retained'" (NAB); interview with Levinas in Cohen, *Face to Face with Levinas*, 24–25: "This ethical exigency undermines the Hellenic endorsement, still prevalent today, of the *conatus essendi* . . . Ethics is, therefore, *against nature* because it forbids the murderousness of my natural will to put my own existence first . . . The word of God speaks through the glory of the face and calls for an ethical conversion, or reversal, of our nature . . . God does indeed go against nature, for He is not of this world. God is other than being"; Marion, *Reduction and Givenness*, 11, speaking of the breakthrough of Husserl's principle of all principles: "Because intuition is broadened, there appears more than it seems; namely, exactly as much as intuition in its broadened sense gives to be seen by the phenomenological, and therefore antinatural, gaze." Perhaps a more fitting term than "antinatural" is "supernatural," "preternatural," or even "paranatural." The radicality of the phenomenological reduction is the necessary visual corrective to broaden indefinitely the horizon for vision, even opening to the possibility of impossibility, the saturation of saturation. Faith, hope and love are those (theological) virtues that can be exercised only in the abyss of this rationally justified opening.

37. See, for instance, Kant, *Critique of Pure Reason*, 226 [A 156, B 195]: "If a cognition is to have objective reality, i.e., if it is to refer to an object and have in that object its signification and meaning, then the object must be capable of being *given* in some way . . . To give an object—if this is not again to mean to be given it only indirectly, but is to mean, rather, to exhibit it directly in intuition—is nothing other than to refer the presentation of the object to experience (whether actual, or at least possible, experience)" (translation modified according to footnote 188). For a genealogy of givenness according to Marion, especially tracing its usage in Heidegger, see Marion, *Reason of the Gift*, 19–49.

38. Marion, *Reduction and Givenness*, 33. For Marion, givenness is not equivalent to the idea of the gift although the plot of givenness is bound up in the possibility of the gift as such. In order for Marion to justify his third reduction, it is necessary for him to demonstrate compellingly the genuine possibility of the gift as such and then to go beyond the gift by reducing it to givenness. Cf. Marion, *Being Given*, 71–118;

ness signifies the process by which a given phenomenon gives itself on its own accord. It refers both to the phenomenon given and to the advent of its self-giving. Givenness traverses into the depths of phenomenality, passing beyond metaphysics, ontology, causality, conceptuality, noumenon/phenomenon distinctions, objectivity and subjectivity. It seeks to discover a phenomenon in its most raw and original form. By way of the phenomenological reduction, givenness attempts to behold a phenomenon without condition or contamination, without bias or projection, without assumption or mastery. A phenomenon shows itself in its appearance and "the privilege of appearing in its appearance is also named manifestation—manifestation of the thing starting from itself and as itself, privilege of rendering *itself* manifest, of making *itself* visible, of showing *itself*."[39] Givenness allows a phenomenon the freedom of manifestation by itself, in whatever manner it may show itself or not show itself. It implies a passivity of intentionality and intuition, whereby the intuiting subject does not act on the phenomenon to determine its phenomenality and appearing, but rather acquiesces to the determination of the phenomenon itself, "as on a screen; all the power of this given comes from crashing down on this screen, provoking all at once a double visibility . . . first, that of the given . . . [and second], the visibility of *l'adonné* ["the gifted"]."[40] The phenomenon, in effect, gives sight to the human subject rather than the subject setting the limits and conditions for the possibility of appearing.[41] As evidenced in chapter 1, Marion's application

---

Marion's discussion with Jacques Derrida in Caputo and Scanlon, *God, the Gift, and Postmodernism*, 54–78.

39. Marion, *Being Given*, 8.

40. Marion, *In Excess*, 50. Cf. ibid., 24–25: "Now, this datum gives itself to me, because it imposes itself on me, calls me, and determines me—in short, because I am not the author of it. The datum merits its name by its being a *fait accompli*, such that it happens to me, and in which it is distinguished from all forseen, synthesized, and constituted objects, since it happens to me as an event. This unforeseen happening marks it as given and attests in it to givenness"; cf. Caputo and Scanlon, *God, the Gift, and Postmodernism*, 58. N.B.: Though the language of sight (appearing, visible/invisible, seeing, etc.) is employed typically in regard to phenomenality and givenness, phenomenal manifestation is not exhausted by the sense of sight alone, but should be considered in the broader sense of perceptibility, especially in the Husserlian sense of immanently given intuition to consciousness. In other words, the language of sight is translatable into other metaphors of empirical intuition, for example, either in its literal sense of seeing or its figurative sense of perception in general; cf. Husserl, *Idea of Phenomenology*, 8–9.

41. Cf. John 9:39–41: "Then Jesus said, 'I came into this world for judgment, so that those who do not see might see, and those who do see might become blind.' Some Pharisees who were with him heard this and said to him, 'Surely we are not also blind, are we?' Jesus said to them, 'If you were blind, you would have no sin; but now you are saying, "We see," so your sin remains'" (NAB). In this context, Jesus seems to refer especially to the "blindness" of sin and doubt, but perhaps this text also can shed light

of givenness developed as a critique of the concept of givenness as used by Husserl and Heidegger. In order to understand Marion's use of givenness, it is necessary to retrace its application in Husserl and Heidegger, as well as Marion's critique of Husserl and Heidegger. By tracing the evolution of givenness as the conceptual core of phenomenology, we will clarify its import for understanding the phenomenality of the Eucharist in terms of givenness in the most critical manner. Clearly understanding givenness will contribute greatly to understanding the phenomenology of manifestation of Marion as distinct from the phenomenology of proclamation of Ricoeur and Levinas.

## A. Givenness in Husserl

The notion of givenness in Husserl aims at an objective manifestation of essences of ideal objects in consciousness. Husserl develops what can be called an "eidetic phenomenology" that works to uncover the most originary forms of phenomena as they give themselves. By way of the phenomenological reduction, Husserl arrives at two distinct realms of phenomenality: (1) consciousness and (2) the world (in relation to consciousness).[42] Both consciousness and the world are given; both are given in proportion to the radicality of the reduction. In Husserl, the phenomenological reduction brackets everything transcendent (outside of consciousness) and any preconceived judgments about spatiotemporal factual being in order to arrive at absolute phenomenological givenness: "*a pure phenomenon, which exhibits its intrinsic (immanent) essence* (taken individually) *as an absolute datum*."[43] The realm of the pure phenomenon is none other than the realm of consciousness, or cognition: "in givenness we see *that the object is constituted in cognition*."[44] According to the reduction, Husserl draws the distinction between that which is given absolutely (immanent to consciousness) and that which is not given or given only partially (transcendent to

---

on the subversion of the transcendental ego in terms of givenness and the priority of the self-manifestation of the phenomenon.

42. Husserl, *Ideas I*, 89–90: "*With an absolutely unconditional* universality and necessity it is the case that a physical thing cannot be given in any possible perception, in any possible consciousness, as something really inherently immanent. Thus there emerges a fundamentally essential difference between *being as mental process and being as a physical thing* . . . Thus the physical thing is said to be, in itself, unqualifiedly transcendent. Precisely in that the essentially necessary diversity among modes of being, the most cardinal among them all, becomes manifest: the diversity between *consciousness and reality*."

43. Husserl, *Idea of Phenomenology*, 35; cf. Husserl, *Ideas I*, 61.

44. Husserl, *Idea of Phenomenology*, 59.

consciousness).[45] In an instance of absolute givenness, "*perception and perceived* form *essentially an unmediated unity, that of a single concrete cogitatio.* Here the perceiving includes its Object in itself in such a manner that it can only be separated abstractively, only as an *essentially non-selfsufficient* moment, from its Object"; in an instant of absolute givenness, *noema* and *noesis* form an inseparable unity.[46] For Husserl, "absolute givenness is an ultimate" whereby instances of immanent absolute givens attain universal status, that is, absolutely given, once and for all.[47] Partial (transcendent) givenness occurs whenever a mental process is directed to something beyond (or outside of) the mind, for example, "all acts directed to physical things or to realities of whatever sort."[48] Husserl employs the example of the givenness of redness in a living intuition to demonstrate the distinction between absolute (immanent) givenness and partial (transcendent) givenness: redness connected to a particular object is reduced in order to "fully grasp in pure 'seeing' the *meaning* of the concept of redness in general, redness *in specie*, the *universal* 'seen' as *identical* in this or that."[49] In this case, "redness *in specie*" constitutes the indubitable *evidence* of givenness, for "*givenness extends just as far as actual evidence*."[50] "Redness," therefore, is to be understood as a phenomenon that is given absolutely and originally, not merely as a concept that gives the full, rational legitimacy of a phenomenon (as in Kant) but as a phenomenon given absolutely and universally in itself, by itself.[51] Husserl bases such an instantiation on what he determines to be the "principle of all principles" for phenomenology: "*every originarily giving intuition is a source of right for cognition*—that *everything* that offers itself *originarily* to us *in intuition* (in its fleshly actuality, so to speak) *must simply be received for what it gives itself*, but without *passing beyond the limits in which it gives itself*."[52] For Husserl there are many modes of givenness, but it is only in cognition, or consciousness, where something is truly given and evidentially "seen."[53] Yet according to Husserl's principle of all principles, it

45. Husserl, *Ideas I*, 78–80, 100–104.

46. Ibid., 79–80. *Noema* refers to the phenomenon that gives itself to consciousness, and *noesis* refers to the process of assimilating the phenomenon in its immanent givenness within consciousness.

47. Cf. Marion, *Reduction and Givenness*, 33.

48. Husserl, *Ideas I*, 79.

49. Husserl, *Idea of Phenomenology*, 45.

50. Ibid., 58.

51. Cf. ibid., 7–8, 23–24, 40, 44, 54.

52. Husserl, *Ideas I*, 44 (English translation taken from Marion, *Being Given*, 12).

53. Cf. Husserl, *Idea of Phenomenology*, 59, for example, speaking of the pluriformity of givenness: "The givenness of the *cogitatio*, the givenness of the *cogitatio preserved*

is not cognition itself that determines what is given, but that which is given offers itself "in the flesh" to cognition where that which gives itself can be received as an instance of absolute, universal givenness. Such giving "in the flesh" only occurs in the sphere of experience (*Erlebnis*), that sphere where intuition acts as a source to legitimate knowledge, where "it gives" (*es gibt*) intuition and intuition gives itself to cognition, where the "x" (phenomenon) takes control of the process of givenness and thereby an intuition is given, in short where the phenomenon gives *itself* (*sich gibt*).[54] This understanding of phenomenality allows for a spontaneity of self-giveness of things and prevents a predetermination of conditions that otherwise would dictate how a phenomenon may give itself. Therefore no human subject has the right to exclude anything that may give *itself* in experience; no a priori conditions of possibility may be enforced, but rather a phenomenon "*must simply be received for what it gives itself*, but without *passing beyond the limits in which it gives itself*." Reversing the Kantian understanding of phenomenality, the transcendental ego relinquishes its sovereignty in determining the rules according to which a thing may appear and instead allows that which appears to determine "*the limits in which it gives itself*."[55] This humbled self permits the possibility of detecting and describing phenomena that do not even exist per se, but nonetheless appear, such as in the aforementioned paradoxical instance identified by Alexius Meinong: "'it gives' objects, of which it is valid to say, 'it gives' not objects as such" (*es gibt Gegenstände, von denen gilt, es dergleichen Gegenstände nicht gibt*).[56] Furthermore, Husserl emphasizes the

---

*in a fresh recollection*, the givenness of the *unity of appearance* enduring in the phenomenal flux, the givenness of *change* itself, the givenness of *things* to the 'outer' sense, the givenness of the different forms of imagination and memory, as well as the givenness of *perceptions* and other sorts of *representations* which unify themselves synthetically in many ways in fitting associations. Of course there is also *logical givenness*, the givenness of *universals*, of *predicates*, of *states of affairs*, etc.; also the givenness of *something absurd*, of *something contradictory*, of *something which does not exist*."

54. Cf. Marion, *Reduction and Givenness*, 53: "[In Husserl] the term 'phenomenon' does not apply first, nor only, to the object that appears, but indeed to a lived experience in which and according to which it appears; this duality alone will allow one to think absolute givenness, intentionality, and the couplet, noesis/noema. Even and especially if one takes intentionality into account, *Erscheinung* is approached on the basis of the immanence of *Erlebnis*—and therefore, inevitably, never on the basis of the appearing of the object itself, which is by definition conditioned."

55. Cf. Kant, *Critique of Pure Reason*, 229 [A 159, B 198]: "The fact that principles occur anywhere at all is attributable solely to pure understanding. For pure understanding not only is our power of rules regarding what happens, but is itself the source of principles, the source according to which everything (whatever we can encounter as an object) is necessarily subject to rules. For without rules there could never be for appearances any cognition of an object corresponding to them."

56. Meinong, "Über Gegenstandstheorie," 9 (translation my own).

correlation between an appearance and that which appears in order to draw the distinction and integral relationship between partial (transcendent) and absolute/universal (immanent) givenness.[57] It is only by way of intentionality that one becomes conscious of something outside the self and an object becomes immanent to consciousness:

> We have the givenness of the pure *cogitatio* as an absolute possession, but not the givenness of outer things in external perception, although such a perception makes a claim to be giving the existence of these things . . . we directly "see," we directly grasp what we intend in the act of "seeing" and grasping . . . The "seeing" or grasping of what is given, insofar as it is actual "seeing," actual self-givenness in the strictest sense and not another sort of givenness which points to something which is not given—that is an ultimate.[58]

Here again, Husserl points to the primacy of the "pure *cogitation*" of cognition, showing the possibility of a phenomenon moving from the realm of partial givenness (transcendent realm) to that of absolute/universal givenness (immanent realm) where the phenomenon is given "in the flesh" in itself and by itself. Immanent data of consciousness maintain a universal character inasmuch as they are not subject to misappropriation or even misinterpretation due to their intimate intuition within consciousness. These are not external (transcendent) data, but pure data that warrant no other contingency or rationale for their givenness.

## B. Application 1: The Appearance of the Eucharist

The notion of givenness as found in the work of Husserl offers valuable insights into the apprehension (as much as is possible) of the phenomenality of the Eucharist. First, Husserlian givenness allows the invisible to appear

57. Husserl, *Idea of Phenomenology*, 11.

58. Ibid., 39–40; cf. Husserl, *Ideas I*, 92–93: "It is therefore fundamentally erroneous to believe that perception (and, after its own fashion, any other kind of intuition of a physical thing) does not reach the physical thing itself. The latter is not given to us in itself or in its being-in-itself. There belongs to any existent the essential possibility of being simply intuited as what it is and, more particularly, of being perceived as what it is in an adequate perception, one that is presentive of that existent itself, 'in person,' *without any mediation by 'appearances'* . . . The perception of a physical thing does not presentiate something non-present, as though it were a memory or phantasy; perception makes present, seizes upon an it-self in its presence 'in person'"; cf. Marion, *Visible and the Revealed*, 56: "Since intuition gives in the flesh, the Kantian caesura between the (solely sensible) phenomenon and the thing-in-itself must disappear."

to consciousness, to be received in intuition as a sacrament-phenomenon shows itself by itself. The Husserlian principle of principles gives the invisible the full right to appear through visible mediation. Since, in the Eucharist, the invisible is inseparable from the visible as such, the transcendence of the eucharistic species becomes immanent through an objectively manifest intuition. Such a pure intuition gives confidence to the receptivity of the invisible as it remains within the pregnancy of sacramental visibility. The invisible is borne in the visible, allowing the invisible to attain to the status of phenomenological validity. The invisible can be constituted as such insofar as the objective visibility of the sacrament really appears to consciousness.[59] Because the eucharistic species (simultaneously as the accidents of bread and wine and the [transubstantiated] substances of Christ's body and blood) are given objectively to consciousness, a possibility opens for receiving whatever it may be that these particular species, as objective phenomena, have to offer, as they give themselves to intuition. For Husserl, if "it gives" (*es gibt*) no appearance in that which appears, "it gives" no phenomenality of which to speak, no detectable nor evident essence of which to speak: "The 'existence' of the *cogitatio* is guaranteed by its absolute self-givenness, by its givenness in pure evidence (*Evidenz*). Whenever we have pure evidence (*Evidenz*), the pure viewing and grasping of something objective directly and in itself, we have the same guarantees, the same certainties."[60] Therefore the sensuous perception of the eucharistic species results in an immanent phenomenon of absolute givenness within consciousness. For the universality of the given intuition of the eucharistic species, intending what it does (namely, transubstantiation and its ensuing effects in the life of the recipients/community of faith) and appearing as it does (regardless of color, shape, texture of bread and wine, as long as the species are truly bread and wine) in each and every eucharistic liturgy, presents an instance of absolute givenness.[61] In effect, the Eucharist migrates from the status of a transcendent (not immanent to cognition) given to the sphere of an "absolutely immanent datum (given/

59. Cf. Husserl, *Idea of Phenomenology*, 9–10: ". . . the things come to be *constituted* in these mental processes, although in reality they are not at all to be found in them. For 'things to be given' is for them to be *exhibited* (represented) as so and so in such phenomena."

60. Ibid., 6.

61. Cf. ibid., 44: "Thus one has to get especially clear about the fact that we accord the status of absolute self-givenness to the absolute phenomenon, the *cogitatio* which has undergone reduction, not because it is a particular, but because it displays itself in pure 'seeing' after phenomenological reduction, *precisely as absolute self-givenness*. But in pure 'seeing' we find that universality no less displays *just* such an absolute givenness"; cf. Husserl, *Ideas I*, 82 (footnote 137): "The fundamental supporting stratum of all reality is corporeality."

*cogitatum*)" as it gives itself as "an originary giving intuition that is a source of right for cognition." In the Eucharist, the invisible is precisely the visible in a hypostatic intermingling in which there is no demarcation between that which is given to consciousness and that which would seem to be referred to beyond that which is given to consciousness (namely, the invisible).[62] In the Eucharist, the invisible shows itself in the visible. The "general essence of meaning" of the Eucharist is absolutely and immanently given in "general 'seeing.'"[63] In the givenness of the Eucharist, Christ definitively means and irrevocably gives his very flesh and blood, given "in the flesh" (*leibhaft*) and unto death, in short, given absolutely: "This is my body, which will be given for you; do this in memory of me . . . This chalice is the new covenant in my blood, which will be shed for you" (Luke 22:19–20).[64]

Such an application of the Husserlian notion of givenness offers ample fodder for a critical and meaningful sacramental theology, lending a fertile basis for one to understand more precisely the human-divine intimacy achieved in the offering and reception of the Eucharist: "On that day you will realize that I am in my Father and you are in me and I in you . . . Whoever loves me will keep my word, and my Father will love him, and we will come to him and make our dwelling with him."[65] Interpersonal and sacramental perichoresis obtains through the application of Husserl's concept of immanent givenness to conscious experience of the Eucharist. A mutual in-dwelling occurs according to the reach of eidetic interpenetration of conscious spiritual life. Perhaps this is why the practice of Exposition of the Blessed Sacrament continues to be such a powerful experience for believers, not just as a spectacle, but as a real event of communion between Christ and his witnesses.

62. Cf. Husserl, *Idea of Phenomenology*, 35.

63. Ibid., 45–46.

64. Cf. ibid., 48–49: "Hence phenomenological reduction does not entail a limitation of the investigation to the sphere of genuine (*reell*) immanence, to the sphere of that which is genuinely contained within the absolute this of the *cogitatio*. Rather it entails a limitation to the sphere of things that are *purely self-given* . . . self-given in the strictest sense—in such a way that nothing which is meant fails to be given"; cf. Husserl, *Ideas I*, 92; Marion, "La phénoménalité du sacrement," 74–75.

65. Cf. John 6:51, 56: "I am the living bread that came down from heaven; whoever eats this bread will live forever; and the bread that I will give is my flesh for the life of the world . . . Whoever eats my flesh and drinks my blood remains in me and I in him" (NAB).

## C. From Husserl to Marion

The idea of givenness in Marion very closely follows its original use in Husserl. For Marion, givenness is a matter of appearance and manifestation for conscious recognition. Yet Marion claims to radicalize the phenomenological reduction even further than Husserl by unbinding givenness from ideal objectivity alone. Whereas Husserl regarded givenness as the pathway for ideal objects to present themselves to consciousness, Marion views givenness as the fundamental dynamism of all phenomenal appearing, ideal object or otherwise. Like Husserl, Marion privileges the immanence of the given phenomenon but instead does not limit immanence to the noetic matrix of the given in consciousness. In effect, Marion expands Husserl's principle of all principles by crossing out its final clause. This clause is spelled out further in Husserl's negative formulation of the principle: "the *norm* that we should follow as phenomenologists: *to claim* [*in Anspruch zu nehmen*] *nothing that we cannot render essentially evident to consciousness itself* in its pure immanence."[66] Marion objects to Husserl's proposed limits on the possibilities of givenness itself, all the while admitting to the limits of human perception and recognition.[67] For Husserl, "consciousness therefore determines phenomenality by reducing every phenomenon to the certitude of an actual presence, far from phenomenality requiring that consciousness be itself determined by the conditions and the modes of givenness—which are always multiple and disconcerting."[68] Instead, Marion proposes to unfetter givenness from the alleged limits to which consciousness would confine phenomena. This is to say that for phenomenology, possibility trumps the certitude of actual presence. Moreover, this is to say that the possibility of the new and unprecedented phenomenon be liberated from the constraints of the sum total of past actualized phenomena and patterns of appearance. The future must remain an open horizon of possibility—a future that unfolds according to givenness manifest in the elusive present. It is possible that a phenomenon indeed passes beyond the limits of consciousness, in which case the phenomenon itself need not be annulled. This "passing beyond" is what Marion calls "paradox," and further, the "saturated phenomenon." In *Reduction and Givenness*, Marion admits that this critique begins with

66. Husserl, *Ideas I*, 136 (§59), as quoted in Marion, *Reduction and Givenness*, 49.

67. See Marion, *Being Given*, 319: "Givenness often gives the given without measure, but the gifted always keeps within its limits. By excess or by default, givenness must in many cases renounce appearing—be restricted to abandon. Phenomenality always admits limits, precisely because givenness, which transgresses them, gives itself over to my finitude."

68. Marion, *Reduction and Givenness*, 51.

Heidegger and that Marion simply extends it further. In order to view this extended critique of Husserl's original program, let us turn to givenness as it plays out in the work of Heidegger.[69]

## D. Givenness in Heidegger

Whereas Husserl's phenomenology is based on ideal objectivity, Heidegger moves beyond the supremacy of the "sphere of things" (*Sachsphäre*) in order to ground phenomenality in the lived experience (*Erlebnis*).[70] In such a broadening, to speak of givenness does not then require speaking exclusively in terms of subject/object. Rather, in Heidegger's notion of givenness, an object does not give itself but a signification or meaning gives itself.[71] The signification of meaning constitutes the human subject; the subject does not constitute the signification of meaning because it is precisely the signification of meaning that is given to the subject: "it gives itself by itself" (*sich selbst an ihm selbst zeigt*). All giving of meaning takes place in the context of "an immediate environment," in the world that surrounds us (*Umwelt*): "the meaningful is primary and immediately given to me without any mental detours across thing-oriented apprehension. Living in an environment, it signifies to me everywhere and always, everything has the character of the world. It is everywhere the case that '*it worlds*' [*es weltet*]."[72] Every meaning or signification is given as a global one and so appears in an expansive context of world givenness. Furthermore, Heidegger asserts the fundamental notion of *Ereignis*—the happening of an event and the ensuing appropriation of the event by the subject—showing that the given is not an object, but the process of an event's unfolding, in short, the conscious unfolding of givenness.[73] Heidegger's phenomenality of *Erlebnis* and *Ereignis* overcomes

69. See ibid., 51.

70. Heidegger, *Towards the Definition of Philosophy*, 55: "In immediate observation I do not find anything like an 'I,' but only an 'ex-perience [*Er-leben*] of something,' a '*living towards something*'"; cf. Pascal, *Pensées*, 128 (396): "Two things teach man about his whole nature: instinct and experience" (translation my own).

71. Heidegger's notion of givenness falls between that of Paul Natorp (1854–1924) and Heinrich Rickert (1863–1936). According to Natorp, the pure given is meaningless in itself but acquires meaning only once taken up by understanding; the given needs the transcendental ego, otherwise the given would not appear. Natorp in effect gives up givenness. Rickert, on the other hand, opposed Natorp's understanding of (non-)givenness and instead asserted that givenness is itself the first category of understanding, and likewise the first judgment, for example, "This is given."

72. Heidegger, *Towards the Definition of Philosophy*, 58.

73. Ibid., 55–56, 60: "However simply and primitively the interrogative experience gives itself, in respect of all its components it is peculiarly dependent. Nevertheless,

the flat Husserlian phenomenology of objectivity by introducing a revised notion of givenness that serves as a way to ask the question about Being (*Sein*) in terms other than is-ness or presence, for according to Heidegger, "the Being of entities (beings) 'is' not itself an entity (being)" (*Das Sein des Seienden »ist« nicht selbst ein Seiendes*).[74] Heidegger broadens Husserl's notion of phenomenality based on a presence of the here and now to an excessive phenomenality based on the "opening of Being" as the fundamental character for the manifestation of all being-phenomena; Heidegger initiates "the phenomenality of *Being* itself."[75] Thus Being is what ultimately gives, not as a being but as the phenomenal playing-field of the disclosure of beings as such. Heideggerian phenomenology, however, is less a question of beings appearing as such, but more of one concerning the overall experience of their phenomenality, their phenomenalization, their givenness, "the interpretation of beings with regard to their Being."[76] Heidegger defines the phenomenon in the same way as Husserl—"what shows itself on the basis of itself"[77]—yet in Heidegger there is found a subtle reversal of the transcendent/immanent relation as found in Husserl:

> Transcendence, for Heidegger, does not pass beyond the immanence of the phenomenon; on the contrary, if the phenomenon is valid as a being, then the Being that offers being to itself becomes, in the capacity of phenomenality, the transcendent par

from this experience a ground-laying and essential insight can now be achieved. (Characterization of the lived experience as event [*Er-eignis*]—meaningful, not thing-like.) . . . an *event of appropriation* [*Ereignis*] (non-process, in the experience of the question a residue of this event). Lived experience does not pass in front of me like a thing, but I appropriate [*er-eigne*] it to myself, and it appropriates [*er-eignet*] itself according to its essence. If I understand it in this way, then I understand it not as process, as thing, as object, but in a quite new way, as an event of appropriation."

74. Heidegger, *Being and Time*, 26 (§2). A metaphysical notion of presence as "self-sustaining existence" in effect can cover up the notion of givenness; cf. Marion, *Reduction and Givenness*, 62; also Marion, *Crossing of the Visible*, 5: "The relief of the visible comes to it from the invisible, which lifts it by deepening and crossing it, to the point of uprooting it from the *humus* of flatness where one encounters only unidimensional perception . . . the visible increases in direct proportion to the invisible. The more the invisible is increased, the more the visible is deepened." This notion of the invisible offering relief to the visible will have significant import for the phenomenality of the Eucharist, as will be demonstrated further below.

75. Marion, *Reduction and Givenness*, 60.

76. Ibid., 63.

77. Marion, *Being Given*, 184: "Intuition is itself attested by itself without the background of a reason still to be offered. Thus the phenomenon according to Husserl answers in advance to the phenomenon according to Heidegger—what shows itself on the basis of itself. This is clear: what shows itself on the basis of itself as pure apparition of self without remainder, and not of an other than self that does not appear (a reason)."

> excellence. *Sein ist das transcendens schlechthin* ("Being is transcendence as such"). The transcendence of Being does not leave being behind it, but rather pushes it to the end. The transcendence of phenomenality does not pass through the immanence of the phenomenon, but much rather leads it to its end.[78]

Heidegger recognizes the essential movement of phenomenal manifestation—from unapparent to apparent, from non-appearance to appearance, from concealment to disclosure:

> Manifestly, [a phenomenon] is something that proximally and for the most part does *not* show itself at all: it is something that lies *hidden*, in contrast to that which proximally and for the most part does show itself; but at the same time it is something that belongs to what thus shows itself, and it belongs to it so essentially as to constitute its meaning and its ground.[79]

Within this phenomenal movement of manifestation, there is always something that remains hidden; specifically, for Heidegger, Being itself remains hidden, or more precisely, the "truth of Being" (*Wahrheit des Seins*) remains hidden:[80] "That which in the phenomenon requires the phenomenological work of unveiling, precisely because of itself it remains concealed, is nothing less than the (always veiled) unveiling of the truth."[81] The ground and source of all phenomenality is the disclosure-concealment dynamic of Being that only can be given intuitively and enigmatically through the inquiry of *Dasein*.[82] Being, however, can never be disclosed, exhausted or comprehended fully by *Dasein* because Being remains "nothing of a being, and is nothing visible . . . for Being can never be found as uncovered or exposed; only beings can and must be."[83] Therefore Being is perceptibly pal-

78. Marion, *Reduction and Givenness*, 64 (English translation of German text my own).

79. Heidegger, *Being and Time*, 59 (§7).

80. Ibid.

81. Marion, *Reduction and Givenness*, 219 (endnote 50).

82. Cf. Schalow, *Heidegger and the Quest for the Sacred*, 34: "Phenomenologically speaking, the more radical and extreme the questioning becomes, the more directly can the inquirer be admitted into the realm of disclosure. This disclosedness is formed in part by a projection which brings to the forefront Dasein's potentiality to be. Thus, Dasein's selfhood is granted as an outgrowth of its 'surpassing beyond' and over to those possibilities which encompass a network of worldly involvements, of being-in-the-world. Heidegger describes this process of surpassing, which epitomizes and brings to light our thrownness *into* the world, 'transcendence.'"

83. Marion, *Reduction and Givenness*, 61; cf. ibid., 60: "The phenomenon had to pass from evident present [as in Husserl] to the enigma of play within it [as in Heidegger]

pable and detectable by *Dasein*, not in the same sensuous way as beings but rather "in the fact that something is, and in its Being as it is; in Reality; in presence-at-hand; in subsistence; in validity; in Dasein; in the 'it gives' ["*es gibt*"]."[84] The inquiry of the analytic *Dasein* is so absolute and fundamental for Heidegger, that any subjective terms regarding *Dasein's* inquiry into its (and the world's) raison d'être (for example, spirit, soul, consciousness, ego, reason, subject, person) must be bracketed out in order to prevent the blocking of any interrogation of the Being of *Dasein* and to avoid the "Cartesian-Hegelian metaphysics of subjectivity."[85] In other words, *Dasein* must be neutral in order to be self-authentic. The opening to the questioning of Being rules within the inescapable realm of lived experience (*Erlebnis*) and the ensuing appropriation of lived experience (*Ereignis*) by the analytic *Dasein*. Heidegger even maintains a diametrically oppositional relationship between faith and uninhibited *Dasein*: "the unconditional character of faith, and the problematic character of thinking, are two spheres separated by an abyss."[86] For Heidegger, the problem with faith vis-à-vis philosophical thinking is that an a priori answering to the question of Being hinders, or even usurps, *Dasein's* neutral freedom and agency to inquire about the question of Being.[87] All must halt before the supreme analytic *Dasein* in order to arrive at "the understanding of the Being of this being (projecting upon the mode of its unconcealedness [*Unverborgenheit*])."[88] *Dasein* must

between the unapparent and the apparent only in order to be able to give rise to the phenomenality of Being, which, par excellence, is covered over in the very uncovering of beings—since it brings about that uncovering"; cf. Heidegger, *Being and Time*, 269 (§44): "Dasein, as constituted by disclosedness, is essentially in the truth. Disclosedness is a kind of Being which is essential to Dasein. '*There is*' *truth* [*Wahrheit gibt »es«*] *only in so far as Dasein is and so long as Dasein is.* Entities are uncovered only *when* Dasein *is*; and only as long as Dasein *is*, are they disclosed."

84. Heidegger, *Being and Time*, 26 (§2).

85. Derrida, *Of Spirit*, 23; cf. 18, 17: "These terms and concepts have thus no rights in an analytic of *Dasein* which seeks to determine the entity which we ourselves are . . . Now who are we? Here, let us not forget, we are first and only determined from the opening to the *question of Being*. Even if Being must be given to us for that to be the case, we are only at this point, and know of 'us' only this: the power or rather the possibility of questioning, the experience of questioning."

86. Heidegger, *What Is Called Thinking?*, 177.

87. Cf. Vedder, *Heidegger's Philosophy of Religion*, 76–77: "Only a ratio that abandons the revelation of faith is capable of actualizing the philosophical way of thinking. The existentiell commitment to faith alone will never find the formal indications for understanding the ontological structure of factical Dasein. Only through the ontological analysis does it become understandable that theology presupposes something that is not pre-given in Dasein, or in being . . . the question of being does not exist for the believer because this question is already answered out of faith."

88. Heidegger, *Grundprobleme der Phänomenologie*, §5, *GA* [*Gesamtausgabe*] 24

remain unhampered by any sort of theological baggage that would impose itself on the open question of Being a priori. The agency and purview of *Dasein* is absolute, exercising an absolute hermeneutic task at the service of the self-disclosure of Being.

### E. Application 2: The Hidden Invisible of the Eucharist

In contrast to Husserl's location of givenness primarily within the realm of objects, especially the objectivity within cognition, Heidegger emphasizes givenness within the real-life experience, more broadly speaking.[89] In so doing, Heidegger recognizes the ordinary nature of all phenomena as bearing an ever-concealed hiddenness that allows phenomena to appear as such, a hiddenness that must remain as a backdrop in order to enable phenomena to disclose themselves, to appear against this backdrop of hiddenness. More specifically, for Heidegger, Being (*Sein*) serves as the condition for the possibility of the uncovering of beings, though Being itself can never be uncovered: "Being does not open like beings are uncovered, if only because its opening precedes uncoveredness and renders it possible."[90] Furthermore, Heidegger's understanding of the relationship between Being and beings creates a space for the phenomenality of the invisible as such. Marion wonders:

> If we want to maintain the title of phenomenon for Being—at the risk of an extremely dangerous ambiguity—it would be necessary to think a phenomenon that is not exhausted in presence here and now, since it is defined only by being able to refuse itself to such presence. To render phenomenal not that which, being invisible, could become visible, and therefore become a being, but, paradoxically, to render phenomenal that which, invisible as such, could not in this way become visible in the mode of a present being—can this task be taken on, or even formulated?[91]

The phenomenality of the Eucharist can assume such a task in order to give phenomenal credence, in terms of givenness, to the invisible as a legitimate

---

[English translation, 21; modified], as quoted in Marion, *Reduction and Givenness*, 64–65.

89. Cf. Marion, "La phénoménalité du sacrement," 74: ". . . nothing shows *itself*, that does not first give *itself* and in the measure in which it gives *itself*, since in effect a phenomenon cannot show *itself* insofar as it does not give *itself* in real-life experience, than it commits itself in the flesh and in person in the realm of conscience."

90. Marion, *Reduction and Givenness*, 61.

91. Ibid.

phenomenon, not as a visible being but as invisible [ ].[92] Heidegger's juxtaposition of Being with beings opens a playing-field of phenomenality that does not restrict appearing to visible beings alone. In addition, just as *Dasein* is called to interpret the Being of beings, a living faith is called to discern the invisible mysteries of God in the visible manifestation of the sacrament. Christ, the A and the Ω, is the hermeneutical key to unlocking the hidden invisible givenness of the Eucharist just as "the question of Being can be reached only when the questioning is guided by a *questioning to the very end* [*Zu-Ende-fragen*], namely, a *questioning that returns to the beginning* [*in den Anfang Hineinfragen*], that is, when it is determined by the sense of the phenomenological principle radically understood—that of the thing itself—*to allow being to be seen as being itself in its Being* [*Seiendes als Seiendes selbst in seinem Sein sehen zu lassen*]."[93] Just as Heidegger's goal of the phenomenological reduction is to "(lead) phenomenological vision back from the apprehension of a being, whatever may be the character of that apprehension, to the understanding of the Being of this being (projecting upon the mode of its unconcealedness [*Unverborgenheit*])."[94] a similar goal is at work in sacramental theology: *fides quaerens intellectum* (Anselm). To probe the phenomenon of revelation at work in the sacrament, Heidegger's concept of Being's self-showing can serve as a fitting analogue. In approaching the mystery of God's self-disclosure in the Eucharist, the believer is called to contemplate not only the physical elements set before him but, above all, he is pressed to contemplate how the invisible Deity is manifest in and through the visible elements, all the while remaining concealed beneath them. Altogether, this is an event of revelation—the self-manifestation of divinity in

92. For specific and concentrated application of Heideggerian phenomenology to liturgical phenomena, see Lacoste, *Experience and the Absolute*; Schrijvers, "Jean-Yves Lacoste: A Phenomenology of Liturgy"; Rivera, "Toward a Liturgical Existentialism"; Rivera, "Corpus Mysticum and Religious Experience: Henry, Lacoste and Marion"; Schrijvers, *An Introduction to Jean-Yves Lacoste*; Gschwandtner, *Postmodern Apologetics?*, 163–83; Schrijvers, "God and/in Phenomenology: Jean-Yves Lacoste's *Phenomenality of God*."

93. Heidegger, *Prolegomena zur Geschichte des Zeitbegriffs*, §14, *GA* 20, 186 [English translation, 137; modified], as quoted in Marion, *Reduction and Givenness*, 64. While this is a connection that Heidegger himself would refuse vehemently in order to protect the neutrality of *Dasein*, I take liberties and make it here because I do not hold the necessity of an absolute separation between religious faith and the task of philosophy; the same *Logos*-principle is at work in both. In fact, I would argue along with Augustine, Karl Barth, Hans Urs von Balthasar, and many others that Christ the *Logos* enlightens *Dasein* by providing it with the urgent questions to ask in the first place, for example, see Matt 16:15: "Who do you say that I am?" (NAB).

94. Heidegger, *Grundprobleme der Phänomenologie*, §5, *GA* 24 [English translation, 21; modified], as quoted in Marion, *Reduction and Givenness*, 64–65.

finite and particular existents. The discovery of Being by *Dasein* is therefore analogous to the discovery of the invisible mysteries of divine life by faith.[95]

Finally, Heidegger's expansive notion of givenness offers to the phenomenality of the Eucharist an experience and event of the signification/meaning of Christ's self-giving, in a word, the happening of the paschal mystery. Through a "kairological understanding of history"[96] and "the self's 'reawakening' in the *kairological* moment,"[97] "*faith is the believing-understanding mode of existing in the history revealed, i.e., occurring, with the Crucified.*"[98] This is to say that a Heideggerian hermeneutic of givenness, when applied to the Eucharist-phenomenon, opens new vistas for understanding oneself vis-à-vis the relationship between the hidden and the revealed. New ways-of-being-in-the-world are disclosed inasmuch as one is attuned to the revelatory givenness and giving-ness of the play between visible and invisible. The possibility of appropriating the paradoxical mode of existence disclosed in the paschal mystery is opened before *Dasein* according to the concealed-unconcealed *es gibt* of the Eucharist.

## F. From Heidegger to Marion

Toward the end of his book *Reduction and Givenness*, Marion calls into question Heidegger's critique of Husserl. Heidegger critiques Husserl for "miss[ing] the *Seinsfrage* ["question of being"] and that it thus contradicts its own principle of returning to the things themselves."[99] However, Marion wonders if this critique might be reversed: if the Being of beings, in the end, does not offer "the ultimate and irrevocable *Sache selbst* ["thing itself"]," then it remains possible that Heidegger missed the radicality of Husserl's original claim:

> In other words, Heidegger's slogan against Husserl—that the possibility of phenomenology surpasses its actuality—could be turned back against the undertaking of *Sein und Zeit*: the *ultimate* possibility of phenomenology would consist in the question of Being no more than it is exhausted in the objectity of the constituted object; beyond the one and the other equally, a

95. Cf. Rom 1:20: "Ever since the creation of the world, [God's] invisible attributes of eternal power and divinity have been able to be understood and perceived in what [God] has made" (NAB).

96. Vedder, *Heidegger's Philosophy of Religion*, 74.

97. Schalow, *Heidegger and the Quest for the Sacred*, 31.

98. Heidegger, *Pathmarks*, 45.

99. Marion, *Reduction and Givenness*, 161.

> final possibility could still open to it—that of positing the *I* as transcendent to reduced objectity, but also to the Being of beings, that of positing itself, by virtue of the reduction carried out to its final consequences, outside of Being. Outside of Being?[100]

Marion claims the possibility that the phenomenological reduction leads to the final possibility of positing the ego outside of Being—and not only this—but positing phenomenality as beginning not from the ego, but from the phenomenon. Indeed, "to the thing itself." Here is the provocation of Marion's project: a reduction to givenness, an inversion of intentionality.[101] So much reduction, so much givenness. Marion responds affirmatively to the question, "Outside of Being?" To shed the strictures of Being and its question is to open phenomenality to its ultimate possibilities—possibilities already giving themselves. The newness is not in the discovery of brand new phenomena, but in further recognition of what has been giving itself all along, as well as the open possibilities of what may give itself in the future. Marion's transgression beyond the question of Being opens to a further question that aims at the "wonder of all wonders" and the phenomenon par excellence. Marion wonders what sort of phenomenon could serve as a model of utmost possibility—not a possibility limited in some fashion, but a possibility exceeding every imaginable limit, namely, the impossible that nevertheless remains the utmost for possibility—an inverted metric with neither beginning nor end.[102] This inversion, à la Levinas, allows Marion to posit the call of givenness as most anterior and originary, as most giving and unlimited: "In the pure form of the call a reduction is carried out: nothing manages to give itself as a phenomenon if a response does not give itself over to it as to an originary claim."[103] The affirmative response to the call of givenness in the form of abandonment by the human subject is the result of the reduction deployed to its fullest potential: the ego is converted

100. Ibid., 162.

101. Marion admits to have followed Levinas on the inversion of intentionality, but claims to go beyond Levinas in the reduction to givenness, the face of the other—ethical exigency—simply being a mode of givenness. See Marion's essay on Levinas in Bloechl, *Face of the Other*, 225: "Such a reversal of intentionality and phenomenality, passing from the object which is visible and aimed at to the face which aims and is thus non-visible, radically alters the entire horizon of phenomenological analysis, as we have all indeed noticed. In that much, we have all become Levinasians, and definitively."

102. See Marion, *Visible and the Revealed*, 45: "Thus, following the guiding thread of the saturated phenomenon, phenomenology finds its ultimate possibility: not only the possibility that surpasses actuality, but the possibility that surpasses the very conditions of possibility, the possibility of unconditioned possibility—in other words, the possibility of the impossible, the saturated phenomenon."

103. Marion, *Reduction and Givenness*, 198.

into the *interloqué* (*der Angesprochene*), "the called/the gifted."[104] So much reduction, so much givenness. The further the reduction is exerted, the more phenomenality gives to view. Vision is in fact saturated and bedazzled, blinded by the luminous flood of givenness. A continuity of recognition can be traced from Plato's cave to Marion's donative/erotic reduction.[105] It is because of Marion's critique of the reductions of Husserl and Heidegger—in some ways a return to Husserl through a critique of Heidegger—that he is able to propose a third reduction: the reduction to givenness, and at the same time, the reduction to love.

In supplying the necessary warrants for the third reduction to givenness, Marion in effect opens the possibility of using phenomenology to explore religious phenomena, that is, phenomena that give themselves in religious contexts. One can assess the plausibility structures, the coherence, the logic and patterns of religious phenomena such as theophanies, prayer, worship, exegesis of sacred texts, oracles and prophecy—in sum, the possibility of divine revelation and the possible human responses to it. Is Marion, then, contradicting the Heideggerian rule of delimiting *Dasein*, in warding off any scent of theology—to maintain its neutrality and the integrity of the philosophical task? Yes and no. Marion indeed is calling into question the protection of *Dasein*'s neutrality inasmuch as "neutrality" implies a subjective imposition of limits for phenomenality. The fear of contaminating *Dasein*'s neutrality causes an obstruction of possibility for that which gives itself. Marion argues that *Dasein* and the question of Being are not ultimate; that which gives itself—the phenomenon—is ultimate. However, at the same time, Marion does not claim to be converting phenomenology to a pure theology by introducing the possibility of the saturated phenomenon with its ensuing configurations and paradigmatic content. Rather, he insists that "with the question of a phenomenon taking saturation to its maximum, it is not straightaway or always a question of debating the status of the theological in phenomenology, but at the outset and in the first place of a possible figure of phenomenality as such."[106] This should allay any concerns that phenomenology has smuggled in theology defiantly through the back door.

104. See ibid., 200–202.

105. See Plato, *Rebublic*, Book VII, in *Complete Works*, 1132–37.

106. Marion, *Being Given*, 234.

## G. Application 3: Saturating Sacramental Encounter of the Eucharist

Despite Heidegger's insistence that philosophical and theological investigation must remain mutually exclusive, Marion's reduction to givenness may offer great promise for a fresh, liberating and captivating critical hermeneutic for sacramental theology, since the Christian faith tradition is one steeped in manifestation.[107] Marion has stretched convincingly the phenomenological method to its assurgent application in theology. His trilogy on the phenomenological method—*Reduction and Givenness*, *Being Given*, *In Excess*—has caused a wave of consternation among some (philosophers?), and elation among others (theologians?).[108] While Marion is not alone in employing the phenomenological method in the theological realm (see the work of Henry, Chrétien, Ricoeur, Levinas, Sokolowski, et al.), his contributions directly stretch the method as developed by Husserl and Heidegger.[109] Even though Husserl and Heidegger identified and worked along (but without crossing) a distinct border that separated theology from philosophy, Marion regards such partitioning as unwarranted. For Marion, the question of divine revelation remains pertinent in the realm of critical philosophy inasmuch as the question of divine revelation is a question about possibility. For "higher than actuality stands *possibility*. We can understand phenomenology only by seizing upon it as a possibility."[110] While Marion is careful to draw the distinction between the phenomenon of "revelation" and that of "Revelation," he establishes his primary task as that of challenging the principle of sufficient reason, in any of its avatars (for example, the ego, *Dasein*, "immutable laws of nature," etc.) as authoritative for phenomenality.[111]

107. Cf. Marion, *In Excess*, 29: "Why do [theologians] not undertake, or undertake so little (Hans Urs von Balthasar remains here insufficient and exceptional), to read phenomenologically the events of revelation recorded in the Scriptures, in particular the New Testament, instead of always privileging ontic, historic, or semiotic hermeneutics?"

108. Cf. Janicaud, *Phenomenology and the "Theological Turn"*, for a general presentation of the issues at stake.

109. Cf. Marion, *Reduction and Givenness*, 203–5, on Marion's proposal of a third phenomenological reduction: an *epoché* that discloses the original form of givenness in phenomena; "so much reduction, so much givenness."

110. Heidegger, *Being and Time*, 63 (§ 7).

111. Marion draws the distinction between "revelation" and "Revelation" by designating "revelation" as "an appearance that is purely of itself and starting from itself, that does not subject its possibility to any preliminary determination" (*Visible and the Revealed*, 47), and by defining "Revelation" as "(of God by himself, *theo*logical) . . . assum[ing] the phenomenological figure of the phenomenon of revelation, of the paradox of paradoxes, of saturation to the second degree. To be sure, *R*evelation (as

As mentioned above, one of Marion's primary targets of critique is the transcendental logic of Immanuel Kant. In his *Critique of Pure Reason*, Kant asserts four "principles of pure understanding" that he views to be sine qua non transcendental conditions of possibility for understanding: (1) axioms of intuition [quantity], (2) anticipations of perception [quality], (3) analogies of experience [relation], and (4) postulates of empirical thought as such [modality].[112] Essentially, for Kant, these are the boundaries, or limits, of phenomenality. Kant draws the distinction between noumena and phenomena and carefully identifies what he sees to be the conditions for any and all phenomenal appearing to consciousness. Marion challenges this notion

---

actuality) is never confounded with *r*evelation (as possible phenomenon)" (*Being Given*, 367 [endnote 90]). This distinction in Marion is complicated with his nuanced portrayal of "revelation" in *Being Given*: "If the Revelation of God as showing himself starting from himself alone can in fact ever take place, phenomenology must redefine its own limits and learn to pass beyond them following clear-cut and rigorous procedures. That is to say, it must design one of its possible figures as a paradox of paradoxes, saturated with intuition to the second degree, in a word, a phenomenon of revelation" (242). In his 1992 essay, "The Saturated Phenomenon" (in Marion, *Visible and the Revealed*, 18–48), he defines "revelation" more modestly and even includes the phenomena of the idol and the icon as different modes of revelation. In his 1997 book, *Being Given*, Marion appears to conflate the respective meanings of "revelation" and "Revelation," with the sole difference being that "revelation" indicates possibility, while "Revelation" indicates actuality. More specifically, Marion understands "Revelation" to mean any particular content of divine revelation (for example, Islam, Buddhism, Judaism, Hinduism, Christianity, etc.), whereas "revelation" means merely the possibility of the paradox of paradoxes, saturation to the second degree. Cf. the following essays for a discussion of Marion's attempt to locate revelation within the field of phenomenology: Westphal, "Vision and Voice"; Westphal, "The Importance of Overcoming Metaphysics for the Life of Faith"; Burch, "Blurred Vision: Marion on the 'Possibility' of Revelation."

112. Cf. Kant, *Critique of Pure Reason*, 229–302 [A 159–235; B 159–294]. More specifically, Kant describes the four principles of understanding as (1) axioms of intuition whose principle is that "all intuitions are extensive magnitudes" (quantity), (2) anticipations of perception whose principle is that "in all appearances the real that is an object of sensation has intensive magnitude, i.e., a degree" (quality), (3) analogies of experience whose principle is that "experience is possible only through the presentation of a necessary connection of perceptions" (relation), and (4) postulates of empirical thought as such whose principles include (*a*) "what agrees (in terms of intuition and concepts) with the formal conditions of experience is *possible*," (*b*) "what coheres with the material conditions of experience (with sensation) is *actual*," and (*c*) "that whose coherence with the actual is determined according to universal conditions of experience is *necessary* (exists necessarily)" (modality). In sum, "for Kant, a phenomenon appears, therefore, only in a site that is predefined by a system of coordinates, a system that is itself governed by the principle of the unity of experience." Marion, *Visible and the Revealed*, 38. However, for Marion, the saturated phenomenon surpasses all Kantian predetermined principles of understanding to the measure that it eludes cognitive limitation in the form of the paradox. See Marion, *Being Given*, 199–221; Marion, *Visible and the Revealed*, 18–48.

directly with his own original concept of the "saturated phenomenon" (*phénomène saturé*). Marion contends for the side of possibility, construing the possibility of revelation as that which would occur in the form of the saturated phenomenon par excellence. He does this to oppose those who would deem the phenomenon of revelation as "impossible."[113] Breaking through the aporia of revelation, Marion demonstrates the various ways in which Kant's principles of pure understanding do not take into account the full and excessive possibilities of phenomenality: (1) quantity is challenged by the phenomenon of the event, (2) quality is beset by the phenomenon of the idol, (3) relation is absolved by the phenomenality of the unsubstitutable, auto-affecting flesh, and (4) modality is surpassed by the phenomenon of the icon.[114] For Marion, the event, the idol, the flesh, and the icon are all particular forms of the saturated phenomenon, as indicated above. Yet he goes even further to apply his theory in the case of Christ as an instance of Revelation.[115] Christ is an instance, not only of the saturated phenomenon, but an instance of the saturation of saturation, doubly paradoxical insofar as he assumes the form of a radical Gift that floods the horizon of phenomenality, appearing as a shortage, and bearing the name "the abandoned."[116] Christ saturates quantity in the form of his eventfulness; he saturates quality

113. I recall Marion saying once in class at the University of Chicago (Spring Quarter, 2009, Swift Hall, Room 106) that "the fact that a line can be drawn between the possible and the impossible suggests the possibility that such a line can be crossed."

114. Cf. Marion, *Being Given*, 225–33.

115. Cf. ibid., 234–41.

116. Cf. Mark 15:34: "And at three o'clock Jesus cried out in a loud voice, '*Eloi, Eloi, lema sabachthani*?' which is translated, 'My God, my God, why have you forsaken me?'" (NAB); Ps 22:2: "My God, my God, why have you abandoned me? Why so far from my call for help, from my cries of anguish?" (NAB); Isa 52:14: "Even as many were amazed at him—so marred was his look beyond that of man, and his appearance beyond that of mortals" (NAB); Isa 53:2–3: "He grew up like a sapling before him, like a shoot from the parched earth; there was in him no stately bearing to make us look at him, nor appearance that would attract us to him. He was spurned and avoided by men, a man of suffering, accustomed to infirmity, one of those from whom men hide their faces, spurned, and we held him in no esteem" (NAB); John 1:10–11: "He was in the world, and the world came to be through him, but the world did not know him. He came to what was his own, but his own people did not accept him" (NAB); Marion, *Being Given*, 238, 246: "The unbearable therefore suspends perception in general, beyond the difference between hearing and sight, because it results from the thorough saturation of the figure of Christ. And this paradox culminates in the resurrection itself; for, since it by definition passes beyond what this world can receive, contain, or embrace, it can let itself be perceived only by terrifying, to the point that this terror sometimes suffices to designate it by denegation . . . I will name the phenomena of revelation (saturation of saturation), where the excess of the gift assumes the character of shortage, with the name the *abandoned* (*l'abandonné*)."

in the form of his bedazzling appearance; he saturates relation in the form of his incarnate flesh that cannot be circumscribed by the world of common-law phenomena but rather transgresses them through his apophatic epiphany; and he saturates modality in the iconic form of his person, whereby instead of the ego constituting him to its liking, he constitutes the human subject by his loving and forgiving gaze. In this way Marion contrasts Kant's position in which there is no room for the phenomenon of revelation, let alone divine Revelation. Marion weds the notion of givenness with the particularities of phenomenal possibility in his construal of the phenomenon of revelation: the saturated phenomenon that appears on the limited horizons of intentionality, saturating the intentional aim of the human subject with unrelenting intuition. For Marion, not only is Christ the doubly saturating phenomenon, Christ is to be worshipped and adored insofar as his bedazzling divinity calls forth such an absolute response, according to its unreserved giving to the point of abandonment. The Eucharist is the fullest expression of this total self-giving as it extends the sacrificial offering of Christ crucified, as well as the redemptive grace (gift) of his resurrection from the dead, under the most humiliating appearance of food and drink. It would be too reductionistic to limit a description of the Eucharist to the eucharistic species (bread become body, wine become blood) alone. Without doubt, this is a phenomenon involving persons. It exhibits an intrinsic iconicity that must be explored through Marion's illuminating hermeneutic of the saturated phenomenon.

## III. Iconicity as Gateway to Ultimate Reality as Revealed in the Eucharist

Taking one form of the saturated phenomenon as posited by Marion, let us turn to the efficacy of the icon as a portal to ultimate reality as manifest in the Eucharist.[117] In his early work *The Idol and Distance* (1977), Marion proposes a thoroughly apophatic theology in response to Nietzsche's pronouncement, "God is dead!" For Marion, the key question from which to frame a response to this tremendous proclamation is, "*What* God is dead?" Marion replies, "The God of *metaphysics* is dead." In Marion's conception, the God of metaphysics is not the one, true and living God about whom the Scriptures testify, but an idol to be razed. For Marion, the juxtaposi-

117. "Ultimate reality" is a term in vogue today that refers to that which one holds to be absolutely the case, especially concerning the question of the divine. This term is inspired largely in part by Paul Tillich's notion of "ultimate concern." See Tillich, *Systematic Theology*, 1:3–15.

tion of the idol vis-à-vis the icon is a key paradigm for approaching and understanding the question of divine denomination, or (un-)naming God.[118] The idol is fashioned according to humanity's attempt to envisage the divine whereby "human experience precedes the face that (a particular) divinity assumes in it . . . the idol fixes the divine for us permanently, for a commerce where the human hems in the divine from all angles."[119] The idol, formed strictly according to human determination, acts not as a translucent mediator that discloses divine mystery, but as a mirror reflecting only the human onlooker, exhausting every aim, allowing no invisibility to illuminate the gaze—in effect burying the gaze through narcissistic inversion.[120] As such, a philosophical or theological thought that "expresses a concept of what it then names 'God'" functions precisely as an idol: "The concept consigns to a sign what at first the mind grasps with it (*concipere, capere*); but such a grasp is measured not so much by the amplitude of the divine as by the scope of the *capacitas*, which can fix the divine in a specific concept only at the moment when a conception of the divine fills it, hence appeases, stops, and freezes it."[121]

A prime example of such an instance is Descartes's naming of God as *causa sui*, that is, God as the cause of Godself.[122] In this particular example, Descartes superimposes the category of causality onto God, thus determining God qua God within the limits of human reason and understanding. The human gaze becomes transfixed upon its glamorous idol that merely confirms a particular mode of knowledge and the presuppositions of its neat and tidy logic, namely, a sterile rendering of "more of the same." If God is conceived and approached in solely human terms and categories, God is reduced to a supreme being among all beings, a primordial cause among causes, the God of onto-theology—essentially an existent among existents,

118. Although both the idol and the icon function as saturating phenomena for Marion, the usage of these terms here is derived primarily from his pitting of them in *God without Being*.

119. Marion, *Idol and Distance*, 5; cf. Marion, *God without Being*, 9–10: "The idol presents itself to man's gaze in order that representation, and hence knowledge, can seize hold of it . . . it captivates the gaze only inasmuch as the gazeable comprises it."

120. Marion, *God without Being*, 12–13.

121. Ibid., 16.

122. Ibid., 16, 35–36.

a creature among creatures.[123] Such is the fate of the conceptual idol of ultimate reality.[124]

The icon, on the other hand, "does not result from a vision but provokes one."[125] The icon maintains the presentation of the invisible by summoning the gaze to surpass itself by preventing a freezing of the visible, instead "giving rise to an infinite gaze."[126] In the icon, the human seeker is met by the counter-gaze of the re-presentative icon; the icon bears an "intention that envisages," coming to it from an "elsewhere whose invisible strangeness saturates the visibility of the face with meaning."[127] When gazing upon the icon, one must "[renounce] all grasping (*aisthesis*)" and "[submit] to an apocalyptic exposure": "we become a visible mirror of an invisible gaze that subverts us in the measure of its glory."[128] Unlike the idol, which fixes the concept as constitutive of the essence of God, "the icon obliges the concept to welcome the distance of infinite depth . . . indeterminable by concept."[129] The concept is no longer employed to determine an essence but rather to determine an *intention*: "that of the invisible advancing into the visible and inscribing itself therein by the very reference it imposes from this visible to the invisible."[130] In the event of the mutual beholding of the personal icon and the human person, a profound union occurs, which "increases in the measure of distinction, and reciprocally."[131] A person lives and breathes in the measure that she is not reduced to a thing, to presence, to substance, or to any other criterion that renders her to be the self-same phenomenon as her personal onlooker. There are similar traits between those who gaze upon one another, to be sure, but it is precisely the iconic distance between persons that promotes their loving communion as others. In the icon, gazes cross one another, whereas in the idol, one gaze freezes the other in a lifeless

123. Cf. Tracy, *Analogical Imagination*, 409: "For these reasons, the major explicitly analogical traditions in theology have correctly insisted that in the theological use of analogies, the dissimilarities between God and world are as great as the similarities; the *via eminentiae* is possible only on condition of its constant fidelity to the *via negationis*."

124. Even the predicate "ultimate reality" can become a conceptual idol!

125. Marion, *God without Being*, 17.

126. Ibid., 18.

127. Ibid., 21.

128. Ibid., 22.

129. Ibid., 23.

130. Ibid.

131. Ibid. Cf. ibid., 104: "Distance: the gap that separates definitively only as much as it unifies, since what distance gives consists in the gap itself"; and Marion, *Idol and Distance*, 156: "Distance brings about separation in order that love should receive all the more intimately the mystery of love. Alterity grows as much as union—solely in distance, anterior and perennial, permanent and primordial."

form. Distance obtains through the course of personal othering and mutual reciprocity. The icon thereby becomes the paradigmatic figure of intersubjective distance and a communion of persons.

In the phenomenality of the Eucharist, the Person of Christ offers himself without remainder, that is, he gives all of himself to the person who is his beloved without holding anything of his Person back. As a saturated phenomenon of revelation—doubly saturating as it is doubly paradoxical—the Eucharist exhibits a "givenness without intuition by excess . . . without one being able to decide between excess and shortage . . . where the excess of the gift assumes the character of shortage, with the name the *abandoned* (*l'abandonné*)."[132] That is, one cannot decipher the reason for the lack of intuition given by the phenomenon of the Eucharist, all the while groping for an adequate intuition of Christ that would satisfy the premade concept of Christ, whether in the form of caricature or idol. The very nature of the sacrament holds the given in suspense between faith and doubt, between presence and absence, between excess and shortage, between body and bread, between blood and wine, between the divine and the human. In word and ritual the Eucharist is given as an iconic sacrament at the intersection of infinite divinity and finite humanity. The limitations of human perception and cognition require the appearance of the abandoned phenomenon of saturation, taking on the character of a shortage of intuition (for example, "It still looks and tastes like bread and wine") so that the counter-gaze of the divine countenance is not too overpowering for communion to obtain.[133] The monstrosities of both God (in the form of a "consuming fire") and humanity (in the form of a deranged and sinful [non-]person)—though

132. Marion, *Being Given*, 246. Cf. ibid., 319: "Givenness often gives the given without measure, but the gifted always keeps within its limits. By excess or by default, givenness must in many cases renounce appearing—be restricted to abandon. Phenomenality always admits limits, precisely because givenness, which transgresses them, gives itself over to my finitude."

133. Marion, "La phénoménalité du sacrement," 72: "It is not solely a question here of constituting objects from transcendental subjectivity, those experts by the initiative of an intentionality and those certified by the assurance of an intuitive repleteness, but to receive the phenomena that show *themselves* from the intentionality of God, such that reveal themselves in and from Godself, in the encounter of our waiting, forecast and design, according to the deployment of an intuition 'too' (Mk 9:3) powerful for our capacity, the glory even of God." As a result of the shortage of intuition, itself a product of the saturation of saturation, the iconic phenomenon of revelation must be perceived by a non-intentionality of faith. See Marion, *Prolegomena to Charity*, 100–101: "Freed from intentionality, love in the end would be defined, still within the field of phenomenology, as the act of a gaze that renders itself back to another gaze in a common unsubstitutability . . . But to render oneself other, to surrender this gaze to the gaze of the other who crosses me, requires faith."

entirely incommensurable in kind—must empty themselves in order to commune intimately with one another.[134] Force must yield to gentleness and to the freedom of response through the distance of alterity between divine and human. The stubbornness of sinful humanity also must forego its insistence to determine truth for itself—what is possible and impossible, what is good and evil.[135] In this iconic encounter of persons, identity does not sublate difference because difference promotes and perpetuates union. A hypostatic union is made possible between divine and human through the kenotic self-giving begun by divine initiative.[136] The phenomenality of the icon is redoubled in the phenomenality of the Eucharist as a phenomenon of revelation par excellence. Saturation itself is saturated for the sake of love, subverting expectation and reversing degenerate patterns of nature and history. In order to tease out the relationship between distance, difference and communion, let us examine more closely Marion's conception of the process of divine revelation under the aegis of the Dionysian mystical tradition.

## IV. The Space of Revelation

In both *The Idol and Distance* and *God without Being*, Marion draws from the apophatic theological framework of Dionysius the Areopagite (ca. sixth century AD).[137] Marion issues a critique of Thomas's prioritization of the (analogous) predicate "Being" (*esse/ens*) for God while seeking to retrieve Dionysius's preference for the term "Goodness" that opens the necessary

134. Cf. Deut 4:24: "For the LORD, your God, is a consuming fire, a jealous God" (NAB); Isa 33:14: "On Zion sinners are in dread, trembling grips the impious: 'Who of us can live with the consuming fire? Who of us can live with everlasting flames?'" (NAB); Nah 1:5–6: "The mountains quake before him, and the hills dissolve; the earth is laid waste before him, the world and all who dwell in it. Before his wrath, who can stand firm, and who can face his blazing anger? His fury is poured out like fire, and the rocks are rent asunder before him" (NAB); Heb 12:29: "For our God is a consuming fire" (NAB).

135. See John Paul II, *Veritatis splendor*, 35–37.

136. See Sokolowski, *Christian Faith and Human Understanding*, 70: "The Eucharist is not just the action of the Church but the action of Christ himself. And still more precisely, the Eucharist is the moment during which *God* acts, the moment at which the Creator achieves his second, more perfect creation and reveals to believers and to all the world who and what he is. The Eucharist is the definitive action of the Church, of Christ, and of God. Everything else the Christian does takes its bearings from this decisive sacrament and sacrifice."

137. For a recent erudite treatment of Marion's Dionysian influence, see Jones, *A Genealogy of Marion's Philosophy of Religion*.

distance for the human person to respond with an inexhaustible offering of praise to a non-essentialized God—a "God without Being":

> To begin with, [Dionysius] does not pretend that goodness constitutes the proper name of the Requisite, but that in the apprehension of goodness the dimension is cleared where the very possibility of a categorical statement concerning God ceases to be valid, and where the reversal of denomination into praise becomes inevitable. *To praise* the Requisite *as* such, hence *as* goodness, amounts to opening distance. Distance neither asks nor tolerates that one fill it but that one traverse it, in an infinite praise that feeds on the impossibility or, better, the impropriety of the category. The first praise, the name of goodness, therefore does *not* offer any "most proper name" and decidedly abolishes every conceptual idol of "God" in favor of the luminous darkness where God manifests (and not masks) himself, in short, where he gives himself to be envisaged by us.[138]

In effect, goodness does not so much name God, by fixing God in temporal-spatial dimensions or philosophical concepts or even biblical metaphors, as expresses the recognition of an opening of distance that allows lovers to pursue one another in the luminous darkness of interpersonal manifestation.[139] In this case, distance indeed functions as a concept, not merely as another term within the index of divine predicates but as signifying the acquiescence of the human subject to the iconic phenomenon of divine revelation—a saturated phenomenon that bedazzles the human subject with an infinite and excessive gaze of invisibility, manifest in the visibility of the face and in the givenness of the call.[140]

Marion expands on the Dionysian notion of distance by identifying the dynamic movement that traverses the distance: agapic love. Agapic love is characterized by Marion in terms of the gift (*le don*) and giving (*donation*):

138. Marion, *God without Being*, 76. Cf. Marion, *In the Self's Place*, 16: "God, if he reveals himself, reveals himself before being praised, and the praise is deduced from God by his definition, *Deus laudandus*."

139. Cf. Marion, *Idol and Distance*, 9, 24: "The icon properly manifests the nuptial distance that weds, without confusing, the visible and the invisible—that is, the human and the divine . . . [God] is the Unthinkable, insofar as He reveals the distance of Goodness in the encounter of creation."

140. Marion, *God without Being*, 95, 100–101; cf. Marion, *Idol and Distance*, 144: "To move from a model of language in which the speaker makes an effort to take possession of meaning to a model in which the speaker receives meaning, with the Name, through homology: 'to say divinely.'"

> In the distance, only *agapē* can put everything on earth, in heaven, and in hell, in giving, because *agapē* alone, by definition, is not known, is not—but gives (itself). At the heart of *agapē*, following its flux as one follows a current that is too violent to go back up, too profound for one to know its source or valley, everything flows along the giving, and, by the wake traced in the water, but without grasping anything of it, everything indicates the direction and meaning of distance.[141]

In this passage Marion demonstrates how *agape* eludes the ontological categories of Being/being (but rather "is not") in favor of an iconic and unlimited reality—one in which "love is not spoken, in the end, it is made" (*L'amour ne se dit pas, à la fin, il se fait*).[142] Thus distance provokes an apophatic "mute decency" (silence), admitting that "among the divine names, none exhausts God or offers the grasp or hold of a comprehension of him."[143] Yet Marion is careful to qualify such a claim by negating the tempting concession of intellectual laziness or complacency:

> The unthinkable, as the distance of Goodness, gives itself—not to be comprehended but to be received. It is therefore not a question of giving up on comprehending (as if it were a question of comprehending, and not of being comprehended). It is a question of managing to receive that which becomes thinkable, or rather acceptable, only for the one who knows how to receive it. It is not a question of admitting distance despite its unthinkability, but of preciously receiving the unthinkable, as the sign and seal of the measureless origin of the distance that gives us our measure. If love reveals itself hermetically as distance (which is glossed by *cause* and *goodness*) in order to give itself, only love will be able to welcome it.[144]

This is an agapic, rather than a Gnostic, conception of the human-divine relationship, achieved according to the immeasurable order of agapic, interpersonal love: to know is to love according to the logic of love along the

141. Marion, *God without Being*, 106; cf. Marion, *Idol and Distance*, 153: "Anterior distance conceives us because it engenders us. Anterior distance demands to be received because it more fundamentally gives us [the chance] to receive ourselves in it."

142. Ibid., 107 (154 in original French text).

143. Ibid., 106. Cf. Marion, *In the Self's Place*, 289: "Now, since by definition the unnameable cannot be named by *a* name, it is fitting, before taking any other steps, to admit that all names are in a sense suitable to God, since precisely none can name him adequately. The endless proliferation of divine names constitutes the first and indispensable step in their institution."

144. Marion, *Idol and Distance*, 155.

"horizon of 'love without being.'"[145] Here reason operates according to the power of love (not merely desire) that intends the good of the other, and thus the full appearance of the other.[146] Yet the other's appearing is based not on subjective intentionality, but on the acquiescence of the subject to the manifestation of the other—an interpersonal fiat to the saturating iconic encounter of the other. Especially in the case of receiving divine revelation in the form of aperture, one must surrender mastery, give in to the chase, yield to the gaze and pursuit—the simultaneous appearance and absence—of the Lover.[147] Marion insists not that "God is," but that "*G×d gives*" (thereby overcoming onto-theo-logy): "The giving, in allowing to be divined how 'it gives,' a giving, offers the only accessible trace of He who gives."[148] God is

145. Horner, *Jean-Luc Marion*, 135. Cf. Marion, *Visible and the Revealed*, 74: "But in this case, to *see* the invisible face, I must *love* it. Love, however, comes from charity. In consequence, one must hold that the natural phenomenon of the face of the other cannot be discovered except through the light of charity, that is, through the 'auxiliary' of Revelation. Without the revelation of the transcendence of love, the phenomenon of the face, and thus of the other, simply cannot be seen. This is an exemplary case of 'Christian philosophy,'" and 152: "Only love can give access to the 'great reason.' The love revealed by the Word, hence by the *Logos*, is deployed as a *logos*, hence as a rationality. And a rationality by full right, because it allows us to reach the closest and most internal phenomena, those experienced by the flesh which intuition saturates . . . But Christ has not only shown the logic of love, he has demonstrated and proven it in facts and acts by his passion and his resurrection"; Marion, *Prolegomena to Charity*, 87: "Loving no longer consists trivially in seeing or in being seen, nor in desiring or inciting desire, but in experiencing the crossing of the gazes within, first, the crossing of aims."

146. Cf. Pascal, *Pensées*, 423–24 (277–78): "The heart has its reasons of which reason knows nothing: we know this in countless ways. I say that it is natural for the heart to love the universal being or itself, according to its allegiance, and it hardens itself against either as it chooses. You have rejected one and kept the other. Is it reason that makes you love yourself? It is the heart which perceives God and not the reason. That is what faith is: God perceived by the heart, not by the reason" (translation my own); and Marion, *Prolegomena to Charity*, x: "Love deploys the rationality of those who stage objectivity without entering into it, the actors acted by and acting through their final desire—to love and to be loved."

147. Cf. Song 7:10–12, 8:14 (RSV): "I am my beloved's, / and his desire is for me. / Come, my beloved, / let us go forth into the fields, / and lodge in the villages; / let us go out early to the vineyards, / and see whether the vines have budded, / whether the grape blossoms have opened / and the pomegranates are in bloom. / There I will give you my love . . . Make haste, my beloved, / and be like a gazelle / or a young stag / upon the mountains of spices."

148. Marion, *God without Being*, 105. The significance of the crossing out of the word "God" with the cross of St. Andrew "demonstrates the limit of the temptation, conscious or naïve, to blaspheme the unthinkable in an idol. The cross does not indicate that G×d would have to disappear as a concept, or intervene only in the capacity of a hypothesis in the process of validation, but that the unthinkable enters into the field of our thought only by rendering itself unthinkable there by excess, that is, by criticizing our thought. To cross out G×d, in fact, indicates and recalls that G×d crosses out our

recognizable in the manifold gifts that pour forth from God, the givenness of all reality, and ultimately the very *es gibt* of Godself, i.e., "*G×d gives*."[149] It is through God's givenness that creation springs forth through distance: "*Because* it forever 'remains in an inaccessible light' (1 Timothy 6:16) the unthinkable calls to participation beings that have no common measure with it—no common measure other than a reciprocal disproportion in distance."[150] This participation in the divine givenness is constituted by receptivity and reciprocity on the part of humanity: "Man therefore does not receive the gift as such except in welcoming the act of giving, that is, through repetition by giving himself . . . Only the gift of the gift can receive the gift."[151] While Marion avoids establishing a vacuously cyclic economy of exchange (within which no authentic gift can be given and received as such due to the phenomena of debt, currency, supply/demand, etc.), he suggests that the phenomenological reduction to givenness (which includes in itself the erotic reduction) lets phenomena appear as they give themselves "in the flesh," rather than obscuring the possibility of their giving by deciding upon a priori conditions for their phenomenality.[152] A path for the possibility of the phenomenon of revelation is opened thereby, one that does not draw a line in the sand between what we can know with certainty and what we cannot, any more than one may attempt to draw an impassable (impassible) line between beings (*Seiendes*) and Being (*Sein*). What matters in the end, as well as in the beginning, is not what we can know with certainty, but what we can know with assurance, namely, that we are loved. The Eucharist gives itself as love, and for that reason, as a gift that can be received to the degree that it is given away. She who receives the Eucharist must become a sincere

---

thought because he saturates it; better, he enters into our thought only in obliging it to criticize itself. The crossing out of G×d we trace on his written name only because, first, He brings it to bear on our thought, as his unthinkableness. We cross out the name of G×d only in order to show ourselves that his unthinkableness saturates our thought—right from the beginning, and forever . . . Distance implies an irreducible gap, specifically, disproportion . . . Doubtless it will not be named 'Being,' since Being is of a kind with being by virtue of ontological difference appropriated to itself through *Ereignis*. Doubtless it will not be recognized in any being (and especially not a being 'par excellence'), since being belongs to this side of distance. Doubtless we will name it G×d, but in crossing G×d with the cross that reveals him only in the disappearance of his death and resurrection. For the other term of distance, G×d, strictly does not have to be, nor therefore to receive the name of a being, whatever it may be. *G×d gives*" (Marion, *God without Being*, 46, 105, respectively).

149. Ibid., 105.

150. Marion, *Idol and Distance*, 156.

151. Ibid., 166.

152. Cf. Horner, *Jean-Luc Marion*, 135–46, on the "erotic reduction" proposed in Marion's *Le phénomène érotique*.

gift of herself in order to have received the Eucharist authentically, which itself is nothing other than the sincere and total self-giving of Christ.[153] In the Eucharist, kataphatic denomination gives way to apophatic de-nomination.[154] The distance of goodness creates the necessary space for the gift to appear, for love in the making. Next let us procure the implications of apophatic de-nomination in the work of Marion in order to appreciate more fully the call and response of eucharistic manifestation.

## V. Opening onto a Third Way?

According to Marion, the Eucharist gives a presence and an absence, an assertion (of faith) and a denial (of sensual perception) due to the paradoxical saturation of saturation. He has suggested that the most appropriate human response to doubly saturating givenness is praise and adoration. As evidenced above, much of the impetus for Marion's theological constructions derives from the writings of Dionysius, who is considered rightly an apophatic theologian. In his early work, *The Idol and Distance*, Marion positions himself clearly in the arena of apophatic theology, in response to the pretentious kataphatic onto-theology that suffered its demise at the hands of the nineteenth- and twentieth-century "masters of suspicion." In fact, Marion devotes an entire chapter to the thought of Dionysius in this work. Likewise, *God without Being* sounds a dark and opaque Dionysian tone. However, Marion can be seen nuancing an overtly apophatic position in his 1997 presentation, "In the Name: How to Avoid Speaking of 'Negative

153. See the Second Ecumenical Vatican Council, *Gaudium et spes*, 24: "Furthermore, the Lord Jesus, when praying to the Father 'that they may all be one . . . even as we are one' (Jn 17:21–22), has opened up new horizons closed to human reason by indicating that there is a certain similarity between the union existing among the divine persons and the union of God's children in truth and love. It follows, then, that if human beings are the only creatures on earth that God has wanted for their own sake, they can fully discover their true selves only in sincere self-giving." Translation taken from Flannery, *Vatican Council II*, 189–90.

154. In the way of review, "kataphatic theology" (from the Greek verb *kataphaíno*, meaning "to declare, make known, appear, make clear" [*kata*-, "downwards"; *phasis*, "an assertion"]) refers to the profusion of predication of the divine, for example, "God is good, God is merciful, God is omnipotent," etc. "Apophatic theology" (from the Greek verb *apopheíso*, meaning "to negate/deny" [*apo*-, "away from"; *phasis*, "an assertion"] refers to the ensuing negation or denial of all positive predication of the divine in order to lead toward transcendence and union with the divine (*theosis*), for example, "God is not good but beyond goodness as we know it." Apophatic theology is also associated with the notion of "unknowing" (*agnosía*) which denotes being liberated from concepts proffered by the created world. Cf. McGinn, *The Foundations of Mysticism*; O'Rourke, *Pseudo-Dionysius and the Metaphysics of Aquinas*; Louth, *The Origins of the Christian Mystical Tradition*.

Theology.'"[155] In this essay, Marion presents what he calls a third way for (un-)naming the divine—a third way beyond kataphatic or apophatic proposals alone. Prescinding from a predominant apophatic paradigm (or at least the caricature thereof), Marion suggests a third way to which both kataphatic and apophatic configurations must yield. In this essay Marion still refers to his position as Dionysian, but further attempts to dissolve a binary "metaphysics of presence" by asserting a ternary route of de-nomination whereby language functions pragmatically and liturgically by "transporting itself in the direction of Him whom it denominates."[156] Marion claims a pathway that is allied neither with kataphaticism nor apophaticism exclusively, but transcends both tendencies through a responsorial of praise that employs language in order to provoke the extension of distance between God and human that swells to the measure of sincere love. Language functions solely as vehicle of the erotic intentionality of the human subject, met by the iconic demonstration of divine glory: "excess conquers comprehension and what language can say."[157] In effect and in the end, words are swallowed up by the Word: "*the theologian must go beyond the text to the Word.*"[158]

It is not by coincidence that Marion gives the name *Hors-texte* ("outside of the text") to the second part of *God without Being*. Language is used to comport one to God, only then to give way to silence. One is left to wonder if Marion's position in his essay, "In the Name," can in fact be called a nuanced position. It appears that he is left conceding to the conceptual idol-smashing power of the apophatic. However, the nuance of Marion's 1997 essay is to be found especially in his brief reference to the Heideggerian phenomenological "as." Though Marion assesses Dionysius's use of the preposition "as" (ὡς) in *The Idol and Distance* as well as "In the Name," the mention of Heidegger's phenomenological "as" suggests a betrayal of the primacy of givenness insofar as it signifies "the interpretive comprehension of what is aimed at on the basis of and to the measure of the intonation of the one who intends."[159] For Heidegger, the event of appropriation (*Ereignis*) is shaped by the construction of meaning "when entities within-the-world are discovered along with the Being of Dasein—that is, when they have

155. Caputo and Scanlon, *God, the Gift, and Postmodernism*, 20–53 (including response of Jacques Derrida). Revised in Marion, *In Excess*, 128–62.

156. Caputo and Scanlon, *God, the Gift, and Postmodernism*, 27.

157. Ibid., 40.

158. Marion, *God without Being*, 149; cf. ibid., 157: "In short, *the 'progress' of theology works only to overcome the irreducible delay of the eucharistic interpretation of the text in relation to the manifestation of the Word.*"

159. Caputo and Scanlon, *God, the Gift, and Postmodernism*, 30. Also, see Marion's reflection on the Heideggerian phenomenological "as" in Marion, *Givenness and Hermeneutics*, 47–63.

come to be understood."[160] The phenomenological "as" acts as a mediator of the distance between the perceiving subject and the self-disclosing phenomenon, especially in the instance of divine revelation.[161] However, it is precisely this phenomenological "as" that opens the possibility of the third way that Marion proposes in "In the Name." Without the kataphatic sway of the linguistic "as," there would be no intentionality to be saturated. The kataphatic "as" paves the way for the aperture of absence to cross the threshold of visibility, only to disappear therein. Distance is created as language serves as a bridge to span the abyss between God and creature without absolving it. Language functions pragmatically instead of predicatively or nominally: "It is no longer a matter of naming or attributing something to something, but of aiming in the direction of . . . , of relating to . . . , of comporting oneself towards . . . , of reckoning with . . .—in short of dealing with . . ."[162] Words are at the service of givenness but only as a means to an end. Speech and language function to carry the human subject to the threshold of doubly saturating phenomena only to become a stammering of *glosseis* ("utterances") signifying the swooning of lovers.[163]

In spite of Marion's proposal of a third way beyond the kataphatic or apophatic alone, one may be left to wonder if he (unintentionally) claims the third way as guise for an ultimately covert aphophatic theology. Kataphatic predication of God aligns with common-law phenomena where a given phenomenon is met with an adequate corresponding concept supplied by intentionality. Herein emerges the temptation of onto-theology, a subjective managing of divine givenness with handy concepts and categories. Marion clearly works to avoid this extreme. Apophatic de-nominating, on the other hand, suggests the phenomenality of either a poor phenomenon or a saturated phenomenon. Either not enough intuition is given for a prearranged concept or an overabundance of intuition is given that cannot be allocated by any combination of concepts. Marion's third way is comparable to the phenomenon of revelation that assumes the form of a paradox of all paradoxes, though appearing as a shortage of intuition, as if nothing gives itself. And that is precisely the point: "nothing is the something of

160. Heidegger, *Being and Time*, 192 (§ 32).

161. Ibid., 189–90 (§ 32): "The 'as' makes up the structure of the explicitness of something that is understood. It constitutes the interpretation . . . If the 'as' is ontically unexpressed, this must not seduce us into overlooking it as a constitutive state for understanding, existential and *a priori*."

162. Caputo and Scanlon, *God, the Gift, and Postmodernism*, 30.

163. Cf. 1 Cor 13:1: "If I speak in human and angelic tongues, but do not have love, I am a resounding gong or a clashing symbol."

that which is no thing."[164] A phenomenon does indeed give itself, initiating a double phenomenality in which the invisible gives itself in and through the visible. The invisible as such gives no thing since its intrinsic nature is beyond the world of objects and things. Yet the invisible nonetheless relies on the visible world to manifest itself to an embodied consciousness. This is where Marion's proposed third way can be reinstated as an apophatic position since in the saturation of saturation a deficiency of intuition transpires. Nevertheless, Marion's nuance is to be found in his notion of the double phenomenality of the revelatory phenomenon whereby the invisible manifests itself in and through the visible. In addition, one might ask if the invisible likewise relies on language to manifest itself. Is not an incarnational and sacramental theology consonant with the iconicity of language? However, Marion suggests that in the superabundance of the phenomenon of revelation, language must falter and eventually be abrogated. Must language give leave to the power of manifestation, or does not manifestation of the invisible rely on the sacramental efficacy of the written text and the spoken word for its communicability?[165] To return to Heidegger, disclosure of meaning occurs in and through language—language as flesh of thought rather than as dispensable vessel for the transport of the subject to the auto-manifesting phenomenon alone. If "language is the house of Being," is it permissible to prescind so rapidly and amnestically from language within a sacramental view of the cosmos?[166] These questions will be taken up further below, especially in chapter 4, but for now the task is to gauge the import of Marion's third way of doubly saturating givenness for interpreting the phenomenality of the Eucharist.

## VI. The Double Phenomenality of the Sacrament: Where the Invisible and the Visible Collide

In applying the phenomenological concept of givenness in the realm of theology, Marion is not guilty of a "sleight of hand" (as some—Janicaud, et al.—may think), sneaking in theology through the back door of phenomenology. Instead, Marion attempts to approach a phenomenon such as the Eucharist in terms of its publicness and possibility, just as in approaching any other phenomenon. Simply because it takes place under the roof of a church does not thereby disqualify the phenomenon from critical appraisal; if anything,

164. Nancy, *Noli me tangere*, 92.

165. Cf. Chauvet, *Symbol and Sacrament*, 190–227.

166. See Heidegger's "Letter on Humanism," in Heidegger, *Basic Writings*, 239: "Language is at once the house of being and the home of human beings."

a phenomenon that occurs at the heart of the life of a community of faith demands even more attention and consideration than commonplace phenomena. In "La phénoménalité du sacrement" Marion designates the classic medieval depiction of the sacrament as his point of departure—the juxtaposition of the *sacramentum* and the *res sacramenti*: "the duality of a sign (*sacramentum*) and what is signified (*res sacramenti*)."[167] This duality constitutes the mystery of the one-flesh union between Christ and his Church as "the flesh (the physical body and the sensing soul) finds itself in this hypostatic point united to divinity in Christ, so that it is able to deploy this unique communion in certain gestures and acts that also articulate according to the symbol of the thing and grace."[168] In effect, it gives (*es gibt*) a double phenomenality: "one unique and very visible (the thing that one calls a *sacramentum*), one part appearing as a phenomenon already constituted (the worldly thing: bread, wine, water, oil, etc.), visible among other visibles of the world, but the other part also as the intermediary, not yet constituted as such, toward another term, remaining invisible (the 'thing' [*res*] accomplished by the sacrament, *res sacramenti*, the grace sanctified by Christ) and yet assumed to be constituted in the same phenomenon."[169] Marion highlights the paradoxical phenomenality of the sacrament, composed of one part visible and the other part invisible. Invisibility does not imply necessarily unreality and a complete lack of evidence, but it very well may imply absence, concealment, hiddenness and spirit. In fact, "the *res sacramenti*, the grace of Christ, will never appear to the contrary as such in the light of this world; it will never be numbered among the worldly phenomena, even if from the sacramental acts it performs each instant of our lives after baptism—for their visibility will never extend beyond intra-worldly things toward 'that which no eye has seen' (1 Cor 2:9)."[170] Nonetheless, the invis-

167. Rahner, *Church and the Sacraments*, 34; cf. the Council of Trent, in Denzinger and Schönmetzer, *Enchiridion symbolorum*, 1639: "The very holy Eucharist has, certainly, this in common with the other sacraments, that it is 'the symbol of a holy thing and the visible form of an invisible grace'" (*Commune hoc quidem est sanctissimae Eucharistiae cum ceteris sacramentis, 'symbolum esse rei sacrae et invisibilis gratiae formam visibilem'*; translation my own).

168. Marion, "La phénoménalité du sacrement," 59; cf. Eph 5:32: "This is a great mystery, and I mean in reference to Christ and the Church" (NAB).

169. Ibid., 61.

170. Ibid., 62; cf. Rahner, *Church and the Sacraments*, 37: "By such 'natural symbols' or intrinsically real symbols, we mean for our purpose here, the spatio-temporal, historical phenomenon, the visible and tangible form in which something that appears, notifies its presence, and by so doing, makes itself present, bodying forth the manifestation really distinct from itself. With natural symbols, the sign or symbol as a phenomenon is intrinsically linked to what it is a phenomenon of, and which is present and operative, even though really distinct."

ible *res sacramenti* depends on the visible *sacramentum* in order to manifest itself as a phenomenon, recognizable in human intuition. In the Eucharist, the grace of God appears in *sacramentum*; the visibility of the Eucharist gives appearance to the invisibility of grace.[171] The Eucharist gives itself to be received in intuition fully, yet to an intuition bound to the finite limits of sensuosity. The *res sacramenti* is perceived as a shortage by the senses but as excessive to the soul, resulting in an enraptured and ecstatic response of praise and thanksgiving. In the Eucharist, the sign and referent are united as one, yet distance is maintained insofar as invisibility and incomprehensibility remain. However, in order for one to recognize the fertile givenness of the invisible *res sacramenti*, a phenomenological conversion must occur on the part of the subject: ". . . the spiritual discipline of phenomenology is a true conversion of the sense of intentionality, which is first the forgetting of consciousness, and then its discovery of itself as given."[172] Not only is the recognition of the givenness of consciousness required, but also the humility to say to Christ, "Master, I want to see" (Mark 10:51), for "to all who received him, who believed in his name, he gave power to become children of God" (John 1:12). Intentionality is relinquished in order to receive divine saturating grace.[173] In order to see grace, sight must undergo an inversion—a denegation of visibility; to see is to unsee, to receive is to give up.[174] This is the essence of a counter-experience and the demands of conversion (*metanoia*). The sacrament, in particular the Eucharist, confronts the arrogance of self-sufficiency and the feeble attempts of finite creatures at delimiting the infinite. The *res sacramenti* depends on the *sacramentum* for paradoxical phenomenality to obtain, yet for paradoxical phenomenality to be recognized as such, intentionality must give itself up voluntarily in affirmative response to the call of givenness issued through a paradox of all paradoxes.

In sum, Marion's elaborated hermeneutic of givenness can be applied in conceiving the Eucharist as a doubly paradoxical event and icon—a saturation of saturation.[175] With a conception of givenness as an iconic event, a

171. Cf. Marion, "La phénoménalité du sacrement," 71: "God, when God gives, never gives less than Godself. God causes in person: 'it is God alone who accomplishes the interior effect of the sacrament' and 'the power of the sacrament comes only from God.'"

172. Ricoeur, *Husserl*, 10 (as quoted in Horner, *Jean-Luc Marion*, 25).

173. See Marion, *Prolegomena to Charity*, 71–101.

174. Cf. John 9:40–41: "Some of the Pharisees who were with him heard this and said to him, 'Surely we are not also blind, are we?' Jesus said to them, 'If you were blind, you would have no sin; but now you are saying, "We see," so your sin remains'" (NAB); Matt 10:39: "Whoever finds his life will lose it, and whoever loses his life for my sake will find it" (NAB); 2 Cor 5:7: "For we walk by faith, not by sight" (NAB).

175. Cf. Marion, speaking of the gift in the discussion between himself and Derrida,

spontaneity and freedom opens within the phenomenality of the Eucharist. No longer is it entirely predictable or controllable, but it is allowed to manifest according to its own giving. Marion locates sacramental dynamism in the manifestation of the invisible in and through the visible—the invisible incarnate. The Eucharist is the sacrifice of Christ in which the Word of God "*is said as it is given*."[176] Even the proclamation of God's Word (in the Person of Christ) can be reduced to its primordial givenness. For Marion, the textual witness serves only to "tell an event . . . the text assures us a negative of the event that alone constitutes the original."[177] The goal of biblical exegesis, for instance, becomes an aiming through the text to the event—the event as referent.[178] Marion suggests an absolute hermeneutic that "shines by its absence" and "disappears to the benefit of the eucharistic moment."[179] Christ only then is recognized as "the nontextual Word of the words . . . [who] speaks to the extent that he blesses."[180] In the end, "the referent is not taught, since it is encountered by mystical union" and the Word is known "nonverbally, in flesh and Eucharist."[181] Union with Christ in the Eucharist demands the dissolution of hermeneutics—a shipwreck of speech and text upon the

---

in Caputo and Scanlon, *God, the Gift, and Postmodernism*, 57: "If everything which appears has come unto us as given, one of the most decisive characters of any phenomenon establishes it as an event, which definitively happens." Similar to Marion is the thinking of Rahner on the Eucharist as event, in Rahner, *Church and the Sacraments*, 82: "Indubitably the celebration of the eucharist is an absolutely central event in the Church"—not one belonging to the remoteness of a distant past that came and went, but rather "the free decision of absolute obedience and unconditional, unreserved love constitutes one of those moments of history in which a temporality becomes the definitive, the enduring and the eternal, not just a moment in which something evaporates into the void of the past . . . what happened there as event once and for all is. It *is*"; Rahner, *Eucharist*, 14; and, Rahner, *Church and the Sacraments*, 39: "This visible form is itself an effect of the coming of grace; it is there because God is gracious to men; and in this self-embodiment of grace, grace itself occurs." Notice here Rahner's event-characterization of grace: grace *occurs* in the sacrament. However, Marion locates the event of manifestation in the phenomenon's givenness, whereas for Rahner the eventfulness of the sacrament is an enduring moment of presence rooted in history. For a complementary study on Marion's phenomenology of the Eucharist, see Gschwandtner, *Degrees of Givenness*, chapter 7.

176. Marion, *God without Being*, 142. Cf. Marion, *Reason of the Gift*, 69: "The question of sacrifice concerns, then, first and above all the act of making something sacred and of wresting it from the profane (the act opposed to that of profanation), an act of which sacrifice is only a result that it limits itself to recording, without explaining it."

177. Marion, *God without Being*, 144–45.

178. Ibid., 148.

179. Ibid., 150.

180. Ibid., 150–51.

181. Ibid., 155.

shores of saturated self-giving.[182] The epiphany of Christ in the Eucharist is a matter of manifestation, not proclamation. For Marion, "*the 'progress' of theology works only to overcome the irreducible delay of the eucharistic interpretation of the text in relation to the manifestation of the Word*," to the extent that "the texts themselves [do not] make the event . . . [but] the event alone makes them."[183] With such a view of the Eucharist and its ambivalent relationship with language and texts, a patent apophatic theology results, in which "it is a question not so much of speaking as of struggling . . . between the idol and distance, one must choose."[184] All of the idols emerging from language must be emptied in order for the glorious distance between God and humanity to give itself as the welcome medium of lovers.

In examining these key texts, it becomes clear that, for Marion, the phenomenality of the sacrament can and should be reduced to the eventfulness of manifestation, resulting in a response of adoration. Human subjectivity is bedazzled by the sheer overpowering appearance of Christ, who doubly saturates intuition by his radiant anamorphosis that "assumes the character of shortage, with the name *the abandoned* [*l'abandonné*]."[185] Not only does the phenomenality of the event engender an infinite hermeneutic, the Eucharist begets an absolute hermeneutic that shines by its absence and disappears to the benefit of the eucharistic moment. Even Marion's most recent reflections

182. See Marion, *Givenness and Hermeneutics*, 41–43: "Hermeneutics does not give a meaning to the given, by securing and deciding it, but each time, it gives *its* meaning, that is to say the meaning that shows that given as itself, as a phenomenon which is shown in itself and by itself. The *self* of the phenomenon rules in the final instance all the givenness of meaning: it is not a givenness by the '*I*' of a meaning constituted by it into an object to this very object, but to let its own meaning come to the object, acknowledged more than known. The meaning given by hermeneutics does not come so much from the decision of the hermeneutic actor, as from that which the phenomenon itself is (so to speak) waiting for and of which the hermeneutic actor remains a mere discoverer and therefore the servant." Note that this quote is in reference to any given phenomenon, let alone the saturating givenness of the Eucharist.

183. Marion, *God without Being*, 157, 224.

184. Ibid., 162, 169.

185. Marion, *Being Given*, 246; cf. ibid., 123–31, on the notion of "anamorphosis," which refers to the possibility of paradoxical phenomenality, that is, a double phenomenality at work in a given phenomenon. For example, 130–31: "To appear by touching me defines anamorphosis. The phenomenon crosses the distance that leads it (*ana-*) to assume form (*-morphōsis*), according to an immanent axis, which in each case summons an *I/me*, according to diverse modalities (arrival, happening, imposing), to a precise phenomenological point . . . It *gives* itself because it crosses its phenomenological distance by arising from its nonseen into its final visibility, in a thrust that I have to receive, therefore contain, eventually fend off as a violence. It gives *itself* since anamorphosis (in arriving at, happening to, and imposing itself on) attests that it possesses phenomenality's center of gravity, since it imposes its constraints on the *I/me*."

on the erotic phenomenon speak of a speechlessness that accompanies the phenomenon of sexual climax: "Of eroticization, this erased phenomenon, one can say nothing, even to oneself, even from lover to lover. The words are lacking."[186] In a phenomenon that displays a similar character to that of the Eucharist, the erotic phenomenon—as it "invade[s] all of the horizon of manifestation, but withdraws itself and disappears immediately"—is construed by Marion as a phenomenon of iconic eventfulness; all hermeneutics and language are reduced to the event itself, the manifestation itself.[187] Absolute primacy is accorded the phenomenon (as manifestation) itself, while all accompanying speaking of the phenomenon is shed as an old skin, or even more precise: all words are shattered by the magnitude of the saturated phenomenon's force. A dialectic of manifestation ↔ proclamation does not obtain, but proclamation is seen as a nuisance to the lucidity of manifestation. To let appear includes a stoppage of utterance and an attunement to the silent self-attestation of the phenomenon's unique mode of manifestation. The human subject is always at the mercy of the phenomenon, held at bay only to endure the surging tidal wave of the saturated appearance.[188]

One final point of note in Marion's phenomenological method that concerns the study at hand is his use of the language of witness. It is not that the vocabulary of "witness" and "attestation" is entirely absent from Marion's oeuvre. On the contrary, it is employed to reinforce the primacy of manifestation. A telling section of *Being Given*, subtitled "The Paradox and the Witness," makes this clear. Here again Marion relates the inversion of subjectivity. Instead of a human subject constituting a phenomenon according to the whims of intentionality, one is constituted by the phenomenon itself, becoming its witness. Phenomena themselves give meaning rather than

186. Marion, *Erotic Phenomenon*, 144.

187. Again, see Marion, *Givenness and Hermeneutics*, 45–47, "Thus, hermeneutics depends on the question and answer structure, that is to say the call and response structure, hence of the structure of the given articulated on the visible: hermeneutics itself is a special case of the play between what is given and what is shown, between the call of the given and the response (through the meaning) of what shows up in it. Hence a first thesis: hermeneutics must be understood according to the understanding of the given, through the call and answer figures. It is not that hermeneutics exceeds givenness or substitutes itself to it, but that it displays itself in it, almost as a special case of the original relationship between what gives itself and what shows itself." In other words, for Marion, hermeneutics itself consists of givenness. Every interpretation is comprised of given meanings, that is, meanings given from the phenomenon itself rather than affixed to the phenomenon by the interpreting subject.

188. Marion, *Being Given*, 264, 266: "To receive, for the receiver, therefore means nothing less than to accomplish givenness by transforming it into manifestation, by according what gives itself that it show itself on its own basis . . . The receiver answers for what shows itself because he answers to what is given—first by receiving itself from it."

a human subject assigning their meaning. The manifest event is the original, providing its own self-disclosed meaning. The role of the witness is not to elaborate on the phenomenon's appearing, but to give a "simple, luminous witness": "Here the witness himself is not invested in the phenomenon, nor does he invest it with . . . ; rather, he finds himself so invested, submerged, that he can only register it immediately."[189] Subjectivity becomes a sounding-board for the phenomenon, rather than a meaning constructing testator. Marion goes so far as to refer to the "auto-manifestation" of the saturating phenomenon, making the human subject "*hostage*."[190] Given this conception, one is left to wonder whether Marion's "turning of the tables" on the transcendental ego is, in the end, truly iconic. In spite of Marion's effort to give human subjectivity a face inside his primary concern of giving the phenomenon a face—giving itself as a self—is the face of the human subject ultimately erased in the name of saturation and the "subjectivity" of the phenomenon?[191] For Marion insists that "before the not yet phenomenalized given gives itself, no filter awaits it."[192] However, is not the face of the human subject, who brings phenomenality into play according to a unique and unrepeatable "I," revealed as such inasmuch as one exhibits a unique symbolic order in which to assimilate and relate any and all phenomena?[193]

189. Ibid., 217–18.

190. Ibid., 218–19: "Though paradoxical, or precisely for that very reason, the saturated phenomenon should in no way be understood as an exceptional, indeed vaguely irrational (to say it plainly, 'theological'), case of phenomenality. Rather, it accomplishes the coherent and rational development of the most operative definition of the phenomenon: it alone appears truly as itself, of itself, and on the basis of itself, since it alone appears without the limits of a horizon or reduction to an I and constitutes itself, to the point of giving *itself* as a *self*. I will therefore name this apparition that is purely of itself starting from itself, this apparition that does not submit its possibility to any prior determination, an auto-manifestation"; and Marion, *Visible and the Revealed*, 144, cf. 142–44.

191. Marion, *Being Given*, 265: "Therefore the receiver who presents and renders visible should see. He is in play like vision, exerts an aim, exposes a face, which one will have to look in the face as a personal other. He must therefore say the 'I' that says it all." It is likewise important to note the fine line Marion draws between an instance of a saturated phenomenon and any and all phenomena; cf. Marion, *Visible and the Revealed*, 126: "The banality of the saturated phenomenon suggests *that the majority of phenomena, if not all* can undergo saturation by the excess of intuition over the concept or signification in them. In other words, the majority of phenomena that appear at first glance to be poor in intuition could be described not only as objects but also as phenomena that intuition saturates and therefore exceed any univocal concept." This fine line of distinction between the saturated phenomenon and all other phenomena heightens the questions at stake here.

192. Marion, *Being Given*, 265.

193. Cf. Chauvet, *Symbol and Sacrament*, 84–88, for example, 84–85: "Reality is never present to us except in a mediated way, which is to say, *constructed* out of the

In reversing the Kantian paradigm of subjectivity, does Marion give the phenomenon too much vis-à-vis hermeneutic subjectivity, thereby making of the human subject a frozen idol, paralyzed by the (personified) gaze of the phenomenon? Does not iconicity live by the forms of dialectic, of trilectic, of fecundity? It is not time now to attempt to answer these questions, but they will reemerge in chapter 4 after examining the thought of Ricoeur and Levinas—the thinking that thinks phenomenality in terms of proclamation and attestation.

Through the course of this chapter, the tonality of Marion's phenomenology of givenness has been demonstrated amply: the manifestation of manifestation. Beginning with Meinong's paradox, it was shown how the Eucharist fits the criteria of the doubly saturating phenomenon of revelation, paradox of all paradoxes. In order to secure the credibility of this claim, it was necessary to retrace the trajectory of the idea of givenness as employed by Husserl, Heidegger, and Marion. It was likewise necessary to review Marion's leveling of Kant's stringent categories of pure understanding by raising the question of the saturated phenomenon. Thereby attaining the appropriate warrant for considering the Eucharist through a phenomenology of givenness, a fuller description of the Eucharist as a paradigmatic phenomenon of revelation was provided in terms of its eventfulness, iconicity, and double phenomenality. Marion's affinity for Dionysian apophaticism was recalled in order to sketch the contours of the human response to the phenomenon of divine revelation. This response takes the form of adoration and praise in the course of a swelling distance between God and humanity, not a distance of separation but a distance of loving union through which blessing is bestowed via absence. Finally, we considered the role of the witness in Marion's matrix of givenness. It is fitting to end chapter 2 with the question of the witness, as this question will figure prominently in the phenomenological projects of Ricoeur and Levinas. With all of the potency given in Marion's attention to givenness and love, there remains something wanting. Perhaps this vacancy is none other than the language and testimony of lovers, in a word, the ethics of love and justice.

---

symbolic network of the culture which fashions us. This *symbolic order* designates the system of connections between the different elements and levels of a culture (economic, social, political, ideological—ethics, philosophy, religion . . .), a system forming a coherent whole that allows the social group and individuals to orient themselves in space, find their place in time, and in general situate themselves in the world in a significant way—in short, to find their identity in a world that makes 'sense,' even if, as C. Lévi-Strauss says, there always remains an inexpungible residue of signifiers to which we can never give adequate meanings"; and Chauvet, *Sacraments*, 13–17, and 2: "The *symbolic order* precisely designates this meaningful organization of the many elements that compose a properly human existence. It precedes every single person since it is within it that one becomes a 'subject' (or a 'person')."

# chapter 3

# Paul Ricoeur and Emmanuel Levinas: Thinkers of Proclamation and Attestation

## I. On the Way to Discourse

IN CHAPTER 2, THE idea of givenness, signified by the phrase *es gibt* ("it gives"), was shown to function at the heart of the thought of Jean-Luc Marion. In chapter 3, while maintaining a similar revisionist pattern of de-centering the self-constituted ego, Paul Ricoeur and Emmanuel Levinas will be met as advocates of "the other" in an alternative tenor—that of proclamation and attestation.[1] While both Ricoeur and Levinas are phenomenologically similar to Marion in many respects, it will be demonstrated that the former dwell on the dynamic of testimony, in the form of proclamation, while the latter accentuates the operation of anterior, pre-linguistic givenness, in the form of manifestaion. Where, for Marion, the priority of givenness is signified by the *es gibt* ("it gives"), Ricoeur and Levinas pave the way for a construal of a hermeneutically charged givenness that can be signified by *es gibt als* . . . ("it gives as . . .") and *es gibt nach* . . . ("it gives according to . . .").[2] For Ricoeur, givenness is interpreted as, and according to, textual

1. It is important to recall that the terms "testimony" and "attestation" are very similar yet not univocal. "Testimony" is that which is attested by a witness, as in "a witness gives testimony." "Attestation" is the act of bearing witness to . . . (an event, a concept, a truth, another, that something is the case). I follow Jean Greisch's careful treatment of the two terms in his article "Testimony and Attestation."

2. The ellipsis (. . .) that follows *es gibt als* and *es gibt nach* signifies possibility and variability in terms of testimonials, hermeneutics, and the multiple witnesses to that which gives itself. For more on the phenomenological "as," see Sokolowski, *Presence and Absence*, 41–49.

mediation; and for Levinas, givenness is a byproduct of the originary call to become responsible for the other. Situating both Ricoeur and Levinas in the same chapter is not to suggest that they say virtually the same thing. On the contrary, each thinker offers a peculiar phenomenological perspective that cannot be conflated or synthesized into a single vision. Nonetheless, a hypothesis will be submitted that correlates the thinking of the two in such a way as to suggest a brand of thought representative of the paradigm of proclamation and attestation. It will be proposed that a witness becomes witness insofar as one speaks. The thinking of Ricoeur and Levinas will be called upon to give witness to the phenomenality of proclamation and testimony, completing the "trilectic of testimony" set forth in chapter 1.

One might find it odd that for a book on the Eucharist, especially as considered within a Roman Catholic context, two non-Catholic philosophers are relied upon heavily. Indeed, this is an odd combination but that is its point. To put Marion, Ricoeur and Levinas in conversation around the question of the Eucharist will (1) prove that the method of phenomenology has vast potential for fruitful innerreligious and interreligious dialogue, and (2) enhance Catholic eucharistic theology by unmasking its deficiencies in conversation with Protestant and Jewish thought and their primary hermeneutic of proclamation and attestation. In this chapter, the work of Ricoeur and Levinas will be treated separately, first that of Ricoeur followed by that of Levinas. A direct comparison between Ricoeur, Levinas and Marion, and the application of their respective phenomenological contributions to the question of the Eucharist, will follow in chapter 4.

## PAUL RICOEUR: WITNESS TO THE ABSOLUTE

### II. Paul Ricoeur and the Challenge of Hermeneutics to Phenomenology: A Critique of Husserlian Idealism

Paul Ricoeur could be described aptly as a thorn in the side of phenomenology insofar as he razes the bastions of phenomenological idealism and objective purity in the name of hermeneutics. One could go so far as to say that Ricoeur appears as an (altruistic) deconstructionist of phenomenological certainty. For Ricoeur, universal claims are arrived at only by way of the particular; better put, the universal is held in perpetual suspense according to the ever-unfolding hermeneutics of the particular. The following reflections on the way Ricoeur thinks the phenomenon will demonstrate this to be the case. The investigation of Ricoeur's hermeneutical phenomenology will proceed along four steps: (1) the critique Ricoeur levels at Husserlian idealism, (2) Ricoeur's conception of the symbol and metaphor as heuristics to the invisible, or absolute, (3) the place of kerygma (proclamation) in Ricoeur's thinking, and (4) the function of attestation in Ricoeur's ethical paradigm. First, let us proceed by attending to Ricoeur's revised phenomenological proposal.

Ricoeur has been earmarked as one of the pivotal proponents of the linguistic turn in the history of philosophy. He pays careful attention to the function of language and interpretation in all philosophical methods, especially in the phenomenological method. He always chooses the long route in attempting to answer any question set before him. The long route consists of whatever detours are necessary in order to arrive at the most adequate (but never entirely definitive) responses to a pressing question for philosophical inquiry. Yet Ricoeur does not mandate that theology be bracketed from critical philosophical inquiry, but sees a continuity of reason operating in each realm with the same rigor:

> The incessant work of philosophical discourse [is] to put itself into a relation of proximity with kerygmatic and theological discourse. This work of thought is a work that begins by listening, and yet within the autonomy of responsible thought. It is an incessant reform of thinking, but within the limits of reason alone. The "conversion" of the philosopher is a conversion within philosophy and to philosophy according to its internal exigencies. If there is only one *logos*, the *logos* of Christ requires me as a philosopher nothing else than a more complete and more perfect activation of reason; not more than reason, but *whole* reason. Let us repeat this phrase: whole reason.[3]

Here Ricoeur reveals his fidelity to Kantian thought: religion within the limits of reason alone. It is within the limits of reason that Ricoeur sets out on the long route for developing a critical phenomenological method that recognizes the enmeshment of every phenomenon in a density of texts. For Ricoeur, as for Marion, philosophy and theology are not mutually exclusive domains even though they may have distinct discourses. Both fields lay claim to reasonableness tethered to a principle of coherence, intelligibility and logic, in a word, *logos*. *Logos* resists all reductionisms and intellectual despondencies. It is always led by questioning, and for questioning, nothing is ever out of bounds. Honest and responsible thinking is ever open to possibility. Whole reason is interdisciplinary in nature and relies on a *logos*

3. Ricoeur, *Conflict of Interpretations*, 403.

shared in common for meaning-making and truth-seeking. This is the vital human task.

For Ricoeur, the human being is language and "language is the medium of our thinking."[4] Ricoeur follows the transcendental aesthetics of Kant and the existential ontology of Heidegger in order to recognize the contextual matrix of phenomenality: the *Sitz-im-Leben* of every phenomenon.[5] In Kant, a phenomenal intuition is synthesized with a correlating concept by the image-producing imagination; while in Heidegger, a particular percept is wedded to a universal concept by the reflective ontological analytic *Dasein*.[6] In both cases, it is the human being who imagines (Kant) and understands (Heidegger), in a word, it is the human being who interprets. As Heidegger makes clear, no interpretation is made without presuppositions, without pre-understandings, or without pre-ontological projection (*Vorhabe, Vorsicht, Vorgriff*).[7] Yet this is not all. Heidegger goes on to posit discourse (*Rede*) as "the articulation of the *Verständlichkeit* ("intelligibility") of the *Da* of *Dasein*," thereby "mak(ing) understanding possible just because it lets something be seen *as* something through its pointing out."[8] In other words, language is what allows phenomena to become intelligible—to be understood. Language is the vehicle that brings phenomena to the light of understanding, copulating percepts with concepts, thereby rendering percepts (that is, manifested phenomena) intelligible. In this sense, language is the incarnating and appropriating principle of manifestation, giving

4. Klemm, *Hermeneutical Theory of Paul Ricoeur*, 26, 62.

5. Cf. Ricoeur, *Hermeneutics and the Human Sciences*, 108: "The most fundamental condition of the hermeneutical circle lies in the structure of pre-understanding which relates all explication to the understanding which precedes and supports it . . . In what sense is the development of all understanding in interpretation opposed to the Husserlian project of *ultimate* foundation? Essentially in the sense that all interpretation places the interpreter *in medias res* and never at the beginning or the end." In Ricoeur's view, the original *Sitz-im-Leben* of a text—that is, authorial intention, original situation, and original addressee—is displaced by a new *Sitz-im-Leben* of the reader that is characterized by the possibility of multiple interpretations and a variety of particular contexts for interpretation. This displacement occurs through the process of distanciation; cf. Ricoeur, *Hermeneutics and the Human Sciences*, 110–11: "The concept of distanciation is the dialectical counterpart of the notion of belonging, in the sense that we belong to an historical tradition through a relation of distance which oscillates between remoteness and proximity. To interpret is to render near what is far (temporally, geographically, culturally, spiritually)."

6. Cf. Klemm, *Hermeneutical Theory of Paul Ricoeur*, 32.

7. Cf. Heidegger, *Being and Time*, 191–92 (§ 32): "Whenever something is interpreted as something, the interpretation will be founded essentially upon a fore-having, fore-sight, and fore-conception. An interpretation is never a presuppositionless apprehending of something presented to us."

8. Klemm, *Hermeneutical Theory of Paul Ricoeur*, 36–37, 40.

phenomena "in the flesh" (*Leibhaftigkeit*) to be understood *as* such. Phenomena appear "in the flesh" insofar as they are disclosed by language.[9] This process does not happen in an a-temporal realm of abstraction, but in time: "temporality is both the meaning of the being of *Dasein* and also that in which the as-structure of understanding and interpretation is grounded."[10] It is time that allows for the ecstatic appearing of phenomena in and through language; phenomena stand out to understanding insofar as they are articulated in language over the course of time.

Ricoeur directly assumes Heidegger's advancements of the interpretive process in his critique of Husserlian idealism. Whereas for Husserl, "*to each psychic lived process there corresponds through the device of phenomenological reduction a pure phenomenon, which exhibits its intrinsic (immanent) essence* (taken individually) *as an absolute datum*," for Ricoeur "all phenomenology is an explication of evidence, an evidence of explication" and "in spite of its intuitive kernel, this experience remains an interpretation."[11] Instead of positing the transcendental ego as the indubitable foundation of phenomenality, a self is given to the ego by the text according to its "universal

9. Cf. Heidegger, *Being and Time*, 204 (§ 34): "The totality-of-significations of intelligibility is *put into words.* To significations, words accrue" (*Das Bedeutungsganze der Verständlichkeit* kommt zu Wort. *Den Bedeutungen wachsen Worte zu*); and "The way in which discourse gets expressed is language. Language is a totality of words—a totality in which discourse has a 'worldly' Being of its own; and as an entity within-the-world, this totality thus becomes something which we may come across as ready-to-hand." Also cf. ibid., 202 (§ 33): "When considered philosophically, the λόγος itself is an entity, and, according to the orientation of ancient ontology, it is something present-at-hand . . . Along with the formal structures of 'binding' (synthesis) and 'separating' (diaeresis)—or, more precisely, along with the unity of these—we should meet the phenomenon of the 'something as something' ["*etwas als etwas*"], and we should meet this as a phenomenon. In accordance with this structure, something is understood with regard to something: it is taken together with it, yet in such a way that this confrontation which *understands* will at the same time take apart what has been taken together, and will do so by Articulating it *interpretively*."

10. Klemm, *Hermeneutical Theory of Paul Ricoeur*, 38.

11. Husserl, *Idea of Phenomenology*, 35, and Ricoeur, *Hermeneutics and the Human Sciences*, 127–28. Cf. Husserl, *Idea of Phenomenology*, 9, 50: "Therefore, we also find in the case of the phenomenon of perception what we found in the case of consciousness of universals, namely, that it is a consciousness which constitutes something self-given which is not contained within what is occurring [in the world] and is not at all found as *cogitatio* . . . Thus as little interpretation as possible, but as pure an intuition as possible (*intuitio sine comprehensione*). In fact, we will hark back to the speech of the mystics when they describe the intellectual seeing which is supposed not to be a discursive knowledge. And the whole trick consists in this—to give free rein to the seeing eye and to bracket the references which go beyond the 'seeing' and are entangled with the seeing, along with the entities which are supposedly given and thought along with the 'seeing,' and, finally, to bracket what is read into them through the accompanying reflections."

power of world disclosure."[12] Language serves as the medium between the teleological ideal of logicity and the mute elemental experience proceeding from an *Ursprung* (ground, origin, soil).[13] Just as in Heidegger, every experience occurs within a world that gives a totality of references (*Bewandtnisganzheit*), having the structure of meaningfulness (*Bedeutsamkeit*), in Ricoeur both subject and phenomenon are encompassed by the ontological conditions of finitude and belonging.[14] In other words, Ricoeur transposes Heidegger's notion of "being-in-the-world" to the "relation of belonging": a human subject and world are placed face to face in a relation that is at once particular, historical and textual. Ricoeur emphasizes intentionality over against elemental intuition.[15] For him, "the symbolic *manifestation* of a *thing* is a matrix of symbolic meanings as words . . . [wherein] manifestation and meaning are strictly contemporaneous and reciprocal."[16] This is not only the case for a symbol-phenomenon per se, but for Ricoeur the cosmos itself is saturated with symbolic meanings.[17] A phenomenon becomes manifest insofar as it is rendered *as* such verbally. While phenomena may give meanings that are in principle univocal, these meanings "do not immediately reveal their univocity. They must, in Husserl's terms, be submitted to the work of elucidation (*Aufklärung*)."[18] However, Ricoeur and Husserl differ on how this elucidation transpires. Husserl insists that "phenomenology does not 'create' but only 'finds,'" but in Ricoeur's estimation, "phenomenology seeks to go beyond a static description of experience, a mere geography of the layers of meaning," and through intentional explication creates meanings.[19] This process of fashioning new meanings is a fourfold route that begins with naïve description and ends (or begins anew) with appropriation of meaning. The process can be outlined as follows:

12. Ricoeur, *Interpretation Theory*, 95.

13. Cf. Klemm, *Hermeneutical Theory of Paul Ricoeur*, 63.

14. Cf. ibid., 89, and Ricoeur, *Hermeneutics and the Human Sciences*, 105.

15. Ricoeur, *Hermeneutics and the Human Sciences*, 106: "The Husserlian demand for the return to intuition is countered by the necessity for all understanding to be mediated by an interpretation."

16. Ricoeur, *Symbolism of Evil*, 11.

17. Ricoeur, *Figuring the Sacred*, 61.

18. Ricoeur, *Hermeneutics and the Human Sciences*, 121.

19. Ibid., 127.

Ricoeurian Hermeneutic Schema

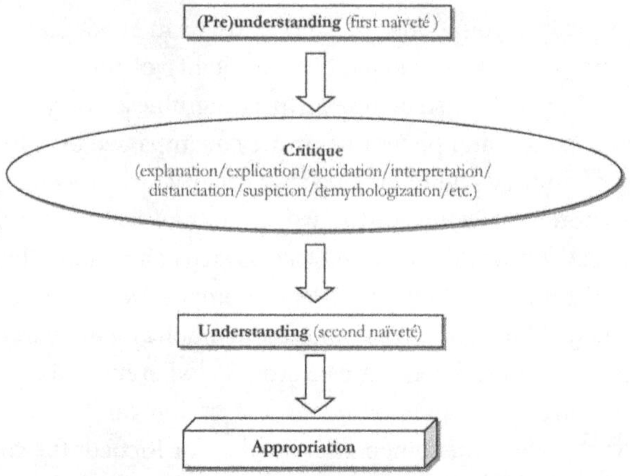


The first step signifies the immediacy of belief—literal and direct renderings of texts at face value, primitive assimilation of symbols, pre-critical consciousness. The second step of critique recognizes that "something has been lost, irremediably lost" of pre-modern innocence.[20] Critique prevents (pre)understanding from traversing along in ignorance by de-centering its unchecked presuppositions, biases and blind spots in favor of "truthfulness, intellectual honesty (and) objectivity."[21] Critique interrogates (pre)understanding by submitting it to the scrutiny of hermeneutic rigor, including a hermeneutic of suspicion. Critique asks the question of meaning via the intricacies of symbolic and metaphorical disclosure, contextual orientation, and historical particularity. A new (yet unfinished) understanding emerges from critique, reoriented and enlightened, though still naïve insofar as hermeneutics never arrives at a point of rest—at a point of absolute certainty, of complete or total understanding. Post-critical understanding must be put through the ringer of hermeneutics, elutriated through the decanting of critique, refined in the fires of suspicion's kiln. An understanding of second naïveté is the arrival at meaningfulness wherein event is surpassed by meaning through intentional exteriorisation.[22] Reality is re-written through an iconic metamorphosis in which a distance is opened between text and subject; new possible ways of being-in-the-world are disclosed.[23] The key

20. Ricoeur, *Symbolism of Evil*, 351. For a biblical account of the mutation of innocence in the opening Genesis narratives, see André LaCocque's trilogy: *The Trial of Innocence*, *Onslaught against Innocence*, and *The Captivity of Innocence*.

21. Ricoeur, *Symbolism of Evil*, 350.

22. Ricoeur, *Hermeneutics and the Human Sciences*, 134–35.

23. Cf. Ricoeur, *Interpretation Theory*, 42–43.

question is distilled as, "What meaning does the phenomenon have for us?" This question leads to the final step of appropriation. Appropriation (*Aneignung*) signifies a "'playful' transposition of the text" whereby what was initially alien is made one's own; event is surpassed by meaning only to become event again: the event of appropriation.[24] And yet it could be said that the eventfulness of the latter is surpassed again by meaning, namely, the attested meaning of the life of the one who appropriates. In other words, our lives become texts and bear an indelible character of action, communicated in the forms of language, symbol and testimony. Ricoeur never loses sight of the ontological concern for the genealogy of being—from texts to action and back again. A hermeneutic circle can be identified:

Hermeneutic Circle of Appropriation

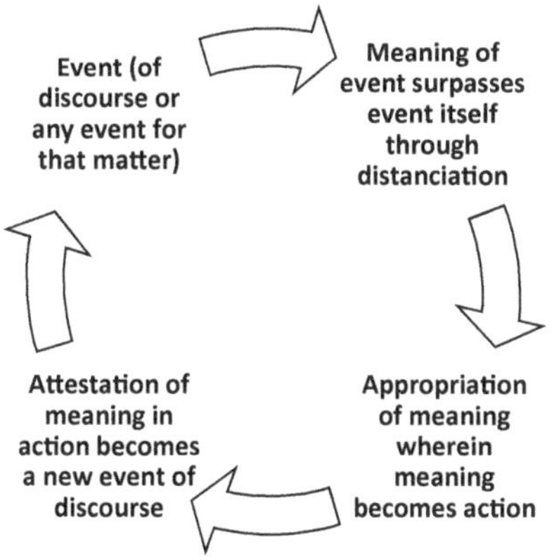
Event (of discourse or any event for that matter)
Meaning of event surpasses event itself through distanciation
Appropriation of meaning wherein meaning becomes action
Attestation of meaning in action becomes a new event of discourse

24. Ricoeur, *Hermeneutics and the Human Sciences*, 183, 185. It is important to note the subtle distinction between "event" and "event of discourse." When Ricoeur refers to the "event-meaning dialectic," he is referring specifically to the "event of discourse." However, Ricoeur seems to expand the notion of "event of discourse" to refer to any event-experience in general; cf. Ricoeur, *Interpretation Theory*, 16: "My experience cannot directly become your experience. An event belonging to one stream of consciousness cannot be transferred as such into another stream of consciousness. Yet, nevertheless, something passes from me to you. Something is transferred from one sphere of life to another. This something is not the experience as experienced, but its meaning. Here is the miracle. The experience as experienced, as lived, remains private, but its sense, its meaning, becomes public. Communication in this way is the overcoming of the radical non-communicability of the lived experience as lived . . . The event is not only the experience as expressed and communicated, but also the intersubjective exchange itself, the happening of dialogue." On the notion of appropriation as action, see Ricoeur, *Freud and Philosophy*, 382: "A meaning that exists is a meaning caught up within a body, a meaningful behavior . . . Every enacted meaning is a meaning caught up within the body; every praxis involved in meaning is a signifying or intention made flesh, if it is true that the body is 'that which makes us be as existing outside of ourselves.'"

According to this model, a perpetual manifestation ↔ proclamation ↔ attestation trilectic—the trilectic of testimony—appears wherein manifestation = event; proclamation = meaning; and testimony = event and/or meaning. The process can be described in this way: (1) an event occurs; (2) the event is rendered meaningful and intelligible in and through language; (3) the meaning of the event is appropriated by a person, the meaning becoming incarnate in the life of the person; (4) the life of the person becomes a living testimony—a text of action—that gives itself over *as* meaning to be interpreted and appropriated anew. Through this progressive process, being makes its way through the conduits of manifestation, proclamation and attestation—event and meaning and event again.

In sum, Ricoeur's attention to "the fullness of language" and to the layers of interpretation involved in every phenomenological experience challenges the presuppositions of Husserlian idealism.[25] Ricoeur's challenge will appear again in chapter 4 vis-à-vis the notion of givenness in Marion: in Ricoeur's conception, consciousness is not merely a *tabula rasa* upon which given phenomena incessantly crash down upon it, but rather it is colored and shaped within a particular milieu, according to a symbolic order in which all phenomena appear *as* such and are in turn assimilated and appropriated.[26]

## III. Symbol and Metaphor as Heuristics of the Invisible: *Es Gibt Als . . .*[27]

Given the overarching concern of this book, namely, the phenomenality of the Eucharist, it will prove helpful to examine briefly the place and phenomenality of the symbol and the metaphor in Ricoeur's hermeneutical theory. For the Eucharist is a phenomenon that claims to display a plurivocity of meanings concerning things hidden and revealed, that is, phenomena invisible and visible, unsaid and said. The Eucharist claims a double phenomenality (as pointed out by Marion) comprised of multiple dimensions, at once distinct and thereby efficacious. Insofar as the visible is not reduced to the invisible, and vice versa, the phenomenon of the Eucharist maintains its integrity and sacramental genius. In a similar fashion, both symbol and metaphor refract univocity by means of their opacity. Living symbols and

25. Ricoeur, *Symbolism of Evil*, 357.

26. In contrast, see Marion, *In Excess*, 50.

27. Due credit for the origin of this notion, *es gibt als . . .* , must be attributed to my mentor at Loyola University Chicago, John P. McCarthy, who, to my knowledge, was the first to coin this phrase in the course of a conversation we had on this very topic.

metaphors are perpetually pregnant with meaning insofar as they maintain their genius of double meanings; they bear fruitful potential to generate new meanings and paradigms for understanding reality as long as they are not reduced to a single, univocal, literal meaning. For Ricoeur, symbol and metaphor appear at the heart of his hermeneutics as they themselves are instances par excellence of ways in which meaning is made. When it comes to the phenomenon of the sacrament, symbol and metaphor are helpful for approaching the Eucharist heuristically. This is to say that, in chapter 4, the Eucharist will not be rendered as simply a symbol or a metaphor, though it may be conceived as such from a reduced hermeneutics of language and text. Rather, it will be shown that the logic of the symbol and metaphor may be employed as a heuristic to discover the logic of the Eucharist, which, though functioning as both symbol and metaphor on a first level of reflection, transcends such analyses upon ascending levels of reflection. The logic of the Eucharist will be proved to surpass the logic at work in the symbol and the metaphor.

First, it is necessary to provide working definitions for symbol and metaphor as they appear in the work of Ricoeur. While both symbol and metaphor are considered "double-meaning expressions," metaphor functions solely in the linguistic realm whereas symbol "brings together two dimensions, we might even say, two universes, of discourse, one linguistic and the other of a non-linguistic order."[28] Therefore symbol functions to its full degree insofar as it first operates metaphorically, for "the symbol, in effect, only gives rise to thought if it first gives rise to speech."[29] For instance, take the example of the *cathedra*, the chair in a cathedral upon which the bishop of a diocese symbolically sits. The Latin word, *cathedra*, can be rendered as "chair," "seat," or "throne," used to designate the physical object "there." Yet the word designates much more than an instance of physical "chair." It signifies the office, identity, jurisdiction, power, teaching authority, etc., of the bishop. The symbol of the *cathedra* gives rise to thought—first the literal reference to the chair-object, second to the invisible attributes of the person, office and mission of the bishop. The symbol functions along a pathway of meaning: (1) the manifestation of the chair itself, (2) the ensuing naming of the "chair" as such and that to which it refers, namely, office, authority, etc.—a process of naming wherein the literal signification yields to the symbolic signification without dispensing of the literal signification altogether, and (3) an unfolding generation of endless exegesis. The role of the phrase et cetera ("and others") is crucial here, for a symbol functions insofar as it does

28. Ricoeur, *Interpretation Theory*, 53–54.

29. Ibid., 55.

not cease in giving meanings without limit; a symbol's meaning is never exhausted, unable to be definitively defined: et cetera, et cetera, et cetera . . . A symbol means . . . and more. It is like the effect obtained in putting two mirrors face to face—an infinite explication of meaning, a recursive reflection between the literal and symbolic significations.

The symbol is an instance par excellence of the manifestation ↔ proclamation dialectic. The symbol lasts as long as the dialectic remains intact. "Manifestation" signifies the literal signification of the symbol, for example, the givenness of the chair itself as well as the givenness of the meanings (latent or otherwise) of "chair," "bishop," "authority," et cetera, while "proclamation" signifies the verbal rendering and announcement of meanings generated by the symbol, that is, the linguistic and metaphorical potencies of the symbol. The symbol enters the sphere of meaning only by the gateway of language, yet not only language but also testimony: whereas "metaphor occurs in the already purified universe of the *logos*," the symbol "hesitates on the dividing line between *bios* and *logos*. It testifies to the primordial rootedness of Discourse in Life. It is born where force and form coincide."[30] Here "force" signifies the potency of natural symbols—of the cosmos imbued with a surplus of meaning, for example, symbols such as "sky," "mountain," "sea." "Form" signifies the linguistic transposition of manifest phenomena, that is, the naming of the phenomena for the sake of intelligibility and understanding, for example, "this is sky," "this is mountain," "this is sea." A more pragmatic example employing the above mentioned symbol *cathedra* is the act of the pope making a dogmatic pronouncement *ex cathedra*. To make a dogmatic pronouncement *ex cathedra* means for the pope to proclaim a point of doctrine that is universally binding and infallible insofar as it proceeds "from the chair" of the successor to the Petrine office.[31] The phrase *ex cathedra* signals the power of the symbol *cathedra*; the teaching exhibits potency insofar as the interplay between literal and symbolic significations obtains—insofar as the "dogma" is wedded to the "chair" of the office of Peter. Such an act is symbolic due to its "rootedness of Discourse in Life." How so? The act is symbolic in that it proceeds from the power of the sacred—the overwhelming manifestation of the *mysterium fascinans*

30. Ibid., 59. Cf. Ricoeur, *Rule of Metaphor*, 361–62: "Poetic discourse brings to language a pre-objective world in which we find ourselves already rooted, but in which we also project our innermost possibilities. We must thus dismantle the reign of objects in order to let be, and to allow to be uttered, our primordial belonging to a world which we inhabit, that is to say, which at once precedes us and receives the imprint of our works. In short, we must restore to the fine word *invent* its twofold sense of both discovery and creation."

31. Cf. Vatican Council I (1870), Denzinger and Schönmetzer, *Enchiridion symbolorum*, ¶ 1839 (3073–74).

*et tremendum*—the "Life-discourse" that drives all discourse only to disappear therein. The "Life-discourse" is proclaimed through a metaphorical construal of meaning—one that "gives rise to thought" without eclipsing or exhausting the originating power of the "Life-discourse." The office of the pope, and of any authority for that matter, stems from the authority of life—the authority of biological (and zoe-ological) forces that ultimately cannot be tamed or mastered. Yet authority (most of all, ecclesial authority) promises new life through a logical ordering of existence, especially through the play of the metaphor. One responds in reverence where one at once looks into an abyss and finds security, that is, the point of intersection between "form and force," the dialectic between *bios* and *logos*, a discourse rooted in the primordial Life-discourse of being. The symbol itself exhibits a double phenomenality at the intersection between meaning given and meaning made—a perpetual generation of meanings. Let us now turn our attention to Ricoeur's understanding of metaphor as it relates to the creation of meaning.

In *The Rule of Metaphor*, Ricoeur gives a topography of the operation of symbol and metaphor, especially emphasizing the relationship between the verbal and the non-verbal. Ricoeur takes up the notions of "verbal icon" and "seeing as," advanced in the work of Marcus B. Hester. In the work of Hester, a disciple of Wittgenstein, the verbal icon functions to produce imaginative possibilities of "seeing as." Ricoeur comments that for Hester, poetic language (ruled by the metaphor) "is that language game (to use Wittgenstein's terms) in which the aim of words is to evoke, to arouse images."[32] In this conception, reading becomes "a suspension of all reality and 'an active openness to the text.'"[33] Poetic language becomes iconic insofar as its reading is characterized by suspension and openness, resulting in a hermeneutic without boundaries. Poetic language opens the way for interpreting the ambiguous in which the metaphorical "is" is accompanied by the literal "is not." "Seeing as" draws from the storehouse of images from one's history and lived experience in order to aim at a sensible configuration of the ambiguous phenomenon; the verbal becomes the "vassal to the non-verbal." More precisely, in the case of analogy, a referential (metaphysical) movement from the visible to the invisible obtains.[34] In such a schema, "the circle of the heliotrope," that is, "the sun," predominates the metaphorical discourse: light—the invisible yet visible phenomenon that makes all else appear, that gives growth and ultimately drives all biological processes in

32. Ricoeur, *Rule of Metaphor*, 248.

33. Ibid.

34. Cf. ibid., 340.

Earth. The sun serves as a fitting model for the dual phenomenality of the metaphor, involving both a natural given meaning and a host of responsorial meanings. The sun performs as an integral phenomenon of nature but further lends itself as a locus of meaning-making due to its central role in the solar system. Ricoeur goes so far as to identify the "soul" of interpretation stemming from metaphor: "metaphor is living by virtue of the fact that it introduces the spark of imagination into a 'thinking more' at the conceptual level. This struggle to 'think more,' guided by the 'vivifying principle,' is the 'soul' of interpretation."[35] Metaphor lives insofar as it functions according to its abrasive, perturbing (yet life giving) apophantic is/is not. The power of its negation within its assertion is the fundamental principle of the metaphor's generativity. The metaphorical "is" generates to the extent that it resists univocity. To say "time is a healer," is to say at once "time is not a healer." The power of the metaphor resides in its paradoxical nature—to mean two things simultaneously and more besides.[36]

Meaning and truth are disclosed through the metaphor to the degree that reading is characterized by suspension and openness—to risk "seeing *as*." Thereby the traditional phenomenological notion *es gibt* ("it gives") becomes modified to *es gibt als* . . . ("it gives *as* . . ."). The ellipsis is important here as it connotes dynamic and open-ended possibility instead of a static and already decided actuality. Toward the end of *The Rule of Metaphor*, Ricoeur reproves Heidegger for submitting a "determined ontology, in which the neutral is more expressive than the personal and in which the granting of being at the same time assumes the form of something destined. This ontology proceeds from a listening turned more attentively to the Greeks than to the Hebrews, more to Nietzsche than to Kierkegaard. So be it. It is appropriate that we in turn be attentive to this ontology without soliciting it."[37] Ricoeur also asserts that, for Heidegger, *es gibt* is the key word that carries the mark of this determined ontology. What is Ricoeur's ultimate aim in attending to Heidegger's ontology without soliciting it? The clue is given in the conclusion of his book as Ricoeur esteems speculative thought as that which "bases its work on the dynamism of metaphorical utterance, which it construes according to its own sphere of meaning."[38] Ricoeur, in

35. Ibid., 358.

36. Cf. Klemm, *Hermeneutical Theory of Paul Ricoeur*, 127: "The possibility of such self-recognition through poetic texts depends upon the efficacy of a logic of overturning and superabundance, which Ricoeur says is the 'logic' of the metaphoric process itself: meaning discovered/created in the image formed when a kinship has been seen through contradiction."

37. Ricoeur, *Rule of Metaphor*, 369.

38. Ibid., 370.

the end, points to the power of poetic discourse and locates its dynamism in its primordial and hidden dialectic: "the dialectic that reigns between the experience of belonging as a whole and the power of distanciation that opens up the space of speculative thought."[39] Speculative thought is none other than that signified by the expression "seeing as," which recognizes the potency of meanings in all discourse and leaves room for possibility within all inquiry. Speculative thought inhabits the virtual space of investigation wherein hypothesis, risk and dialectic create an ever expanding horizon for thinking.[40] Yet dialectic does not rule out the possibility of finding satisfactory, or even definitive, answers: "Dialectic provides us with a universal technique of questioning, without concern for man's ability to answer; but man would not pose questions if he had no hope of answering them . . . For this reason, the absence of prospective resolution required by the neutral character of the art of the dialectic is one thing; the actual incompletion of a project that by definition includes the very prospect of its accomplishment is something else again."[41] Such sentiments resonate with Ricoeur as he makes recourse to dialectic without foregoing the quest for meaning for which one is compelled to live and even to die.

Again, to round out this brief investigation of the symbol and the metaphor in Ricoeur's thought, language is the vehicle that mediates meaning, for "the symbol, in effect, only gives rise to thought if it first gives rise to speech."[42] And it is in the metaphorical-linguistic aspect of the symbol that language "captures the foam on the surface of life," where "expression creates being . . . one would not be able to meditate in a zone that preceded language."[43] For Ricoeur, "there is no symbolism before man speaks, even if the power of the symbol is grounded much deeper. It is in language that the cosmos, desire, and the imaginary reach expression; speech is always

39. Ibid., 371.

40. Cf. ibid., 365: "So, once more, the task of speculative discourse is to seek after the place where appearing means 'generating what grows' . . . The 'flowers' of our words—*Worte, wie Blumen*—utter existence in its blossoming forth."

41. Ibid., 314–15, Ricoeur here quoting from Pierre Aubenque's *Le problème de l'être chez Aristote: Essai sur la problématique Aristotélicienne* (1962).

42. Ricoeur, *Interpretation Theory*, 55.

43. Ibid., 63, and Ricoeur, *Rule of Metaphor*, 254. Here Ricoeur is quoting from Gaston Bachelard's *The Poetics of Space* (1958). Ricoeur quotes Bachelard at greater length in endnote 62: "The essential newness of the poetic image poses the problem of speaking being's creativeness. Through this creativeness the imaging consciousness proves to be, very simply but very purely, an origin. In a study of the imagination, a phenomenology of the poetic imagination must concentrate on bringing out this quality of origin in various poetic images."

necessary if the world is to be recovered and made hierophany."[44] With such an emphasis on language in mind, the augmented *es gibt als* . . . signifies the contextual and hermeneutic layers surrounding every appearing phenomenon. In Ricoeur's estimation, for a phenomenon to show itself, it will appear *as* such through the mediation of language. We will suspend a direct application of the heuristic of symbol and metaphor to the Eucharist until chapter 4.

## IV. The Primacy of Proclamation Inside of Living Dialectic

Having explored the place of the symbol and the metaphor in the the hermeneutic theory of Ricoeur, we now will distill these reflections in order to arrive at the heart of Ricoeur's depiction of the religious phenomenon: kerygmatic proclamation.[45] We have seen that, for Ricoeur, symbols declare meaning through an intention of signifying and that even natural realities take on a symbolic dimension only through the universe of discourse.[46] In the following analysis, proclamation will serve as a signal word signifying all

44. Ricoeur, *Conflict of Interpretations*, 13. Cf. Ricoeur, *Interpretation Theory*, 57: "There is no need to deny the concept in order to admit that symbols give rise to an endless exegesis. If no concept can exhaust the requirement of further thinking borne by symbols, this idea signifies only that no given categorization can embrace all the semantic possibilities of a symbol. But it is the work of the concept alone that can testify to this surplus of meaning"; and Ricoeur, *Hermeneutics and the Human Sciences*, 116: "The linguistic sign can *stand for* something only if it is *not* the thing. In this respect, the sign possesses a certain negativity. Everything happens as if, in order to enter the symbolic universe, the speaking subject must have at his disposal an 'empty space' from which the use of signs can begin. The *epoché* is the virtual event, the imaginary act which inaugurates the whole game by which we exchange signs for things and signs for other signs. Phenomenology is like the explicit revival of this virtual event which it raises to the dignity of the act, the philosophical gesture. It renders thematic what was only operative, and thereby makes meaning appear as meaning."

45. Cf. Ricoeur, *Conflict of Interpretations*, 382: "There has always been a hermeneutic problem in Christianity because Christianity proceeds from a proclamation. It begins with a fundamental preaching that maintains that in Jesus Christ the kingdom has approached us in decisive fashion. But this fundamental preaching, this word, comes to us through writings, through the Scriptures, and these must constantly be restored as the living word if the primitive word that witnessed to the fundamental and founding events is to remain contemporary. If hermeneutics in general is, in Dilthey's phrase, the interpretation of expressions of life fixed in written texts, then Christian hermeneutics deals with the unique relation between the Scriptures and what they refer to, the 'kerygma' (the proclamation). This relation between writing and the word and between the word and the event and its meaning is the crux of the hermeneutical problem. But this relation itself appears only through a series of interpretations."

46. Cf. Ricoeur, *Symbolism of Evil*, 14.

modes of discourse, including the metaphorical dimension of the symbol. Especially in the case of the religious phenomenon, proclamation will be shown to be the primary term for Ricoeur—that is, proclamation over and against manifestation.

To begin, Ricoeur asserts that a religious fact "is never a naked mute experience, but one which is documented in texts—the Old Testament, the Gospels, the Koran, for the Western tradition—the meaning of which is forever being reinterpreted in a cultural tradition that differs from the one they were written in."[47] In other words, the religious fact is borne by meaning that is transcribed into written texts comprised of a variety of forms and genres.[48] Ricoeur identifies what he sees to be the most significant vicissitude that a phenomenology of religion is required to confront: "to the *linguistic* mediation a *cultural* and *historical* mediation is added, of which the former is a mere reflection . . . This weighty fact condemns phenomenology to run the gauntlet of a hermeneutic and more precisely of a *textual* or *scriptural* hermeneutic."[49] The unavoidable gauntlet that Ricoeur identifies recalls the above section on Ricoeur's critique of Husserlian idealism. For Ricoeur, no *es gibt* is receivable in its naked immediacy, but instead appears in and through language and its interpretation: *es gibt als* . . . Not only this, but Ricoeur asserts that language and the art of interpretation are themselves embedded in an ever-shifting cultural-historical matrix that cannot be bracketed in the name of the phenomenological *epoché* without retrograding back into a blissful first naïveté. It is at this point that Ricoeur can be called rightly "the owl of Minerva," insofar as he acknowledges the lag-time of philosophy to depict a historical state of affairs, conducting its rumination during the belated upshot of history.[50] At the threshold of this gauntlet, one has no choice but to take the long route in order to resist the temptation of claiming to have crossed its finish line; for this gauntlet admits no finish line nor does it bequeath a crown of laurels. The gauntlet of hermeneutics calls for perseverance without the promise of a final word on

47. Ricoeur, *Main Trends in Philosophy*, 386.

48. Cf. Ricoeur, "Toward a Hermeneutic of the Idea of Revelation," in Ricoeur, *Essays on Biblical Interpretation*, 73–118.

49. Ricoeur, "Experience and Language in Religious Discourse," in Janicaud, *Phenomenology and the "Theological Turn"*, 130. Cf. ibid.: "To speak of 'linguistic mediation' is already to summon up the grand edifices of speech and writing that have structured the memory of events, words, and personalities—all equally endowed with a founding value. To put it briefly: religion is like language itself, which is realized only in different tongues. The comparison can be pushed even farther, to the degree that the difference between religions duplicates that of different tongues, sometimes fixing and consolidating it, if it does not serve to establish it."

50. Cf. Kearney, *On Paul Ricoeur*.

the matter. The sun may set on one day's conversation, only to rise again at the morrow of resumed discussion. Yet, for Ricoeur, a promise remains on the future horizon, summoning the contestants onward in hope.

In a Christian tonality, in which Ricoeur indigenously speaks, "the God who is coming is opposed to the God of present manifestation." For the Christian disciple, "the meaning of the Resurrection is in its future, the death of death, the resurrection of all from the dead. The God who is witnessed to is not, therefore, the God who is but the God who is coming."[51] Thus Ricoeur's hermeneutics of proclamation finds its impetus in an "eschatology of the sacred" rather than a "presence of the sacred" or "manifestation of the sacred."[52] Yet for all this, Ricoeur refuses to eschew being. It is at this point that Ricoeur parts company with Marion's notion of "God without being," instead opting "to honor this struggle with words" as presented in biblical texts.[53] For Ricoeur, we cannot undo the encounter between sacred texts and the history of their translation, exegesis and inculturation.[54] All the same, Ricoeur is sympathetic with the Bultmannian project of demythologization insofar as it contributes to the necessary stage of critique from a first naïveté to a second naïveté, unmasking cultural accoutrements and

51. Ricoeur, *Conflict of Interpretations*, 406. Cf. ibid.: "The 'already' of his Resurrection orients the 'not yet' of the final recapitulation. But this meaning reaches us disguised by the Greek Christologies, which have made the Incarnation the temporal manifestation of eternal being and the eternal present, thus hiding the principal meaning, namely, that the God of the promise, the God of Abraham, Isaac, and Jacob, has approached, has been revealed as He who is coming for all. Thus disguised by epiphanic religion, the Resurrection has become the pledge of all divine presence in the present world: cultic presence, mystic presence. The task of a hermeneutics of the Resurrection is to reinstitute the potential of hope, to tell the future of the Resurrection."

52. Cf. Kearney, *On Paul Ricoeur*, 28.

53. LaCocque and Ricoeur, *Thinking Biblically*, 361. Cf. ibid., 359: "But it still needs to be shown that neither this logic nor this rhetoric contribute to reinforcing the current vogue for irrationalism. In short, it still needs to be shown that thinking in terms of love does not demand a new *sacrificium intellectus*, but rather another reason . . . To put this a better way, would a theology of love that sets out to do without ontology be in a better position to conclude a new pact with Western reason, on the level, for example, of the criticism this latter exercises today as regards its own totalizing or foundational claims? This would be the case if, in rejoining philosophy in the midst of its crisis, the theology of love were to invent a new pact capable of supporting the comparison with the one once formulated in support of the Judeo-Christian conjunction with Hellenistic neo-Platonism and then with medieval neo-Aristotelianism. Without this pact, declaring themselves totally foreign to Greek thought, identified globally with the metaphysics of being, do Jewish and Christian thought not 'disenculture' themselves and consent to their marginalization?"

54. Cf. ibid., 331.

mythical adaptations in order to bring the kerygmatic kernel to the light of understanding, only then to be appropriated in ethical action.

In his 1978 essay "Manifestation and Proclamation," Ricoeur directly juxtaposes the two entitled notions in order to promote a living dialectic between a hermeneutics of religious language (proclamation) and a phenomenology of the sacred (manifestation).[55] Here we will pick up where we left off in chapter 1 in analyzing this dialectic that can be observed (whether dead, alive or distorted) in every religious phenomenon. In this essay, Ricoeur posits Rudolf Otto and Mircea Eliade as exponents of the phenomenology of the sacred. These thinkers identify those elements in religious experience that are not inscribable within the categories of linguistic proclamation and its ensuing interpretation.[56] Otto's notions of the "numinous" and the "*mysterium fascinans et tremendum*," coupled with Eliade's concept of "hierophany," assume the form of pre-verbal manifestation. They are saturating phenomena that are not translatable into language directly, yet nonetheless reveal themselves through types of symbolic discourse (myths, poetry, etc.) and ritual.[57] Both Otto and Eliade point to a cosmos that is permeated with a translucence of meaning. Ricoeur, following their lead, identifies

55. Cf. Ricoeur, *Figuring the Sacred*, 48–67. Yet it will be shown that, despite his promotion of the dialectic, Ricoeur himself displays a tendency to dwell on the side of proclamation. See, for example, Ricoeur, *Figuring the Sacred*, 71: "In Christianity there is a polarity of proclamation and manifestation, which Mircea Eliade does not recognize in his homogeneous concept of manifestation, epiphany, and so forth. I wonder whether there is not also, in the Hebraic and Christian traditions, a polarity of another kind, the charismatic, which is linked to language. For us, manifestation is not by necessity linked to language. The word 'sacred' belongs to the side of manifestation, not to the side of proclamation, because many things can be sacred without being a text . . . manifestation is not verbal by origin. But I think that there is something specific in the Hebraic and Christian traditions that gives a kind of privilege to the word"; and Ricoeur, *Freud and Philosophy*, 525: "To be sure, I speak of the Wholly Other only insofar as it addresses itself to me; and the kerygma, the glad tidings, is precisely that it addresses itself to me and ceases to be the Wholly Other . . . Thereby it becomes an event of human speech and can be recognized only in the movement of interpretation of this human speech."

56. Ricoeur, *Interpretation Theory*, 60: "We are warned from the very beginning that we are here crossing the threshold of an experience that does not allow itself to be completely inscribed within the categories of *logos* or proclamation and its transmission or interpretation. The numinous element is not first a question of language, if it ever really becomes one, for to speak of power is to speak of something other than speech even if it implies the power of speaking. This power as efficacity *par excellence* is what does not pass over completely into the articulation of meaning." Recall Ricoeur's understanding of symbol as that which maintains both linguistic and non-linguistic dimensions, for example, cf. ibid., 54: "A symbol always refers its linguistic element to something else."

57. Cf. ibid., 62: "For if no myth narrated how things came to be or if there were no rituals which re-enacted this process, the Sacred would remain unmanifested."

what he sees to be the crux of the manifestation ↔ proclamation dialectic: the apparently bound symbolism of the cosmos in which "symbols come to language only to the extent that the elements of the world themselves become transparent, that is, when they allow the transcendent to appear through them."[58] What Ricoeur means here is that "a symbol is bound to the configuration of the cosmos."[59] Ricoeur finds there to be a "logic of meaning of the sacred universe," namely, "a law of correspondences" that constitutes the "logic of manifestation."[60] One example of such a correspondence cited by Ricoeur is "the correspondence between the macrocosm and the microcosm—for example, the hierogamy of earth and sky agrees with the union of male and female."[61] Another example would be the cyclic movement of celestial bodies reflecting the cyclical processes of life, death and regeneration. An example of Ricoeur's claim that "symbols come to language only to the extent that the elements of the world themselves become transparent," would be the symbol of the sun as a bringer of life and light. The sun becomes transparent to a meaning that transcends the physical phenomenon of the sun itself, but nevertheless appears through it.[62] The infinite meanings conveyed by the phenomenon of the sun appear insofar as the sun functions as a fertile symbol rather than a frozen idol.[63] Were the sun to function as an idol, it would refuse to become transparent to the multitude of meanings that its phenomenal appearance engenders. By considering the difference between idol and symbol, Ricoeur begins his exposition on the hermeneutic of proclamation.[64]

Ricoeur notes that in the Hebraic domain, a perpetual struggle obtains between devotion to the one, true God, YHWH, and the host of idols that assault a monotheistic (or at least henotheistic) faith. Ricoeur suggests that

58. Ricoeur, *Figuring the Sacred*, 53.

59. Ibid.

60. Ibid., 54–55. I would submit that this also could be called the "logic of givenness" as proposed in the thought of Marion.

61. Ibid., 54.

62. For example, cf. Ps 19:2–7: "The heavens declare the glory of God, / the sky proclaims His handiwork. / Day to day makes utterance, / night to night speaks out. / There is no utterance, / there are no words, / whose sound goes unheard. / Their voice carries throughout the earth, / their words to the end of the world. / He placed in them a tent for the sun, / who is like a groom coming forth from the chamber, / like a hero, eager to run his course. / His rising-place is at one end of heaven, / and his circuit reaches the other; / nothing escapes its heat" (TNKH translation, JPS).

63. Recall the notion of a "verbal icon" treated above.

64. Ricoeur, *Freud and Philosophy*, 530–31: "An idol is the reification of the horizon into a thing, the fall of the sign into a supernatural and supracultural object . . . the idols must die—so that symbols may live."

"with the Hebraic faith the word outweighs the numinous . . . the instruction through Torah overcomes any manifestation through an image. A theology of Name is opposed to any hierophany of an idol."[65] A theology of history that elevates the "word" becomes opposed to a theology of the sacred that elevates the "numinous"—the location and material of hierophanic manifestation. Thus a desacralizing tendency transpires following the mission of proclamation—the idol-smashing power of the word is unleashed to ward off any possibility of bowing before an idol.[66] Ricoeur identifies the genius of proclamation within the Judeo-Christian tradition—one filled with various forms of discourse (parabolic, prophetic, eschatological, etc.) that operate according to the "logic of limit-expressions."[67] Such discourse challenges conventional wisdom based on the logic of correspondences by intensifying and transgressing colloquial expressions through the employment of the paradox and hyperbole. Limit-expressions reorient only through the passage of disorientation, "rupturing ordinary speech" and "exploding a once-harmonious universe."[68] The effect of proclamation's power is a desacralization of the cosmos—an overturning of values in order to submit a surpassing claim to authenticity and fidelity to an ultimate concern (Tillich) more ultimate than that formerly established. Yet for all this, Ricoeur proposes a unified dialectic that harnesses the polarity between manifestation and proclamation in order to promote the unique strengths and contributions of each. Ricoeur suggests that this dialectic provides a healing balm for the growing and pervasive secularization of culture, as well as for the hyper-sensitivity to the holy that distorts and idolizes the natural symbolic display of the cosmos. For instance, while a thinker like Sigmund Freud may be regarded as a Goliath of modernity, threatening the very existence and legitimacy of religious faith, Ricoeur finds the manifestation ↔ proclamation dialectic to be an intervening mediator between the reasonable accusations posed by Freud and the distortions that obtain within his method.[69] The

65. Ricoeur, *Figuring the Sacred*, 56.

66. For instance, see Mark I. Wallace's introduction to Ricoeur, *Figuring the Sacred*, 9: "Ricoeur understands *revelation* in performative, not propositional, terms: it is an event of new meaning between text and interpreter, rather than a body of received doctrines under the control of a particular magisterium. He refers to the disclosive power of figurative (including sacred) texts as an 'areligious sense of revelation' just insofar as any poetic text—by virtue of its powers of metaphorical reference—can become a world that I inhabit and within which I project my innermost possibilities."

67. Ibid., 57.

68. Ibid., 60.

69. Ricoeur, *Freud and Philosophy*, 531: "The fact that a destructive hermeneutics is justified according to the requirements of faith itself does not imply an acceptance *in toto* of the psychoanalysis of religion within the framework thus outlined. On the

dialectic prevents an interpreter from reducing religion to only one of its dimensions while neglecting the rest.

Having now come to the end of considering Ricoeur's proposal of the manifestation ↔ proclamation dialectic, let us submit the argument that, despite his attempt to adhere to a balanced and complementary dialectic, Ricoeur privileges one side of the dialectic over the other, namely, Ricoeur assigns primacy to proclamation. This claim is suggested in light of the whole of Ricoeur's writing on the subject. While Ricoeur writes, "the subtle equilibrium between the iconoclastic virtualities of proclamation and the symbolic resurgence of the sacred has expressed itself throughout the history of Christianity as a dialectic of preaching and sacraments," it is telling to note that he refrains from referring to the sacramentality of the cosmos in his assessment of the phenomenology of the sacred.[70] In fact, Ricoeur appears to collapse "sacrament" into "kerygma": "the sacrament, we could say, is the mutation of sacred ritual into the kerygmatic realm."[71] Yet there is more. Ricoeur writes, "for in Christianity the liturgical kernel represents the Eucharist, as a kind of text that tells the story of the Last Supper."[72] For Ricoeur, the Eucharist is not so much a matter of a manifestation of presence as it is an instance of textual proclamation. He concedes that this "liturgical text that tells the story of the Last Supper," in the last resort, refers to a "sacred act," and that he "recognizes something *revealing* that is not frozen in any ultimate or immutable text," but Ricoeur makes this concession reluctantly: "I am frightened by this word 'sacred.'"[73] In the end, "Christianity proceeds from a proclamation. It begins with a fundamental preaching that maintains that in Jesus Christ the kingdom has approached us in decisive fashion."[74] It is in his attention to language, interpretation and proclamation that allows Ricoeur to prioritize testimony as constitutive of ethics. By examining the relation of testimony to ethics, we will be able to interpret the Eucharist, above all, as an ethical phenomenon.

contrary, we must once more come to grips with Freud, we must confront his hermeneutics with the hermeneutics of Eliade, Van der Leeuw, Barth, and Bultmann, in order to construct what we can say positively and negatively about the psychoanalysis of religion." Note here that representatives of both manifestation and proclamation are cited: Eliade and Van der Leeuw representative of the former, and Barth and Bultmann representative of the latter.

70. Ricoeur, *Figuring the Sacred*, 67.

71. Ibid.

72. Ibid., 71.

73. Ibid., 72.

74. Ricoeur, *Conflict of Interpretations*, 382.

## V. Attestation as Vector to the Ethical: *Es Gibt Nach . . .*

The final point of analysis in the thought of Ricoeur that concerns us and the topic at hand is the place of testimony and attestation in his philosophical and theological vision. After having explored Ricoeur's proposal of the manifestation ↔ proclamation dialectic, it is necessary to examine the role of testimony and attestation within this dialectic. Further, it has been surmised above that *es gibt als . . .* adequately expresses Ricoeur's suggested hermeneutic revision of phenomenology. Here we will submit an additional revision of *es gibt* in light of the prominent role of testimony and attestation in Ricoeur's thinking: *es gibt nach . . .* ("it gives *according to . . .*"). The ellipsis here refers to the source of the testimony—the one who attests. Within both dynamics of manifestation and proclamation, testimony resides. Meaning and truth are exposited to the degree that testimony is active in the process of communication.

To begin with, Ricoeur posits that the "kerygma is itself expressed in a witness . . . the kerygma is also a Testament."[75] Ricoeur recognizes that Christian preaching hinges on testimony: the testimony of the historical community that surrounded Jesus during the time of his earthly sojourn, the testimony of successive generations that bases itself on the former testimony, the testimony of the canonical texts that express meaning and truth through a variety of forms and genres. The fact of testimony cannot be bypassed: "it is in the speech of the one giving testimony that one believes."[76] Testimony is the most integral feature of kerygmatic proclamation. In Ricoeur's conception, testimony is formed not only by witnessing to an event, it also is aimed at by expressive intentionality.[77] Ricoeur refuses to reduce testimony to an event's manifestation but rather maintains a dialectic of testimony between the poles of manifestation and proclamation. For Ricoeur, attestation—that is, "the act of testifying, of bearing witness"—assumes the following three

75. Ibid., 386.

76. Ricoeur, *Oneself as Another*, 21. Cf. Rom 10:17: "So faith comes from what is heard, and what is heard comes by the preaching of Christ" (RSV).

77. Recall Ricoeur's critique of "pure intuitionism" in Husserl's phenomenology, and Ricoeur's juxtaposition of "witness to event" and "witness of intentionality"; cf. Ricoeur, *Conflict of Interpretations*, 386, 389: "The kerygma is not first of all the interpretation of a text; it is the announcement of a person . . . But demythologization is distinguished from demystification by the fact that it is moved by the will to better comprehend the text, that is, to realize the intention of the text which speaks not of itself but of the event"; and Ricoeur, *Symbolism of Evil*, 167: "But *how* does the myth signify this plenitude? The essential fact is that this intuition of a cosmic whole, from which man is not separated, and this undivided plenitude, anterior to the division into supernatural, natural, and human, are not *given*, but simply *aimed at*. It is only in intention that the myth restores some wholeness."

primary forms: (1) personal attestation to an event, (2) self-attestation of the event itself, and (3) self-attestation of conscience itself. Each of these three forms of attestation in the thought of Ricoeur will be considered in turn.

The first form—personal attestation to an event—is the most evident and common notion of the three mentioned. The significant trait of this form of testimony, for Ricoeur, is its personal character of uniqueness. Testimony to an event appears insofar as it is the testimony of someone. Here, testimony is not synonymous with evidence that could appear in any form whatsoever—object, traces of fingerprints at the scene of a crime, a video-recording, etc. The act of attestation runs deeper; this is an act wherein "the specificity of testimony consists in the fact that the assertion of reality is inseparable from its being paired with the self-designation of the testifying subject. The typical form of testimony proceeds from this pairing: I was there."[78] The "I was there" of the testimony raises the question of trustworthiness: can I trust this "I" who "was there"? Ricoeur points out the problematic character of the boundary between reality and fiction revealed by a phenomenology of memory: is the recounting of this event true to what actually happened? In the act of attestation, only a fine line can be drawn between discourse ("Just the facts, ma'am, just the facts") and narrative (imaginative interpolation, creative story-telling), if any line can be drawn at all. In addition, "it is the witness who first declares himself to be a witness."[79] It is in this act of self-designation that "no one [else] testifies for the witness."[80] A dialogical situation is inaugurated as the witness makes this self-declaration before another and asks to be trusted by the other. The phenomenon of promise-making enters here as the act of being true to one's word. A public space of witness is opened where the possibility of suspicion breeding controversy arises at the appearance of multiple (and usually conflicting) testimonies. This is the space where testimony submits itself to the possibility of critique and requires interpretation. Such a space reinforces the demand for objectivity in testifying, but is not for this reason justified in naïvely trimming away narrative from discourse as if all of our personal histories are not enmeshed in stories. A phenomenon of biographical attestation can be observed in which each witness is heard one by one and the quality and trustworthiness of the witness is authenticated on personal terms. It is here that the possibility of false testimony lurks. The testimony of a personal witness "is not perception itself but the report, the story, the narration of the event. It consequently transfers things seen to the level of

78. Ricoeur, *Memory, History, Forgetting*, 163.

79. Ibid., 164.

80. Paul Celan, *Atemwende* (1967), quoted in Greisch, "Testimony and Attestation," 81.

things said."[81] In this sense, testimony is at the service of judgment insofar as it requires interpretation, evaluation and discernment as to its veracity.[82]

The second form of attestation proposed by Ricoeur is the self-attestation of the event itself, the paradigmatic instance being the self-attestation (self-revelation) of the absolute. It is this form of attestation that aligns the thought of Marion and Ricoeur in closest proximity, though not in a univocal sense. The manifestation side of Ricoeur appears most clearly in this particular form of attestation. In the first sense of this second type of attestation, testimony "*gives* to interpretation a content to be interpreted," while in the second sense it "*calls for* an interpretation."[83] Ricoeur identifies this first sense as "the aspect of *manifestation* in testimony" that signifies an immediacy of the absolute that gives itself originally to someone to interpret.[84] Without the immediacy of the givenness of the absolute, interpretation would have nothing to interpret except other alleged interpretations of interpretations ad infinitum. At this point, one may ask, what is "the absolute"? In the thinking of Ricoeur, the absolute is akin to the numinous (Otto), but even more originary insofar as the absolute gives itself in the form of a transcendent idea mediated in experience, in turn mediated by testimony and language. The absolute is an idea that appears in experience and history, though it is neither experience nor history per se because it transcends experience and history, only giving signs of itself therein. Neither can the absolute be identified with the testator to the absolute since the absolute appears as something entirely other, in which the testator becomes involved and to which s/he must give answer. In his 1972 article, "The Hermeneutics of Testimony," Ricoeur demonstrates a careful reading of Jean Nabert's *Le désir de Dieu*, especially of Book III, subtitled, "*Métaphysique du témoignage et herméneutique de l'absolu.*" "*Le désir de Dieu*" is ambiguous as it can be translated "yearning for God" or "yearning of God." The ambivalence of this title inspires Ricoeur's designation of the two traits of this particular form of testimony indicated above: (1) the absolute gives itself to be interpreted,

81. Ricoeur, "Hermeneutics of Testimony," in Ricoeur, *Essays on Biblical Interpretation*, 123.

82. Recall the hermeneutical matrix of truth, knowledge, and testimony introduced in chapter 1.

83. Ricoeur, "Hermeneutics of Testimony," in Ricoeur, *Essays on Biblical Interpretation*, 143.

84. Ibid., 144. Cf. ibid., 134: "There is no witness of the absolute who is not a witness of historic signs, no confessor of absolute meaning who is not a narrator of the acts of deliverance," and 145: "If interpretation is possible, it is because it is always possible, by means of this gap (between apparentness and hiddenness of the event), to mediate the relation of meaning and event by another meaning which plays the role of interpretation with regard to their very relation."

and (2) the absolute calls for an interpretation. Thereby the absolute is not synonymous with God per se but akin to the limit-concept of God in a Kantian sense. It is analogous to Heidegger's *Sein* insofar as it shows itself in and through the mediation of existents, while itself remaining hidden. Yet, in Ricoeur's understanding, the absolute can be attested to only by an original and absolute affirmation, which involves the divestment (*dépouillement*) of self-consciousness in order to "receive the meaning of events or perfectly contingent acts which would attest that the unjustifiable is overcome here and now."[85] Self-consciousness must divest itself since it is not able to apprehend itself and the idea of the absolute in the same instance. The absolute signifies the immediacy of its manifestation to consciousness, leaving a residue of its force in the wake of language, denomination, and the testimony of its witness. The absolute demands nothing less than an absolute response on the part of the witness to its manifest idea. Essentially, it is the question, "What matters most?"

In addition to the fundamental question of life's meaning, the theodicy question, too, appears at the center of Ricoeur's hermeneutics of testimony. Testimony to the absolute proffers proleptic evidence of vindication through "freedom in the light of hope." An eschatological vision of the ultimate triumph of justice is proclaimed by the power and assurance of the absolute, and this is where philosophy is brought to the threshold of theology, confessing that it has done all the thinking it can muster on its own. It is at this crucial point that testimony signals "both a manifestation and a crisis of appearances," where there is "no manifestation of the absolute without the crisis of false testimony, without the decision which distinguishes between sign and idol."[86] The ultimate testimony to this decision is the witness in suffering, the witness to the point of death, in a word, the martyr. The martyr testifies to "something or someone which goes beyond him."[87] In this sense a "criteriology of the divine" (Nabert) demonstrates the beyond of

85. Ibid., 121. Also see ibid., 120: "This original affirmation, for a reflexive philosophy, is in no sense an experience. Although numerically identical with real consciousness in each person, it is the act which accomplishes the negation of the limitations which affect the individual destiny. It is divestment (*dépouillement*). It is by this 'divestment' that reflection is brought to the encounter with contingent signs that the absolute, in its generosity, allows to appear of itself. This divestment (*dépouillement*) is not only ethical but speculative; it is when the thought of the unconditioned has lost all support in the transcendent objects of metaphysics, when it has renounced all the objectifications that understanding imposes. It is then that the claim of the absolute, reduced to the depth of an act immanent to each of our operations, remains steady for something like an experience of the absolute in testimony."

86. Ibid. 146.

87. Ibid.

the absolute to which the martyr testifies. The martyr relinquishes his life in pointing to the beyond-himself. The martyr accepts the fate of his premature death in a personal judgment that clings to the sign of the absolute, forsaking the idols of false testimony. In other words, the apophatic divestment of all kataphatic predication of the divine resembles the apophatic divestment of self-consciousness "in fear and trembling" (Kierkegaard) before the assurance of the veracity and vindication of the absolute. In both cases an endless exegesis prevails as one gives oneself up—divests oneself—in worship before the sign of the promise—a promise that lingers on the horizon of "the evening of life" (John of the Cross): "a man becomes a martyr because he is first a witness . . . The witness is the man who is identified with the just cause which the crowd and the great hate and who, for this just cause, risks his life."[88] For Ricoeur, it is Jesus who is the paradigmatic instance of this testator, who lays down his life for the cause of truth.[89] It is the original affirmation—a thetic judgment that testifies to the unseen manifestation and immediacy of the absolute—that guides the martyr's resolve to undergo death for the sake of the (unnamable) Name.[90] Of this Name there is no limit to its interpretation.

The third, and final, form of attestation found in the thought of Ricoeur is the self-attestation of conscience in which "it is the self who calls the self and bears witness to its ownmost power of being."[91] By "bearing witness to its ownmost power of being," the self "measure(s) the inadequation of its actions to its most profound being . . . always in relation to some demand marked with the distinction between good and evil."[92] In good

88. Ibid., 129. Cf. John of the Cross, *Collected Works*, 90, 178: "When the evening comes, you will be examined in love. Learn to love as God desires to be loved and abandon your own ways of acting . . . When faith reaches its end and is shattered by the ending and breaking of this mortal life, the glory and light of the divinity, the content of faith, will at once appear"; 1 Cor 13:12: "At present we see indistinctly, as in a mirror, but then face to face. At present I know partially; then I shall know fully, as I am fully known" (NAB); 1 John 3:2–3: "Beloved, we are God's children now; what we shall be has not yet been revealed. We do know that when it is revealed we shall be like him, for we shall see him as he is. Everyone who has this hope based on him makes himself pure, as he is pure" (NAB).

89. Cf. John 10:18, 37: "No one takes [my life] from me, but I lay it down on my own accord . . . For this I was born, and for this I have come into the world, to bear witness to the truth" (RSV).

90. Cf. Acts 5:41: "So they left the presence of the Sanhedrin, rejoicing that they had been found worthy to suffer dishonor for the sake of the name" (NAB); 3 John 7: "For they have set out for the sake of the Name and are accepting nothing from the pagans" (NAB).

91. Ricoeur, *Figuring the Sacred*, 271.

92. Ibid., 271–72.

Kantian form, conscience activates a deontological ethics and asks, what should I do in the face of radical evil given the moral demands put on me by my neighbors? But for Ricoeur this conscience is formed precisely vis-à-vis others in which a triad of passivities—that of the flesh, of the foreign, and of the relation of the self to itself (conscience)—"becomes *the* attestation of otherness."[93] Again, for Ricoeur, the passivity of the foreign—of "the other than self"—is not a passivity of immediacy but is mediated by speech.[94] Facing others, conscience is constituted by way of attestation and the self and, in turn, comes to the truth about itself, both in terms of evaluating past action and of opening to possibilities of the loftiest potential of future action.[95] However, the route to the truth about oneself must pass through the wrack of suspicion: "it haunts attestation, as false testimony haunts true testimony."[96] Yet "the *assurance of being oneself acting and suffering* . . . remains the ultimate recourse against all suspicion; even if it is always in some sense received from another, it still remains *self*-attestation."[97] Conscience then is reassured of its veracity through an ethical course of action in the world: "living well with and for others in just institutions."[98] The conscious resolve to live for the cause of justice finds its footing in the self-attestation of conscience. By setting forth possible ways of being-in-the-world in relation to others, conscience rises above solipsism and thus serves as a vector to the ethical.

In closing this exegetical section on Paul Ricoeur as a thinker of proclamation and attestation, let us draw our attention, once again, to the second revision of *es gibt*: *es gibt nach* . . . ("it gives according to . . ."). The significance of this Ricoeurian-inspired revision is that it highlights the function of testimony at work in all phenomenality occurring at the intersection of event and meaning. Testimony is always a personal testimony, whether in the form of manifestation (given in person) or that of proclamation (personal witness). A phenomenon gives itself insofar as it gives itself *as* a who, *to* a who, *attested by* a who. Characteristic of every phenomenon is (1) its self-attestation (manifestation/givenness), (2) its ensuing interpretation (proclamation/hermeneutics), and (3) its efficaciousness for shaping

93. Ricoeur, *Oneself as Another*, 318.

94. Ibid., 329: "There is not a single one of our analyses in which this specific passivity of the self affected by the other than self is not announced . . . [an] ordered exchange between the grammatical persons."

95. Ibid., 341: "Conscience is, in truth, that place par excellence in which illusions about oneself are intimately bound up with the veracity of attestation."

96. Ibid., 302.

97. Ibid., 22–23.

98. Ibid., 330; cf. 352.

conscience (attestation/testimony of the absolute), inspiring a consideration of ethical action. Ricoeur would concede that a phenomenon first is manifest before it is interpreted, but simply for this reason he would not collapse the manifestation ↔ proclamation dialectic to phenomenal manifestation alone. Rather, for Ricoeur, meaning is made inasmuch as it is given, and meaning is given inasmuch as it is made. In the end, hermeneutics is not merely the residue of the saturated phenomenon; hermeneutics is the hypostatic "*logos*" that renders phenomena recognizable *as* such, given "in the flesh," and thereby intelligible.[99]

## EMMANUEL LEVINAS: WITNESS TO GLORY

### VI. The Challenge of the Other to Phenomenology

Emmanuel Levinas could be called the advocate of alterity within the history of Western philosophy, for his entire oeuvre rests on the priority of the other (*l'autre*), or more precisely, the other (*l'autrui*).[100] For his part, Levinas, in positing ethics as first philosophy, suggests a philosophy of passivity wherein substitution—one-for-the-other—assumes the core tenet. Yet this vocation to "responsibility for the other is of the order of a 'summons,' not of manifestation."[101] Concerning the religious phenomenon in particular, Levinas can be positioned squarely on the side of proclamation, for he

99. Cf. Ezek 3:1–3: "And he said to me, 'Son of man, eat what is offered to you; eat this scroll, and go, speak to the house of Israel.' So I opened my mouth, and he gave me the scroll to eat. And he said to me, 'Son of man, eat this scroll that I give you and fill your stomach with it.' Then I ate it; and it was in my mouth as sweet as honey" (RSV). Phenomenality is enmeshed in textuality.

100. While most English translations of Levinas's works reflect his tendency (though not constancy) to capitalize such words as *l'Autre*, *l'Autrui*, *Désir*, *l'Infini*, *le Même*, *le Dire*, *le Dit*, etc. (the Other, the Other, Desire, the Infinite, the Same, the Saying, the Said, etc.), I will refrain from capitalizing any such terms for the sake of clarity and from preventing the possibility of interpreting such words as implicitly referring to the divine. Even though Levinas at times associates a word such as *l'Infini* with divinity, on a first-level reflection it is not his (or my) intention to do so. A second point of clarification: for Levinas, *l'Autre* is "the other" generally speaking, that is, the signal term for "alterity," while *l'Autrui* is the term he uses for "the personal other." When pertinent, I will signify parenthetically, for example, "the other (*l'autrui*)," when a precise and context-specific meaning of "the other" is intended explicitly. Otherwise, I am content to allow the ambiguity in the term "the other" to prevail. For, as we will see, every said retains an ambiguity that signifies the signification of the sign given from the saying; cf. Levinas, *Otherwise than Being*, 152.

101. Ricoeur, "Emmanuel Levinas: Thinker of Testimony," in *Figuring the Sacred*, 119.

insists that "Jewish monotheism does not exalt a sacred power, a *numen* triumphing over other numinous powers but still participating in their clandestine mysterious life."[102] Instead, for Levinas, "it is precisely a word, not incarnate, from God that ensures a living God among us . . . God is real and concrete not through incarnation but through Law, and His greatness is not inspired by His sacred mystery. His greatness does not provoke fear and trembling, but fills us with high thoughts."[103] It is clear that Levinas's texts exhibit a predilection for proclamation over and against manifestation. His hermeneutical matrix is permeated with the language of word, law, ethics and testimony. According to Ricoeur's assessment of testimony in the thought of Levinas, testimony can be characterized by the dimensions of height and exteriority, by which, the glory of the infinite assumes the role of transcendent height that can be testified to only by the assignment of responsibility: "But at the moment when the glory of the infinite, escaping every theme, risks falling into the ineffable, ethical discourse starts up again, or rather speaks—for there is finally no other testimony rendered to height, to the glory of the infinite, than the testimony of exteriority, of the assignment of responsibility."[104] In the Christian tradition, if the Eucharist claims to be a pronouncement of a Word from the Infinite, Levinas's suggestion that this discourse is mediated according to an ethical discourse of the assignation of responsibility, is entirely pertinent. Levinas's thinking serves as the paradigmatic vector to the ethical. The following reflection on Levinas's work will proceed along three steps: (1) his challenge to Husserlian idealism, (2) his proclamatory ethical vision via such notions as the saying, the said, and infinity, and (3) the notion of testimony running as a crimson thread throughout his work. While Levinas holds much in common with both Marion and Ricoeur, his contributions are unique and offer the final thrust needed to stretch the one-dimensional manifestation ↔ proclamation dialectic into a two- and then three-dimensional trilectic of testimony: manifestation ↔ proclamation ↔ attestation.

## VII. The Counter-intentionality of Un-manifestation: The Face That Speaks

Much like Ricoeur, Levinas seeks to challenge Husserlian idealism, not so much by a hermeneutics of text (as in Ricoeur), but according to the

102. Levinas, *Difficult Freedom*, 14.

103. Ibid., 144–45.

104. Ricoeur, "Emmanuel Levinas: Thinker of Testimony," in *Figuring the Sacred*, 124.

recognition of the other. Levinas similarly takes issue with Husserl's confidence in the asserted nakedness of phenomenal disclosure—what could be called an intuitionism of manifestation. While Levinas appreciates Husserl's quest for the un-ensconced phenomenon, Levinas's overriding concern is that phenomena have a tendency of being reduced to more of the same through the assimilating powers of conscious intentionality; phenomena become enslaved to the throes of totality, even in the name of intuition. The transcendent phenomenon, having become immanent to consciousness, is eaten and digested by the almighty human subject, with the net effect of the phenomenon's assimilation to the same as a conscious datum.[105] Through immanent appearance, the phenomenon is managed by consciousness, manipulated and catalogued along with the rest. Manifestation as disclosure is the rule, and phenomena are borne as succinct *noemata* for noetic appraisal. Even the uniqueness of the other (*l'autrui*) is effaced and rendered an alter-ego. Levinas challenges the notions of consciousness and immanence in Husserl, as they "gather up the manifestation of manifestation."[106]

In contrast, Levinas seeks to break up and awaken consciousness by "jolting the 'dogmatic slumber' which sleeps at the bottom of every consciousness resting on its object."[107] In Levinas's analysis, the synchrony of the given is preceded and outdone by the dia-chrony of the other.[108] Phenomenality is not a matter of gathering up appresentations of the present, but of recognizing the trace of an immemorial past that refuses to be phenomenalized in a manifestation of the present, and is attested instead by the costly demands of the other who faces me. Consciousness is dethroned and immanence undercut by the epiphany of the face (*le visage*) of the other (*l'autrui*)—the apparition of the face that is "a surplus on the inevitable paralysis of manifestation," for the face speaks the first discourse of "an opening

105. Levinas, *Existence and Existents*, 35: "Let us take some time to look at the example of food; it is significant for us because of the place it occupies in everyday life, but especially because of the relationship between desire and its satisfaction which it represents, and which constitutes what is typical of life in the world. What characterizes this relationship is a complete correspondence between desire and its satisfaction. Desire knows perfectly well what it wants. And food makes possible the full realization of its intention. At some moment everything is consummated."

106. Levinas, *Basic Philosophical Writings*, 134. Cf. Levinas, *Outside the Subject*, 94–95: "A Transcendence that is inseparable from the ethical *circumstances* of the responsibility for the other, in which the thought of the unequal is thought, which is no longer in the imperturbable correlation of the noesis and the noema, which is no longer the thought of the same. But, as non-transferable responsibility, it has received its uniqueness of self from the epiphany of the face in which a different requirement than that of the ontologies is taking on meaning."

107. Levinas, *Basic Philosophical Writings*, 136.

108. Cf. Levinas, *Time and the Other*, 103.

in the opening"—a living visitation that says "Do not kill me."[109] The face of the other (*l'autrui*) speaks a content, maintaining its relational distance and proximity from the one spoken to.[110] It cannot be reduced to categories of givenness, manifestation or appearance. Deflecting the domineering force of vision, the face disappears among the invisible contours of speech. The face is at once "a seigniory and defenselessness itself": "humility unites with elevation (and) announces thereby the ethical dimension of visitation."[111] The face establishes the ethical relationship between myself and the other (*l'autrui*) who faces me—the other (*l'autrui*) as my master insofar as she speaks the first word to me, commencing the discourse, teaching me something I do not know already.[112] For "a relation between terms that resist totalization, that absolve themselves from the relation or that specify it, is possible only as language . . . , [and] to have meaning is to teach or to be taught, to speak or to be able to be stated."[113] Language: the sine qua non for intersubjectivity and the epiphany of the other.

For Levinas, the vis-à-vis, that is, the face-to-face, is the primordial structure of all phenomenality. However, Levinas describes the form of the face-to-face relationship as asymmetrical. The other (*l'autrui*), vis-à-vis me,

109. Levinas, *Humanism of the Other*, 31.

110. Cf. Levinas, *Collected Philosophical Papers*, 115, 125: "The kerygma . . . [is] a *proximity* between me and the interlocutor, and not our participation in a transparent universality. Whatever be the message transmitted by speech, the speaking is contact . . . Proximity is not an intentionality . . . The contact in which I approach the neighbor is not a manifestation or a knowledge, but the ethical event of communication which is presupposed by every transmission of messages, which establishes the universality in which words and propositions will be stated."

111. Levinas, *Alterity and Transcendence*, 104, and Levinas, *Humanism of the Other*, 32. Cf. *Alterity and Transcendence*, 104–5: "So what distinguishes the face in its status from all known objects comes from its contradictory nature. It is all weakness and all authority." Recall the possibility of the paradoxical phenomenon related in chapter 2 of this study.

112. Cf. Levinas, *Totality and Infinity*, 101. Cf. ibid., 171, 174, 180: "The calling in question of the I, coextensive with the manifestation of the Other in the face, we call language. The height from which language comes we designate with the term teaching . . . Teaching signifies the whole infinity of exteriority . . . Language does not exteriorize a representation preexisting in me: it puts in common a world hitherto mine. Language *effectuates* the entry of things into a new ether in which they receive a name and become concepts . . . [and is an] *offering* of the world, this offering of contents which answers to the face of the Other or which questions him, and first opens the perspective of the meaningful . . . To see the face is to speak of the world . . . Teaching is a discourse in which the master can bring to the student what the student does not yet know. It does not operate as maieutics, but continues the placing in me of the idea of infinity. The idea of infinity implies a soul capable of containing more than it can draw from itself."

113. Ibid., 97.

is not my equal but my superior. The other (*l'autrui*) obliges me to bear the responsibility of her life, of her destiny, of her death. I am accused and held hostage by the visage of my neighbor, better put, the visage of the stranger.[114] In all ways I am "my brother's keeper."[115] Assuming responsibility for my neighbor is also spoken: "Here I am!" (*me voici*), spoken not by my neighbor but by me. This response is invoked by my neighbor who precedes me and implicates me by her very epiphany—her voice invokes the assignation of responsibility for her in me. I am not only responsible for her, but for all.[116] This magnitude of responsibility confers a kenotic selfhood that can never evade its existential obligation to the others: "as responsible, I am never finished with emptying myself of myself."[117] Such an ironic reversal of the primacy of subjective consciousness, Levinas calls "counterconsciousness."[118] He does not thereby supplant a "totality of consciousness" with a "totality of language," for "all linguistic totalities are transcended by, and owe their existence to, the relation of speaking—a relation that escapes from all attempts to reduce speech to an object, a topic, or a theme."[119] The locus of relationality, around which Levinas's thinking revolves, resists all totalization. Relationality, rather, refers to the enigmatic playing field of phenomenality upon which phenomena inhabit a phenomenology of sociality wherein "(phenomenological vision is) found in the company human beings keep among themselves, between beings who speak to one another, and of whom it is said that they 'see one another.'"[120] In this domain, the other assumes the form of transcendence, coming over me as a paroxysm, evoking the an-archic responsibility in me, which is "anterior to all the logical delib-

114. Levinas oftentimes assumes a hyperbolic discourse in order to break up a solipsistic consciousness, for example, cf. Cohen's introduction to Levinas, *Time and the Other*, 25: "To think otherwise, for Levinas, is to undergo the *emphasis*, the *hyperbole*, the *superlative*, the *excellence* which escapes thought while determining it. It is to recognize the dative, the 'to the other' and the 'for the other,' which overdetermines the nominative. It is to enter into a *disorientation* which is neither an opinion, a prejudice, a dogma, nor a truth, but the wonder proper to ethical significance."

115. Cf. Gen 4:9: "The LORD said to Cain, 'Where is your brother Abel?' And he said, 'I do not know. Am I my brother's keeper?'" (TNKH translation, JPS).

116. Cf. Ricoeur, "Emmanuel Levinas: Thinker of Testimony," in *Figuring the Sacred*, 125: "The self is not the ego. Yet it remains that the place of the self is inexpugnable. 'The self is a *sub-jectum*; it is under the weight of the universe, responsible for everything.'" Ricoeur here is quoting from Levinas, *Otherwise than Being*, 116.

117. Levinas, *Basic Philosophical Writings*, 144.

118. Cf. Levinas, *Entre Nous*, 58, and Marion, *Being Given*, 266–67, where Marion employs the term "counter-intentionality."

119. Peperzak, *To the Other*, 30.

120. Levinas, *Time and the Other*, 97.

eration summoned by reasoned decision."[121] Nevertheless, "the order of truth and knowledge has a role to play in that peace of proximity and in the ethical order it signifies. To a very great extent, it is the ethical order of human proximity that brings about or summons that of objectivity, truth and knowledge."[122] This is an order where "meaning means" and meaning cannot be reduced by a phenomenological *epoché*.[123] For Levinas, signification makes perception possible because it "precedes givens and illuminates them."[124] However, in spite of his appreciation for contemporary philosophy's attention to history and cultural plurality, Levinas aims at a more "fundamental movement, pure transport, absolute orientation, sense," which he calls "desire for others."[125] This desire is at once receptive and creative—a liturgical work, an "investment at a loss" that "*never returns to the same*."[126] The almighty ego is emptied to such a degree that it acts not for itself but for the world to come—not even a promised world to come for itself, but for the world to come for successive generations.[127] This desire for others is

121. Ibid., 111. Cf. ibid., 109: "I have attempted a 'phenomenology' of sociality starting from the face of the other person—from proximity—by understanding in its rectitude a voice that commands before all mimicry and verbal expression."

122. Levinas, *Alterity and Transcendence*, 141.

123. Ibid., 172, and further: "I cannot further explain this moment in which, in the weight of being, rationality begins. A first notion of signifying, to which reason may be traced, and that cannot be reduced to anything else. It is phenomenologically irreducible: meaning means." Cf. Levinas, *Basic Philosophical Writings*, 102: "But *is not the one-for-the-other meaning itself*? A signifyingness of meaning more ancient than manifestation of being."

124. Levinas, *Humanism of the Other*, 12. Cf. ibid., 11: "To be given to consciousness, to glimmer for it, the given would have to be previously placed on an illuminated horizon, similar to the word that receives the gift of being understood from a context to which it refers. Signification would be the very illumination of this horizon. But the horizon does not result from an addition of absent givens, because each given already needs a horizon to define and give itself. This notion of horizon, or *world*, conceived on the model of a language and culture—with all the historical adventure and 'already done' this entails—is then the place where signification is situated"; and ibid., 18: "There does not exist any *signification in itself* that a thought could reach by hopping over the reflections—distorting or faithful, but sensible—that lead to it. To reach the intelligible we must cross through history, or relive duration, or go from concrete perception and the language installed in it. All things picturesque in history, all the different cultures, are no longer obstacles that separate us from the essential and the intelligible; they are the paths by which we can reach it. Furthermore, they are unique pathways, the only possible paths, irreplaceable, and consequently implicated in the intelligible itself!"

125. Ibid., 30.

126. Ibid., 28, 26.

127. Cf. ibid., 28–29: "Our era . . . is action for the world to come, surpassing one's era, it is the surpassing of self that requires the epiphany of the Other, and this is the depth of the thesis upheld in these pages . . . There is something base and vulgar in an

a hunger not satisfied, a "love without lust," a mysterious bush engulfed in flames yet not consumed.[128] Desire for others assumes a pragmatic form in its work toward justice for all in which "language is justice."[129]

Lastly, a word must be said on the notion of kerygma in Levinas, for kerygma serves as the gateway for phenomenal appearance.[130] For Levinas, the linguistic mode of a phenomenon is part and parcel of its appearing. Without signification and language, a phenomenon does not appear *as* such. Levinas insists that "the *appearing* of a phenomenon is inseparable from its *signifying*, which refers to the proclamatory, kerygmatic intention of thought. Every phenomenon is a discourse or a fragment of a discourse."[131]

---

action conceived only for the immediate, that is, for nothing but our lifetime. And there is great nobility in energy liberated from the embrace of the present. To act for distant things at a time when Hitlerism triumphed, in the deaf hours of that night without hours, to act independently of any evaluation of the 'forces in presence,' was undoubtedly the height of nobility"; and cf. Levinas, *Alterity and Transcendence*, 109: "The saintliness of the human cannot be expressed on the basis of any category. Are we entering a moment in history in which the good must be loved without promises? Perhaps it is the end of all preaching. May we not be on the eve of a new form of faith, a faith without triumph, as if the only irrefutable value were saintliness, a time when the only right to a reward would be to not expect one? The first and last manifestation of God would be to be without promises." Here Levinas can be distanced from Ricoeur's eschatological vision of promise promoted in preaching.

128. Levinas, *Alterity and Transcendence*, 129; cf. Levinas, *Humanism of the Other*, 30: "Is the Desire for Others appetite or generosity? The Desirable does not satisfy my Desire, it hollows me, nourishing me somehow with new hungers. Desire turns out to be bounty." Cf. Levinas's interview response in Robbins, *Is It Righteous to Be?*, 108: "I think that responsibility is the love without concupiscence of which Pascal spoke: to respond to the other, to approach the other as unique, isolated from all multiplicity and outside collective necessities. To approach someone as unique to the world is to love him. Affective warmth, feeling, and goodness constitute the proper mode of this approach to the unique, the thinking of the unique."

129. Levinas, *Totality and Infinity*, 213. Cf. ibid., 71–72, 200: "*We call justice this face to face approach, in conversation* . . . Justice consists in recognizing in the Other my master . . . To speak to me is at each moment to surmount what is necessarily plastic in manifestation . . . This bond between expression and responsibility, this ethical condition or essence of language, this function of language prior to all disclosure of being and its cold splendor, permits us to extract language from subjection to preexistent thought, where it would have but the servile function of translating that preexistent thought on the outside, or of universalizing its interior movements."

130. Cf. Peperzak, *Beyond*, 58: "The affirmative character of identification is *kerygmatic*: to identify a being is to pronounce a kerygma or proclamation; consciousness proclaims this phenomenon to be this and such . . . Every phenomenon is (a) Said (*Dit*). The exhibition of being, its disclosure or manifestation, the very idea of phenomenality presupposes *and* conditions a particular mode of language: the *apophantic* language of gathering identification and thematic presentification of a said; kerygmatic proclamation; phenomenology."

131. Levinas, *Collected Philosophical Papers*, 112.

Phenomena appear insofar as they bear meaning.[132] Once again, as in Ricoeur, *es gibt* must be revised to *es gibt als* . . . In this way, Levinas views language as the basis of all phenomenality; the basis of language is conversation, and the basis of conversation is the uttered epiphany of the face and the ensuing response of the pupil whose self-assured consciousness has been contravened and subverted. Within a kerygmatic context, Levinas develops the concepts of "the saying" (*le dire*) and "the said" (*le dit*). These concepts are crucial for Levinas's phenomenological project. They are not univocal. The saying precedes and gives rise to the said; the saying is originary whereas the said is derived from the saying. The saying issues from the beyond—from the mouth of infinity—and inaugurates the discourse of life and phenomenality. Let us now turn our attention to the relationship between the saying and the said in the thought of Levinas and their pertinence to a phenomenological portrayal of human life.

## VIII. The Enigma of the Saying and the Precipitation of Ethics

Conversation begins with the spoken epiphany of the face of the other (*l'autrui*) that commands responsibility of the one spoken to. The one spoken to continues the conversation with her response, either in the affirmative "Hello," or in the negative of ignoring the invocation of the other.[133] In the affirmative "Hello" or "Here I am," the one spoken to chooses to accept the call to proximity in relation to the other, thereby entering the realm of the surplus of sociality.[134] The surplus extends from the primordial saying that encompasses all conversation without being reduced to everyday parlance. The saying is the first word of discourse—a word from . . .—a tran-

132. Cf. ibid., 109–11: "Being is manifested with a theme . . . a being is manifest as a being on the basis of its meaning . . . The setting forth of meaning . . . must first name beings, proclaim them as this or that . . . The priority of the a priori is a *kerygma* which is neither a form of imagination nor a form of perception."

133. Cf. Levinas, *Alterity and Transcendence*, 98.

134. Levinas, *Outside the Subject*, 142: "In everyday language we approach the other person. The *Saying* is not exhausted in the giving of meaning as it inscribes itself—fable—in the Said. It is communication not reducible to the phenomenon of the *truth-that-unites*: it is a non-indifference to the other person, capable of ethical significance to which the statement itself of the Said is subordinate. The proximity that declares itself in this way is not a simple failure of the coinciding of minds that truth would bring with it. It is all the surplus of sociality. Sociality that is also irreducible to *knowledge* of the other; it is delineated in language after an entirely different model than intentionality, despite all the importance given to the *Said* in language and that is further emphasized in a rhetoric already departing from the everyday logos."

scendent word that is traceable only in the heart of the summoned and the discourse of the said. Whereas the said is historical, particular and culturally charged, the saying is invisible, unmanifest and diachronically comes to pass before it is ever recognized as having passed. The saying is the infinite beyond of discourse, the realization that there is always more to be said, the . . . which goes before and behind all discourse. Such discourse is one in which "in approaching the other I am always late for the meeting."[135] Diachrony has irrupted a synchronous display of the appresentation of beings to consciousness. Two nontransferable epochs converge on the fold of the saying and the said: the saying connotes an immemorial past, while the said signifies ethical discourse between persons—the trace of the saying.[136] The infinite speaks through the finite said, for "its signification has let itself be betrayed in the logos only to convey itself before us. It is a word already stated as kerygma in prayer or blasphemy. It thus retains in its statement the trace of the excession of transcendence, of the beyond."[137] While the saying is of a non-phenomenological order, it permits itself to be thematized in order to show itself: "thematization is then inevitable, so that signification itself show itself, but does so in the sophism with which philosophy begins, in the betrayal which philosophy is called to reduce."[138] The saying of the infinite is not provable in the realm of manifestation, but only attested to in the course of conversation and ethical responsibility.[139]

It is through the attested saying that ethics unfolds, for the saying is the primordial utterance from which no one can escape.[140] Yet this utterance

135. Levinas, *Otherwise than Being*, 150.

136. Cf. ibid., 149: "The unheard-of saying is enigmatically in the anarchic response, in my responsibility for the other. The trace of infinity is this ambiguity in the subject, in turns beginning and makeshift, a diachronic ambivalence which ethics makes possible."

137. Ibid., 151.

138. Ibid., 151–52. Cf. Levinas, *Humanism of the Other*, 40: "Illeity is the origin of the otherness of being, in which the *in itself* of objectivity participates by betraying it."

139. Levinas, *Otherwise than Being*, 152: "The Infinite would be belied in the proof that the finite would like to give of its transcendence; entering into conjunction with the subject that would make it appear, it would lose its glory"; and cf. Prov 25:2: "It is the glory of God to conceal a matter, / And the glory of a king to plumb a matter" (TNKH translation, JPS).

140. Cf. Ps 139:4–13: "There is not a word on my tongue but that You, O Lord, know it well. You hedge me before and behind; You lay your hand upon me. It is beyond my knowledge; it is a mystery; I cannot fathom it. Where can I escape from Your spirit? Where can I flee from Your presence? If I ascend to heaven, You are there; if I descend to Sheol, You are there too. If I take wing with the dawn to come to rest on the western horizon, even there Your hand will be guiding me, Your right hand will be holding me fast. If I say, 'Surely darkness will conceal me, night will provide me with cover,' darkness is not dark for You; night is as light as day; darkness and light are the same. It was

comes to speech only in my dealings with my neighbor, with the stranger. The stranger summons me immediately and always. I cannot run from this summons; if I do, I only hear it louder. To ignore this summons is to kill my neighbor; to kill my neighbor is to kill myself. The sway of justice cannot be resisted. The possibility of responding to the stranger is the possibility of language, the possibility of conversation. To say "Hello," or "Here I am," is to begin breathing life into the stranger; the stranger becomes my neighbor; all unique strangers become my neighbors. Justice rules friendship, justice rules lovers. The saying allows itself to be betrayed once in its thematization for the sake of its epiphany, but it will not let itself be betrayed twice by a rejection of its humble advent. The neutral illeity of the saying is reflected in the advent of the third party on the scene. Justice and its demands speak upon the arrival of the neutral third party who pulls at the asymmetry of the self-other relationship only to reinstate it. As the saying is attested further by the antiphony of the said, the glory of the infinite shines through just relationships among neighbors. Ethics precipitates in the wake of the enigmatic saying and the trace of its riveting summons in the said.

Levinas's work bears a poetic quality, even as it attempts to speak frankly and without any hint of mysticism. To sum up his genealogy from the saying to ethics: the call of the other and my responsibility for him is the basic anthropological structure described through Levinas's vocative reduction.[141] Interpersonal ethical relationship is the fundamental force before and behind every phenomenal recognition, interpretation and appropriation. Without the call of the other, enigma slips away, and so does the idea of the infinite. Without the idea of the infinite, no steady responsibility for the other obtains, for the vocation of responsibility is without limit. For Levinas, the saying is another way to refer to the infinite, and the said is another way to refer to the human witness to the infinite. The said—discourse—is the playing field of ethics where the other calls to me and I in turn, become responsible for him. Ethics transpires through the course of conversation, yet its impetus extends from a transcendent elsewhere attested in the intersubjective relationship, not as an event of manifestation but as a prophetic word of the other issuing from my own lips.

---

you who created my conscience . . ." (TNKH translation, JPS).

141. Lacoste reflects similarly on Levinas's "saying" in the domain of sacramental theology. See Lacoste, *La phénoménalité de Dieu*, and Schrijvers, "God and/in Phenomenology," 87: "Lacoste concurs with Levinas' analysis: to reduce the saying of the other to yet one more representation of my own consciousness is to deny the humanity of the other."

## IX. Testimony to Glory: The Ambiguity of Every Said

The final stage of analyzing Levinas as a thinker of proclamation and attestation is to focus on the place of testimony in relation to the saying and the said. First of all, for Levinas, "saying is witness; it is saying without the said, a sign given to the other . . . a fraternity, a proximity that is possible only as an openness of self, an imprudent exposure to the other, a passivity without reserve, to the point of substitution."[142] Secondly, the saying is announced in the (said) voice of the one who opens himself in passivity to responsibility for the other, saying "Here I am!"—a response that "brings me out of invisibility, out of the shadow in which my responsibility could have been evaded."[143] The secret of Gyges is broken here in that there remains no need to become invisible when one is living justly.[144] A neutral illeity is begotten upon the emergence of the third party within the surplus of sociality, stretching the You-I dialogue to a social trio demanding the law of justice. In obedience to the order of signification given to the one who accepts responsibility for the other, one becomes a prophet, bearing the other in the same, announcing a word that does not originate with oneself but proceeds from another, namely, a word of glory.[145] The prophetic voice—the glory of the infinite—is the one that "commands me from my own mouth."[146] Thus subjectivity takes on an ambiguity and ambivalence in which the infinite does not announce itself as a theme but is attested to in the said that points to the saying—the accusative "Here I am" by which I testify to the infinite; it is here that I am "the author of what was, *without my knowledge*, inspired in me—to have received, whence we know not, that of which I am the author."[147] Glory is glorified in its absence, in the testimony of the trace in which the infinite speaks only to disappear therein, having already come in the disguise of the stranger and her demand on me. Only in alterity is love possible—love, whose very positivity lies in its negativity.[148]

The transcendence of glory, the upward anchor of love, signifies the vertical dimension of testimony, that sense of elevation that is prior to

142. Levinas, *Otherwise than Being*, 150–51.

143. Ibid., 150.

144. Cf. Plato, *Republic* 359c–360d.

145. Cf. Levinas, *Basic Philosophical Writings*, 146: "Prophesying is pure testimony, pure because prior to all disclosure; it is subjection to an order before understanding the order."

146. Ibid., 104.

147. Ibid., 105.

148. Cf. Levinas, *Existence and Existents*, 35.

objectivity, culture, aesthetics and consciousness—an elevation that "ordains being" and gives rise to the phenomenon of erecting altars that extend toward the heavens.[149] The glory of the significance of the trace "consists in signifying without making appear, if it establishes a relation with illeity—a relation, personal and ethical, a relation, obligation, that does not unveil—if, consequently, the trace does not belong to phenomenology, to comprehension of *appearance* and *dissimulation*, it could at least be approached by another path, by situating that significance from the phenomenology that it interrupts."[150] This quote shows the radicality of Levinas's vocative reduction, posing a threat to the hubris of phenomenology itself. As a trace of the infinite, the illeity of the ethical relationship disrupts the synchronous stream of phenomenological manifestation. Proclamation collides with manifestation to say that the other cannot be described in terms of unveiling (*alétheia*) and appearance alone. Levinas claims to recognize a command from eternity that plays itself out in the intersubjective demands of justice. He locates this command at the heart of the drama of the People of Israel. Torah issues a freedom of responsibilities that requires consent prior to freedom and non-freedom, prior to choice, prior to the temptation of temptation.[151] Torah is a summons from the depths of eternity—a summons that expresses an immovable actuality prior to all possible responses, descriptions and testimonies, expressing itself in the possibilities of responsibility.[152] For this reason, the saying itself is non-phenomenological because it is pure actuality—an actuality that necessarily goes before all potentiality and possibility, but nevertheless is attested in the latter.[153] This is to suggest

149. Levinas, *Humanism of the Other*, 36.

150. Ibid., 41.

151 See Levinas's Talmudic lecture, "The Temptation of Temptation," in Levinas, *Nine Talmudic Readings*, 30–50.

152. Even though Levinas does not describe the infinite or the saying in terms of actuality, I find it helpful to do so in order to set up the return to classic metaphysics as a timeless expression of transcendence and as the unexpected threshold of phenomenological inquiry. In the final chapter, I will argue that Levinas's disruption of phenomenology aligns with the disruption of metaphysics as a science of actuality.

153. See Levinas, "The Temptation of Temptation," in Levinas, *Nine Talmudic Readings*, 43: "The adherence to the good of those who said 'We will do and we will hear' is not the result of a choice between good and evil. It comes before it . . . This undoubtedly indicates that the doing which is at stake here is not simply *praxis* as opposed to theory but a way of *actualizing without beginning with the possible*, of knowing without examining, of placing oneself beyond violence without this being the privilege of a free choice. A pact with good would exist, preceding the alternative of good and evil." Cf. Levinas, *Time and the Other*, 92: "I have not proceeded in a phenomenological way. The continuity of development is that of a dialectic starting with the identity of hypostasis, the enchainment of the ego to the self, moving toward the maintenance of this identity,

that at the threshold of possibility for phenomenology is the possibility of actuality, and moreover, the admission that possibility depends on it. This is, again, the possibility of impossibility, the possibility (from a finite vantage point) of the infinite, the possibility of a non-possibility, namely, the un-possibility called actuality. In this sense phenomenology is interrupted by a bygone and irretrievable past that awakens the incipit word of phenomenology: to the other who calls me. This awakening is without self-interest, as self-interest is emptied by disinterestedness toward the other. Illeity is the term that signifies the indiscriminate call of the other, of every other, which bears within itself a trace of the nonnegotiable infinite. Levinas's notion of illeity can be likened to Ricoeur's notion of "the absolute":

> The saying in the said of the witness born signifies in a plot other than that which is spread out in a theme, other than that which attaches a noesis to a noema, a cause to an effect, the memorable past to the present. This plot connects to what detaches itself absolutely, to the Absolute. The detachment of the Infinite from the thought that seeks to thematize it and the language that tries to hold it in the said is what we have called *illeity*. One is tempted to call this plot religious; it is not stated in terms of certainty or uncertainty, and does not rest on any positive theology.[154]

Only a trace of the absolute—of illeity—can be detectable on the horizon of phenomenality via an ethical, sincere and veracious proclamation of testimony.[155] In other words, testimony is not proof positive of transcendence

toward the maintenance of the existent, but in a liberation of the ego with regard to self. The concrete situations that have been analyzed represent the accomplishment of this dialectic"; Levinas, *Entre Nous*, 112–13: "In knowledge, one is two, even when one is alone . . . This is the excellence of the multiple, which evidently can be thought as a degradation of the one. To cite another verse, created man is blessed with a command to 'multiply.' In ethical and religious terms: you will have someone to love, you will have someone for whom to exist, you cannot be just for yourself. He created them man and woman at the outset, 'man and woman created He them.'" Also, recall one of the ancient rabbinic methods of biblical exegesis, *remez*, in which allegorical meanings are unfolded from the text in proportion to the multiplicity of texts and paradigms brought together in proximity, for example, narrative, parables, apocalyptic, Mishna, Gemara, Talmud.

154. Levinas, *Otherwise than Being*, 147.

155. Cf. Levinas, *Basic Philosophical Writings*, 103, 107: "My responsibility for the other is precisely this relation with an unthematizable Infinity. It is neither the experience of Infinity nor proof of it: it *testifies* to Infinity. This *testimony* is not appended to a 'subjective experience' in order to proclaim the ontological 'conjuncture' disclosed by the subject. This testimony belongs to the very glory of the Infinite . . . It is the Saying that, unencumbered by any possessions in being, achieves the extradition of sincerity. No Said recovers sincerity, and none is adequate to it. Saying without said, apparently

or infinity, but simply an ambiguous trace of an anarchic saying to which I attest in my encounter with the face of the other; insofar as I speak, I give witness to that which speaks in me. In sum, *es gibt* of manifestation is modified, as informed by the work of Levinas, to *es gibt als* . . . and *es gibt nach* . . . of proclamation. What gives, gives *as* the saying of the infinite—a trace in my affirmative responsorial said, "Here I am!," to the other who beckons me. What gives, gives *according to* the prophetic witness of my affirmative response to the other—a word of the other (*l'autrui*) spoken in the same (*moi*). Phenomenality is awakened by a proclaimed word issued from eternity and attested in intersubjective discourse of uprightness. A covenant relationship is established between me and the other according to the unevadable leverage of the other's call and my responsibility for him. I am my brother's keeper after all.

## X. Segue

Having sketched the thinking of Ricoeur and Levinas as proclamation and testimony, as well as the thinking of Marion as manifestation and adoration, we will proceed to chapter 4 that will recall Marion's description of the Eucharist as self-manifestation, contrasted with the proclamatory hermeneutic of Ricoeur and Levinas. Without backtracking over fundamental grammars in sacramental theology as alluded to in chapter 2, for example, *sacramentum*, *res sacramenti*, etc., we will attempt to develop an augmented understanding of the Eucharist as manifestation-proclamation-attestation. Beginning with the manifestation ↔ proclamation dialectic, a trilectic of testimony will be submitted that harnesses the creative genius of Marion's, Ricoeur's and Levinas's thought in conversation. From chapter 2, we have, at this point, a preliminary submission of the Eucharist as manifestation. Through chapter 4, this construal will be revised through its exposure to the gauntlet of hermeneutics and the exigencies of the other. The apparatus of the trilectic of testimony will be employed as a heuristic model by which to situate the respective positions and contributions of Marion, Ricoeur and Levinas. At the end of chapter 4, a renewed interpretation of the Eucharist will be submitted that bears the promise of confronting contemporary

---

a talking for nothing, a sign given to the other, 'as simple as "hello,"' and, within the Saying, a sign given of this giving of a sign—the pure transparency of confession—testimony . . . In the game that activates the cultural keyboard of language, sincerity and testimony signify through the very ambiguity of every said, through the greeting it offers to the other (*autrui*)—the resounding 'in the name of God' of all language. But prophecy, through its ambiguities, is not the last resort of a lame revelation. It belongs to the glory of the Infinite."

hermeneutics of suspicion surrounding the religious phenomenon. Chapters 5 and 6 will set out, in turn, to extend the proposal of chapter 4 into a reflective discourse—chapter 5 serving as poetic imagination, chapter 6 serving as transcendental reflection—in order to weigh the truth-claims that surfaced in chapter 4.

# *chapter 4*

# The Eucharist as Manifestation-Proclamation-Attestation

"*But dialecticians ask* . . ."[1] It is through a living dialectic that a religious phenomenon such as the Eucharist is prevented from becoming stale and insipid. Dialectic is an opening, a refusal to reduce all sides of a phenomenon to a single face, to a solitary position. The most appropriate approach to the ambiguity and saturating givenness of the Eucharist is humble inquiry.[2] Through open investigation, without pretention, we will recommence our fervent quest to render the phenomenality of the Eucharist meaningful, intelligible and relevant. We will proceed under the hope that the Eucharist "*is not lacking in reason*."[3] Held in great regard is the method of rational dialectic that inspired Plato's dialogues, Thomas's *quaestiones disputatae* and his recurring refrain, *non solum* . . . *sed etiam* . . . ("not only . . . , but also . . ."). Yet, as indicated in chapter 1, we do not propose a synthesis, sublation, or reduction to one side of the dialectic alone. Rather, we follow Ricoeur's proposal of the unresolved dialectic as the centrifugal force of truth—truth that is given and said in proportion to the fertile tension of the dialectic, a concentrated unity in difference. Another name for such a unity in differ-

1. De Lubac, *Corpus Mysticum*, 228 (quoting from Algerius of Liège, *De sacramentis*).

2. Cf. Jas 4:1–3: "What causes wars, and what causes fightings among you? Is it not your passions that are at war in your members? You desire and do not have; so you kill. And you covet and cannot obtain; so you fight and wage war. You do not have because you do not ask. You ask and do not receive, because you ask wrongly, to spend it on your passions" (RSV).

3. Cf. de Lubac, *Corpus Mysticum*, 233 (quoting from Hildebert, *Versus de mysterio missae*).

ence is paradox. It will be argued that the Eucharist gives itself according to the paradox of the cross—the "*logos* of the cross."[4] Chapter 4 will maintain a phenomenological discourse, working carefully to describe the primary dimensions of the phenomenality of the Eucharist, suspending judgment on these descriptions until chapter 6. The order of reflection in chapter 4 will proceed as follows: (1) to recall how Marion frames the Eucharist as manifestation and adoration, (2) to set forth an interpretation of the Eucharist as proclamation and attestation in light of Ricoeur's and Levinas's proposals of a revised phenomenology, and (3) to situate Marion's, Ricoeur's and Levinas's contributions to understanding the Eucharist within the heuristic model of the trilectic of testimony, as introduced in chapter 1.

## I. *Venite Adoremus*: Divine Love Manifest in Saturation

To recall our analysis in chapter 2, Marion opens space for the possibility of phenomena that give themselves to a degree of excess that saturates intentionality. To describe this kind of paradoxical givenness, Marion employs the term "saturated phenomenon"—one that cannot be categorized as a kataphatic common-law phenomenon or an apophatic deficiency of intuition.[5] In the former, intentionality corresponds adequately with intuition in the form of a concept; in the latter, intentionality flounders in a dark abyss where intuition is found lacking for the aim of intentionality. In the case of the saturated phenomenon, intuition exceeds the intentional aim, leaving the human subject stupefied and mystified by the overcoming sway of the imperturbable phenomenon. In all three cases—the common law phenomenon, the phenomenon lacking in intuition, and the saturated phenomenon—the phenomenon shows itself from itself according to its degree of auto-manifestation, or givenness.[6] In all ways the phenomenon is master of its own manifestation, regardless of the role human subjectivity plays in the phenomenon's appearing. This conception is more akin to Newtonian empiricism (in which, for example, the reality of space is as it is in itself, independent of objects that occupy it), than to a Leibnizian relativism (in which, for example, the reality of space amounts to a relative positioning of objects in relation to one another).[7] Further, Marion rejects Kantian transcendental idealism in favor of anterior givenness. First a phenomenon

4. Cf. Chauvet, *Symbol and Sacrament*, 527–28.

5. Cf. Marion's essay "In the Name," in Caputo and Scanlon, *God, the Gift, and Postmodernism*, 39–41; Marion, *Being Given*, 221–33 (§23).

6. Cf. Marion, *Being Given*, 222.

7. Cf. Patricia W. Kitcher's introduction to Kant, *Critique of Pure Reason*, xxxv.

gives itself, then it is interpreted; the interpretation does not add anything to the phenomenal manifestation, it merely reports on what has been seen.[8] This distinction between what appears and its interpretation secures the rights of phenomenal manifestation, that is, human subjectivity is restricted from encroaching upon the absolute agency of a phenomenon's capacity to show itself in any way or to any degree whatsoever. No (Kantian) a priori limits are permitted to impose on the free play of phenomenality. However, the reverse prevails: the phenomenon is permitted to encroach on human subjectivity—to impose its intuitional gallantry on the shortcomings of intentionality. In the end, the saturated phenomenon threatens the perpetuity of the intuition ↔ intentionality dialectic without abolishing it.

The Eucharist, for Marion, is a paradigmatic instance of the revelatory phenomenon. The intuitional excess that proceeds from the Eucharist overtakes the intentional gaze of the human subject, appearing in the form of a shortage, a lack, a trace. The Eucharist bears the sacramental claim: a manifestation of the invisible in the visible. To adore Christ in the Eucharist is to worship a personal phenomenon that perplexes the intentional aim: "I see only bread and wine!" Yet the self-attestation of the phenomenon gives to intentionality that which it cannot bear: living flesh and blood of a divine-human person "given up for you." A double phenomenality obtains: one part visible (*sacramentum*), the other part not visible (*res sacramenti*).[9] Altogether, for Marion, the phenomenon of the Eucharist is ultimately an original event of manifestation of a person in flesh and blood—an irreversible givenness of giving-ness in the Person of Christ, given to the point of abandonment. Christ the Word is known not through words but rather "nonverbally, in flesh and Eucharist."[10] This disclosure is precisely the advent of the logic of the cross. The primordial Word speaks in the silent tenor of his passion and death: a mute corpse, at once human and divine, signals the stoppage of discourse at the heights of manifestation.[11] Yet the heights

8. Cf. Marion, *Being Given*, 216–19. Cf. Hart, *Kingdoms of God*, 141: "We may say, then, that as a matter of principle phenomenality must be granted unlimited extension so as not to exclude anything that gives itself, in whatever way, from whatever 'region of being,' to intentional experience and how to value what is given depends on the degree of intuitive fullness that it yields."

9. Cf. Merleau-Ponty, *Visible and the Invisible*, 251, 257: "The invisible is not another visible ('possible' in the logical sense) a positive only *absent* . . . The invisible is . . . what, relative to the visible, could nevertheless not be seen as a thing."

10. Marion, *God without Being*, 155.

11. Cf. von Balthasar, *Theo-logic*, 2:72: "This end is death, which, bringing the Son to silence, gives the loudest tidings of the Father: through the 'wordless word' (William of Saint Thierry), which Thomas of Celano calls the *lingua tertia* [third tongue]." The *lingua tertia* can be likened to Marion's proposal of a "third way"; cf. "In the Name," in Caputo and Scanlon, *God, the Gift, and Postmodernism*, 20–53.

of this manifestation remain sacramental—it is not frozen in the paralyzed flesh of Christ to become an idol of remorse, but is rather a portal—an icon—to an infinite hermeneutic of meaning of "this one here, given up for you." The giving-ness of love is given to the point of abandonment all the way through to the glory of resurrection. The gift repels its consignment to a sterile economy of exchange in order to open onto an infinite horizon of plentitude. In good Heideggerian fashion, phenomenal manifestation obtains inasmuch as phenomenal concealment: "an absolute hermeneutic is announced, and not only does it reveal nothing, but it shines by its absence; barely named, it disappears to the benefit of the eucharistic moment (Luke 24:28–33)."[12] The human subject lies bereft of any manipulation or steering of this revelatory phenomenon, but for this reason is not disqualified from participating in it.[13] Indeed, the human subject is witness to the iconicity of the Eucharist but only insofar as faithfully telling the phenomenon according to its own mode of manifestation.[14] There remains an intractable distance between the giving divine-human phenomenon and the gifted human subject (*l'adonné*). The gifted only can perceive the phenomenal trace

12. Marion, *God without Being*, 150. Cf. Chauvet, *Symbol and Sacrament*, 74, 404: "That the non-face of the crucified One be the 'para-doxical' trace of Divine Glory, that the face of God show itself only by erasing itself, that we think of God less in the metaphysical order of the Unknowable than in the symbolic and historical order of the unrecognizable—quite clearly this is the 'folly' which the theologians attempt to express through their discourse . . . The twofold movement of procession and recession (procession even in recession) we attribute theologically to God, especially in the 'paradoxical' revelation of the glory of God in the face of the Crucified, belongs also to humankind; at least our meditation on Heidegger's Being, all the way to its being crossed out, has allowed us to think this."

13. Marion, *God without Being*, 169, 179: "What the consecrated host imposes, or rather permits, is the irreducible exteriority of the present that Christ makes us of himself in this thing that to him becomes sacramental body. That this exteriority, far from forbidding intimacy, renders it possible in sparing it from foundering in idolatry, can be misunderstood only by those who do not want to open themselves to *distance*. Only distance, in maintaining a distinct separation of terms (of persons), renders communion possible, and immediately mediates the relation. Here again, between the idol and distance, one must choose . . . The bread and the wine must be consumed, to be sure, but so that our definitive union with the Father may be consummated in them, through communion with the ecclesiastical body of his Son. *The eucharistic present is deduced from the real edification of the ecclesiastical body of Christ*."

14. Cf. ibid., 196: "Only the Father can manifest the Lordship of Jesus, just as only Jesus can recognize a disciple as his own. In this sense, the confession of faith, while supremely implicating the believer, has nothing of a self-implication about it: not only does it not suffice to implicate oneself in it to verify it, but to pretend to do so would constitute the supreme imposture. The confession of faith passes through the one who speaks, but it comes from much further away and it goes much further. It passes right through him, coming from the mystery . . ."

of the passing of the gift as it "assumes the character of shortage, with the name the *abandoned* (*l'abandonné*)."[15]

Theology then assumes a eucharistic locus where "*only the bishop merits, in the full sense, the title of theologian*" since "only the celebrant receives authority to go beyond the words as far as the Word, because he alone finds himself invested by the *persona Christi*."[16] Further, "*theology cannot aim at any other progress than its own conversion to the Word*, the theologian again becoming bishop or else one of the poor believers, in the common Eucharist. Once all is given, it remains to say it, in the expectation that the Said itself should come again to say it."[17] In this manner the Christian disciple is divested of all pretentiousness to give meaning to the Eucharist; all meaning comes directly from the divine Expositor who alone knows from whence and whither he comes.[18] Therefore, in Marion's understanding, the Eucharist, as a sacrament, necessitates a part that remains invisible, elusive to the senses, and apparently absent. Such a part, in relation to the common law phenomena of visibility, maintains the welcome aperture between creatures and creator. It is precisely this distance that characterizes a sacrament as such—a distance and relationality that opens the possibility for a doubly saturating manifestation and fecund communion.

What attitude is precipitated by this graceful appearing? For Marion, the attitude immediately engendered by such unbounded love is none other than adoration, such as that expressed in the classic eucharistic hymns of Thomas Aquinas:

*Adoro te devote, latens Deitas,*
*Quae sub his figuris vere latitas.*
*Tibi se cor meum totum subicit*
*Quia te contemplans totum deficit.*

*Pange, lingua, gloriosi*
*Corporis mysterium*

15. Cf. Marion, *Being Given*, 246.

16. Marion, *God without Being*, 153.

17. Ibid., 158.

18. Cf. von Balthasar, *Theo-logic*, 2:11, 66–67: "Theo-logic begins with the self-revelation of the triune God in the Incarnation of the divine Logos, and the Logos is the Word, the Son, and the expositor [*Ausleger*] . . . The man Jesus presents himself (at least in Johannine terms) primarily as the expositor of the Father . . . Christ, going beyond the law and the prophets, presents himself as the expositor of God as he is in himself. Indeed, he unveils in his own visibility the invisible God, even while simultaneously leaving this God his fatherly invisibility."

*Sanguinisque pretiosi,*
*Quem in mundi pretium,*
*Fructus ventris generosi,*
*Rex effudit gentium.*[19]

Adoration is that movement of the heart—the core of one's being—whereby one receives such a boundless gift only in giving this gift away.[20] Self-donation is the *forma Christi* whereby one becomes an *alter Christus*, a subsidiary manifestation of that original incarnate manifestation of divine grace.[21] This metamorphosis is disclosed in the ecclesiastical context, but remains to be contemplated. Marion's theology of the Eucharist results in an attitude of perpetual adoration and contemplation, not only (though most especially) of the eucharistic species, but of the entire cosmos. This could be described as a Bonaventurian recognition of a sacramentally charged cosmos: meaning is all around us, we only have to open our eyes and behold it as it gives itself without measure.[22] The cosmos is translucent, revelatory

19. Thomas Aquinas, *Devoutly I Adore Thee*, 68–69, 88–89: "Devoutly I adore You, hidden Deity, / Under these appearances concealed. / To You my heart surrenders self / For, seeing You, all else must yield . . . Acclaim, my tongue, this mystery / Of glorious Body and precious Blood / Which the King of nations shed for us / A noble womb's sole fruitful bud."

20. Cf. Marion, *Prolegomena to Charity*, 130: "Henceforward the disciples, that is to say the Church, that is to say humanity, finally reconciled with its destiny, no longer has but one function and one mission in a thousand different attitudes: to bless, so as thereby to welcome and acknowledge, the gift of the presence of God in and as his Christ."

21. Cf. ibid., 152: "Our flesh becomes word in order to bless the trinitarian gift of the presence of the Word, and to accomplish our incorporation in Him." Here flesh becomes word only to become flesh once again, namely, the "in*corp*oration" into the *Corpus Christi mysticum*.

22. Cf. Luke 9:32: "Peter and his companions had been overcome by sleep, but becoming fully awake, they saw his glory and the two men standing with him" (NAB), and Ps 19. Cf. also Marion, *Visible and the Revealed*, 126: "The banality of the saturated phenomenon suggests *that the majority of phenomena, if not all* can undergo saturation by the excess of intuition over the concept or signification in them. In other words, the majority of phenomena that appear at first glance to be poor in intuition could be described not only as objects but also as phenomena that intuition saturates and therefore exceed any univocal concept. Before the majority of phenomena, even the most simple (the majority of objects produced technically and reproduced industrially), opens the possibility of a doubled interpretation, which depends upon the demands of my ever-changing relation to them. Or rather, when the description demands it, I have the possibility of passing from one interpretation to the other, from a poor or common phenomenality to a saturated phenomenality. That is, 'those things that are the clearest and the most common are the very things that are most obscure, and understanding them is a novelty [*nova est intentio eorum*].'"

and iconic, disclosing a refulgence of divine glory before which the intentional aim withers.[23] Therefore Christ, the divine Expositor, gives himself hypostatically in the humble forms of human flesh, bread become Body and wine become Blood, in order to reveal the life-giving manifestation of his eternal countenance.[24] In response to this paradoxical givenness of glory, the human person becomes enraptured by the divine gaze of compassion, captivated by its manifest lucidity, overtaken by this personal and total gift of self. For Marion, prayer is praise:

> In this sense, what we understand by the term "eucharistic contemplation" here assumes its true meaning: summoned to distance by the eucharistic present, the one who prays undertakes to let his gaze be converted in it—thus, in addition, to modify his thought in it. In prayer, only an "explanation" becomes possible, in other words, a struggle between human impotence to receive and the insistent humility of God to fulfil. And without defeat in this combat, thought will never carry the least speculative victory. Eucharistic contemplation, in this sense, would

23. Cf. 2 Cor 3:17–18: "Now the Lord is the Spirit, and where the Spirit of the Lord is, there is freedom. All of us, gazing with unveiled face on the glory of the Lord, are being transformed into the same image from glory to glory, as from the Lord who is the Spirit" (NAB).

24. Cf. Ps 80:4: "O Lord of hosts, restore us; Let your face shine upon us, that we may be saved" (NAB). It must be noted here that Marion is careful to draw the distinction between "sacrament" and "icon." See Marion, *Crossing of the Visible*, 77: "The Incarnation, which delivers the person of Christ and the divine nature, only prolongs the presence of this nature in the Eucharist, where no face accompanies it, and vice versa: it grants legitimacy to the icon, a perpetual visage of Christ waiting for his return, with the sacramental accompaniment of the divine nature. It is precisely this distortion of the economy that prevents the danger of the idol: the Church can never identify the nature and the hypostatic visage of its Christ in a single liturgical performance, nor yield to the ultimate temptation of summoning as a demon that which it should dominate. Hence the importance of not including the common icon under the title 'sacrament.' The icon thus strictly retains its paradoxical legitimacy as τύπος: a sign and not (a) nature of the invisible—appearing at a distance from the invisible, precisely because the invisible marks it all the way through." Yet in referring to the manifestation of Christ's countenance in the Eucharist, I am taking liberties in light of Marion's discussion of "the eschatological and the universal," and his exegesis of Matt 25:31–46, in *Being Given*, 91–94: "It is beneficial to us that [Christ] depart, for the impossibility of empirically identifying the givee par excellence, Christ, allows his role to proliferate: the absent but still to come givee opens the universal place of his own face to every human face . . . The withdrawal of Christ permits the 'least of [his] brethren' to come forward and expose himself to the gift as a face of the givee." This connection is very important as it links Marion's thinking of the Eucharist as "blessing" to its ethical dimensions as "gift." In this way, the face of "the least of these" testifies to the face of Christ. This is a prime instance of the dynamic of testimony at work within the rubric of manifestation.

> become an urgency: "Not only do we not sin by adoring Him, but we sin by not adoring Him" (Saint Augustine).[25]

Indeed, eucharistic contemplation is an urgency for Marion. Once one recognizes the sheer givenness of the cosmos, and especially the utter givingness of divine grace, one immediately falls to one's knees. To recognize givenness becomes the first step in achieving a Christian ethics. Contemplation is prior to action. For how does one know how to act without first contemplating the givens in the playing field of action? How does a scientist propose a hypothesis without first assessing the givens of a problematic? In sum, for Marion, givenness is first philosophy and the gateway to all subsequent reflection and praxis. Likewise is givenness the primary hermeneutic entry point for understanding and contemplating the eucharistic phenomenon, the sacrament par excellence that claims a double-phenomenality.[26] More will be said in chapter 5 about the personal dimensions of the Eucharist as disclosed according to the erotic reduction. For now, let us proceed to consider the unique contributions of Ricoeur and Levinas for a phenomenology of the Eucharist.

## II. The Eucharist as Speech and Text: How to Interpret Love-Kerygma?

It is now time to aim at a rapprochement between the thinking of Ricoeur and Levinas and apply it to the Eucharist, interpreting it according to the modified phenomenological rubrics: *es gibt als* . . . and *es gibt nach* . . . This section will proceed along the following three steps: (1) the Eucharist considered in relation to *es gibt als* . . . , (2) the Eucharist considered in relation to *es gibt nach* . . . and its precipitating ethical dimensions, and (3) placement of Ricoeur's and Levinas's thinking within the model of the trilectic of testimony.

First, as demonstrated in chapter 3, Ricoeur and Levinas stretch phenomenological givenness, especially the notion of *es gibt*, according to the hermeneutical receptors of givenness. Ricoeur approaches the religious phenomenon through the generative phenomenality of metaphor and symbol. Levinas, for his part, assesses the religious phenomenon through its upshot of the call of the other. Both Ricoeur and Levinas regard the linguistic and dialectical components of a phenomenon as indispensable and primary,

25. Marion, *God without Being*, 182. Cf. de Lubac, *Corpus Mysticum*, 230: "St. Augustine . . . certainly had no inclination to deny the obscurity essential to faith, or to contest the penitential submission that it demands of our understanding."

26. Cf. Marion, *In Excess*, 1–29.

over and above (though without dispensing entirely of) the manifestation component. For Ricoeur and Levinas, a religious phenomenon such as the Eucharist depends on its linguistic comportment to appear *as* such. For them, the Eucharist would only ever appear *as* . . . A primordial, universal and pure givenness may be possible in theory but not in practice—for what human subject could receive any phenomenon (including the Eucharist) apart from its filtration along the historical, cultural, linguistic and ethical pathways that constitute a human person's existence? If the Eucharist means anything, it means only *as* . . . and *according to* . . . Ricoeur and Levinas would find no possible way for a human subject to divest herself completely of the manifold filters of appropriation that render a phenomenon recognizable *as* such and intelligible and meaningful.

From a Ricoeurian outlook, metaphor and symbol serve as paradigmatic heuristics for approaching the double phenomenality of the Eucharist. In metaphor, an "is/is not" paradox emerges from the play of the copula, for example, "time is a healer." In the phenomenality of metaphor, a plural phenomenality gives rise to thought. It is clear enough to talk about "time" and "healer" as signifiers for their respective referents. This is to construe truth as correlation: each signifier corresponds with its respective referent, and language seems to serve thereby as a means to differentiate and signify one thing from another. However, the flipside of the metaphor—its creative and generative potential—demonstrates a concomitant (invisible) given alongside the first and plainer (visible) given. The concomitant reality arises from the "is not" of the "is/is not" paradoxical potency of the metaphor. The meanings of "time" and "healer" may be plain enough, but the pairing of "time" and "healer" seems to contradict common logic and meaning because "time" is not a "healer" per se. Yet within this paradox (not outright contradiction) a meaning emerges that resonates as true. The veracity of the metaphor does not lie in its efficaciousness of correspondence, but in its ability to produce meaning. "Time is a healer" is to say that the passing of time allows anger to dissipate, or that the passing of time helps one forget the immediacy of sorrow, or that the possibility of remembrance engenders a proximity between oneself and a loved one who has died, or . . . , ad infinitum. The simple metaphorical statement, "time is a healer," demonstrates innumerable meanings and plurality of possibility for truth's expression.

The symbol serves as an even better heuristic for approaching the phenomenality of the sacrament, so much that some go so far as to say that the phenomenality of the symbol is precisely and ultimately the phenomenality of the sacrament. Recall Zwingli, Calvin, and many other theological positions of Reformed Christianity. As Ricoeur notes, the symbol "brings together two dimensions, we might even say, two universes, of discourse, one linguistic [i.e., metaphorical] and the other of a non-linguistic order."[27] Taking the example of the Eucharist, Jesus breaks apart bread, gives it to his disciples to eat and says (in Greek translation), Λάβετε, τοῦτό ἐστιν τὸ σῶμά μου ("Take; this is my body"); likewise he gives to his disciples a chalice from which to drink and says, Τοῦτό ἐστιν τὸ αἷμά μου τῆς διαθήκης τὸ ἐκχυννόμενον ὑπὲρ πολλῶν ("This is my blood of the covenant, which is poured out for many").[28] The metaphorical play of the "is/is not" between the subjects and predicates in these words is clear: bread/body, wine/blood. However, these statements are not only metaphorical, but symbolic insofar as they bring together two universes: one linguistic, the other non-linguistic. Both a linguistic paradox and a non-linguistic paradox appear: an order of proclamation and an order of manifestation. The linguistic order of ritual serves to evoke the non-linguistic order concerning personal, communal and cosmic salvation. The linguistic order is the means by which the disclosure-concealment of manifestation comes to light. If Jesus did not announce the bread to be (εἶναι) his body, and the wine to be (εἶναι) his blood, the disciples would not be able to receive them *as* such.

At this point, let us take a detour away from direct reflection on the thought of Ricoeur and Levinas to consider a brief proposal regarding the *es gibt als* . . . This "*as* such" indicated above, does not signify a mere prepositional simile, but signifies a transformative ontological conjunction at the crux of sacramental phenomenality.[29] The difference between "as" functioning as a preposition and "as" functioning as an ontological conjunction is the difference between "truth as adequation" and "truth as testimony." In the former, "as" functions to denote the "qua" of something—how it acts in the character, role or capacity of . . . ; in the latter, "as" functions to bridge one's assent to a proposed "such and such is (εἶναι) the case."[30] The latter is

27. Ricoeur, *Interpretation Theory*, 53–54.

28. Mark 14:22–24 (RSV); cf. Matt 26:26–29; Luke 22:17–19; 1 Cor 11:23–26. Obviously, according to critical scholarship in biblical studies and Christology, Jesus most likely would not have said these words in Greek but in Aramaic. Yet the biblical witness that comes down through the canonical textual tradition is the Greek linguistic formulation.

29. I justify the retention of ontology in the course of the predominantly Ricoeurian analysis of this section in order to fashion yet another dialectic between ontology and meontology. However, this notion of "transformative ontological conjunction" is my own.

30. I am arguing here that "as," functioning conjunctionally (in the sense of "according to . . ."), is different than "as" functioning prepositionally in both the Dionysian ὡς and the Heideggerian phenomenological "as." When "as" functions prepositionally, a likeness is manifest between subject and predicate, although within a milieu of ambiguity: "the in-draft of distance multiplies meaning [*sens*] in the name of the meaningless [*l'insensé*] that remains infinitely to be signified." Marion, *Idol and Distance*,

precisely the role of the "*as* such" of the double phenomenality of the Eucharist. An irreversible becoming transpires between subject and predicate: bread becomes Body, wine becomes Blood. The conjunctional "as" serves as an indicator of a metamorphosis of being according to the self-attestation of the absolute. The form of the logical conjunction may serve as a helpful heuristic to understanding this subtle distinction between the prepositional "as" and the conjunctional "as." The logical conjunction is signified by A^B, where ^ means "and." The conjunction is true insofar as both A and B are each and together true. This can be demonstrated by the following Venn diagram when applied to the phenomenality of the Eucharist:

**Where the left circle signifies bread, the right circle signifies body, and the dark grey overlapping of circles signifies the hypostatic reality of the sacrament. The shade of dark grey is the ^ of the A^B.**[31]

186. However, when "as" functions conjunctionally, the subject and predicate are irrevocably conjoined—yoked—so that to pronounce the predicate is to pronounce the subject and vice versa, according to the self-attestation of the absolute. The latter is the genius of the sacrament: a becoming occurs at the intersection of two seemingly oppositional and adversive realms of existence. In the prepositional "as," a human subject places a phenomenon in an a priori symbolic order through the event of appropriation (*Ereignis*). In the conjunctional "as," a human subject adheres to the truth-claim of a phenomenon according to the attestation surrounding the phenomenon's raison d'être, which itself signifies the in-breaking of the absolute. An ontological, and not merely ontic or hermeneutic, metamorphosis obtains.

31. It is important to note that the proposed Venn diagrams in no way intend to undermine the clarity of Catholic teaching on transubstantiation, the Incarnation of Christ, or Trinitarian theology. Rather, they serve as heuristic models for comprehending the paradoxical logic revealed in all three mysteries: unity and difference, singularity and plurality. In each case the crux of the mystery is to be found precisely at the site where the circles overlap, forming a paradoxical reality in which the distinction among circles is not lost, nor is the union of circles mitigated by their simultaneous difference. For instance, this logic is articulated in the *definitio fidei* of the Council of Chalcedon in 451. See Denzinger and Schönmetzer, *Enchiridion symbolorum*, ¶ 302 (148): ". . . οὐδαμοῦ τῆς τῶν φύσεων διαφορᾶς ἀνῃρημένης διὰ τὴν ἕνωσιν, σωζομένης

Given this configuration of the logical conjunction, A^B, the Eucharist obtains inasmuch as the bread-ness and wine-ness subsist (accidentally) in their concomitant relation to the subsistence of the Body and Blood (substantially) of Christ in the very same eucharistic species.[32] The traditional doctrine of transubstantiation can be articulated through this conception: the accident of bread-ness (left circle) remains in the sacrament, while the historically and spatially incarnate and resurrected Body of Christ (right circle) likewise maintains its spatial distinction from the eucharistic species. Yet bread is transubstantiated (overlapping of circles), that is, becomes the body of Christ according to his pronouncement that it is *as* (conjunctionally) *such*, thereby making the historically and spatially incarnate and resurrected Body of Christ synonymous with the eucharistic species. Both the visible and invisible give themselves together in the unified sacramental phenomenon of the Eucharist. This is the same logic of (dialectical/trilectical) hypostasis at work in the doctrines of the Incarnation and Trinity:

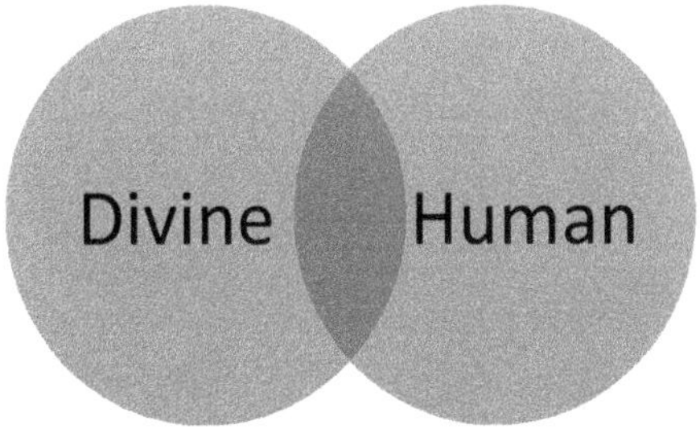


**Where the left circle signifies divinity, the right circle signifies humanity, and the dark grey overlapping of circles signifies the hypostatic union (in difference) of the incarnate Christ: one person, two natures—one nature divine, the other nature human.**

Similar to the doctrine of transubstantiation is the doctrine of the Incarnation. As it was codified especially through the Ecumenical Councils of Nicaea (325), Constantinople (381), Ephesus (431) and Chalcedon (451),

δὲ μᾶλλον τῆς ἰδιότητος ἑκατέρας φύσεως καὶ εἰς ἓν πρόσωπον καὶ μίαν ὑπὸστασιν συντρεχούσης"; Tanner, *Decrees of the Ecumenical Councils*, 2:86: ". . . at no point was the difference between the natures taken away through the union, but rather the property of both natures is preserved and comes together into a single person and a single subsistent being." I am calling this logic the dialectical logic of Christian mystery and revelation.

32. Regarding the tangential question of the doctrine of concomitance in relation to transubstantiation, see Thomas Aquinas, *Summa theologiae*, III.76.1–8.

the doctrine on the Person and natures of Christ is based on the dialectical notion of the hypostatic union: the paradox of two distinct natures in one incarnate Person. Just as the doctrine on the incarnate Word admits no admixture or confusion of the distinct—human and divine—natures in the single Person, Christ, the Eucharist proclaims two distinct phenomenalities in a single unified phenomenon: one visible, the other invisible; one manifest, the other concealed. Let us also consider the doctrine of the Trinity:

Venn Diagram of Logic of Trinitarian Doctrine

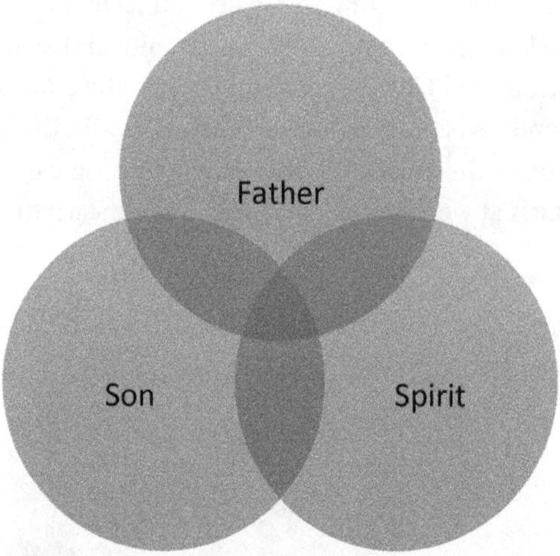


According to this conception, the Father is neither Son nor Spirit, the Son is neither Father nor Spirit, and the Spirit is neither Father nor Son. Yet *as* (conjunctionally) the Father is in the Son, so the Son is in the Father, and so on. The center point of this Venn diagram shows the trilectical overlapping of all three circles to signify the doctrine of the Trinity: three distinct Persons in one God, sharing the same divine substance. Making reference to the doctrines of the Incarnation and the Trinity is helpful for understanding the doctrine of transubstantiation in the Eucharist. All this is to say that the operation of language, for example, even that of the small word "as," radically functions to bring phenomena to light and bears the power to enact the double phenomenality of the sacrament, whereby two phenomenalities are conjoined in a singular unified phenomenon.[33]

In addition to the double-phenomenality-making function of language inside the Eucharist is Ricoeur's prioritization of kerygmatic proclamation.

33. Cf. Levinas, *Humanism of the Other*, 13: "In the *this as that*, neither the *this* nor the *that* is given forthwith, outside of discourse."

Not only is it necessary to note that the above treatment of the conjunctional "as" is a highly Catholic move (observing how the function of language applies to the dynamic of manifestation, namely, the doctrine of transubstantiation), it is likewise important to observe that Ricoeur, as a Reformed Christian, would disagree most likely with such a move. For Ricoeur, the Eucharist functions as a mode of discourse that operates according to the logic of limit-expressions. The Eucharist does not so much give a transubstantiated substance as it proclaims and attests to new and possible ways-of-being-in-the-world. It speaks at the limits of a human person's finitude, mortality and rationality. The liturgical form of the Eucharist proclaims a narrative ever new and imaginative, composed of a host of limit-expressions that disorient only to reorient according to the dialectical cruciform pattern of Christ the Testator. Such an understanding of the Eucharist persists in contemporary Protestant and Evangelical settings, and stems originally from the thought of Luther and Calvin on the Eucharist: remembrance and word of promise, testimony and hope. For Ricoeur, the Eucharist is essentially a kerygmatic phenomenon—a word of divine grace that is conferred in preaching and ritualized in a word oriented sacrament: "for in Christianity the liturgical kernel represents the Eucharist, as a kind of text that tells the story of the Last Supper."[34] Furthermore, this Eucharist-word-phenomenon functions in signifying the fact that "the kingdom of God has approached us in decisive fashion," as well as the hoped-for eschatological vindication that attends the revelation of the just ones.[35] In Ricoeur's conception, the Eucharist is fundamentally a ritual enactment of a prophetic word of hope that transforms its hearers according to its stunning power of disorientation and desacralization, razing all idols that clutter up the pathway of the divine kerygma. The pattern of Christ's life—a life lived to death for the causes of justice and truth—functions as the paradigmatic way-of-being-in-the-world, proclaimed and attested in the liturgical rite of the Eucharist.

While the above assessment of metaphor and symbol as heuristics to understanding the double phenomenality of the Eucharist, as well as a construal of the Eucharist according to its kerygmatic function of proclamation, are primarily Ricoeurian contributions, Levinas, too, helps to overcome the innate egoistic hunger for (more) manifestation by recognizing the priority of the word from the other. For Levinas, not only do phenomena depend on their linguistic transport to be recognized by the human subject, the human subject is mastered first by the encounter of the face of the other who speaks. Since the call to be responsible for the other is the most anterior

34. Ricoeur, *Figuring the Sacred*, 71.

35. Ricoeur, *Conflict of Interpretation*, 382.

phenomenon before all other phenomena (even before givenness), the word from the visage of the other serves to establish the playing field of all phenomenal perception to come thereafter. For all appearing matters little if the primordial face of the other is ignored. Phenomena have meaning inasmuch as they proceed from the original phenomenon that gives meaning to the whole of existence: "It is I, the other. Do not kill me." My proximity to the other establishes the point of reference between me (*moi*) and all other phenomena. From this originary focal point of reference, I behold the sum of appearances within my lifetime, always in the context of ethical exigency. The Eucharist matters not, unless it is a phenomenon that promotes the cause of justice—the care of my neighbor, the rescue of the stranger.

In an insightful article, Michael Purcell examines Levinas's phenomenology of eating by juxtaposing two radically divergent interpretations of consuming the eucharistic species: (1) a destructive and totalizing eating that assimilates and incorporates the Eucharist into the same (self), and (2) a taking and eating that bears meaning in its configuration as substitution, one-for-the-other.[36] In the former, the Eucharist is converted simply into more of the same, digested by the human subject, fulfilling the base desire for food and drink; whereas in the latter, the alterity of Christ in the Eucharist is promoted to the measure that Christ has promoted and continues to promote the alterity of the recipient, coming as "the one so utterly consumed by responsibility *for* the Other that he lets himself be taken *by* the Other."[37] Christ exemplifies the form of being taken hostage to the extreme: his cause for justice and truth escalates to his arrest, trial, condemnation and crucifixion. Christ's passion is said proleptically in the final meal shared with his friends, in which he gives his body and blood as food and drink—the same body and blood soon to be given up for them to the point of abandonment and God-forsakenness on the cross. According to this manner of receptivity, the recipient of the Eucharist is thus summoned to become an *alter Christus*—an ethical charge to become one-for-the-other, according to the needs and demands of the other, in daily living.[38] In this sense, one's food is not merely that which is eaten, digested and assimilated by the body for nourishment, rather one's food is "to do the will of him who sent me, and to

36. See Purcell, "An *Agape* of Eating."

37. Ibid., 334.

38. Matt 16:24–25: "Then Jesus said to his disciples, 'Whoever wishes to come after me must deny himself, take up his cross, and follow me. For whoever wishes to save his life will lose it, but whoever loses his life for my sake will find it'" (NAB). Cf. Purcell, "*Agape* of Eating," 334: "Ultimately, the signification of the eucharist is not ontological but ethical . . . Eucharistically speaking, eating is no longer simply for the sake of eating, nor is it for the sake of oneself; it is the one-for-the-other of responsibility."

accomplish his work."[39] My relationship to food and drink is a relationship subordinate to my relationship to the personal other (*l'autrui*). The former relationship exists to serve the latter.

In this way, the phenomenon of the Eucharist issues an ambivalent and inquisitive proclamation for its recipient: (1) Do you receive me as plain food and drink to satisfy your menial desire, or (2) Do you receive me as the personal pattern of living a life according to the priority of substituting yourself one-for-the-other? When thought along these lines, the Eucharist becomes a daunting phenomenon that one dares to receive only with fear and trepidation. To receive the Eucharist as the radically substituted Christ is to accept the summons to responsibility for the other and the exigencies of responsibility. In this conception, "the sacred" is defined as the place where the ethical charge of responsibility is lived out, rather than an off-limits locale where the numinous is manifest. In the Eucharist, Christ offers the paradigmatic form of authentic living, testifying to the primordial voice of the saying, according to which his life becomes an offering, one-for-the-other.

Before considering the notion of testimony in the phenomenological thinking of Ricoeur and Levinas, the notion of the saying in Levinas must be examined as a fitting analogy for the invisible phenomenality of the Eucharist. At this point it should be clear that, thinking the Eucharist through the thought of Levinas, the Eucharist may be regarded as an entirely personal, or better "prosopic," phenomenon.[40] It directly involves persons in a relational face to face setting. Yet for Levinas, the face to face is not a matter of manifestation but of proclamation—a phenomenality initiated by the non-visible saying that beckons from a diachronic distance of the immemorial past.[41] A trace of this elusive saying can be detected in the said

39. John 4:34 (RSV).

40. See Levinas's response in an interview featured in Robbins, *Is It Righteous to Be?*, 255–56: "I was led to Matthew 25, where the people are astonished to hear that they have abandoned and persecuted God. They eventually find out that while they were sending the poor away, they were actually sending God himself away. I always said later on, after I became acquainted with the concept of the Eucharist, that the authentic Eucharist is actually in the moment when the other comes to face me. The personality of the divine is *there*, more so than in the bread and wine."

41. See Levinas, *Levinas Reader*, 148, 187 (endnote 3): "Naturally, this is a way of saying that in social relations the real presence of the other is important; but above all it means that this presence, far from signifying pure and simple coexistence with me, or expressing itself through the romantic metaphor of 'living presence', is fulfilled in the act of hearing, and derives its meaning from the role of transcendent origin played by the word that is offered. It is to the extent that the word refuses to become flesh that it assures a presence among us . . . But all signification does not derive from experience, does not resolve into a manifestation. The formal structure of signifyingness,

wherein I utter my "anarchic response, in my responsibility for the other."[42] In the phenomenon of the Eucharist, the response of Christ for us is audible: "I give myself up for you." An ironic change in positions subverts the primacy of the ego through the backdoor: the epiphany of the Lord of the universe comes in the form of slave, servant and hostage in order for the ego to recognize its poverty, returning the primacy of place, once again, to the other. One who receives the Eucharist willfully accepts responsibility for the other just as Christ willfully accepted responsibility for her to the point of his death for her.[43] The saying, in this context, can be heard as the voice of the ever hidden and incomprehensible God the Father, who issues the command to be responsible for the stranger in just, that is, righteous and holy, living. It is this saying to which Christ is found obedient; it is this saying that remains in the aftermath of the death of the just one for all of those who bear the possibility of following in his stead.[44] Thinking the Eucharist through the logic of Levinas, its double phenomenality is not a matter of visible-invisible, revealed-concealed, but of call-response: the call of the saying and its trace in the pattern of living put on display in Christ, and the ensuing response of the recipient of the Eucharist: to become as Christ in accepting the summons to responsibility and substitution, one-for-the-other.

In like fashion, Christ in the Eucharist epitomizes the tenderness and gentleness of the feminine genius set forth by Levinas. In the Eucharist, the epiphany of Christ is at once that of the lover and beloved. In his radical form of substitution, Christ aims at the frailty (*faiblesse*) of the other, fearing

---

the-one-for-the-other, does not from the first amount to a 'showing oneself.' Suffering for another, for example, has a meaning in which knowing is adventitious."

42. Levinas, *Otherwise than Being*, 149.

43. Cf. Phil 2:5–8: "Have among yourselves the same attitude that is also yours in Christ Jesus, / Who, though he was in the form of God, / did not regard equality with God something to be grasped. Rather he emptied himself, / taking the form of a slave, / coming in human likeness; / and found human in appearance, he humbled himself, / becoming obedient to death, even death on a cross" (NAB); and Luke 22:27: "For who is greater: the one seated at table or the one who serves? Is it not the one seated at table? I am among you as the one who serves" (NAB); and John 13:12–15: "So when he had washed their feet [and] put his garments back on and reclined at table again, he said to them, 'Do you realize what I have done for you? You call me "teacher" and "master," and rightly so, for indeed I am. If I, therefore, the master and teacher, have washed your feet, you ought to wash one another's feet. I have given you a model to follow, so that as I have done for you, you should also do'" (NAB); and John 10:17–18: "For this reason the Father loves me, because I lay down my life, that I may take it again. No one takes it from me, but I lay it down on my own accord. I have power to lay it down, and I have power to take it again; this charge I have received from my Father" (RSV).

44. Cf. Wis 1:12—2:24.

for her and coming to her assistance.[45] Herein Christ "indulges in compassion, is absorbed in the commonplace of the caress."[46] Coming as food and drink, Christ symbolically and literally gives himself as nourishment for the weary one, sacramentally caressing and soothing the beloved in all her integral dimensions.[47] Christ invites the stranger to his "warmth [and] gentleness of intimacy," the hospitality and welcome of a safe-haven, a new and secure dwelling for the beloved.[48] Likewise does Christ assume the place of the beloved: an advent of humility under the appearance of bread and wine, food and drink—a frailty that speaks a word of tenderness to be recognized in the voice of the stranger.[49] It is me (*moi*) who am to care for the stranger, to assume the responsibility for her in her frailty and vulnerability. To consume Christ, the stranger, is to willfully accept the stranger's needs as paramount, to welcome her into myself as a sanctuary of care, to become her lover and friend insofar as her servant.[50] This is not a mute receptivity of a mute transubstantiated host, but a lively and sonorous dialogue of care and compassion—a dialogue in which words spark action and desire is not satiated but rekindled with each new loving word and caress, speaking life and peace into the other who first gave life to me in the summons provocatively proclaimed in my response: Here I am (for you)!

45. Cf. Levinas, *Totality and Infinity*, 256: "Love aims at the Other; it aims at him in his frailty [*faiblesse*] . . . To love is to fear for another, to come to the assistance of his frailty. In this frailty as in the dawn rises the Loved, who is the Beloved . . . The epiphany of the Beloved is but one with her *regime* of tenderness"; and Eph 5:25–27.

46. Levinas, *Totality and Infinity*, 257; cf. Isa 66:12–13: "As nurslings, you shall be carried in her arms, and fondled in her lap; / As a mother comforts her son, so will I comfort you; in Jerusalem you shall find your comfort" (NAB); and Ps 131:1–2: "Lord, my heart is not proud; nor are my eyes haughty. / I do not busy myself with great matters, with things too sublime for me. / Rather, I have stilled my soul, hushed it like a weaned child. / Like a weaned child on its mother's lap, so is my soul within me" (NAB).

47. Cf. Matt 11:28–29: "Come to me, all you who labor and are burdened, and I will give you rest. Take my yoke upon you and learn from me, for I am meek and humble of heart; and you will find rest for yourselves. For my yoke is easy, and my burden light" (NAB); and Matt 23:37: "Jerusalem, Jerusalem, you who kill the prophets and stone those sent to you, how many times I yearned to gather your children together, as a hen gathers her young under her wings, but you were unwilling!" (NAB).

48. Levinas, *Totality and Infinity*, 152–56.

49. Cf. Matt 25:31–46; Isa 11:1: "But a shoot shall sprout from the stump of Jesse, and from his roots a bud shall blossom" (NAB); Isa 53:2–3: "He grew up like a sapling before him, like a shoot from the parched earth; / There was in him no stately bearing to make us look at him, nor appearance that would attract us to him. / He was spurned and avoided by men, a man of suffering, accustomed to infirmity, / One of those from whom men hide their faces, spurned, and we held him in no esteem" (NAB).

50. Cf. Song 5:16: "This is my beloved and this is my friend, O daughters of Jerusalem" (RSV).

In Ricoeur's exegesis of the metaphor and the symbol, and in Levinas's exegesis of personal responsibility and alterity, a double phenomenality is evinced that makes the double-phenomenality claim of the Eucharist not so unusual. This is to say that in the phenomenality of the metaphor, the symbol, and the relationality between oneself and another, more-than-meets-the-eye is the norm and underlying logic. These phenomena themselves operate according to a seen-unseen, call-response structure; their very operation is based on this structure bearing a double phenomenality. In all three cases, the logic of proclamation runs deeper than a minimalist surface view of the phenomenon. In all three cases, a very real invisible dimension is at play that is not a derivative or abstraction of the visible, but rather comes to light in the seen and the heard, speaking its trace in the visible, the historical, the linguistic. In this way do the metaphor, the symbol, and personal relationality serve as heuristics and actual components of the religious phenomenon, such as that of the Eucharist.

## III. Glorious Food, Drink and Responsibility: Absolute Attestation

To round out our application of Ricoeur's and Levinas's thinking pertaining to the Eucharist, it is necessary to turn to an interpretation of the Eucharist according to its various modes of attestation. Here, the aim will be to recall Ricoeur's three forms of attestation (as expounded in chapter 3), while situating Levinas's notion of attestation of/to glory as overlapping with the self-attestation of the absolute and of conscience, and to apply these various forms of attestation to the phenomenality of the Eucharist. To recall, Ricoeur's first form of attestation is the personal attestation to an event. In the phenomenality of the Eucharist, a church—a community of believers—attests to the person, Jesus of Nazareth, specifically as an attestation to his personal identity and the meaning of his life for us.[51] Though often characterized in epic proportion (and rightfully so), the person of Jesus is first attested as an in-the-flesh, historical, actual human being. That Jesus lived historically, in the flesh, ate and drank, etc., is of chief importance for the meaning, significance and truth of his life and person. The refutations of Gnostic interpretations of Jesus appear relatively early in the textual witnesses to the life of Christ: it is clear that Jesus was no mere phantasm or apparition.[52] Secondly, a simultaneous (though posterior to fleshly recogni-

51. Cf. the Niceno-Constantinopolitan Creed: "For us men and for our salvation, he came down from heaven . . ."

52. Cf. Luke 24:36–43: "As they were saying this, Jesus himself stood among them,

tion) attestation of Jesus's divine filiation and nature follows a verification of his spatio-temporal physical existence. Incarnation, or more precisely, hypostatic union, is the term used to signify the unique constitution of Jesus's personhood—one person with two natures, at once truly human and consubstantial with God the Father. This tenet of Christian faith is understood according to the logic of hypostasis, as illustrated above. It expunges the inaccuracies of pantheism, monophysitism, and Nestorianism in favor of a piercing pronouncement of Christ's incarnate Person *as* (conjunctionally) true human *and* true God. Yet the doctrine of the Incarnation, as it was articulated eventually in the Ecumenical Councils of the first few centuries AD, has developed gradually and has been inferred *a fortiori* through further theological reflection on the testimony of the original historical community that surrounded Jesus and on the traditions handed on to successive generations. Scripture holds innumerable texts that speak of testimony and witness. One such text, à propos to personal attestation to the Christ-event is 1 John 1:1–4:

> That which was from the beginning, which we have heard, which we have seen with our eyes, which we have looked upon and touched with our hands, concerning the word of life—the life was made manifest, and we saw it, and testify to it, and proclaim to you the eternal life which was with the Father and was made manifest to us—that which we have seen and heard we proclaim also to you, so that you may have fellowship with us; and our fellowship is with the Father and with his Son Jesus Christ. And we are writing this that our joy may be complete. (RSV)

---

and said to them, 'Peace to you.' But they were startled and frightened, and supposed that they saw a spirit. And he said to them, 'Why are you troubled, and why do questionings rise in your hearts? See my hands and my feet, that it is I myself; handle me, and see; for a spirit has not flesh and bones as you see that I have.' And when he had said this he showed them his hands and his feet. And while they still disbelieved for joy, and wondered, he said to them, 'Have you anything here to eat?' They gave him a piece of broiled fish, and he took it and ate it before them" (RSV); and Ignatius of Antioch (d. ca. AD 110), *Letter to the Smyrnaeans*, in Richarson, *Early Christian Fathers*, 113: "Regarding our Lord, you are absolutely convinced that on the human side he was actually sprung from David's line, Son of God according to God's will and power, actually born of a virgin, baptized by John, that 'all righteousness might be fulfilled by him,' and actually crucified for us in the flesh, under Pontius Pilate and Herod the Tetrarch . . . For it was for our sakes that he suffered all this, to save us. And he genuinely suffered, as even he genuinely raised himself. It is not as some unbelievers say, that his Passion was a sham. It's they who are a sham! Yes, and their fate will fit their fancies—they will be ghosts and apparitions. For myself, I am convinced and believe that even after the resurrection he was in the flesh."

This text is an ideal instance of personal attestation to the Christ-event: that which was made manifest (φαίνω)—that which the witnesses heard, saw and touched. It concerns the word of life (λόγου τῆς ζωῆς) that must be attested (μαρτύρομαι) and proclaimed (ἀπαγγέλλω) in order for others to enter into fellowship (κοινωνία) with the community of believers, and that the joy of these original witnesses may be full. This text signifies a mode of personal attestation: the attestation is credible inasmuch as it proceeds from the original and authentic witnesses to the Christ-event, namely, the apostolic witnesses.

Therefore the name of the letter wherein this text appears is indispensable: the first letter of John. Whether John the apostle actually wrote the letter or not is, in the end, incidental insofar as the crucial point is that the letter's identity is enmeshed in the original apostolic community, and for that reason has been deemed canonical. Yet the designation John remains important, for this is an account according to John, rather than according to an anonymous witness. The potency of the textual witness is determined according to the measure of its specific personal character and attribution. The letter is not associated with a purely anonymous witness, which would render the text spurious and inauthentic. It is a mode of personal attestation whereby the event is proclaimed with conviction according to "this one here," namely, John, or at least in a vein connected to John the apostle. Anonymity is not without fruit in the realm of ideas, but when it comes to testimony, an anonymous witness carries little clout; add one's personal name to the testimony, and the testimony functions according to the witness's credibility, public reputation and conviction. The credibility and authenticity of the witness stands or falls on the basis of his or her personal character and public recognition, as well as on the degree to which the witness is implicated in the trial.[53] Concerning those original witnesses to Christ and his life and death, many of them held fast to their testimony to the point of death, sealing their personal testimony with their own blood, just as Christ did.[54]

The eucharistic context is nestled within this community of martyrs, that is, witnesses. Not only this, but the eucharistic liturgy signifies a

53. Aristotle says as much in *Rhetoric*, Book I, §15 (1375b27–1376a33): "By ancient witnesses I mean the poets and all other notable persons whose judgments are known to all . . . There are also those witnesses who share the risk of punishment if their evidence is pronounced false. These are valid witnesses to the fact that an action was or was not done, that something is or is not the case . . . Most trustworthy of all are the ancient witnesses, since they cannot be corrupted."

54. Cf. Mark 6:17–29, Acts 6:8—8:3, and Acts 12:1–2: "About that time King Herod laid hands upon some members of the church to harm them. He had James, the brother of John, killed by the sword . . ." (NAB).

common union (communion) among those who partake: "The cup of blessing that we bless, is it not a participation [κοινωνία] in the blood of Christ? The bread that we break, is it not a participation [κοινωνία] in the body of Christ? Because the loaf of bread is one, we, though many, are one body, for we all partake of the one loaf."[55] The dynamism of the Eucharist arises in its unified diversity—the plurality of personal uniqueness that reveals an epiphany of the cosmic universal (catholicity) through a gathering up of personal particularity: "now you are Christ's body, and individually parts of it."[56] Liturgical movement proceeds from the lives of the saints that attest to the life of Christ; Christ's life would not become manifest were it not for the personal witness of others.[57] Even in the case where one personally encountered Jesus in the flesh, solitary testimony must be ratified by additional witnesses—a community of witnesses.[58] Finally, concerning the Eucharist

55. 1 Cor 10:16–17 (NAB); cf. 1 Cor 12:12–26.

56. 1 Cor 12:27 (NAB).

57. Cf. John 1:6–8, 15, 19: "A man named John was sent from God. He came for testimony, to testify to the light, so that all might believe through him. He was not the light, but came to testify to the light . . . John testified to him and cried out, saying, 'This was he of whom I said, "The one who is coming after me ranks ahead of me because he existed before me"' . . . And this is the testimony of John . . ." (NAB); John 1:40–42, 45–46: "Andrew, the brother of Simon Peter, was one of the two who heard John and followed Jesus. He first found his brother Simon and told him, 'We have found the Messiah' (which is translated Anointed). Then he brought him to Jesus . . . Philip found Nathanael and told him, 'We have found the one about whom Moses wrote in the law, and also the prophets, Jesus son of Joseph, from Nazareth.' But Nathanael said to him, 'Can anything good come from Nazareth?' Philip said to him, 'Come and see'" (NAB); Eucharistic Prayer I, Roman Rite: "For ourselves, too, we ask some share in the fellowship of your apostles and martyrs, with John the Baptist, Stephen, Matthias, Barnabas, [Ignatius, Alexander, Marcellinus, Peter, Felicity, Perpetua, Agatha, Lucy, Agnes, Cecilia, Anastasia] and all the saints." In all of these cases, Jesus is attested to by specific persons in order to be brought to light before other persons so that they, in turn, would share in their fellowship. The latter example is cited in order to show the personal and memorial context of the Eucharist: its veracity comes largely in part from the host of personal witnesses that attest to its truth and meaning; cf. Heb 12:1.

58. John 20:1–29; Deut 19:15: "One witness alone shall not take the stand against a man in regard to any crime or any offense of which he may be guilty; a judicial fact shall be established only on the testimony of two or three witnesses" (NAB); Matt 18:16; Matt 18:20: "For where two or three are gathered together in my name, there am I in the midst of them" (NAB); Gal 1:18; 2:1–2, 9: "Then after three years I went up to Jerusalem to confer with Cephas and remained with him for fifteen days . . . Then after fourteen years I again went up to Jerusalem with Barnabas, taking Titus along also. I went up in accord with a revelation, and I presented to them the gospel that I preach to the Gentiles—but privately to those of repute—so that I might not be running, or have run, in vain . . . and when they recognized the grace bestowed on me, James and Cephas and John, who were reputed to be pillars, gave me and Barnabas their right hands in partnership, that we should go to the Gentiles and they to the circumcised" (NAB).

directly, we need look no further than the testimony of Paul (the earliest written account of the institution of the Eucharist in Scripture), within the larger testimonial context of Scripture: "For I received from the Lord what I also handed on to you . . ."[59] The identity of Paul as a legitimate apostle in relation to the community of the original twelve apostles is imperative for the credibility of the injunction to repeat the memorial ritual of the Lord's Supper. In sum, the (phenomenological) truth and meaning of an event can never stand on its own, but always must be attested personally in order to make its appearance, both for those who witness the event directly and for those who were not privy to the event's original self-disclosure. Even those who were at the scene of an event remain under the shroud of the event's elusiveness, obscurity and ambiguity; every event is received as a fragment to be interpreted and proclaimed to others by way of personal testimony.

The second form of attestation, explicated by Ricoeur and reflected in the notion of the saying in Levinas, is the self-attestation of the event itself, especially the (non-)phenomenality of the absolute. It is first necessary to propose a link between Ricoeur's notion of the absolute and Levinas's notion of the saying, especially since Levinas suggests that the absolute is "an abusive word," as it smacks of totality.[60] While Ricoeur identifies this form of testimony as "the aspect of *manifestation* in testimony," Levinas is careful to prevent the notion of the absolute from being reduced to phenomenal manifestation, or simply part of the cognitive process of gathering up more of the manifestation of manifestation. Instead, for Levinas, the saying belongs to an order of non-phenomenality, and is beyond representation.[61] The saying posits itself only as a trace in the testimony of responsibility in the summoned. A moment of manifestation does occur in Levinas's proposal, but it often comes disguised under the term "epiphany of the face of the other" (*l'autrui*)—a manifestation that is more in the form of a word from the other than an appearance as such, in order to keep alterity unsullied by the ma-

59. 1 Cor 11:23; cf. 1 Cor 11:23–34.

60. Levinas, *Time and the Other*, 107: "The exteriority of the face is extra-ordinary. It is extra-ordinary for order is justice. It is extra-ordinary or absolute in the etymological sense of this adjective, as always separable from every relationship and synthesis, tearing itself away from the very justice where this extraordinary enters. The absolute—an abusive word—could probably take place concretely and have meaning only in the phenomenology, or in the rupture of phenomenology, which the face of the other calls forth." Cf. Levinas, *Otherwise than Being*, 147: "The saying in the said of the witness born signifies in a plot other than that which is spread out in a theme, other than that which attaches a noesis to a noema, a cause to an effect, the memorable past of the present. This plot connects to what detaches itself absolutely, to the Absolute. The detachment of the Infinite from the thought that seeks to thematize it and the language that tries to hold it in the said is what we have called *illeity*."

61. Cf. Levinas, *Otherwise than Being*, 150.

nipulative tendencies of the ego over the various modes of manifestation.[62] The face appears inasmuch as it speaks. In any case, the point here is to show that a linkage between Ricoeur's notion of the absolute and Levinas's notion of the saying is not without warrant.

Both the absolute and the saying, first of all, are not to be identified with the testator or the testator's conscience: the absolute and the saying are entirely other than the testator. In both cases, the consciousness of the testator must be divested according to the counterconsciousness of an obsession of proximity with the transcendent other: "an event that strips consciousness of its initiative, that undoes me and puts me before an Other in a state of guilt; an event that puts me in accusation—a persecuting indictment, for it is prior to all wrongdoing—and that leads me to the *self*, to the accusative that is not preceded by any nominative."[63] The imposing force of the other—ultimately of the absolute or the saying—merits an original affirmation on the part of the testator, a thetic judgment that functions as an assurance of the ecstatic beyond of the absolute or the saying. For both Ricoeur and Levinas, the authentic testator's life assumes the pattern of sacrifice: the one-for-the-other of substitution whereby the witness attests to that which is beyond himself in the *Gestalt* of love. This could be called the eucharistic form, as expounded above, wherein Christ speaks the utmost expression of substitution "in which Christ, the perfect 'one-for-the-other' of substitution and expiation, draws close in the proximity and sensibility of sacrament and evokes responsibility in us such that we, sharing in this meal, are constituted no longer according to the for-itself of subjectivity, but as the one-for-the-other of responsibility."[64] In this way, the participant in the *koinonia* in the body and blood of Christ attests in faith to the *logos* of the absolute, appearing in the figure of the Pasch.

The third form of attestation occurring in the thought of Ricoeur, coinciding with Levinas's notion of "the subjectivity of the subject that makes itself a sign," is the self-attestation of conscience.[65] In this form of attestation, the self "bears witness to the glory of the Infinite" as well as "to its ownmost power of being."[66] For both Ricoeur and Levinas, this form of attestation

62. Cf. ibid., 151–52: "Thematization is then inevitable, so that signification itself show itself, but does so in the sophism with which philosophy begins, in the betrayal which philosophy is called upon to reduce."

63. Levinas, *Entre Nous*, 58–59.

64. Purcell, "*Agape* of Eating," 336.

65. Levinas, *Otherwise than Being*, 151.

66. Ibid., and Ricoeur, *Figuring the Sacred*, 271. Cf. Levinas, *Entre Nous*, 128–29, 132: "Does the 'knowing' of the prereflexive consciousness of self *know*, properly speaking? A confused consciousness, an implicit consciousness, preceding all intention—or

is characterized as radical passivity of the subject vis-à-vis the other. The Eucharist is, again, a phenomenological episode par excellence wherein this peculiar form of attestation is inscribed. In the eucharistic liturgy we are reminded of who we ought to be, we undergo an examination of conscience in the context of a proclamation announcing the most profound possibilities of our being. Jesus occupies center stage of this anthropophagous counter-theurgy in which we are reminded of our primary raison d'être: to love one another as Christ has loved us.[67] This anamnestic dialogue between God and humanity, mediated by the God-human Christ—the *logos* made flesh—piques conscience according to its own self-attestation inspired by the in-breaking of the other. Into conscience is breathed the "I believe that I can" that overcomes its contrary of suspicion through "the *assurance of being oneself acting and suffering*."[68] Through eucharistic liturgy, conscience overcomes the post-lapsarian suspicion of total depravity by receiving anew the vision of its rectitude and virtue. Conscience again outstrips listless lassitude according to a fresh *metanoia*, a renewed conversion to Christ, the prophetic voice of the other spoken in the same. Conforming to the pattern of Christ's servitude becomes possible in receiving the Eucharist as that which feeds conscience and nourishes hope by giving up oneself for the other.[69]

In retrospect, the three forms of attestation—personal attestation to an event, self-attestation of the absolute, and self-attestation of conscience—are all evident in the Eucharist. All three forms coincide in this prosopic phenomenon of ultimate concern (Tillich). The Eucharist, thereby, could be called a phenomenon of attestation. Yet, as we will see below, that is not all. Attestation itself must become incarnate through the modes of manifestation and proclamation, for attestation both appears and announces itself.

---

returned from all intention—is not act, but pure passivity. Not only by virtue of its being-without-having-chosen-to-be, or its fall into a jumble of possibles already realized before all assumption, as in the Heideggerian *Geworfenheit*. 'Conscience' that, rather than signifying a knowledge of self, is a self-effacement or discretion of presence . . . In the deposition by the *I* of its sovereignty of self, in its modality as hateful self, ethics, but probably also the very spirituality of the soul, signifies. The human, or human inwardness, is the return to inwardness of nonintentional consciousness, to bad conscience, to its possibility of fearing injustice more than death, of preferring injustice undergone to injustice committed, and what justifies being to what secures it. To be or not to be is probably not the question par excellence."

67. Cf. John 15:12: "This is my commandment, that you love one another as I have loved you."

68. Ricoeur, *Course of Recognition*, 91, and Ricoeur, *Oneself as Another*, 22–23.

69. Cf. John 13:14–15: "If I, therefore, the master and teacher, have washed your feet, you ought to wash one another's feet. I have given you a model to follow, so that as I have done for you, you should also do" (NAB).

The Eucharist, therefore, can be called more properly a phenomenon of manifestation-proclamation-attestation. Having traversed the application of the thought of Marion, Ricoeur and Levinas to the Eucharist, we will now proceed to juxtapose their respective positions according to the manifestation ↔ proclamation dialectic, and further, according to the trilectic of testimony. The animation and vivacity of this trilectic will prove generative for advanced understandings of the phenomenon of the Eucharist.

## IV. Unity in Diversity: When Two Worlds Collide

In reflecting on the subjectivity of *eros*, Levinas writes, "Fecundity evinces a unity that is not opposed to multiplicity, but, in the precise sense of the term, engenders it."[70] This was exactly the point made in chapter 1: the law of a living dialectic is the law of unity in plurality. This is not a unity of totality but a unity of difference. The dialectic becomes fecund inasmuch as each of its poles is not reduced to its opposite; the integrity and distinctness of each must be maintained for the dialectic to prove fruitful. Manifestation and proclamation, as two divergent poles of the dialectic, exhibit the tendency to occlude one another. Manifestation innately resists the desacralizing prophetic voice while proclamation resists the sanctioning of sacred places and obsessive-compulsive fixations on the hallowed. One need go no further than the observation of Catholic and Protestant tendencies to offset one another. According to a typical caricature, Catholics accuse Protestants of biblical fundamentalism while Protestants accuse Catholics of idolatry. Stereotypically speaking, in Catholic life and worship, the manifest sacrament is primary, while in Protestant life and worship, the in-breaking power of the proclaimed word is principal. Similar to Protestant Christianity, the antecedence of the divine word is detectable in Judaism as well, wherein divine utterance obliterates the idols that clutter its passageway. We have called upon three thinkers of these three respective faith traditions—Marion (Catholic), Ricoeur (Protestant), Levinas (Jewish)—in order to apply their respective thinking to the question of the phenomenality of the Eucharist, itself a phenomenon attested under the roof of Christianity.[71] The argument has been made that Marion's thinking represents the pole of manifestation,

70. Levinas, *Totality and Infinity*, 273.

71. Unfortunately, this project has neither space nor expertise to treat the phenomenality of the Pesach as well as that of the Eucharist. However, as a sidenote, it is indicative enough to cite the meaning of the word that refers to the liturgical text of the Pesach, "Haggadah": "telling." Telling falls under the rubric of proclamation rather than manifestation.

while Ricoeur's and Levinas's thinking models the pole of proclamation, as well as the neutral play of testimony that ultimately configures the trilectic. The time has arrived to put these three thinkers into irenic conversation and confrontation in order to test the fecundity of the trilectic of testimony. This trilectic, that claims to explicate the phenomenality of the Eucharist will be described anew to allow for the respective positions of Marion, Ricoeur and Levinas to engage in fruitful dialogue.

## A. Marion on the Eucharist

Given the schema of the trilectic of testimony as applied to the question of the phenomenality of the Eucharist, Marion's position is to be located securely within the manifestation pole of the trilectic. Marion understands the Eucharist as a phenomenon of manifestation, yet bearing a dimension of testimony within itself: the primary self-attestation of the Eucharist with a secondary and incidental witness to its appearing. This can be described in terms of the self-attestation of the Eucharist as event, as well as the self-attestation of the absolute in the form of the Eucharist. However, for Marion, the Eucharist is primarily a matter of apparition, namely, of the Christ-event. Even though Marion posits Christ as the chief hermeneut of an infinite hermeneutics, these hermeneutics are concerned exclusively with the manifestation of Christ's Person—an "in-the-flesh" saturating phenomenon that appears according to its peculiar mode of auto-manifestation. The role of the witnesses in relation to the event is minimal and subordinate to the primacy of the auto-manifestation of the phenomenon itself by itself. For Marion, the Eucharist is in no way primarily a phenomenon of proclamation, but rather a phenomenon of manifestation wherein "an absolute hermeneutic is announced, and not only does it reveal nothing, but it shines by its absence; barely named, it disappears to the benefit of the eucharistic moment . . . where the Word in person, silently, speaks and blesses, speaks to the extent that he blesses . . . pass[ing] through every text and all speech, toward, again, the absolute referent ('I am,' Luke 24:39 = John 8:24 and 58 = Exodus 3:14) . . . the carnal Word [who] comes to the community."[72] Christ is only and finally recognized in the breaking of the bread. According to Marion, this relationship between Christ the Word and hermeneutics can be called a *theo*logy rather than a theo*logy*: the enfleshed Word is both referent and hermeneut whose in-the-flesh manifestation is the core of the Eucharist. In this conception, the chief witness of the incarnate Word is

72. Marion, *God without Being*, 150–52; cf. Marion, *Prolegomena to Charity*, 124–52.

the bishop, or priest in his stead, insofar as he alone "receives authority to go beyond the words as far as the Word, because he alone finds himself invested by the *persona Christi*."[73] Ultimately, Christ the Word is known "nonverbally, in flesh and Eucharist."[74] The form of blessing of the Eucharist is not that of words, but that of a saturating theophany of negative certitude in which hands are extended in love only to be nailed brutally to a cross of wood.[75] The cruciform is not speech but silent blessing: an expression of love that saturates according to its overflowing givenness and its recognition of divine giving-ness. Herein appears Marion's greatest case for givenness: the givenness of suffering.[76] Suffering is the phenomenon that stupefies and benumbs, leaving the recipients and bystanders speechless.[77] As a saturating phenomenon, suffering strips the ego of its imperial prerogative and introduces a series of percepts that cannot be paired with concepts. Reason is undone and the question of theodicy becomes first theology. The mute Christ on the cross is the height of his personal manifestation in the flesh, which itself is the memorial acclamation of the eucharistic moment: "when we eat this bread and drink this cup, we proclaim your death, O Lord, until you come again."

## B. Ricoeur and Levinas on the Eucharist

Yet it is exactly here that the proclamation pole of the dialectic intervenes: the crucifixion of Christ is manifest inasmuch as it is told, proclaimed and preached (Ricoeur): "we proclaim your death, O Lord." And further, the Eucharist proceeds from a context of alterity—a *Sitz im Leben*—that is characterized as a summons to responsibility for the other (Levinas). The epiphany of the commanding face precedes and engenders the phenomenality of the Eucharist. Christ, as other, first has recognized me as other and has given

73. Ibid., 153.

74. Ibid., 155.

75. For more on the notion of "negative certitude," see Marion, *Certitudes negatives*; Gschwandtner, *Degrees of Givenness*, 10–14, 130–37; and Gschwandtner, "Marion and Negative Certainty."

76. The "givenness of suffering," as coined here, is not primarily in reference to a particular text of Marion on suffering per se, but rather an extrapolation and application of his proposal of givenness.

77. Yet even here the dialectic starts up again. The proclamation pole contends that the phenomena of pain and suffering appear insofar as they speak, even if this speech is in the form of a scream, desperate profanities, incomprehensible groaning or utterances. For example, see Sophocles, *Philoctetes*, §§730–56: "I am undone, child . . . I am bitten, child . . . Pa-pai, / apappapai, papappapappapappapai" (ἀπόλωλα, τέκνον·βρύκομαι, τέκνον·παπαῖ, / ἀπαππαπαῖ, παπαππαπαππαπαππαπαῖ).

up himself for me so that I may live, in turn, by recognizing the stranger as other and substituting myself for her so that she may live. Neither givenness nor manifestation precedes the epiphany of the face, the summons to responsibility. However, here the manifestation pole of the dialectic breaks in again: the epiphany of the face, while claiming to resist a characterization of manifestation, actually appears insofar as it is an epiphany of the face of a unique and individuated other (*l'autrui*). Who is this other for whom I am responsible if not "this one here"? And the proclamation pole answers, "how can the appearance of "this one here" appear *as* such without its assimilation and appropriation through (1) language—the medium of our thinking, (2) interpretation according to a symbolic universe—in a word, belonging, and (3) a creative and intentional construal understanding "this" as "that"? (Ricoeur) . . . et cetera ad infinitum. The assertions and rebuttals of the manifestation ↔ proclamation dialectic continue in like fashion without end. And this is the point of the dialectic: a world without end due to the incessant creative communicative potential that the dialectic unlocks.

Let us now turn our attention more intently toward the proclamation pole of the dialectic. This is where the respective positions of Ricoeur and Levinas are to be posited, attesting to the phenomenological flexibility that warrants consulting Levinas's work in relation to the question of the phenomenality of the Eucharist, even though he was not an adherent of the Christian faith. It is testimony, as the backdrop of any sort of proclamation, which allows there to be distance between the proclaimer and that which is proclaimed; the testator testifies to that which she is not. By framing the phenomenality of the Eucharist according to a trilectic of testimony, a distance ensues that allows people of divergent belief sets to talk about a religious phenomenon in terms of its publicness, plausibility and intelligibility. The trilectic of testimony allows there to be discussion about a phenomenon that is hypothetical, prioritizing possibility over actuality. Phenomenology, in its descriptive and scientific functionality, neutralizes the playing field of phenomenality to give space for the uncanny and, at the same time, common ground among strangers. By recognizing the phenomenality of testimony, operating in both manifestation and proclamation, all can enter the conversation and acknowledge that testimony serves as the underlying principle of unity inside all phenomenality. In this sense, testimony itself is not absolute, but bears the potential of pointing to the absolute. The question of the specific identity of the absolute can be bracketed in the name of the phenomenological *epoché* in order to trace the phenomenological relations between that which is manifest, that which is proclaimed, and that which is attested. The "that" of the "that which" can be interchangeable and serve as a placeholder within first-level phenomenological description. Whether the "that" is "God," "Jesus," "*Krishna*," "*Allah*," "the self," "sex," "money," "power," "the other," etc., matters little within a first-level phenomenological description. The "that" can simply be considered as an ultimate concern that promises meaning and purpose for spending time and energy in talking about it. However, in the claim at hand, "Jesus as the Christ" has been named the ultimate concern within the phenomenality of the Eucharist, thereby entering into a second-level phenomenological description, but not yet a transcendental, reflective, thetic judgment, a task that will be postponed until chapter 6. In fact, the Eucharist could not be discussed phenomenologically without referring to the primary referent of this phenomenon, namely, Jesus of Nazareth, son of Mary, Son of God. Nevertheless, this assertion of the hypostatic identity of Jesus of Nazareth can be treated at arm's reach because of the phenomenality of testimony that extends such a truth-claim to the decision of faith. Let us then proceed to examine more closely the Ricoeur-Levinas side of the manifestation ↔ proclamation dialectic.

## C. From Contemplation to Ethics in Ubiquitous Temporality

The proclamation pole of the trilectic of testimony signifies the respective positions of Ricoeur and Levinas concerning the priority of proclamation, testimony, and the movement to and from the ethical. It has been mentioned several times above that testimony serves as a vector to the ethical, evinced in the three forms of attestation: the personal attestation to an event, the self-attestation of the absolute, the self-attestation of conscience. This poses a challenge to Marion's phenomenological thinking as manifestation and adoration. Contemplating cosmological saturating givenness could give reason for a perpetual pause, such as those tender moments between lovers in which all worldly concerns vanish as each is enraptured in the loving gaze of the other. And in fact, some people claim to respond to the vocation to the contemplative life that constitutes a unique lifestyle of mystical contemplation. One has only to think of a few of the great mystics to recognize this possibility: Athanasius's Antony, Thérèse of Lisieux, Catherine of Siena, Teresa of Avila, John of the Cross. A phenomenology of givenness quickly lends itself to a theology of givenness, which, in turn, fosters a life of contemplation and adoration. There even can be a temptation to contemplate to the point of abandoning one's concern for one's neighbors. In other words, the ethical imperative to responsibility can be eclipsed by the saturating beauty that surrounds the human subject.[78] Nevertheless, the paradox of

78. In the United States, for instance, this originally contemplative attitude can be disfigured rather quickly: many people can be observed spending all of their waking

the Mary and Martha narrative testifies to the importance of contemplation, even before meaningful service, though here too is evinced a dialectic relationship.[79]

Secondly, Ricoeur's and Levinas's concern with the mediation of language and the hermeneutics of the face to face pull at a presumptive phenomenological auto-manifestation and self-givenness of the phenomenon. For Ricoeur and Levinas, *es gibt* is better put *es gibt als* . . . and *es gibt nach* . . . Yet the dialectic reminds us that this revision does not supplant the original expression, *es gibt*, but simply augments and enhances it. One could say that the *es gibt* depends upon the *als* . . . and *nach* . . . inasmuch as the *als* . . . and *nach* . . . depend upon the *es gibt*. Phenomenality *as* such can be spoken of only in terms that do not jettison either one of the parties of the trilectic. Phenomenality *as* such depends on phenomenality as *such*, and vice versa. As soon as one of the parties takes leave (by force or otherwise), an adequate phenomenological description collapses. This is a serious danger of the phenomenological method: it exalts the *epoché* at the expense of an accurate rendering of phenomenality; the baby can be thrown out oftentimes (and tragically) with the bathwater, the kernel is at risk of being discarded along with the husk. The proposal of the trilectic of testimony seeks to prevent this tragedy from recurring.

---

(and sleeping) moments "enjoying the good things in life," without living in concern for, and solidarity with, their neighbors, and at times and with great regret, myself included. Cf. Eccl 2:24; 3:12–13: "There is nothing better for man than to eat and drink and provide himself with good things by his labors. Even this, I realized, is from the hand of God . . . I recognized that there is nothing better than to be glad and to do well during life. For every man, moreover, to eat and drink and enjoy the fruit of all his labor is a gift of God" (NAB). How quickly a gift of God can die in its failure to bless in the form of Levinasian ethics.

79. Cf. Luke 10:38–42: "Martha, Martha, you are anxious and worried about many things. There is need of only one thing. Mary has chosen the better part and it will not be taken from her" (NAB); Thérèse of Lisieux, *Story of a Soul*, 257–58: "A soul that is burning with love cannot remain inactive. No doubt, she will remain at Jesus's feet as did Mary Magdalene, and she will listen to His sweet and burning words. Appearing to do nothing, she will give much more than Martha who torments herself with many things and wants her sister to imitate her. It is not Martha's works that Jesus finds fault with; His divine Mother submitted humbly to these works all through her life since she had to prepare the meals of the Holy Family. It is only the *restlessness* of His ardent hostess that He willed to correct"; Teresa of Avila, *Interior Castle*, 437: "Believe me, Martha and Mary must join together in order to show hospitality to the Lord and have him always present and not host him badly by failing to give him something to eat. How would Mary, always seated at his feet, provide him with food if her sister did not help her? His food is that in every way possible we draw souls that they may be saved and praise him always."

Third, it is necessary to come to terms with the role of time within the trilectic of testimony at work in eucharistic liturgy. Marion, Ricoeur and Levinas each add a peculiar dimension to the question of liturgical tempo. From Marion's phenomenology of manifestation, the time of the present is primary according to the optic of givenness given in the suspended present. If memory is engaged, it is for the sake of re-presenting the given phenomenon to consciousness in another present recollection. If the future is anticipated, it is for the sake of bracing oneself for oncoming givenness. From Ricoeur's phenomenology of proclamation, the time of the future is primary according to the magnitude of hope. Vindication and the fullness of truth's revelation remain always on the eschatological horizon of resurrection and the temporality of the not yet. Interpretation acts always in anticipation of its consequences, and definitive verdicts are postponed to the degree that the future's revelation is suspended indefinitely. Subjectivity's identity is composed of its latent potential to be realized as the future unfolds—"I believe that I can"—even more than the sum total of its checkered past. Levinas attests to the time of the past—more precisely, the time of the immemorial past. Levinas contests that a past more distant that the historical past cannot be accessed by historical memory, extant texts, ancient archeological artifacts, or even carbon dating. This is the history of the infinite that paradoxically transcends chronological and numerical history but nevertheless is witnessed in the ethical relationship between me and the other. Responsibility and its infinite vocation testify to the immemorial past and the call of the other that always beat me to the scene of recognition and responsive action. Altogether, the temporal loci of Marion, Ricoeur and Levinas contribute to a trilectical comprehension of liturgical tempo.

Eucharistic liturgy is punctuated by temporal fluctuation between past, present and future. This fluctuation occurs so frequently that we could speak of the ubiquitous temporality of liturgy. It is tethered neither to chronological time nor to the time of passing seasons and cycles of life and death. For time eternal is life without the interruption of death's alleged terminus and cessation. Beyond the marketplace notion of chronological time (*kronos*) is the transcendent and interpersonal notion of liturgical time (*kairos*). It is the time of lovers, the dramatic stage upon which time stands still and yet moves faster than the speed of light, the *mise-en-scène* in which past, present and future all bleed into one another without confusing their irreducible difference. The eucharistic prayer of the Roman Rite, in its antiphonal sequence of Preface, Thanksgiving, Epiclesis I, Institution Narrative, Anamnesis, Epiclesis II, and Intercessions, effects a crossfertilization of temporality that bears the fruits of conversion, healing, reconciliation, virtue and peace (*shalom*). Both past and future break into the present, in turn broken apart by its inability to reduce alterity to homogeneity. Past enters into the present through *memoria* in which both historical and immemorial past are witnessed in the *hic et nunc*. Future enters into the present through prophecy and prolepsis whereby the future's consummation is witnessed in its present proclamation. The present makes its great escape at the behest of the rush of past and future, just as the self takes leave of itself in its responsorial of responsibility for the other and worship of divine alterity incarnate. The following figure illustrates these gestures of temporal ubiquity:

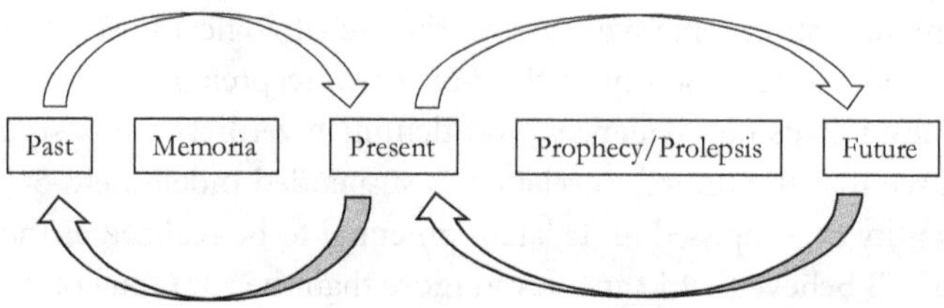


Apocalyptic consequence of a forgotten past is converted into a just and loving present bound in solicitude to an ambivalent past both lamented and celebrated and a resolute future both promised and anticipated. The work of Marion, Ricoeur and Levinas in combination again gives us phenomenological insight into the time of liturgy. Anamnestic contemplation leads to an ethical future filled with hope. Nothing is lost in relation to the transformative power of the cross. The cross of Christ is the redemptive axis point at which a regrettable past is redeemed and an august future is assured. Liturgy, therefore, is witness to creation, witness to redemption.

## V. The Witness

The entire complexity of the Eucharist-phenomenon will be paused at this point in order to isolate just one of its components: its potential recipient. The witness to the Eucharist, in a first-level reflection, occupies the neutral position of the trilectic of testimony, witnessing the interplay between manifestation and proclamation. As a third party witness, however, he or she will be confronted eventually with the truth-claim of the dialectical phenomenon: "Is it true?" Judgment can only be suspended for so long . . . and then it is time for a person to decide for himself or herself whether a phenomenon is true or false to its claims, even amidst the cloudiness of its ambiguity. There is a difference between the responses "I see what you mean" and "I believe."[80] The former conforms to a proposed phenomenological description, while the latter enters the realm of transcendental judgment at the risk of missing the mark. The third party witness has the privilege of recognizing the dialectic before its distortion and breakdown; the witness is duped neither by the totalizing tendency of manifestation, nor the desacralizing iconoclastic force of proclamation. The witness looks, listens and touches, groping for truth and authenticity. While a transcendental reflection on the status of the truth-claim of the Eucharist will be postponed until chapter 6, it is enough for now to indicate that the witness stands at the threshold of doubt and belief; for the home of faith is ambiguity.

The witness recognizes that he or she is surrounded—above and below, before and behind—by the infinite (A–Ω), asking again the question of being betwixt life's bookends of an unfathomable whence and whither.[81] The witness represents the culmination of attestation: (1) personal attestation to an event, (2) self-attestation of the event itself, especially that of the absolute, (3) self-attestation of conscience itself. At the threshold of doubt and belief, the witness is confronted at the crossroads of the multitude of attestation. The witness is engendered by the interplay between the various modes of attestation, summoned to decide personally, thus becoming a witness a second time by proclaiming his or her irrevocable decision to others. At this juncture, the witness, by way of a personal decision of judgment, is incorporated and initiated into a communal *ecclesía*, while a new third party witness arises as onlooker and listener.[82] As taken up in the fertile play of the trilectic of testimony, the witness remains in the struggle between faith and doubt, between the totalizing tendencies of religious truth in the form of manifestation or proclamation. This perpetual tension is necessary for the trilectic not to collapse. All the same, the witness is called to forfeit the temptation of temptation in order to live freely in the eternity of the

80. Cf. John 4:39–42: "Many of the Samaritans of that town began to believe in him because of the word of the woman who testified, 'He told me everything I have done.' When the Samaritans came to him, they invited him to stay with them; and he stayed there two days. Many more began to believe in him because of his word, and they said to the woman, 'We no longer believe because of your word; for we have heard for ourselves, and we know that this is truly the savior of the world'" (NAB).

81. The symbol A–Ω connotes the infinite, wherein the beginning is the end and the end is the beginning.

82. Cf. Acts 1:8: "But you shall receive power when the Holy Spirit has come upon you; and you shall be my witnesses in Jerusalem and in all Judea and Samaria and to the end of the earth" (RSV); Matt 28:18–20: "And Jesus came and said to them, 'All authority in heaven and on earth has been given to me. Go therefore and make disciples of all nations, baptizing them in the name of the Father and of the Son and of the Holy Spirit, teaching them to observe all that I have commanded you; and behold, I am with you always, to the close of the age'" (RSV); and 1 John 1:1–4.

trilectic—not merely exercising a freedom of indifference, but a righteous freedom for excellence.[83] In addition, for the complacent skeptic, to suspend decision indefinitely, for or against, is also to decide.[84] The personal decision of the witness is formulated, in the end, according to the self-attestation of the absolute and the self-attestation of the witness's personal conscience. Accosted by the underlying depth of the infinite (A–Ω), the ultimate concern manifest and proclaimed by the absolute and conscience, and acknowledged in one's finitude, mortality and radical dependence, the moment of decision has arrived. The Eucharist appears as a phenomenon that posits a claim that concerns the human person in an ultimate way: a discourse and manifestation of life, death and salvation; a promise of ultimate hope; a healing balm for suffering; a remedy for waywardness and damage. According to such points of recognition, the Eucharist can be interpreted as a phenomenon of manifestation-proclamation-attestation, exhibiting fruitfulness according to the measure of the dynamic interplay among the distinct parties of the trilectic of testimony.

## VI. The Trilectical Reduction and the Kingdom of God

Recalling the narrative of the various phenomenological reductions from chapter 1, let us resume our inquiry into the possibility of a reduction that is one yet many. If Marion's third reduction to givenness claims to yield access to the paradoxical phenomenon—the saturated phenomenon—and even to the doubly saturated phenomenon, the paradox of all paradoxes—the revelatory phenomenon—then might it be possible to conceive of a reduction that itself operates as paradoxical? In other words, is it possible to construct a reduction of the reduction as a refusal of the temptation to totality? Is it possible to avoid reductionism by appealing to the testimony of the paradox, of the more-than-one, of plurality—a testimony that is itself not yet another totalizing proposal? For instance, could the respective reductions of Marion and Levinas be deployed at the same time? Could the donative/erotic reduction (Marion) be performed alongside the vocative/ethical/(agapic?) reduction (Levinas), all the while being kept in motion by the hermeneutical/testimonial anti-reduction (Ricoeur)? Could the trilectic of

83. See Pinckaers, *Sources of Christian Ethics*, 327–78; Levinas, "The Temptation of Temptation," in *Nine Talmudic Readings*, 30–50; and Wallenfang, "Levinas and Marion on Law and Freedom."

84. Cf. Rev 3:14–16: "To the angel of the church in Laodicea, write this: 'The Amen, the faithful and true witness, the source of God's creation, says this: "I know your works; I know that you are neither hot nor cold. I wish you were either cold or hot. So, because you are lukewarm, neither hot nor cold, I will spit you out of my mouth"'" (NAB).

manifestation ↔ proclamation ↔ attestation serve as programmatic for the most radical reduction yet? Can Hegel's synthesis be suspended perpetually in favor of a vulnerable antinomy of the both/and?[85] Can we conceive of a trilectical reduction that would sustain the tension between Marion's, Levinas's, and Ricoeur's reductions and promote their complementarity? Such a proposal may save phenomenology from its most dangerous weakness, which is also at the same time its most cherished strength: the power of the reduction. The trouble is that the reduction can fall quickly into a brand of reductionism and thereby delimit possibility.

Can we imagine a reduction that includes within itself both givenness and ethical exigency, both manifestation and proclamation, both love and responsibility, both *eros* and *agape*, both interior contemplation and exterior action—without conflation? Not only one, but also the other?[86] This book answers all of these questions in the affirmative and wagers an attempt at exercising such a paradoxical reduction. The recognition of the possibility of the trilectical reduction also reinforces the promises of interdisciplinary studies in the form of liberal arts pedagogy. While all disciplines have their fair share of reductive tendencies, the idea of unity in difference may serve as the antidote to prevent individual disciplines from solipsism. In fact, this book attempts an interdisciplinary study of the Eucharist, incorporating intricate philosophical methods that greatly enhance a postmodern consideration of the Eucharist as a phenomenon. Its underlying premise is that philosophy and theology mutually inform one another. The question of the Eucharist gives new insights to phenomenology, and phenomenology provides helpful schemas through which to understand the Eucharist anew. It has been through the open dialogue between phenomenology and theology that the trilectic of testimony was able to take shape.

In a recent work by Kevin Hart, *Kingdoms of God*, he goes so far as to suggest that a Christian "phenomenological theology would attend to

85. This is not to suggest an eschatological rapprochement between good and evil, but a plurality within goodness itself, a unity in diversity. In the end, there remains a radical difference between contradiction ("Yes" and "No") and paradox ("Yes" and "Yes"). There is no genuine dialectic between good and evil since evil represents no substantial entity but merely a deprivation of goodness. Authentic unity in difference involves complementary givens or sayings, not a disfiguration or distortion of one side of the dialectic alone.

86. Cf. 1 Cor 12:14–17: "Now the body is not a single part, but many. If a foot should say, 'Because I am not a hand I do not belong to the body,' it does not for this reason belong any less to the body. Or if an ear should say, 'Because I am not an eye I do not belong to the body,' it does not for this reason belong any less to the body. If the whole body were an eye, where would the hearing be? If the whole body were hearing, where would the sense of smell be?"

Jesus as phenomenologist, that is, to how he receives phenomena."[87] *Dialectical Anatomy of the Eucharist* has sought to do just that: attend to Jesus as phenomenologist by investigating the phenomeno-logic of the Eucharist. However, Hart's book gives us cause for pause at this point in our study. He reminds us that the motif of the Kingdom (βασιλεία) of God is central to Christian revelation. It is worth recalling some illuminating ideas from his text to underscore the possibility of a trilectical reduction as inspired by the logic of Christian belief, the logic of the both/and. Relying heavily on the classic parable of the Prodigal Son, or of the Manifestation of the Father (as Hart would like it), Hart observes Jesus to exercise a type of phenomenological reduction inasmuch as "in telling a story Jesus brackets everyday life and its worldly logic in order to lead those who hear him to a deeper place."[88] In effect, by bracketing the natural attitude of wordly logic and affairs, Jesus introduces his listeners to what Hart calls the "supernatural attitude" in place of the natural attitude.[89] As the "phenomenality of God," Jesus enacts the "basilaic reduction reveal(ing) that a mode of passivity is primary, that is, being taken outside oneself as the center of activity and being receptive to God's kingly rule."[90] He claims further that this basilaic reduction has two distinct moments: "κένωσις whereby one withdraws from 'the world,' and ἐπέκτασις whereby one stretches into the endless possibilities of the Kingdom . . . In this sense, we may speak of Jesus as the phenomenality of God: He is the light by which we see a relation with the Father made manifest, as open to us in the βασιλεία."[91] Hart perceptively identifies the new world that Jesus the phenomenologist opens: the Kingdom of God. This is the world of eucharistic liturgy in which Christ, the Servant King, lays down his life for his Bride, the Church. Divine *kenosis* gives rise to both *epektasis* and

87. Hart, *Kingdoms of God*, 144.

88. Ibid., 131.

89. Ibid., 149. Cf. ibid., 157; and 171, 177–78: "The Gospels afford us a means by which we can begin a phenomenology of the Christ . . . We see Jesus perpetually confronted with a version of the natural attitude, 'the world,' in its various forms (αἴων, κόσμος, *mundum*, *orbis terrarium*, *imperium mundi*) and responding by leading his audience (and us) back to something that has a prior claim on us, the βασιλεία or Kingdom. The good arrangement and harmony of κόσμος must be led back to a better arrangement and harmony in which the Father is regarded as absolute, not his creation or anything in it . . . For it is life in the Kingdom that is the transcendental attitude for Christianity, an attitude that is also eschatological in that our hope, through Christ, is in the Kingdom coming in its fullness . . . That would be the true supreme phenomenology." Hart's notion of "supernatural attitude" resonates with Ricoeur's notion of the "logic of superabundance." See Ricoeur, *Figuring the Sacred*, 279–83, 315–29.

90. Hart, *Kingdoms of God*, 175, 151, respectively. Cf. ibid., 176.

91. Ibid., 176.

*ekstasis*, inverting the closed circuit of the mechanical economy of exchange and instead opening onto the infinite possibilities of a Kingdom ruled by the eternal law of love. Love has become flesh in order that flesh become love. This is a love of responsibility, fidelity and self-mastery. It has done away with irrational impulses of self-gratification and patterns of entropic vice. According to the paradigm of Christ, the phenomenality of God, virginal fecundity is revealed as the eschatological state of interpersonal communion wherein angels and saints commune with the Most Holy Trinity in the interminate feast of love that is the eternal act of being—the something breathing eternity into eternity, denying the nothingness that never was and that could never be not not.

Rejecting the nullity of plurality, the trilectic of testimony follows the phenomenological attitude revealed by Christ and through Husserl and his daring descendents. To bracket the natural attitude is step one. To bracket the reduction itself is step two, otherwise the phenomenological reduction very well may reduce the phenomenon to givenness alone or ethics alone or some other alone. A reduction of the reduction assures non-reductionism. Attestation has proven to be the third-party witness to the dialectical polarity between manifestation and proclamation, preventing the dialectical fecundity to collapse into another impasse of sterile reductionism. Hart attests to this when he says that "the βασιλεία does not simply or fully show itself; it is here yet to come, and its coming is in the gift of the Father. So its phenomenality cannot be said to abide at the level of givenness, for it is not given all at once; it also needs to be embodied in our actions."[92] Even as a metaphor for the phenomenological attitude, the Kingdom of God implies the logic of the both/and, the joint dynamism of manifestation and proclamation, the phenomenality of interpersonal communion sustained by the *pas de deux* of presence and absence, of sacrament and word, of contemplation and ethics. Step three is to let the plurality of reductions do their work in mutual and complementary communication, generating the perceptible fruit of ethical givenness, of transcendent immanence, of soberly responsible erotic love.

To this point, the fecundity of the trilectic of testimony has been introduced, both in its general application and its specific application to the phenomenality of the Eucharist. However, we are working toward a second analytic moment of transcendental reflection that is to follow the first step of phenomenological description. In order to arrive soundly at this second stage of transcendental reflection—assessing the status of the truth-claim of the Eucharist—an interim reflection will assume the space of chapter 5: a portrayal of the Eucharist as prosopic intercourse between three parties:

92. Ibid., 157.

God, the other and me (*moi*). To enflesh the trilectic of testimony one step further, it must be applied in the domain of dialogue, or conversation. Upon additional phenomenological analysis, it will be suggested that the Eucharist is primarily a phenomenon of conversation among persons. The notion of gift will be defined as conversation.

## *chapter 5*

# The Eucharist as Prosopic Intercourse

## I. Nuptial Contours of Love

Situating the Eucharist according to the structure of the trilectic of testimony hermeneutic holds the peril of impersonality and anonymity: the dominant character of the Eucharist may be lost if thought solely at the level of abstraction. While the manifestation ↔ proclamation ↔ attestation trilectic may be helpful for comprehending the Eucharist in reductive yet non-reductive terms, it nevertheless risks reducing the Eucharist to the abstract and theoretical, in essence disembodying the Eucharist and thereby negating its most fundamental attribute. In order to counteract this tendency of abstraction, we include a chapter that focuses exclusively on the prosopic trait (that is, "relating to the person or face") of the Eucharist. If the Eucharist is interpreted in abstract terms only, it could end up amounting to a faceless host and cup given impersonally to a faceless congregation. This would be the tragic consequence of all rigors of abstraction if not wedded to the concreteness, specificity and uniqueness of persons, who themselves—in themselves—constitute the living phenomenality of the Eucharist.[1] At its heart, the Eucharist claims to offer itself as a personal phenomenon of the nuptial order.[2] It is the gift of the Bridegroom for his Bride. It is the paradoxical movement of two bodies becoming one, yet remaining distinct:

1. Cf. 1 Cor 12.

2. See, for example, John Paul II's Apostolic Letter, *Dies Domini*, 12, 14: "The God who rests on the seventh day, rejoicing in his creation, is the same God who reveals his glory in liberating his children from Pharaoh's oppression. Adopting an image dear to the Prophets, one could say that in both cases *God reveals himself as the bridegroom*

> Husbands, love your wives, as Christ loved the Church and gave himself up for her, that he might sanctify her, having cleansed her by the washing of water with the word, that he might present the Church to himself in splendor, without spot or wrinkle or any such thing, that she might be holy and without blemish. Even so husbands should love their wives as their own bodies. He who loves his wife loves himself. For no man ever hates his own flesh, but nourishes and cherishes it, as Christ does the Church, because we are members of his body. "For this reason a man shall leave his father and mother and be joined to his wife, and the two shall become one flesh." This is a great mystery, and I mean in reference to Christ and the Church.[3]

The author to the church in Ephesus elegantly depicts the essence of eucharistic theology. It must be contextualized within the covenantal marriage relationship, a relationship that involves the sexual complementarity of persons in communion. The Eucharist is sacrament between Christ, the Bridegroom, and the Church, the Bride. It is a relationship at once ethical and loving, responsible and passionate, sacrificial and life-giving. The primary site of the Eucharist is the human body, as Chauvet and Falque have indicated without fail, and not just any anonymous body, but your body and my body and his body and her body.[4] Every body bears a name, and

*before the bride* (cf. Hos 2:16–24; Jer 2:2; Is 54:4–8). As certain elements of the same Jewish tradition suggest, to reach the heart of the '*shabbat*,' of God's 'rest,' we need to recognize in both the Old and the New Testament the nuptial intensity which marks the relationship between God and his people . . . Therefore, if God 'sanctifies' the seventh day with a special blessing and makes it 'his day' *par excellence*, this must be understood within the deep dynamic of the dialogue of the Covenant, indeed the dialogue of 'marriage.' This is the dialogue of love which knows no interruption, yet is never monotonous. In fact, it employs the different registers of love, from the ordinary and indirect to those more intense, which the words of Scripture and the witness of so many mystics do not hesitate to describe in imagery drawn from the experience of married love." For more on the notion of divine eros, see Patterson and Sweeney, *God and Eros*.

3. Eph 5:25–32 (RSV); cf. Rev 19:7; 21:1—22:5; 2 Cor 11:2; Hos 2:16–22; Isa 54:5–6; 62:5; Ezek 16:6–14; Song of Songs.

4. See Chauvet, *Symbol and Sacrament*, 140–51, 355–76; Falque, *God, the Flesh, and the Other*; Falque, *Les noces de l'agneau*; Falque, *Metamorphosis of Finitude*, 3: "[The Son of Man] takes on fully *the corporal modality of the present*, or the gift of the body . . . in the unique, almost conjugal, moment of the act of love, in which his body is given to the other: *Hoc est enim corpus meum*—'this is my body' (Mk 14:22)"; Gschwandtner, "Corporeality, Animality, Bestiality"; and Gschwandtner, *Postmodern Apologetics?*, 205: "The eucharistic act, [Falque] suggests, recapitulates the 'erotic act' of marriage (*NA*, 248). In marriage the chaos of our passions is transformed into order and it prefigures the eschatological bridal supper of Revelation . . . Desire that arises out of our animality is transformed into mutual love that respects alterity (modeled on the Trinitarian relationships). In desire, one embraces one's own body in a way that requires

every name refers to a body—a some-body: "But now thus says the LORD, he who created you, O Jacob, he who formed you, O Israel: / 'Fear not, for I have redeemed you; I have called you by name, you are mine.'"[5] The Eucharist, in the end, is an antiphony bearing a double invocation of persons: the first addressed to humanity by God, the second addressed to God by humanity. The form of this double invocation may be called dialogue, or conversation. Another name for these two terms, similarly implying the notion of communion, is intercourse. Therefore the term intercourse is a most à propos indicator for comprehending the Eucharist in its communal, conversational, nuptial, bodily and personal character. The aim of this chapter will be to recast the traditional notion of gift as "that which is given," or the recently developed phenomenological notion of gift as "that which gives itself according to its particular mode of givenness" (Marion), to a revised phenomenological concept of gift as conversation.[6] The notion of gift as conversation avoids both aporias of extremity: (1) a jejune economy of exchange, and (2) an impersonal, abstract, nameless and solitary gift as *such*, for "hell is the absence of every other."[7] Gift as conversation implies that no gift gives (manifestation) wherein no response responds (proclamation); likewise no response responds (proclamation) wherein no gift gives (manifestation). The notion of gift as conversation is inspired by the dialectic—essentially dialogue—wherein two parties hold and articulate their respective positions without either becoming domineering over the other. And so it is with genuine conversation: there is a give and take, "a time to

differentiation. Desire becomes incarnate in the mutual gift of bodies that enables the incarnation of our flesh: 'My body *becomes flesh for the other, at the same time that the body of the other also transforms itself into flesh for me*' (*NA*, 274). The church shares in this community of bodies. In taking on our flesh, Christ has experienced our pathos; conjugal union between divine and human becomes possible."

5. Isa 43:1 (RSV); cf. John 15:16–17: "You did not choose me, but I chose you and appointed you that you should go and bear fruit and that your fruit should abide; so that whatever you ask the Father in my name, he may give it to you. This I command you, to love one another" (RSV); 1 Cor 1:2: "To the Church of God which is at Corinth, to those sanctified in Christ Jesus, called to be saints together with all those who in every place call on the name of our Lord Jesus Christ, both their Lord and ours" (RSV); Rom 10:13: "For, 'every one who calls upon the name of the Lord will be saved'" (RSV); Acts 2:21: "And it shall be that whoever calls on the name of the Lord shall be saved" (RSV); Joel 2:32: "And it shall come to pass that all who call upon the name of the LORD shall be delivered; for in Mount Zion and in Jerusalem there shall be those who escape, as the LORD has said, and among the survivors shall be those whom the LORD calls" (RSV).

6. Credit for this notion is due to my wife, Megan J. Wallenfang, who coined the term *gift as conversation* in the course of a conversation we were having about this very topic.

7. Marion, *Prolegomena to Charity*, 20.

keep silence, and a time to speak."[8] Communication becomes the most fundamental paradigm of the gift, for it gives (*es gibt*) insofar as it takes two and it speaks.[9] The Song of Songs relates the perennial conversation between bride and bridegroom.[10] The context of this conversation between the two parties is mediated and witnessed by a third party, the daughters of Jerusalem. This third party serves to mediate between the lover and the beloved to ensure the justice, reciprocity, complementarity and consummation of their love for each other, for example, "Eat, friends; drink! Drink freely of love!" and "Where has your lover gone, O most beautiful of women? / Where has your lover gone that we may seek him with you?"[11] The threefold configuration resembles the trilectic of testimony: two dialectical interlocutors with a third neutral party witnessing to the polarity and reciprocity of the dialectic.[12] It is also the case with the phenomenality of the Eucharist: God—self (*moi*)—world is the basic analogically related form of the parties involved in the manifestation, proclamation and attestation of this phenomenon.[13] The form is also that of the sacrament of marriage wherein a woman and man give themselves one to another within and before a community of witnesses, divine and human. In both cases, a trilectic of testimony obtains that undergirds the phenomenality of the sacrament. The fecundity of the dialectical

8. Eccl 3:7 (RSV).

9. Cf. Song 2:8; 5:16: "The voice of my beloved! Behold he comes, / leaping upon the mountains, bounding over hills . . . His speech is most sweet and he is altogether desirable" (RSV); 1:2–3: (Bride) "Let him kiss me with kisses of his mouth! / More delightful is your love than wine! Your name spoken is a spreading perfume—that is why the maidens love you" (NAB); 7:10: (Groom) "And your mouth like an excellent wine—(Bride) that flows smoothly for my lover, spreading over the lips and the teeth" (NAB); 7:10: "And your mouth like choicest wine. 'Let it flow to my beloved as new wine / Gliding over the lips of sleepers'" (TNKH translation, JPS). Note how this latter (more literal) translation gives the image of the lover's mouth/speech awaking the slumber of the beloved.

10. For a masterful exegesis of the Song of Songs, see LaCocque, *Romance She Wrote*.

11. Song 5:1 and 6:1, respectively (NAB).

12. Cf. Eccl 5:9–12: "Two are better than one, because they have a good reward for their toil. For if they fall, one will lift up his fellow; but woe to him who is alone when he falls and has not another to lift him up. Again, if two lie together, they are warm; but how can one be warm alone? And though a man might prevail against one who is alone, two will quickly withstand him. A threefold cord is not quickly broken" (RSV). Note how, in the last verse, the author mysteriously infers three figures from the preceding form of the pair.

13. Cf. Tracy, *Analogical Imagination*, 410, 412: ". . . a pattern of ordered analogical relationships among God-self-world . . . [in which] even the religious silence evoked by an intensified (i.e. mystical) religious experience of the originating event is *theologically* understood *as* silence only on the other side of that speech, that reflective, second-order, kataphatic speech proper to the mystical theologian as speaker."

two-party intercourse engenders and invokes the arrival of a third party to witness to the dialectic in such a way that the neutral third party validates, promotes, and carves out the necessary space for the fruitfulness of the prosopic intercourse of the dialectic to obtain. The child, as the gifted offspring of lovers, becomes witness to conjugal love and intimacy.

The sexual connotation of the term prosopic intercourse should not be left implicit, but rendered explicit as part and parcel of the logic of the Eucharist. The Song of Songs, as a seasoned text of the nuptial and sacramental, is an explicitly sexual, and thereby personal, text.[14] The intimacy of lovers is not concealed from the discourse, but rendered explicit, for example:

> How fair and pleasant you are,
> O loved one, delectable maiden!
> You are stately as a palm tree,
> and your breasts are like its clusters.
> I say I will climb the palm tree
> and lay hold of its branches.
> Oh, may your breasts be like clusters of the vine,
> and the scent of your breath like apples,
> and your kisses like the best wine
> that goes down smoothly,
> gliding over lips and teeth.[15]

This text linguistically brings to light the erotic dimensions of love between the lovers: beauty, pleasure, yearning, sacramentality, mystery, delight. It presents the limen between love and lust, the pivotal question whether or not the beloved becomes for the lover a means to an end or an end in herself. Authentic love remains as such insofar as it does not fail to promote the dialectical tension between its erotic and agapic dimensions.[16] All the same, in an authentically loving relationship, lovers divest themselves physically and psychologically in mutual trust, at the same time becoming their most authentic selves as given one-for-the-other. A certain translucency and nakedness transpires—a nakedness without shame.[17] This explicitness—this nakedness—is likewise evident in Jesus nailed naked to a cross of wood. His body is exposed in its nakedness, given up to the degree of his love: totally,

14. For the convergence of the literal and allegorical meanings of the Song of Songs, see Cavadini, "The Church as the Sacrament of Creation: A Reading of Origen's *Commentary on the Song of Songs*."

15. Song 7:6–9 (RSV).

16. Cf. Benedict XVI, *Deus caritas est*, 1–18.

17. Cf. John Paul II, *Man and Woman He Created Them*, 169–78.

absolutely and irrevocably. Jesus gives all as flesh and says all as word.[18] Jesus abandons himself to you and to me and to him and to her in the Eucharist in as much as he enacted this offering on the hill of death, the place called *Golgotha*, there a body sapped of its life to be anointed with spices: "when we eat this bread and drink this cup, we proclaim your death, O Lord, until you come again."[19] In the conjugal act of sexual intercourse, the spouses donate themselves one to another without reservation. Their consummated union is achieved by a complete giving of self, withholding no part but instead giving all. Such an expression of self-donative love becomes creative: bodies, persons mingled together, speaking the language of gift—given and received, received and given, unlocking the heterosexual procreativity of conjugal love. In like fashion, the Eucharist signifies the self-donation of Jesus's life, body and person, given up for you—you who are a member of the spouse of Christ, the Church, and therefore the one-flesh body of Christ himself.[20] The Eucharist is tied to Jesus's consummating death on the cross whereupon his blood was "shed for you and for the many so that sins may be forgiven." It was on the cross that the Church was conceived: "but one of the soldiers pierced his side with a spear, and at once there came out blood and water."[21] The sexual language of Jesus's body is one of complete self-donation—a body given up for you, entirely exhausted through his act of giving and his life of preaching the good news of God's reign.

So this giving up of flesh and blood is not only a showing, but a telling: the Eucharist is characterized as prosopic intercourse—a narrated giving of flesh, one-for-the-other. This narrative is a story—his story, your story, my story, our story: "I came that they might have life and have it abundantly . . . and I have other sheep, that are not of this fold; I must bring them also, and they will heed my voice."[22] In this story, the characters have names—irreplaceable, incommunicable.[23] The protagonist of this drama is Jesus, but the protagonist matters inasmuch as the cast of characters—each character

18. Cf. Matt 24:35: "Heaven and earth will pass away, but my words will not pass away" (RSV).

19. Cf. Song 8:14: "Make haste, my beloved, and be like a gazelle / or a young stag upon the mountains of spices" (RSV); and Mark 16:1: "And when the Sabbath was past, Mary Magdalene, and Mary the mother of James, and Salome, bought spices, so that they might go and anoint him" (RSV).

20. Cf. 1 Cor 12:27: "Now you are the body of Christ and individually members of it" (RSV); Gen 2:24: "Therefore a man leaves his father and his mother and clings to his wife, and they become one flesh" (RSV); Eph 5:25–32.

21. John 19:34 (RSV).

22. John 10:10, 16 (RSV).

23. Cf. Luke 10:20: "Nevertheless do not rejoice in this, that the spirits are subject to you; but rejoice that your names are written in heaven" (RSV).

unique and unrepeatable. These characters have faces and names—not a nameless, shapeless, anonymous throng. The protagonist indeed testifies, but his testimony itself is mediated by personal testimonies of his testimony, as well as the testimonies of conscience and the absolute. The drama exhibits the form of a trilectic, which analogously mirrors the doctrine of the Trinity, three Persons in one God. We will set our task below to interpret the Eucharist concretely as a phenomenon of conversation, inasmuch as gift can be rendered *as* conversation.

The ensuing discussion will attempt to achieve three goals: (1) to describe the personhood of the Eucharist in light of the thinking of Marion, Ricoeur and Levinas; (2) to describe the conversational character of the Eucharist; and (3) to offer a poetic rendition of the Eucharist in light of the two preceding goals.

## II. The Eucharist as a Phenomenon between Persons

To claim that the Eucharist is essentially a phenomenon between persons is to assume the clarity of the meaning of the term "person."[24] However, the term holds a plurality of meanings according to a multitude of interests. For instance, oftentimes a strict definition of "person" is sought, perhaps one that locates the essence of personhood in consciousness, or self-awareness, or a host of other abilities or competencies, thereby restricting the self-determination of the phenomenon itself, in all of its manifold dimensions. In order not to reduce the notion of person by giving credence to this or that definition according to a particular ideology or self-interest, it is necessary to have recourse once again to a trilectical strategy through the phenomenological method, a trilectic between manifestation, proclamation and attestation. A phenomenological assessment of human personhood will be attempted in light of the complementary insights of Marion, Ricoeur and Levinas. We begin by interpreting human personhood through the framework of givenness (Marion) in conversation with its extended application *as* . . . and *according to* . . . (Ricoeur, Levinas).

First, by way of the hermeneutic of personal givenness, human beings at every stage of life, development and circumstance, speak personhood for themselves with or without the attentive *ob-audire*—receptive listening, recognition and obedience—of their fellows. That is to say that a human

24. For a helpful introduction to the term "person," see Sokolowski's essay "The Christian Difference in Personal Relationships," in Titus, *On Wings of Faith and Reason*, 68–84. For Sokolowski's systematic depiction of the human person as the "agent of truth," see Sokolowski, *Phenomenology of the Human Person*.

being herself testifies to her personal existence (self-attestation) regardless of the intentional validation of this testimony by other human persons. The relationship between givenness and personhood can be set forth in the form of a question: "What relevance does the phenomenological hermeneutic of givenness have for the task of understanding human personhood?" Or, better put: "What relevance does the phenomenological call of givenness have for the event of being(,) understood by human personhood?"[25] This language of "call" and "event of being" will be explored further below, but for now, an argument concerning the phenomenological description of human personhood is ready to be proposed: The vocational givenness of the human person, as the call of pluriformatic alterity prior to her conscious recognition and reception by other human persons, establishes her undeniable fait accompli self-attested personhood and unique identity—a personhood at once radically dependent upon, and constitutive of, the responsibility of her fellow human persons.[26] In other words, the a priori vocational givenness

25. The comma, found here between parentheses, signifies the two possible renderings of the end of the sentence—a double entendre: (1) ". . . the event of being understood by human personhood," and (2) ". . . the event of being, understood by human personhood." In the first rendering, "being" is employed as an auxiliary verb, placing emphasis on the act of understanding (or the event of understanding) whereby the human subject is understood according to the anterior givenness of personhood. In the second rendering, "being" is employed as a non-finite verb (or gerund), placing emphasis on the act of being (or the *event* of being). Both meanings are intended, as both disclose the dimensions of the act of understanding human personhood: (1) a human person understands herself only upon encounter with another person, and (2) only human personhood can understand the event-of-being (*Ereignis*, according to the Heideggerian analytic *Dasein*). The double entendre here surrounding the word "being" was inspired by Marion's play on the word "being" in the title of his book *Etant donné* (*Being Given*); cf. Marion, *Being Given*, 1–2.

26. The pronoun "she" and possessive pronoun "her" (rather than "it/its") will be used in reference to "person" in order to support the living identity of a human person, versus a lifeless, nameless objectification of "person." "She/her" is even preferable to "he/his" because of the genius of receptivity inscribed in the female human body and persona; cf. John Paul II, *Mulieris dignitatem*, 18: "Motherhood implies from the beginning a special openness to the new person: and this is precisely the woman's 'part'"; and ibid., 30: "The moral and spiritual strength of woman is joined to her awareness that *God entrusts the human being to her in a special way*. Of course, God entrusts every human being to each and every other human being. But this entrusting concerns women in a special way—precisely by reason of their femininity—and this in a particular way determines their vocation . . . In this sense, our time in particular *awaits the manifestation* of that 'genius' which belongs to women, and which can ensure sensitivity to human beings in every circumstance: because they are human!"; and John Paul II, *On the Genius of Women*, 28: "Woman is endowed with a particular capacity for accepting the human being in his concrete form." Moreover, the term "vocational givenness" is my own. It is a term that seeks to maintain the dialectical tension between the respective phenomenological reductions of Marion and Levinas, and the dialectical relationship between manifestation and proclamation.

of the human person serves as a silent yet discernable testimony of the reality and there-ness of the self vis-à-vis other selves; vocational givenness phenomenally testifies to the person as such; vocational givenness serves as the preliminary mode of manifestation, proclamation and attestation for the her-there-who-ness bursting forth in self-revelation in the form of a simultaneous call (on the part of the self-revealer) and sensible perceptibility (on the part of the respondent to the self-revealer). Vocational givenness is not synonymous with self-evidence, but rather is that which presents itself as intuition and ethical exigency prior to its recognition by a perceiving and discerning self. However, in addition to the anterior vocational givenness of human personhood, a reciprocal moment of recognition occurs in which one person recognizes another person as such, and simultaneously recognizes oneself as person in relation to other persons. Pushing against the priority of the givenness of manifestation, Levinas insists that the anterior moment of phenomenality is the summons of responsibility issued by the other—a summons extending from the diachronic call of the infinite. Ricoeur agrees with Levinas's prioritization of the various modes of passivity through which a person is constituted: "oneself as another." However, Ricoeur would concede to the anteriority of pre-linguistic manifestation, granted that such manifestation becomes recognizable, intelligible and meaningful only by way of its linguistic mediation (proclamation). Vocational givenness of the human person signifies both personal givenness and the ethical subpoena to responsibility. Through phenomenology, the essence of human personhood is accessed by bracketing and setting aside the calloused natural attitude. This is done, first of all, by attending to the complexity of language games surrounding the mystery of personhood.

The first aporia that confronts the quest for a universal understanding of human personhood is the problem of language.[27] As Boethius wrote in the sixth century AD, "But the proper definition of person is a matter of great perplexity."[28] Further, Boethius's classic definition of person—*naturae rationalis individua substantia* ("an individual substance of a rational nature")—may even confuse the question due to its metaphysical cast.[29] Amidst the contemporary scene of polemics surrounding the establishment of a proper definition of human personhood operates a deceptive language

27. For an important and insightful account of the genesis and evolution of the term and idea "person," see Yannaras, *Person and Eros*, 5–6; Zizioulas, *Being as Communion*, 27–65; Spaemann, *Persons*, 5–40; Kearney, *God Who May Be*, 9–19. Also cf. Buber, *I and Thou*, for a critical argument regarding "I-Thou" language and thinking.

28. Quotation taken from Rolnick, *Person, Grace, and God*, 37.

29. See Boethius, *De persona et duabus naturis*, c. ii; Thomas Aquinas, *Summa theologiae*, I.29.1–4.

game. In reference to some members of the human species, the term "person" is applied without ambiguity or question, while to other members the term "person" is withheld and different language is substituted such as "blastocyst, embryo, fetus, pregnancy, slave, prostitute, illegal alien, vegetable, organism, body"—in essence "it." Even my language of "member" here assumes an organic and inclusive understanding of the human species, and the language game into which I have entered just now will be played out through the remainder of this text. Though the language game is unavoidable, the term "human person" undoubtedly holds pride of place among the various terms that refer to the diverse forms, stages of development, and circumstances of human life. With the term "human person" follows the ensuing dignity, rights and value attributable to the human person as such by other human persons. Thus the language game serves only to establish common understandings of the term "human person," bearing immense ethical implications. The victors of the language game are those who, in the end, call a thing what it is (what gives/says itself) and thereby set forth the most accurate description of a given phenomenon through the mediums of language and hermeneutics. The notions of givenness and call offer an interpretive key through which to uncover, recognize and understand the human person as she gives herself, thus establishing, what could be called, an anthropology of vocational givenness.

With regard to personhood, to what exactly does the above-mentioned "call of pluriformatic alterity" refer? Both Levinas and Marion view the call as intrinsic to phenomenality, though in differing constellations. The call exerts a phenomenological claim on the human subject through the giving intuition (Marion) and ethical exigency (Levinas) of the calling phenomenon, in effect inverting the typical self-referential movement of intentionality. The anteriority of the call reverses the egoistic determination of the phenomenon.[30] Especially in the case of the other person (*l'autrui*), the urgent question is: how am I to be responsible for her? Consciousness is not separate from the call of the other, but is derived from the face-to-face with the other.[31] The dynamic of counter-intentionality is especially true

30. See Marion, *Being Given*, 266–67; Levinas, *Entre Nous*, 58.

31. Cf. Rolnick, *Person, Grace, and God*, 222–23, including a key quotation from Ricoeur: "Otherness is not added on to selfhood from outside, . . . it belongs instead to the tenor of meaning and to the ontological constitution of selfhood" (223); cf. Purcell, "*Agape* of Eating," 318–36, 330: "Consciousness is not the identity of ipseity. The subject rather is a term in a hypostasis with the other, and cannot be adequately expressed as an ego, an I or a oneself," and 332: "It is only because of the in-spiration of the other, that the respiration of the self happens"; and cf. Levinas, *Otherwise than Being*, 105: "But the oneself is hypostasized in another way. It is bound in a knot that cannot be undone in a responsibility for others . . . In the exposure to wounds and outrages, in the feeling

in the case of a human person's encounter with another human person. I (*Je*) do not make myself, rather the other makes me (*moi*) according to my responsibility for her.

In *Being Given*, Marion employs the phenomenon of paternal denomination to demonstrate the phenomenality of the call of the child and the response of the father, shown through the responsorial name given to the child by the father. This passage is worth quoting at length:

> Why does [the father] give [his child] a name? One obvious reply might be that the child does not yet have one and remains anonymous. But in this case, how and with what right does the father call a nameless child by his own name, thereby literally offering no sign that he is from this father? The obvious reply to this is because the father knows, through intimate experience, that this child is born from his own deeds, from his own wife, in his house, in front of him, etc. These excellent reasons nevertheless suffer from a well-known weakness: by definition, in fact on account of the temporal delay of birth's initial belatedness to conception, biological paternity remains without immediate and direct proof, always doubtful (and technologically it will become more and more so in the near future). Every child is born naturally from its mother, but strictly speaking, it always remains of unknown father; there is no child who is not a foundling—that is to say, received. As a result, it has been admitted since time immemorial that the sole proof of paternity resides in the juridical recognition of the child by the father; paternity is accomplished symbolically, not first of all or always biologically. The father becomes one, in all cases and not only in adoption, only by his decision to recognize, ask for, and claim as his own the foundling and natural child . . . The father decides to be father because the child (and the context surrounding his birth) exerts over him a call to recognition in paternity. The child silently calls the father to call him with his name—with the name of the father, with the name that he does not have, which is not and never will be his own. The child thus exercises an anonymous call on the father. When the father recognizes himself as father to the point of recognizing the child as his own, to the point of giving him his name, he does nothing other than,

proper to responsibility, the oneself is provoked as irreplaceable, as devoted to the others, without being able to resign, and thus as incarnated in order to offer itself, to suffer and to give. It is thus one and unique, in passivity from the start, having nothing at its disposal that would enable it to not yield to the provocation." Thus can Luther's quote from the Heidelberg Disputation (¶ 21) be rendered even more precisely: "allow a thing to call itself what it is," instead of "call a thing what it is."

> by calling him in this way, offer a response to the call . . . The father will therefore be born into his own paternity to the extent that he responds to the child's anonymous call with a naming response.[32]

In this passage, Marion claims to demonstrate a verifiable instance of givenness as a personal call of the other. The phenomenon of fatherhood is constituted by an affirmative naming response to the call of the child. Granted that Marion's interpretation of paternal denomination is taken from a particular cultural context, the phenomenality of what he describes assumes a universal figure. In all cases, the ambiguous space between father and child (in terms of biological relationship) opens the way for the call of the child to be issued. The identity of the child's mother is clear but the identity of the child's father transpires through the course of paternal denomination as an affirmative response to the child's silent call to the father to become father. While the broader context of Marion's example is concerned with illustrating the anonymous call as an indisputable mode of givenness, it can be employed to show the vocational givenness and alterity of the human person herself. Marion's example of the invisible call and claim of a child on her father and the father's ensuing response (or lack thereof) sufficiently exposes the vocational givenness of the human person from the origins of her existence as well as the contingent validation of her existence upon the recognition and response of her adult caretakers.[33]

Marion's example also can be transposed into the key of motherhood. A mother is constituted by her response to the call of vocational givenness of her child. As long as a mother affirmatively responds to the call of her living child, *in utero* (in her womb) as well as *extra utero* (outside her womb once born), she paves the way for continued life for her child; if the mother negatively responds to the existence of her living child either by choosing to terminate the life of her child directly or by neglecting to nurture and care for the life of her child, the child will die, the call will be rejected or ignored. In either case, the child's self-attestation is recognizable—a self-attested call that silently cries out: "Here I am! Care for me!" and even "Here I am! Love me!," while simultaneously posing the question, "Who do you say that I am?"[34] The phenomenon of the silent and personal call of a radically vulnerable and dependent human being—a simultaneous call and claim

32. Cf. Marion, *Being Given*, 300–301.

33. Cf. ibid., 293–94.

34. See Lacoste's application of *Mitbefindlichkeit* in "Existence et amour de Dieu," and "De la donation comme promesse," in Lacoste, *La phénoménalité de Dieu*, 130 and 165, respectively.

on other human beings—is the greatest instance of the self-attested vocational givenness of human personhood. This call is most acute in its silent tenor of wombness and embryonicity, that is, the smaller, more hidden and vulnerable a human life, the greater the volume of her silent and personal call into the dark night of phenomenality—a call that seeks validation, an affirmative naming response of the addressee.[35] In fact, the human person perpetually inhabits the space of vulnerability whereby vocational givenness summons other human persons to share in a mutually interdependent existence. The addressee is constituted as fellow through the affirmative response to the silent call of alterity by the caller. True human vocation, therefore, is a life lived in recognition of, and in response to, the call of the other, through a responsorial naming and will to care for another. In this instance, Nietzsche's will to power is subverted by the counter-intentionality of the other, initiating the vocation to a will to care for the other without end.

From conception onward the child *es gibt*—the child "childs" (in the sense of subsistent eventing)—that is, the child appears across the horizon of perceptible phenomenality as originating substantially from something (namely, a gamete) from her father and something (namely, a gamete) from her mother: a reciprocal fusion of life that ecstatically calls out as a distinct, differentiated, self-attested other.[36] Conception—the fusion of maternal and paternal gametes and the rapid and subsequent progression to the single-

35. Cf. Simms, "Milk and Flesh," for example, 23 (quoting R. M. Rilke): "O bliss of the tiny creature who / remains forever in the womb that bore it: / O happiness of the gnat who still leaps *within*, / even on its wedding day: for womb is all."

36. Cf. Yannaras, *Person and Eros*, 28: "The ecstasy, however, of the person, as a recapitulation of essence or nature in the *fact* of its self-transcendence, corresponds not to the intellectual-semiological (and consequently ontic) definition of 'universal' but to its existential-ontological sense. It is nature in general which 'stands out' (*existatai*) in the existential fact of personal otherness, both as self-transcendence and as *relation* with beings—an existential presupposition of the general *disclosure* of beings," and 53: "It is precisely the ecstatic reference of essence or nature, as a fact of interpersonal relation and as a unique and dissimilar pre-conscious cognition, that reveals the form-generating character of the nature and witnesses to the essence (*ousia*) as presence (*par-ousia*)." In other words, personal existence is the mode for the revelation (present-ation) of essential or substantial existence. Cf. Ratzinger, *Truth and Tolerance*, 246: "The being of another person is so closely interwoven with the being of this first person, the mother, that for the moment it can only exist at all in bodily association with the mother, in physical union with her, which nonetheless does not abolish its otherness and does not permit us to dispute its being itself." For the biological factuality of the process of fertilization, cf. Beckwith, *Defending Life*, 65–83; Carlson, *Human Embryology and Developmental Biology*, 32–41; Makabe et al., *Atlas of Human Female Reproductive Function*, 117–75; Schoenwolf et al., *Larsen's Human Embryology*, 39–43 (note the etymology of the word "zygote," from Greek *zugotos*, "yoked"); Veeck and Zaninović, *Atlas of Human Blastocysts*, 16–39.

celled zygotic stage of development—marks the arrival of the person—the incipient phenomenological manifestation and proclamation of self-attested personal givenness and call. Yet as self-attested other, a child as person exists *as* such only in reciprocal relation to other persons, especially the child's parents. The self-attestation of the child comes by way of the *es gibt als* . . . and the *es gibt nach* . . . Likewise, all persons—no matter at what point of development, circumstance or need of care—exist always in reciprocal relation with other persons. Joseph Ratzinger conveys this point in the following dictum fashioned in the context of Christian theology: "the true God is, of his own nature, being-for (Father), being-from (Son), and being-with (Holy Spirit). Yet man is in the image of God precisely because the being for, from, and with constitute the basic anthropological shape."[37] Whether one adheres to the Christian faith or not, this dictum verbally reflects, in a precise way, the human existential situation of radical interdependency—both in terms of psychosomatic care and in terms of self-constitution. In the former sense, no one can exist entirely apart from the help of others in fulfilling one's psychosomatic needs; in the latter sense, no one can know, understand or recognize oneself apart from the structural matrix of personal identity that is constituted vis-à-vis other persons. Ultimately, the ancient maxim, know thyself, is only possible through the help of other selves. Likewise, the Christian maxim, love your neighbor as you love yourself, can be reversed to witness to the dynamic of self-constituting alterity: love yourself as you love your neighbor. In other words, through the redoubling of recognition and respect of otherness, one comes to recognize and respect the otherness of oneself vis-à-vis other selves.[38] To say "love yourself as you love your neighbor" does not result in a Lutherian *incurvatus in se* (a "curving in on oneself"), but in an ever renewed self-identity, self-knowledge and self-love of surprise and wonder. Each and every person (self/*moi*) is unique,

37. Ratzinger, *Truth and Tolerance*, 248; cf. Purcell, "*Agape* of Eating," 329: "If sensibility is understood in terms of proximity rather than knowing, then a subjectivity irreducible to consciousness and thematisation can be described . . . The signification of proximity is experienced in my responsibility for the other. In other words, in the significative structure of this for that, my responsibility is the for of the relationship, one-*for*-the-other"; and Simms, "Milk and Flesh," 26–27: "We begin life not as separate monads, but as mingling presences, as aspects of significant wholes where the newborn's action finds its complement and completion in the actions of the (m)other," and 30, 34: "The infant's body, from the beginning, transcends the matter it is made of by having an intentionality that ties it to the body of the (m)other. Flesh here means the intentional *chiasm*, or entwining, between dyadic bodies, the invisible form of the other that is inscribed in each . . . The *dyad* is actually a *triad*: the flesh of the world, the third, transcends the two."

38. Cf. Marion, *Being Given*, 279–82.

unrepeatable and nontransferable, in a word, *incommunicabilis*.[39] Likewise, each and every person (self/*moi*) exists as an accomplished fact—as a fait accompli—as an emergence of the flesh.[40] Greek philosopher Christos Yannaras puts this fact well:

> The Person of God—not to mention any human person—cannot be fixed or known by objective definitions, analogical correlations or conceptual assessments. For every person is a unique, existential reality, unlike any other and unrepeatable, a reality of absolute existential otherness, refractory of any objectivity that could be defined by the utterances of human language. Our existential otherness becomes known and participated in only in the immediacy of *relationship*. Not only the Person of God, but also any kind of human person, is known only as we realize a relationship with it.[41]

This is to say that whenever adult human beings attempt to set down a definitive definition of human personhood, such a definition always will elude them.[42] This elusion is due to the intrinsic relational character of the human person—a character constrained neither by language of substance, being, individual, essence, nor language of relationality, communicability, rationality, consciousness. Even the relationality that obtains among and between persons largely remains incomprehensible because relation exceeds isolation and manipulation.[43] Furthermore, true relationality suggests an

39. Cf. Rolnick, *Person, Grace, and God*, 4.

40. Cf. Marion, *Being Given*, 270–71, 370 (endnote 31).

41. Yannaras, *Absence and Unknowability of God*, 78; cf. ibid., 71–72: "In other words, the catholicity of the event of knowing through *relationship* preserves the chief elements (otherness and freedom) with which we mark out the *personal* existence of human kind—man or woman as person/personality, with the greater ontological meaning offered by this definition. Apophaticism, then, as an active *abandonment* of the consolidation of knowledge in conceptual categories, is the epistemological position that leads to the dynamics of the ontology of personhood, that is to say, to a conferring of meaning on both the subject and the reality facing it, independent of any kind of *a priori* necessity"; and cf. Buber, *I and Thou*, 6: "As experience, the world belongs to the primary word *I-It*. The primary word *I-Thou* establishes the world of relation."

42. Cf. Simms, "Milk and Flesh," 23 (quoting R. M. Rilke): "And we: spectators, always, everywhere, / turned toward all this and never beyond it. / It overfills us. We arrange it. It falls apart. / We arrange it again, and fall apart ourselves."

43. Cf. Rolnick, *Person, Grace, and God*, 211: "Relation overflows comprehension [Levinas] . . . Personal identity is totally lost if isolated, for its ontological condition is relationship [Zizioulas]"; 220: "Uniqueness is something absolute for the person. The person is so absolute that it does not permit itself to be regarded as an arithmetical concept, to be set alongside other beings, to be combined with other objects, or to be used as a means, even for the most sacred goal. The goal is the person itself; personhood

iconic interplay whereby a reciprocal otherness and saturation obtains and overflows within and through the mutual encounter of persons.[44] In effect, the human person exists as an unfathomable enigma to her own species according to her vocational givenness by which she attests to herself in relation to other persons; for the primordial face of the human person is the face of implicating vocational givenness, and a complementary invocation to responsibility—to live as one-for-the-other.

To recapitulate, recall the proposed argument concerning a phenomenological description of human personhood: The vocational givenness of the human person, as the call of pluriformatic alterity prior to her conscious recognition and reception by other human persons, establishes her undeniable fait accompli self-attested personhood and unique identity—a personhood at once radically dependent upon, and constitutive of, the responsibility of her fellow human persons. Instead of proposing a closed definition of human personhood, this claim obliges one to consider the invitation to be attentive and listen for the silent call of each and every human person—a call contextualized in radical relational interdependency and otherness. One can test the truth-claim of this proposal by reflecting on real-life experience and the aftermath of one's response (or lack thereof) to the clarion call of the other that beckons. For those who find themselves with the capacity to respond with care to the call of others, such people live with great responsibility. To learn from the wisdom of Spiderman: "With great power comes great responsibility." The true human vocation is none other than the courageous acceptance of the responsibility to one's fellows—the will to journey in compassion and solidarity with one's sisters and brothers as far as the road leads.[45] This journey begins by being attentive to the vocational givenness of the human person, appearing and calling out at her phenomenal conception,[46] and thereupon and thereafter proclaiming the personal otherness and distinctness of her existence in relation to other selves—an existence at once fragile and powerful: fragile inasmuch as her radical dependence on others, powerful insofar as her eschatological potentiality and radiant otherness make clear.[47] In sum, the human person

---

is the total fulfillment of being [Zizioulas]"; and 221: "Exactly as the Greek Fathers spoke of the divine persons, we cannot give a *positive qualitative content* to a hypostasis or person, for this would result in the loss of his absolute uniqueness and turn a person into a classifiable entity [Zizioulas]."

44. Cf. Marion, *Being Given*, 232–33.

45. For an entry point into the phenomenology of responsibility, see Levinas, *Otherwise than Being*, 9–11, 135–36.

46. Namely, the event of gamete fusion and subsequent zygotic metamorphosis.

47. Kearney, *God Who May Be*, 12–14.

ecstatically exhibits a personal and vocational givenness beyond expectation and measure.[48]

Why this extended consideration of human personhood? Because the Eucharist is essentially a phenomenon between persons—and not only adult persons, but all persons; and not only able-bodied and able-minded persons, but all persons; and not only Christian persons, but all persons; and not only righteous persons, but all persons.[49] The Eucharist is a personal offering to all persons insofar as "Christ, while we were still helpless, yet died at the appointed time for the ungodly . . . while we were still sinners Christ died for us."[50] The Eucharist is the pinnacle expression of Christ's solidarity with all human persons:

> He came to save all through Himself,—all, I say, who through Him are reborn in God,—infants, and children, and youths and old men. Therefore He passed through every age, becoming an infant to infants, sanctifying infants; a child for children, sanctifying those who are of that age, and at the same time becoming for them an example of piety, of righteousness, and of

48. Cf. Marion, *Being Given*, 199–202.

49. Cf. Eisland, *Disabled God*, 111–12, 114: "The church is thus called first to discern the presence of the disabled God in its midst. One place to begin is to consider the body practices of the church. The body practices of the church are a physical language—the routines, rules, and practices of the body, conscious and unconscious. In the church, the body practices are the physical discourse of inclusion and exclusion. These practices reveal the hidden 'membership roll,' those whose bodies matter in the shaping of liturgies and services . . . Hope and the possibility of liberation welling up from a broken body is the miracle of the Eucharist . . . As the disabled God, Christ has brought us grace and, in turn, makes us a grace to others as physical beings. Jesus Christ, the disabled God and the incarnation of hope, requires that eucharistic theology and ritual be a sacrament of actually existing bodies"; Reynolds, *Vulnerable Communion*; Matt 19:13–15: "Then children were brought to him that he might lay his hands on them and pray. The disciples rebuked them, but Jesus said, 'Let the children come to me, and do not prevent them; for the kingdom of heaven belongs to such as these.' After he placed his hands on them, he went away" (NAB); Matt 21:14–16: "The blind and the lame approached him in the temple area, and he cured them. When the chief priests and the scribes saw the wondrous things he was doing, and the children crying out in the temple area, 'Hosanna to the Son of David,' they were indignant and said to him, 'Do you hear what they are saying?' Jesus said to them, 'Yes; and have you never read the text, "Out of the mouths of infants and nurslings you have brought forth praise"?'" (NAB; cf. Ps 8:3 LXX; Wis 10:21); John 10:16: "I have other sheep that do not belong to this fold. These also I must lead, and they will hear my voice, and there will be one flock, one shepherd" (NAB); Matt 5:44–45: "But I say to you, love your enemies, and pray for those who persecute you, that you may be children of your heavenly Father, for he makes his sun rise on the bad and the good, and causes rain to fall on the just and the unjust" (NAB).

50. Rom 5:6, 8 (NAB).

> submission; a young man for youths, becoming an example for youths and sanctifying them for the Lord. So also He became an old man for old men so that he might be the perfect teacher in all things,—perfect not only in respect to the setting forth of truth, but perfect also in respect to relative age,—sanctifying the elderly and at the same time becoming an example to them. Then he even experienced death itself, so that He might be the firstborn from the dead, having the first place in all things, the originator of life, before all and preceding all.[51]

This description of Christ's incarnation, growth and development—passing as he does through all the stages of human development so as to live in complete solidarity with humanity and accomplish the work of redemption holistically—is entirely pertinent to the question of the phenomenality of the Eucharist.[52] For Christ invites all to this table, to the wedding feast of "the Lamb of God, who takes away the sins of the world!"[53] Personhood allows for the phenomenality of the Eucharist to become incarnate. The Eucharist traces the form of Christ's incarnation, life, death, resurrection and ascension—the pattern of *exitus-reditus* wherein humanity is swept up in a condescending (Athanasius) and re-ascending soteriological itinerary. This is the logical form of the Eucharist that speaks a word and elicits a response. The Eucharist is a phenomenon shared between persons; it is not given to be received by non-human species, but appears as a phenomenon

51. Irenaeus of Lyons, *Against Heresies* 2, 22, 4, in Jurgens, *Faith of the Early Fathers*, 1:87.

52. This is more clearly evident in the Eastern Rite churches in which infants are admitted to the eucharistic table. One also may be led to inquire into the spiritual nourishment of the infant in his or her mother's womb who must in some way be touched by the spiritual blessings of the Eucharist *in utero* through the mother's reception of the Eucharist, due to the mother and child's most intimate symbiotic one-for-the-other relationship. Perhaps a kind of spiritual prelude to baptism for the infant? Furthermore, what does it mean to be conceived within the womb of a woman already baptized, or baptized while the child is still in her womb? Cf. Marion, *Prolegomena to Charity*, 129, 133, 138: "The presence of Christ, and therefore also that of the Father, discloses itself by a gift: it can therefore be recognized only by a blessing. A presence, which gives itself by grace and identifies itself with this gift, can therefore be seen only in being received, and be received only in being blessed . . . Christ, in blessing at the very moment of his ultimate elevation, and precisely because he disappears 'in the very gesture of blessing,' makes himself recognized as such by the disciples . . . The withdrawal of Christ does not make him less present, but more present than his physical presence permitted. Or rather, the new mode of his bodily presence (as the Eucharist) assures us, in the very withdrawal of the former body, a more insistent presence."

53. John 1:29 (RSV); Rev 19:9: "And the angel said to me, 'Write this: Blessed are those who are invited to the marriage supper of the Lamb.' And he said to me, 'These are the true words of God'" (RSV).

proceeding from the person Jesus to human persons who are to become one flesh with him. The inclusive relationality between persons is the sine qua non condition for the possibility of the eucharistic liturgical drama to unfold. The Eucharist bears an anthropological shape that allows humanity to recognize the *theo*logical in Christ and in themselves—a recognition that occurs through the course of the Eucharist as theo*logical* conversation between persons—all persons who themselves breathe personhood into one another according to the affirmative responsibility of one-for-the-other.

## III. The Eucharist as Conversation: From Dialectic to Trilectic and Back Again

The working dialectic between manifestation and proclamation is promoted and maintained by conversation between the two parties of the dialectic. As manifestation and proclamation, the Eucharist necessitates an ongoing conversation between these two poles of the dialectic. Likewise, as it involves two interlocutors concerned with its meaning, the Eucharist takes the form of a conversation between persons, namely, between Christ and his Bride, the Church. Undoubtedly, the language of the Eucharist is the language of gift: "this is my body given up for you; this is my blood poured out for you." In such a formulation, an I-Thou relationship is posited: Christ appears as the *I* offering himself as gift to the *Thou*. However, in order for Christ's eucharistic gift to be received *as* such, the original I-Thou relation demands a role-reversal: Christ becomes the *Thou* and awaits a response from the former *Thou* who is constituted subsequently as a reciprocal *I* insofar as deemed recipient of gift. This role reversal is critical for the play of the gift; without such a reversal, the gift cannot obtain *as* such. At least this is Chauvet's contention. In his magisterial work, *Symbol and Sacrament*, Chauvet argues that a gift is that which constitutes persons as subjects insofar as "the gratuitousness of the gift *carries the obligation of the return-gift of a response*."[54] For Chauvet, the sheer gratuitousness of the gift is met by the gracious super-abundance of the gift that makes the gift refractory to any attempt at its calculation, and bears with it the possibility (and desire!) of a return-gift to be made by the givee. Aiming at the theological concept of grace, Chauvet warns of the danger for the gratuitousness even of grace to become sinister:

> To be theologically Christian, then, a study of grace *must unite the two concepts* we just distinguished [namely, "gratuitousness"

54. Chauvet, *Symbol and Sacrament*, 108.

> and "graciousness"]. To limit oneself to the aspect of gratuitousness would be evil. For to weigh someone down with an avalanche of free liberalities made "without desire of return" is to deprive that person of the inalienable right of response that every recognition of a human being as a subject demands; it is thus to alienate that person, not to recognize that person as "other." The subject can only die, asphyxiated, if it becomes the "object" (that is exactly the word to use!) of free generous gifts which it cannot reciprocate. We said above that every gift obligates; there is no reception of anything *as a gift* which does not require some return-gift as a sign of gratitude, at the very least a "thank you" or some facial expression.[55]

Chauvet's point here is paramount for our consideration of gift as conversation, and for a phenomenological description of the Eucharist as gifted conversation. Chauvet argues that the giver has no difficulty attaining to the status of human subject because it is the giver who gives, who acts, who maintains a level of agency and determination in the act of giving. Yet on the other end of the giving-ness of the gift is the givee whose fate is at stake: Will the givee (1) be rendered a mere mannequin without voice—a perpetual objective *Thou*, or worse, *It*, which only receives this avalanche of gratuitous givenness; or (2) assume a reciprocal role of the giver, issuing a return-gift to the former giver, in effect becoming an authentic human subject and person—an *I* (*moi*) who in turn desires to give and to share in the joy of the givee? Without being trapped in a lock-joint economy of exchange, the obligation of a return-gift that is borne within every gift *as* such is that which animates the human subject, making her a conversation partner instead of a frozen receptacle or pawn of the repressive power of the gift.

The point is that without the "*graciousness of the whole circuit*, and especially of the return-gift," the givee is paralyzed and objectified, stripped of human dignity inasmuch as divested of the potency to issue a return-gift, even in the form of a simple "thank you" or smile. In this manner, the return-gift neither nullifies nor destroys the original gift, but rather validates it and affirms its genius, making it appear *as* such. For a gift is a gift insofar as it is received *as* such. The gift thereby rises to the ethical plane, overturning the bourgeois perpetuation of its own status and place of privilege in the name of the gift—reinforcing the disparities along the fissures of social stratification. Yet more must be said on this crucial topic. In a global climate of growing disparity between the "haves" and the "have-nots," how often are persons asphyxiated by the alleged gratuitousness of their benevolent benefactors?

55. Ibid.

Does the anonymous gift really work? Does the gift that deprives the givee of return-gift truly appear and function as gift? How long will "the poor" remain without name and face, without address and license, without agency and significance? The answer is, as long as the potentate givers deprive their respective givees of the power of the return-gift. The decisive question for ethics today is not what good deed should I do for the stranger, but what gift does the individuated stranger have to offer me (*moi*)? It is I who must divest myself of the power to give in order to receive the passive power of receptivity—powerful insofar as it empowers others. Through such a divestment of my privileged status as egoistic giver, my neighbor is raised to the dignity of an *I*, not simply more of the same, but an *I* as the other. This is precisely the meaning of the Eucharist: illuminated by the rising star of the dark night of phenomenality, the incarnate Word speaks the silent vigil of the arrival of my gift, in effect raising me to the level of person, which he always was and will be forever . . . and so will *I* (*moi*).[56]

This is the manner of the eucharistic gift: a simultaneous offering, summons, vigil, and return-gift—a gracious circuit of amorous gift-giving by mutual lovers. The incarnate sacramentality of divine love demonstrates a paradoxical and dual asymmetry: on the one hand, God's giving-ness is totally other and gratuitous, absolutely sovereign and unmerited, completely saturating and exhaustive; on the other hand, through the Incarnation, God reverses this primordial and diachronic asymmetry in order to breathe life into me, first as a *Thou* and then as an *I* (*moi*), by substituting himself for me that I may respond to him in thanksgiving for this "happy/blessed gift," in εὐ-χαρισ-τία. Just as I sing before him in adoration, she sings over me.[57] Yes, she. How often do exclusive masculine renderings of the Godhead make it virtually impossible to imagine God as receiver of gifts! God as givee! This is the meaning of the Incarnation: in my receiving of the Eucharist, I accept the responsibility of caring for the stranger (Christ!)

56. Cf. Matt 2:9–11: "When they had heard the king they went their way; and behold, the star which they had seen in the East went before them, till it came to rest over the place where the child was. When they saw the star, they rejoiced exceedingly with great joy; and going into the house they saw the child with Mary his mother, and they fell down and worshipped him. Then, opening their treasures, they offered him gifts, gold and frankincense and myrrh" (RSV); Heb 13:8: "Jesus Christ is the same yesterday and today and for ever" (RSV); Rev 1:17–18: "When I saw him, I fell at his feet as though dead. But he laid his right hand upon me, saying, 'Fear not, I am the first and the last, and the living one; I died, and behold I am alive for evermore, and I have the keys of Death and Hades'" (RSV); Rev 22:13: "I am the Alpha and the Omega, the first and the last, the beginning and the end" (RSV).

57. Cf. Zeph 3:17–18: "The Lord, your God, is in your midst, a warrior who gives victory; / he will rejoice over you with gladness, he will renew you with his love; / he will exult over you with loud singing as on a day of festival" (RSV).

in her frailty and vulnerability, to become her lover and friend insofar as her servant.[58] God is not content to give gifts without measure, to usher in grace without response or return-gift. Rather, God awaits our eucharistic response in our praise of responsibility, one-for-the-other.[59] This is the logic and intelligibility of the Eucharist as conversation. In genuine conversation, the *I* speaks a word to the *Thou* while the *Thou* listens attentively. Yet this is not all. At some point—for this to be true conversation—the interlocutors must change places, the *I* becoming the *Thou*, the *Thou* becoming the *I*: a symposium of ideas, an antiphony of dialogue! And so it is with the Eucharist: persons gathered in song around a table of conversation; stories and a meal are shared to bring about a profound sacrificial communion of peace, accord and solidarity, one-for-the-other.

Returning to reflect on the prosopic intercourse of the Eucharist, as introduced above, we are now in a position to assess its iconicity. The Eucharist can be described as an iconic phenomenon between persons—one wherein every person assumes a voice, whether righteous, depraved, agnostic, atheist, *in utero*, comatose, disabled, wounded. Whatever one's circumstance or disposition, it is this they bring to the Eucharist as manifest and proclaimed. The Eucharist bespeaks a manifold testimony of grace and redemption—a religious phenomenon par excellence that appears and speaks at the threshold of our limit-situations. It is this conversant grace that promotes the freedom of all persons in their uniqueness at the eucharistic table. The Eucharist, as gift, is conversation. Hans-Georg Gadamer, in his classic work, *Truth and Method*, recognizes the priority of the question, and the openness the question fosters, in all authentic and fruitful conversation.[60] In this vision for conversation, the *I* belongs to the *Thou* inasmuch

58. Cf. Anselm of Canterbury, "Prayer to St. Paul," in Anselm, *Prayers and Meditations of Saint Anselm*, 153: "And you, Jesus, are you not also a mother? Are you not the mother who, like a hen, gathers her chickens under her wings? Truly, Lord, you are a mother; for both they who are in labour and they who are brought forth are accepted by you"; John 4:7: "A woman of Samaria came to draw water. Jesus said to her, 'Give me a drink'" (NAB); John 12:1–8.

59. Cf. Luke 17:11–19: "On the way to Jerusalem he was passing along between Samaria and Galilee. And as he entered a village, he was met by ten lepers, who stood at a distance and lifted up their voices and said, 'Jesus, Master, have mercy on us.' When he saw them he said to them, 'Go and show yourselves to the priests.' And as they went they were cleansed. Then one of them, when he saw that he was healed, turned back, praising God with a loud voice; and he fell on his face at Jesus' feet, giving him thanks. Now he was a Samaritan. Then Jesus said, 'Were not ten cleansed? Where are the nine? Was no one found to return and give praise to God except this foreigner?' And he said to him, 'Rise and go your way; your faith has made you well'" (RSV).

60. Cf. Tracy, *Analogical Imagination*, 101: "Real conversation occurs only when the participants allow the question, the subject matter, to assume primacy"; Tracy, *Plurality and Ambiguity*.

as the *Thou* belongs to the *I*, and reciprocally so. Gadamer's conception of conversation is that which puts both partners in the dialogue at risk: "they both come under the influence of the truth of the object and are thus bound to one another in a new community."[61] In the Eucharist, all persons, including Christ, come together and risk themselves around the question of truth and its objectivity: what is the case?[62] In the Eucharist, Jesus offers the paradigmatic as the case: "Take this, all of you, and eat of it, for this is my body which will be given up for you. Take this, all of you, and drink from it, for this is the chalice of my blood, the blood of the new and eternal covenant, which will be poured out for you and for many for the forgiveness of sins. Do this in memory of me."[63] This gesture of offering, of supreme gift of self, of a life offered up one-for-the-other, expresses the ultimate among finite possibilities: given to the maximum until there is nothing left to give, in a word, sacrifice.[64]

Even though Christ himself is the protagonist of this drama, he sacramentally absents himself in order to reveal himself as the true one. The appearance of the post-resurrected Christ is met with an accompanying disappearance that opens the iconic distance necessary for correspondence between a set of interlocutors, a community of persons.[65] As it turns out, the logic of the sacrament, on display in the Eucharist, is simply an extension of the basic yet complex logic of perception. Gerard Lukken alludes to this logic in his book, *Per visibilia ad invisibilia*: "The liturgical perception then we experience as being meaningful, because we perceive manifold differences, or at least shadows of differences."[66] Lukken refers to the work of semiotician Algirdas Julien Greimas and his explication of the "semiotic square":

61. Gadamer, *Truth and Method*, 371.

62. Cf. John 18:37–38: "Pilate said to him, 'So you are a king?' Jesus answered, 'You say that I am a king. For this I was born, and for this I have come into the world, to bear witness to the truth. Everyone who is of the truth hears my voice.' Pilate said to him, 'What is truth?'" (RSV).

63. Cf. Tracy, *Analogical Imagination*, 112: "I find myself in another realm of authentic publicness, a realm where 'only the paradigmatic is the real.'"

64. Cf. Marion, "A Sketch of a Phenomenological Concept of Sacrifice," in Marion, *Reason of the Gift*, 69–90.

65. Cf. Chauvet, *Symbol and Sacrament*, 216–20, 161–80; Chauvet, *Sacraments*, 22–28; Marion, *Crossing of the Visible*, 46–87.

66. Lukken, *Per visibilia ad invisibilia*, 270.

Semiotic Square

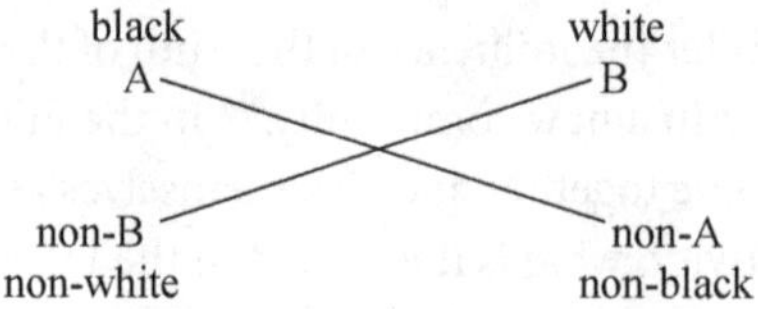


Given the semiotic square, "essential for the elementary structure of meaning is the fact that the negative term is a turning point to a positive contrary term: from 'non black' one comes to the conclusion that one has to do with the color 'white' . . . Essential therefore is that one does not remain stuck to the absence ('non-black'), but that an absence calls a presence ('white') into being."[67] This basic heuristic for semiotic phenomenality is applicable to the Eucharist, though pertaining to an ontological, and not merely ontic or hermeneutic, level. Logically speaking, not only is the phenomenality of the sacrament—at least in a general sense of the term wherein the invisible is manifest, proclaimed and attested in the visible—a possibility, but a necessity. For one to recognize and call a thing "visible," such a denomination demands the concomitant absence and negative term of the "invisible." An overt and exclusive materialism has no way to account for the phenomenality of the invisible except to deny that it exists; in its very denial, the invisible attests to its legitimate phenomenality that in turn makes that of the visible possible.

In the sacrament of the Eucharist, the prototype of Christ remains concealed according to the invisible domain of spirit, while still claiming to give himself prototypically in the materiality therein: Body, Blood, Soul and Divinity.[68] The logic of this double phenomenality opens the necessary distance of freedom and otherness between persons. Since the prototypical Christ withdraws from immediate view in the eucharistic sacrament, he appears precisely therein for faith.[69] Faith can behold Christ—Body,

67. Ibid., 271.

68. Cf. Denzinger and Schönmetzer, *Enchiridion symbolorum*, ¶ 1640 (876): "*. . . et semper haec fides in Ecclesia Dei fuit, statim post consecrationem verum Domini nostril corpus verumque eius sanguine sub panis et vini specie una cum ipsius anima et divinitate existstere*"; Tanner, *Decrees of the Ecumenical Councils*, 2:695: "And it has at all times been the belief in the church of God that immediately after the consecration the true body of our Lord and his true blood exist along with his soul and divinity under the form of bread and wine."

69. Cf. Heb 11:1: "Faith is the realization of what is hoped for and evidence of things not seen" (NAB); Marion, *Prolegomena to Charity*, 101: "But to render oneself other, to surrender this gaze to the gaze of the other who crosses me, requires faith."

Blood, Soul and Divinity—according to its surrendered intentionality, an intentionality inverted before the face of the impossible. Yet intentionality signifies a traversing of distance, an aim that is met by a giving intuition; the intention does not traverse the entire distance, but stretches as far as its finite limits allow. The free intention is met in turn by the free counter-intention through the play of iconicity, the play of conversation, the play of the gift. The prime mediator of this distance of freedom is called, in Christian theology, the divine Spirit: the *nexus amborum* ("the nexus of the two"), the unrevealed Revealer, the vacant place, the vital space between heaven and earth.[70] It is through this space of freedom that the prototype of Christ remains hidden to the "proof" of immediacy and yet apparent and palpable to the decision and testimony of faith. Here the objectivity of truth is "not something already given beforehand to which one only has to adjust oneself with exactitude, but rather a 'making-come-into-being,' and 'advent' which, like a 'fugitive glimpse,' gives itself only in simultaneously 'holding itself back' in a sort of 'suspense' to the person who, against every utilitarian tendency, knows how to respect the 'vacant place' where it discloses itself."[71] In this sense, "faith is chewing, slowly ruminating over the scandal of the Messiah crucified for the life of the world" according to the non-knowledge par excellence—the pneumatic wisdom that is the question of questions.[72] In the end, the Eucharist can be described as a phenomenon guided by the questions of faith: What gives/calls in this phenomenon and what does it mean? The boundless fecundity of the Eucharist is due to the interrogative play around the symbolic phenomenality that both gives meaning (*logos*) to be received (*fiat*), and receives meaning that is given in the course of subjective recognition, interpretation, contemplation and denomination. Christ prototypically absents himself to the senses (for example, to sight and to touch) in the phenomenality of the Eucharist in order to appear and to speak paradigmatically to the subjective intentionality of faith that has been inverted therein. In this way does Christ also put the objective truth status of the claims about his divine-human personhood and identity at arm's reach for the sake of the freedom of faith within the play of conversation, opening the way for a knowledge of faith that phenomenologically operates as the act of attestation.[73]

70. Cf. Chauvet, *Symbol and Sacrament*, 513–15. See Madathummuriyil, *Sacrament as Gift*, for the pneumatological implications of understanding the Eucharist as gift according to a Marionian trajectory.

71. Chauvet, *Symbol and Sacrament*, 117.

72. Ibid., 225, 516, respectively, Chauvet quoting here (in the latter part) from Paul Beauchamp's *L'un et l'autre Testament* (1976).

73. Recall the "Knowledge of Truth Schema" from chapter 1.

In order to understand better these juxtaposed notions of given meaning (*logos*) to be received (*fiat*), and received meaning given by the human subject, let us reflect for a moment on one of the persons who lived in the most intimate proximity to Jesus: Mary, his mother. The testimony about Mary is inseparable from the testimony about Jesus, inasmuch as these two testimonies work together in the formulation of the doctrine of the Incarnation. According to the testimony of the Gospel of Luke, the conception of Jesus in the womb of Mary did not come about as an act of force. Rather, it was through the intercourse of a conversation wherein the gift was offered and received according to Mary's free response of faith: "Behold, I am the handmaid of the Lord; let it be to me according to your word."[74] Mary first receives this eventful meaning mediated by the message of an angel designated by the name "Gabri-el," meaning "God is my strength." The genius of Mary's *fiat*, inscribed in the form of her female body that manifests and speaks the language of receptivity, appears as a portal into the possibility of responding to, and receiving, the gift of God's salvation. Mary's *fiat*, in turn, incarnationally exhibits the prophetic word that bears the other within the same without thereby reducing the other to the same.[75] Jesus becomes incarnate in her flesh—an other within the sameness of her flesh. In following the event of Jesus's conception in her womb, Mary sings a song of praise to magnify the Lord, as well as "[keeps] all these things, pondering them in her heart."[76] Evident in her responses is Mary's personal creativity issuing from her freedom to speak and to give a return-gift to the "Father of lights," from whom comes "all good giving and every perfect gift."[77] Even for Mary, who was in the most intimate relationship with Jesus as his mother, a necessary distance obtains between them that allows both of them to speak to each other in freedom and respect:

> And when they saw him they were astonished; and his mother said to him, "Son, why have you treated us so? Behold, your father and I have been looking for you anxiously." And he said

74. Luke 1:38 (RSV); cf. Latin Vulgate translation: "*ecce ancilla Domini fiat mihi secundum verbum tuum*"; cf. Luke 1:45: "And blessed is she who believed that there would be a fulfillment of what was spoken to her from the Lord" (RSV).

75. Cf. Levinas, *Otherwise than Being*, 149; Levinas, *Totality and Infinity*, 266: "I love fully only if the Other loves me, not because I need the recognition of the Other, but because my voluptuosity delights in his voluptuosity, and because in this unparalleled conjuncture of identification, in this *trans-substantiation*, the same and the other are not united but precisely—beyond every possible project, beyond every meaningful and intelligent power—engender the child"; Rev 19:10: "For the testimony of Jesus is the spirit of prophecy" (RSV).

76. Luke 2:19 (RSV); cf. Luke 1:46–55.

77. Jas 1:17 (NAB).

> to them, "How is it that you sought me? Did you not know that I must be in my Father's house?" And they did not understand the saying which he spoke to them. And he went down with them and came to Nazareth, and was obedient to them; and his mother kept all these things in her heart.[78]

In this scene, the identity of Jesus is manifest according to the degree of his disappearance. Jesus's absence is troubling and perplexing, but nonetheless is necessary for his hypostatic (human/divine) personhood to reveal itself. And again, Mary is described as "keeping all these things in her heart," implying a contemplative consciousness that is at once intentional and intuitive.

Mariology completes the gracious circuit of the Eucharist offered and received as conversational gift. Reflecting on the *fiat* of Mary assists in understanding the Eucharist as fruitful conversation between others. The dialectical relationship between *logos* and *fiat* describes the phenomenality of the Eucharist: the hypostatic union of the *Logos* becoming flesh in and through the faithful *fiat* of the respondent, of the givee who in turn becomes giver. Mary, in becoming one-for-the-other as Jesus's mother, attests to the possibility of accepting the call to responsibility made in the humility of the eucharistic offering, visibly appearing in the forms of bread and wine, invisibly manifest and spoken to an inverted intentionality of faith *as* Body and Blood given up for you. Wherein is the trilectic of testimony? Precisely in the pluriformity of the Word: manifest in flesh and blood; proclaimed in discourse, narrative and conversation; attested in lives that engender the fruits of the Spirit: "love, joy, peace, patience, kindness, goodness, faithfulness, gentleness, self-control."[79] An antiphony of the gift prevails in conversation: partners engaged in lively dialogical play around the object of truth. Antiphony—call and response; question and answer—is the alternation of voices in a symphony of personhood that opens the way for recognizing truth. This opening is made possible by *Hagia Sophia*, the Testator—"the *gift-giving agent* which enables the believer to let God be God and thus to establish a true communication with God . . . the agent of this *enfleshment of the word*" that touches our bodies without "closing up every fissure between body and word."[80] It is the neuter Spirit of Trinitarian theology that resembles the third party of the trilectic of testimony—the neutral party that provides the exigency of accountability to objective truth, paving the way for the fecundity and depth of the trilectic as it witnesses to, and pro-

78. Luke 2:48–51 (RSV).

79. Gal 5:22–23 (RSV).

80. Chauvet, *Symbol and Sacrament*, 514, 526, respectively.

motes the space for, the antiphony of the dialectic between manifestation and proclamation.

## IV. Intimate, Self-Donative Love: The Poetics of the Eucharist

To conclude this chapter, before moving on to the final stage of transcendental reflection (metaphysics), we will consider the language of lovers: poetic discourse. Jennifer Anna Gosetti-Ferencei's book *Heidegger, Hölderlin, and the Subject of Poetic Language* will serve as a helpful guide for accessing the appropriateness and possibilities of poetic discourse. As Marion suggests in his essay critiquing Levinas's reduction to alterity, "not only does love speak—like the face—but it makes possible the most accomplished form of the spoken word—poetry, which tears itself in this way from its ontological determination (Heidegger), in order to take on ethical status."[81] Poetry, from the Greek verb, *poieio* ("to do, make, create, compose"), is a form of discourse that discloses possibility and bears within itself the capacity to open onto new worlds. Heidegger has demonstrated that "the conceptual does not exhaust the realm of the thinkable" since "the concept excludes what it cannot render transparent, thereby exiling it from the sphere of truth and meaning."[82] Likewise, we have argued above that the revelatory phe-

81. Marion, "From the Other to the Individual," in Schwartz, *Transcendence*, 53. Cf. Levinas, *Otherwise than Being*, 199 (endnote 10): "As a sign given of this signification of signs, proximity also delineates the trope of lyricism: to love by telling one's love to the beloved—love songs, the possibility of poetry, of art." For a similar critique of Levinas's reduction to general alterity (rather than specific personal alterity) via John Duns Scotus's notion of singularity, see Falque, *God, the Flesh, and the Other*, 255–77. In response to Marion's and Falque's critique of Levinas, I would argue that Levinas's specification of the personal other as *l'autrui*, rather than merely *l'autre*, implies the uniqueness and individuality of the personal other while maintaining a universal and unconditional summons to responsibility not only for this other but for every other. For Levinas, the covenantal and universal call of responsibility transcends the conditional contours of *haecceitas*. Perhaps *haecceitas* threatens to spoil the resoluteness of responsibility for the other inasmuch as it conditions responsibility by making it contingent on the subjective receptivity of the other's givenness, whether according to physical traits, personality, or perceived degrees of beauty, value, or erotic freight. See again Levinas's interview response in Robbins, *Is It Righteous to Be?*, 108: "I think that responsibility is the love without concupiscence of which Pascal spoke: to respond to the other, to approach the other as unique, isolated from all multiplicity and outside collective necessities. To approach someone as unique to the world is to love him. Affective warmth, feeling, and goodness constitute the proper mode of this approach to the unique, the thinking of the unique." In this text, it is clear that Levinas maintains the notion of individual uniqueness in his conception of the other who faces me (*l'autrui*).

82. Gosetti-Ferencei, *Subject of Poetic Language*, 3–4.

nomenon—or at the very least its possibility—demands the divestment of intentionality and consciousness in order to receive it as such. The concept itself does not encompass the universe. Many phenomena give themselves in ways that escape conceptual limits: "Joy, wonderment, and even, in the wake of Schiller, love can be thought according to Hölderlin only poetically, according not to a conceptual but to a poetic logic."[83] Saturated phenomena, and moreover doubly saturated phenomena, annul every concept that would venture to master them. Whereas the concept demands adequation with a specific object-referent, poetic language "is shown to be an access to truth neither as correctness nor as the correspondence between thought and actuality but as a process of partial, and therefore finite, disclosure."[84] Poetry is at once the language of humility and creativity. It is a melodic responsorial to the vocational givenness of the cosmos and to the call of the other. It is a spontaneous ethical gesture of return-gift to the other who has revealed herself as beautiful, wonderful and unique. By "*troubl(ing) the ordinary distinctions between the real and the imaginary, the verifiable and the elusive*," poetical truth speaks the truth of the paradigmatic, the truer than true, in a word, the absolute. Poetry is the only genre of discourse worthy of the dignity of the absolute because it humbly considers itself to be unworthy according to the comportment of its divestiture, yearning and uprightness.

Because it hearkens beyond the horizon of being, yet all the while evading the temptation to nihilism, "poetical projection is the means by which, in compositional spontaneity, imaginative understanding presses forward into possibilities in transcendence of the given."[85] It is in this way that "poetry is above all an act of creation."[86] The creature, too, is called to create—to become a co-creator with the divine. Meaning not only gives itself, but also is made. Yet this creation of meaning does not give itself over to a blanket relativism in which everything is suddenly equally meaningful and true. Rather, "the poet encounters beings as signs of the destiny of withdrawal and clearing. The poet's naming of the gods is his response to their address; the poet brings us into the 'sphere of decision' as to whether or

83. Ibid., 4.

84. Ibid., 5. Cf. ibid., 6–7: "Heidegger finds in poetic language an alternative to the violence of technological rationality, which defines, reduces, manipulates, and exhausts its object, its 'other' . . . The poem is an 'enigma' we should not wish to solve, but that nevertheless gives direction to thinking"; ibid., 47: "Poetic language is then never a mere grasping hold of, never an expression of a meaning fully explicit, exchangeable between interlocutors."

85. Ibid., 253.

86. Ibid., 258.

not to yield to their claim."[87] The very meaning of holiness is performed by poetic discourse in its responsorial to the call of the divine, of the absolute, of the infinite, of love, of the other. Setting apart truth from falsehood resonates in the ambiguity of the poem that nevertheless expresses an original affirmation of the absolute. Precision of perception and rational discourse is transposed into the key of love that sings with the most fervent resolve and conviction. Poetry is the language of the witness who has come to believe in a testimony of ultimate concern, both given and spoken. This is the language of the Song of Songs and the dozens of Psalms attesting to divine justice, glory and mercy.

In returning to the question of the Eucharist, poetry finds a welcome home. The Eucharist, itself a phenomenon shrouded in the poetic, incites a poetic response by its witness. Poetic discourse is by nature personal and uncanny. It disrupts the typical prosaic discourse of academic writing, yet for this reason is even more necessary and valuable in a postmodern context. To round out this chapter, as well as chapter 6, I will give myself over to transparency to a second degree. I will submit original poetry that will exhibit the potency and meaningfulness of poetic discourse. A turn to poetry will demonstrate a creative output of my personal testimony to the meaning of the Eucharist for me (*moi*). But this is not to be viewed as an isolated or autonomous effort at meaning-making, but one that proceeds from the heart of a community of faith insofar as I am a member of this community. This feeble attempt at poetic discourse will allow the Eucharist to be enfleshed even further. I, who received the gift of the Eucharist even last evening, offer a few humble verses in thanksgiving and praise. May this be but a momentary testimonial mosaic of a surging heart in adoration and contemplation, demonstrating the conversational and ethical nature of the eucharistic gift.

Head bowed low, with body trembling
Admitting my hubris and duplicity I come
Not unaware of the stranger's suffering—yes,
She too bears a name. I must learn her name—her
Sweet name, as you know her sweet name
For it is your name; her name and your name
Mingled together; your names are sweetness itself
She—unrepeatable she!—exudes your glory joy triumphant
A trace of light shimmers upon the horizon yet not destroyed

87. Ibid., 48.

We are not destroyed . . . yet . . . until hope is vanquished
By the throes of careless despair parting
Company with cosmic whisperings alit as
Footprints of . . .
A word distant and near, near in its distance
Jesus, friend in darkest nights and rayonnent of days
Cup of suffering turned springtime pulses
Throb again against the threat of hate which
Never gave ear to listen to the other his
Cry pain ashen bleeding beckons stillness

Why, sparrow, do you sing no more?
This too is resurrection—yes, death, although
Resurrection—alive once more to sing once more
Without cessation pause gap in this life
Breathing rhythms together in song
A share in eternal praise there in the ancient whither
There in the dayspring of belonging
Whence shall come forth she, yes
She who gave me life to conquer fear of her and her kin
Overcoming self-ugliness lackadaisical torpor
Up my soul! Rise to her defense, your defense
Lest you heed the lie—this belch of casual humor
Caressing its own fur and carousing in its shame
Rise, let us be on our way
Liturgical tempo cues our entrance

I rise not on my own power, I, helpless lie
Dormant overwhelmed multitudes needs crave
Gold and silver have I not, but what have I
Give—the power to give; *you* hold the power to
Give gifts without measure, yes, *you*
What is your wish? What is your name?
I will await your gift to me keeping watch
Nighttime wonders unforeseeable horizon spread by your
Gift thank *you* for the gift thank you

*Your* gift you you are we together given

How do you feel? Palimpsest, please proceed at *your* leisure

. ,

?

, , ,

. ;

. . . . . .

? ,

, – ?[88]

88. This wordless sequence of punctuation represents the nature of the responsorial palimpsest that maintains the possibility of creativity and new meanings. It signifies the voice of the other who summons me to responsibility for her. It also represents the unpredictability and incommunicability of the other, as well as the diachronic trace of the saying in the said.

# chapter 6

# Postlude: The Eucharist as Truth

## I. Finitude, Judgment, and Ethical Action

THE EUCHARIST MANIFESTS AND proclaims itself as an ambiguous and enigmatic phenomenon insofar as it is doubly saturated and involves poetic intercourse between persons. As such it calls for a level of transcendental reflection in response to a prior phenomenological description. Chapter 5 concluded with a poetic construal of the Eucharist according to the dialectic between the given meaning (*logos*) received (*fiat*), and the constructed meaning invested in the phenomenon by the human subject. Chapter 6 will attempt a subsequent transcendental response to the preceding phenomenological analysis of the Eucharist as set forth in the previous chapters. As chapter 5 culminated with a personal poetic response to the Eucharist, it will be the task of chapter 6 to take a step backward and reflect on the conditions of possibility necessary for recognizing a phenomenon *as* such and verbally responding to it poetically. Phenomenology, in effect, will be brought into a tensive dialectical relationship with the method of transcendental reflection, also known as metaphysics.[1] In this final chapter we will be inquiring into the possibility of the actuality that makes all possibilities

1. The term "metaphysics" is used in spite of its perennial ambiguity. For the purposes of this chapter, the sense of metaphysics meant, while rooted in the Aristotelian tradition, is above all in reference to the post-Cartesian and post-Kantian conception of metaphysics as the science that examines the universal conditions of possibility for rationality, perception, knowledge, and understanding. For a helpful summary of metaphysics and its historical trajectory, see Grondin, *Introduction to Metaphysics*.

possible.[2] Even though possibility was moments ago exalted through poetic discourse, we find it necessary to locate the transcultural and universal—actual—transcendental conditions for the coherent operation of consciousness, cognition, and meaning-making in order to procure warrant for making a truth-claim in the end. This move may be unsettling for some, especially for those who insist on "purifying" phenomenology from all doctrinal contamination, whether religious, metaphysical or otherwise. I will be careful to maintain the "purity" of the preceding phenomenological investigation while putting the results of phenomenology in conversation with the authority of metaphsyics and its timeless first principles. If Husserl convincingly closed the caesura between noumenon and phenomenon (contra Kant), then I suggest a closure of the caesura between phenomenology and metaphysics, though all the while protecting their distinction and difference in method.

While it is recognized that departing from the poetic to the transcendental so rapidly can, in effect, undermine and curtail the genius of the poetic, it is nonetheless necessary to conclude this study with transcendental reflection in order to carry out the publicness of a project in fundamental theology.[3] If, in the end, all that this text had to say about the Eucharist is that it is an ambiguous and multifaceted phenomenon, why go through all of the scholarly trouble to posit simply that? However, this book attempts to detect an inner logic and, above all, truth amidst its ambiguity and plurality of meanings. The way it will do this is to proceed along the path of transcendental reflection on the phenomenological description laid out in the past five chapters. The dialectic between manifestation and proclamation will be mirrored by the dialectic between phenomenological description and transcendental reflection. The phenomenological and the transcendental—which are often at odds with one another—will be brought together in this final chapter to submit a testimony as to the truth status of the paradigmatic

2. See Gschwandtner, *Degrees of Givenness*, 190: "One would only need to distinguish between possibility and actuality in these [liturgical] events if one were concerned—and of course Marion is concerned—to identify what happens as revelation of the divine, or, even more specifically, as an encounter with the Christian God as the true and only God."

3. Cf. Tracy, *Plurality and Ambiguity*, 43: "Even if we have never heard of the 'heresy of paraphrase,' we know instinctively that we cannot, without loss, translate the meaning of a poem into a prosaic message"; and Levinas, *Alterity and Transcendence*, 172–73: "To seek the definition of meaning is as if one were to try to reduce the effect of a poem to its causes or transcendental conditions. The definition of poetry is perhaps that the poetic vision is more true and, in a certain sense, 'older' than the vision of its conditions. In reflecting on the transcendental conditions of the poem, you have already lost the poem."

phenomenon of the Eucharist: interpersonal sacramental love manifest, proclaimed and attested.

Given this proposal, one might ask what sense it makes to return to Kant after having done away with him. In other words, why go back to concern over transcendental conditions of possibility after phenomenology has liberated itself from the bondage of predetermined subjective impositions on phenomenality? The reason for this inauspicious move is to attempt to ground universal claims to truth in the universal transcendental conditions for meaning-making. This is not to suggest a homogenous culture or univocal mode of expression—a one-size-fits-all order of signification—but it is to argue for a universal basis for meaning-making and truth on which all human reason relies. It will be demonstrated in the following pages that truth is not monadic, but intersubjective. Truth is recognized through the course of communication.[4] As Sokolowski has put it, the human being is "the agent of truth."[5] We are not content to rest our thoughts on probabilities or maybes. We demand to know the truth because we are convinced that the truth will set us free.[6] To approach truth, one must at once reach into the innermost interiority of one's self (*moi*) and stretch outward into the outermost exteriority and distance toward the other. The case for truth is neither solipsistic nor nihilistic. Further, truth does not imply licentious relativism but rather suggests clarity of perception and unambiguous ethical injunction. Knowledge of just action is issued from without, planted as a seed within. Truth must be manifest (*alétheia*), but it also must be proclaimed (*kerygma*), all through the circuit of testimony (*martyría*). If we are able to secure demonstrably the universal and necessary conditions of possibility for discourse and meaning-making, we likewise will guarantee the just sanction for submitting an assertion of truth, in particular, the Eucharist as truth.

4. Cf. Ricoeur, *History and Truth*, 50–51: "Let being be thought in me—such is my wish for truth. And so the search for truth is itself torn between the 'finitude' of my questioning and the 'openness' of my being. It is here that we discover the history of philosophy as the memory of great and singular philosophies: for on the road that ascends from my situation toward the truth, there is only one way of moving beyond myself, and this is *communication* . . . Communication is a structure of true knowledge . . . we should reject any definition of truth which is, as it were, *monadic*, wherein truth would be for each person the adequation of *his* answer to *his* problematic. On the contrary, we now approach an intersubjective definition of truth according to which each one 'explains himself' and unfolds his perception of the world in 'combat' with another."

5. Sokolowski, *Christian Faith and Human Understanding*, 77.

6. See John 8:31–32: "Jesus then said to those Jews who believed in him, 'If you remain in my word, you will truly be my disciples, and you will know the truth, and the truth will set you free'" (NAB).

Transcendental conditions of possibility suggest the limitations of reason. Kant makes this clear in his "Introduction" to the first edition of his *Critique of Pure Reason* when he says that "human reason has a peculiar fate in one kind of its cognitions: it is troubled by questions that it cannot dismiss, because they are posed to it by the nature of reason itself, but that it also cannot answer, because they surpass human reason's very ability."[7] Such questions that surpass reason's very ability include those inquiries into the transcendental principles that ground finite reason itself and serve as the basis and assurance of all coherent discourse and meaning-making. Because human reason is neither the origin of itself nor omniscient in its scope, it asks into the very reason for itself—a reason that is transcendent but nevertheless leaves its trace in the operations of human reason. The quest for the reason of human reason finally leads to what Ricoeur calls "a philosophy of Transcendence—which is what a philosophy of man's limitations is in the last resort."[8] Even with the unlimited stock of possibility served up by phenomenology, we must admit that we are limited. Likewise, even with our multitude of passionate desires that lead us in every which direction, we must admit that we are finite and constricted beings. We are like questions that open onto endless possibilities and yet we must act in this blessed context of possibility's vertigo. To act is to sacrifice possibility by choosing one possibility among the many; to act is to give oneself over to the one, to be faithful to the one. To act is to actualize the possible, or rather to recognize and believe in the actual among the host of possibles.[9] To be free is to bind oneself to an assured actual among the endless possibles issued by imagination. To be free is to be released from the shackles of promiscuous

7. Kant, *Critique of Pure Reason*, 5.

8. Ricoeur, *Freedom and Nature*, 468.

9. See ibid., 93, 122, 418, 447, 479: "Man is man because of his ability to confront his needs and sometimes sacrifice them . . . Though I am not the master of need in the sense of lack, I can reject it as reason for action. In this extreme experience man shows his humanity . . . The limit experience of sacrifice stresses sufficiently that there are other sources of voluntary motivation beside organic concern . . . I am a *problem resolved* as though by a greater wisdom than myself . . . I suffer from being condemned to a choice which concentrates and intensifies my particularity and destroys all the possibles through which I am in contact with the totality of human experience . . . Ah! If only I could grasp and embrace everything!—and how cruel it is to choose and exclude. That is how life moves: from amputation to amputation; and on the road from the possible to the actual lie only ruined hopes and atrophied powers. How much latent humanity I must reject in order to be someone! . . . No longer 'Become all things!' but rather 'Become what you are.' My task is to raise the 'Die and become' to the level of spiritual transcendence where my limitations are transformed in receptivity and patience. To say *yes* remains my act . . . *Yes* to my life, which I have not chosen but which is the condition which makes all choice possible."

desire that paralyze one to act freely. To be free is to tame licentious desire and to sacrifice according to the virtue of self-mastery. To be free is "to swear" an unbreakable oath to the other, "to seven oneself," "to bind oneself by seven things" (שָׁבַע [*shava*])—to commit oneself to the precious pearl that demands nothing less than the most costly, exorbitant and absolute sacrifice.[10] To act is to say "Yes"—a Yes that implies a googolplex of No's that only signify collectively as the negative counterpart to the resolute affirmation of the Yes.[11] If there is any hope in wagering a serious truth-claim, it will be a matter of exceeding the limits of phenomenology only through a paradoxical dialectics of that which proposed to limit phenomenology at the outset: transcendental reflection. The end is the beginning, the beginning is the end. To proceed, we first must clarify the meaning of the notion "transcendental reflection."

## II. From Phenomenology to Transcendental Reflection

What is meant by transcendental reflection? In *Blessed Rage for Order*, David Tracy indicates that the passageway from the meanings gleaned from historical and hermeneutic investigation—which I am including under the rubric "proclamation" as part of the dialectic within phenomenological description—to an assessment of the truth status of these meanings is transcendental reflection.[12] For Tracy, the notion of transcendental reflection refers to a mode of metaphysical reflection, that is, the type of reflection that "mediates the most basic and, hence, most obvious presuppositions of all our thinking and living."[13] In other words, transcendental, or metaphysical, reflection does not claim to introduce anything new to the phenomenologi-

10. See Gen 21:24, 27; 24:7; Deut 6:13; 1 Sam 20:17; Ezek 16:8; Matt 13:44–46.

11. The term "googolplex" signifies the number one with an unlimited series of zeros following it: 1,000,000,000,000,000,000,000, etc. It is known as the number produced by writing as many zeros, following the number one, as a person can until he or she is too tired to continue to do so. Googolplex also can be envisioned as infinity minus one. For our purposes, pure actuality is infinity (*actus purus*) and just human action is infinity minus googolplex, with the remainder of one: my action for which no one else is responsible; the choice of the one demanding the forfeiture of all other possibilities. Cf. Ricoeur, *Freedom and Nature*, 476: "Consent gives me to myself and reminds me that no one can absolve me from the act of *yes*." Ricoeur is referring to consent to the finitude of one's involuntary conditions of being, as well as to the blissful limitations of one's personal freedom and action.

12. Tracy, *Blessed Rage for Order*, 52: "[The theologian] must ask what further discipline will allow him to determine whether his earlier conclusions can legitimately be described not only as accurate meanings but also as true."

13. Ibid., 61, endnote 49.

cal description already made; rather it claims to make explicit the a priori capacities that allow for phenomenological description to identify that which is manifest, proclaimed and attested. To make explicit means to mediate linguistically and conceptually "the basic presuppositions (or 'beliefs') that are the conditions of the possibility of our existing or understanding at all."[14] Transcendental reflection is a mediation of "the conditions of the possibility of experience as such."[15] This prospect is palpably Kantian in its nature, coming to terms with the admissible limits of human cognition, reason and experience through the process whereby reason issues a self-critique of its own ability. However, the First Critique does not imply a cancellation of all universality or objectivity. To the contrary, even Kant maintains "universal conditions of experience."[16] When he relates the synthetic principles of pure understanding—axioms of intuition (quantity), anticipations of perception (quality), analogies of experience (relation), and postulates of empirical thought as such (modality)—he does not have in mind culturally conditioned principles but universal ones. The transcendental turn toward subjectivity, beginning with Descartes, does not disqualify the veracity of objectivity and universal structures of perception and meaning-making. Moreover, the dialectical method proposed in this book admits the possibility, and even necessity, of the complementarity between objective and subjective dimensions of conscious perception and knowledge. As with Husserl, the phenomenon is the noumenon; the datum of consciousness is one with the thing itself.

For Tracy, the method of transcendental reflection bears two primary characteristics: (1) it is capable of articulating conceptual and not merely symbolic categories, and (2) it is able to explicate its criteria for its cognitive claims concerning religious/theistic experience and meanings, two of its fundamental criteria being (*a*) identification of a necessary and sufficient ground in our common experience for such claims, and (*b*) exhibition of an inner coherence and a coherence with other essential categories of our knowledge and belief.[17] This is to say that in following up the task of phe-

14. Ibid., 55–56.

15. Ibid., 63, endnote 64.

16. Kant, *Critique of Pure Reason*, 283: Third postulate of empirical thought as such: "3. That whose coherence with the actual is determined according to universal conditions of experience is *necessary* (exists necessarily)."

17. Tracy, *Blessed Rage for Order*, 55. Transcendental reflection attempts to circumvent the radical suspicions of all claims to truth by calling upon the transcendental to exercise a counter-suspicion on the suspicious. Transcendental reflection subverts suspicion itself when the proposals of suspicion do not acknowledge their own warrants for coherence and intelligibility; cf. Nietzsche, as cited in Palsey, *Nietzsche*, 70, as cited in Tracy, *Plurality and Ambiguity*, 76: "What, then, is truth? A mobile army of

nomenological description, which employs the criterion of relative adequacy (a code word for the principle of sufficient reason) to assess the meaning and meaningfulness of experience, transcendental reflection likewise employs the criterion of relative adequacy to determine the truth status of the meaning and meaningfulness of the experience in asking the question, is this meaning true?[18] In this manner transcendental reflection continues the quest for achieving a thoroughly public theological investigation. To make a truth-claim in a global context of religious pluralism, can one claim, at the same time, an objective and universal truth? Can one make a truth-claim that is true for you, for me, for all? At the very least, this possibility comes to light through the course of conversation—the possibility of adapting oneself to the truth-claim of another, of coming to believe that what the other says is the case. Tracy, substantially influenced by Bernard Lonergan (1904–84), testifies to the possibility of self-transcendence: our ability to ask questions and to allow ourselves an expanding horizon for inquiry. Following his mentor, he opens scientific consideration of the religious phenomenon by allowing the possibility of an expanding horizon. However, while understanding expands through its exposure to alterity in the happening of dialogue with the other, Tracy still contends that the exigencies of reason must remain in force even in a transformative dialogue of alterity.[19] Tracy's point is this:

metaphors, metonyms, and anthropomorphisms—in short, a sum of human relations, which have been enhanced, transposed, and embellished poetically and rhetorically, and which after long use seem firm, canonical, and obligatory to a people: truths are illusions about which one has forgotten that this is what they are; metaphors which are worn out and without sensuous power . . ." Given this text, one could ask Nietzsche, "How is it that what you say makes sense to another?" Nietzsche, and all masters of suspicion, must, in the end, allow suspicion to cast its own suspicious glare upon itself in realizing that its own claims are meaningful and sensible insofar as they too depend on some a priori principle of logic-making and coherence.

18. Cf. Tracy, *Plurality and Ambiguity*, 22–23: "For relative adequacy is just that: relative, not absolute, adequacy. If one demands certainty, one is assured of failure. We can never possess absolute certainty. But we can achieve a good—that is, a relatively adequate—interpretation: relative to the power of disclosure and concealment of the text, relative to the skills and attentiveness of the interpreter, relative to the kind of conversation possible for the interpreter in a particular culture at a particular time. Somehow conversation and relatively adequate interpretations suffice."

19. Cf. Tracy, *Dialogue with the Other*, 41, 44, 46: "To recognize the other *as* other, the different *as* different is also to acknowledge that other world of meaning as, in some manner, a possible option for myself . . . To understand at all is to understand differently. To understand at all is to understand for and within genuine dialogue allowing real manifestations of the other's truth and thereby mutual transformation . . . with the crucial proviso that the demands of reason, including the proper demands of metaphysical and transcendental reflection, must be allowed full sway in every conversation worthy of the name."

when describing, appropriating and attesting to the religious phenomenon in the context of public discourse, the testator must adhere to criteria of adequacy, relevance, coherence and intelligibility in order to assess the religious phenomenon alongside all other phenomena that may be described as they occur in the realm of common human experience and language.[20] The method of transcendental reflection serves as a bridge that mediates the question of truth between the two components of Tracy's revisionist method for Christian theology, namely, (1) Christian texts and (2) common human experience and language. While phenomenological description, including hermeneutic phenomenology, can succeed in articulating the meaning and meaningfulness of the correlation between these two components, it is left for transcendental reflection to render explicit the truth status of religious and theistic claims as they proceed along the same route as do all intelligible phenomena: the route of reason.

Therefore the task of this final chapter will be to show what particular limit-concepts function as fundamental beliefs, or conditions of possibility, for all intelligible human experience as such.[21] However, this task is not identical to the task Kant sets for himself in his *Critique of Pure Reason*, which was to identify the necessary conditions of possibility and concepts to which all objects of experience must necessarily conform in order to appear in human experience. Kant's project, in these terms, has received sufficient critique from Marion concerning the possibility of the saturated phenomenon. Instead, the task of this chapter will be to render explicit those fundamental beliefs to which all reasonable persons adhere—from Kant to Feuerbach to Nietzsche to Freud to Stein to Tracy to Marion to Richard Dawkins, et al.—who claim to pronounce interpretive judgments concerning religious phenomena, either for or against. Judgment can be suspended only for so long; making phenomenological claims in the name of possibility can be sustained for so long. In the end, one must decide, one must judge for oneself, one must interpret, one must testify to truth. Aiming at a thetic judgment through transcendental reflection will posit that which is necessary for any cognitive claims whatsoever, let alone religious and theistic claims.[22] Thetic judgment will not only make a truth-claim for a

20. See Sokolowski, *Phenomenology of the Human Person*, and his portrayal of the human person as a being of language.

21. Cf. Tracy, *Blessed Rage for Order*, 70–71.

22. A "thetic judgment" is "a belief which implies the existence of that which is believed; it is a judgment which posits existence." Ricoeur, "The Hermeneutics of Testimony," in Ricoeur, *Essays on Biblical Interpretation*, 154, endnote 16. A thetic judgment, in contrast to a "categorical judgment," is made without full and exhaustive knowledge of the subject to which truth is predicated. Thetic judgment hovers between ignorance

single segment of the global population, but will make a claim to truth that is indeed universal, even if articulated and expressed through a particular language, culture and social context. Herein emerges the risk of such a bold proposal.

The attempt at a thetic judgment to assess the universal conditions of possibility for all cognitive claims will appear as the most dangerous and presumptuous wager in this investigation. For how can one speak on behalf of all of humanity and make a proposal that claims for itself to be true for all people and for all times? Is not such an argument to be laughed to scorn immediately, especially in the postmodern context in which we now live? Does not such a claim threaten to undo the entire work of phenomenological description that happily opened all windows to let in the fresh air of possibility, in effect clearing the stuffiness of a room full of worn-out and tattered metaphysical baggage? Likewise, does not such an assertion threaten to reinstate those very same totalizing systems of thought that engendered the devastating results of exclusionary ideological imperialisms, and bred the war-bent vermin who carried out the annihilation of their brethren through acts of genocide and unspeakable violence? Would not such a proposal negate the Levinasian project of ethics as first philosophy and the prioritization of the other? Such accosting questions make one tremble in fear and resist any prospects of universal and objective truth-claims. Yet the question of truth remains. It confronts us and summons us to give an account of our dealings with it. The standard of truth remains the benchmark of any statement, proposition, claim to facticity, or even testimony. In a court of law, how can one render judgment on a case if not according to the

---

and omniscience, without belonging to either. The phenomenon of the sacrament, as well as that of human personhood, always will require the response of a thetic judgment due to their enigmatic nature and paradoxical double phenomenality, for example, the visible and the invisible, the said and the saying, presence and absence, the finite and the infinite. Similar to the transition from phenomenology's suspension of judgment to metaphysics's thetic judgment is the transition from general apophatic discourse about the divine to apophantic discourse about the divine as in the work of John Scotus Eriugena. See Falque, *God, the Flesh, and the Other*, 47–76. Falque relates the transition from the apophatic to the apophantic as a "setting of *logos*." Yet for Falque, similar to Marion and the cohort of phenomenologists of givenness, the "setting of *logos*" is ultimately a setting of manifestation: "Manifestation thus legitimately abides with the logos, in phenomenology (the manifest) as in theology (the theophany), deploying a type of discourse which is made the *setting* [*écrin*] without being made a *screen* [*écran*]. The exiting from being by the nihilation of eminence and the struggle against every form of reification of the divine leads Erigena, like Aristotle before him and Heidegger after him, toward a new mode, properly called the 'apophantic' that is *revelatory* of the thing itself (*apo-phaines-thai*)" (ibid., 58). Our contention is that the meaning of *logos* cannot be reduced to manifestation alone (Falque, Marion, et al.), but must be held in tension with the structural exigencies of proclamation (Ricoeur and Levinas).

principle of truth? Does not sworn testimony in a court of law presuppose, not only the possibility, but the actuality of truth—that such and such is truly the case? Would a dethronement of truth really bring about a more just society—one operating on pure relativism, wherein lies were just as valid as truth-telling, wherein the project of assessing the truth status of cognitive claims was aborted according to the agnostic interrogative: "Who knows?" No. It will be demonstrated below, even at the risk of misconstruing the absolute character of truth for the lie of totality, that the very denial of truth ironically attests to its immovable position as that which allows for the possibility of any logical discourse and meaning-making whatsoever.

In order to carry out this demonstration, it will be necessary to pass through an ordered progression of argument. The following text will set out to do three things: (1) make a case for the *logos*-principle as the standard for truth-telling and ethical action; (2) tally the results garnered from the phenomenological description carried out in chapters 4 and 5, and render explicit—through transcendental reflection—the presumed conditions of possibility involved in the cognitive claims that raise the meaning and meaningfulness of the Eucharist to the status of the true; and (3) offer a second personal testimony to the truth of the Eucharist through original poetic discourse. By following these three critical steps, the trilectic of testimony, as originally proposed in chapter 1, will come full circle. The project will have begun and ended with testimony.

## III. The *Logos*-Principle as Anchor of Discourse: Hope in the Midst of Ambiguity

What is the miracle called understanding? What exactly is the wonder in which you understand me, in which this text makes any sense at all? What is the hope we share in finding and making meaning? What, after all, is at the center of our discourse—of you understanding me, and me understanding you? Can this phenomenon be reduced to the evolution of communication taking place within the species we call ourselves, namely, "human"? Can this evolution alone explain how and why we communicate with one another with the goal of being meaningful? Can all communication be reduced to a complex process whereby members of our species strive to gratify our ultimately base desires, whether nutritional, sexual, emotional, material? Is not even the negation of such desires—fasting, abstinence, solitude, elected poverty—a covert acting on the basis of desire, in the name of desire, perhaps in confidence of some reward awaiting one in heaven, or the gratification of a superiority complex, or the attainment of a kind of spiritual perfection? Perhaps. Perhaps not. In any case, these questions attest to the process of understanding—the process of rendering something meaningful. The question remains: what holds this process together? In a word, *logos*.[23] This ancient Greek word carries with it many meanings—one only has to peruse a Greek lexicon to find this to be true, to be the case. The term *logos* can mean: something said (for example, "word, saying, message, teaching, talk, conversation, question, statement"), account, reckoning, collection (that is, a "gathering up"), reason, mind, grounds, rationality, charge, matter, thing, subject, book, something thought, maxim, proverb, tradition, sentence, narrative, measure, order, explanation, assertion, promise, report, power to speak, opinion, principle, proposition, definition, etc. So what? Precisely! *Logos* is the term—indeed polysemic in its many meanings—that signifies the *what* of discourse—the something, the *that*, the *which*, the *who*, the *why* of discourse. *Logos* is the principle of coherence, intelligibility and rationality of discourse—the meaning-making principle, that by which anything has a chance of making any sense at all—discourse itself.[24] Without

23. See Lacoste's essay "On Knowing God through Loving Him: Beyond 'Faith and Reason,'" in Bloechl, *Christianity and Secular Reason*, 127: "An affirmation as old as philosophy itself, and which is a philosophical affirmation: human beings are defined specifically by *logos*, called *ratio* in Latin, and accordingly, by 'reason' and 'rationality' . . . All that is given is grasped through the *logos*"; and Lacoste, *Experience and the Absolute*, 106: "The intelligibility of the world is an elementary given of experience. We are not only questioning and interpreting animals who cannot live without wishing to understand: the real is also given to us as something we can acquire and that organizes knowledge [*le savoir*], as something we can question and to which we can respond correctly. Before us, we find a cosmos and not chaos. The facts are ordered by laws. We always encounter an order."

24. Cf. Merleau-Ponty, *Merleau-Ponty Reader*, 438–39: "Being. Show that the 'sensible' as such is transcendence, i.e., accessibility of the unaccessible. The '*Logos* of the aesthetic world': this 'reverse side' of the quale, of the projective pellicule, the tacit sense and teleology. This sense is inseparable from the appearance, from the body. It makes the world be 'flesh.' And that it is cumulative. It is this Logos that we unveil by reascending from 'my perceptions,' which are doubtful one by one, to the world as the place of inscription and sedimentation, agency of truth. It is the place of the (verbal) *Wesen*. Rays of *ester*. Here 'perception' and 'perceived' are *inscribed together*. The 'someone' of perception (the one who perceives is 'no one,' and it is as well an 'other'). Differentiation with the horizons of indifferentiation. It is the mass of sensible Being. It is this *Logos* that exists and will always remain the source of sense (*Sinnsquelle*). Not without doubt in its content (it varies with cultures, the 'Nature' of each is 'subjective')—but in its carnal structure—i.e., a kind of *Erfüllung* which is not Spinozist adequation, which is the encasement of *ek-stasis*, going as far as the fundamental 'there is' (*Welthesis*). The capacity for all knowledge, of all *thought* (*Erzeugung* of the invisible), is found in this *Logos* of the visible world: [traditionally], sedimentation, taking support upon sensible Presence, insofar as it has a double ontological ground—(to see is to have the invisible since it is to have an *Urstiftung*)"; and Levinas, *Humanism of the Other*, 22, 25: ". . . the ideal of unity that is the force of the Truth and the hope of understanding among

the *logos*-principle there would be only gibberish. Even if gibberish were meaningful, it would be due to the *logos*-principle. Even the musical phenomenon is guided by the *logos*-principle, whether the music is from the East or from the West, tonal or atonal—if one claims it to be meaningful, it is due to the *logos*-principle. The *logos*-principle is not only the common ground of communication, it can be described as the very ground of communication itself. To try and refute this argument, one would have to apply the very same *logos*-principle in formulating an argument. The *logos*-principle is neither bound to any culture or cultures, nor is it circumscribable by a set of signs, symbols or patterns. It is the rule of the cosmos itself. It is the meaning-making principle inscribed in the whole of the cosmic order wherein realities give themselves *as* meaningful and take on meaning from human subjective assignment and denomination. Even more, it is according to the *logos*-principle that this or that meaning is judged to be true, that is, adequate to experience. Without the notion of a *logos*-principle, the prospect of a public and fundamental theology would be absurd. In fact, the prospect of any theo*logy*, or any *-logy* for that matter, would be absurd—absurd insofar as *logically* absurd . . .

Through this brief *logical* discourse, the first condition of possibility for any cognitive claim whatsoever has been demonstrated sufficiently: the a priori function of what can be called the *logos*-principle.[25] Every sign, symbol, text and word depends on such a principle for it to become discernable and meaningful. It is necessary to render such a *logos*-principle explicit in order to carry out a properly public and fundamental theo*logy*. The *logos*-principle is not itself a phenomenon, but a limit-concept that refers to that which permits all phenomena to be recognizable and rendered intelligible.

---

people . . . the unity of sense without which there is no sense"; and Gadamer, *Truth and Method*, 361: "What emerges in [dialogue's] truth is the logos, which is neither mine nor yours and hence so far transcends the interlocutors' subjective opinions that even the person leading the conversation knows that he does not know"; and Heidegger, *Being and Time*, 56, 58 (§ 7): "Furthermore, because the *λόγος* is a letting-something-be-seen, it can *therefore* be true or false . . . And because the function of the *λόγος* lies in merely letting something be seen, in *letting* entities be *perceived* [im *Vernehmenlassen* des Seienden], *λόγος* can signify the *reason* [*Vernunft*]"; and Stein, *Knowledge and Faith*, 9: "Both Husserl and Thomas were convinced that a λόγος is the force behind all that is, and that our understanding can uncover step by step first one aspect of this λόγος, then another, and so on, as long as it moves ahead in accordance with the principle of the most stringent intellectual honor."

25. Cf. Kant, *Critique of Judgment*, 400: "When we *reflect* . . . we need a principle just as much as we do when we determine, where the underlying concept of the object prescribes the rule to judgment and so takes the place of the principle. The principle by which we reflect on given objects of nature is this: that for all natural things *concepts* can be found that are determined empirically."

It also could be called "ground" or "horizon," but *logos*-principle seems to convey better the underlying linguisticality of all meaning-making. Without such a principle, life would be a blur, and this assertion, too, can be surmised only from the impetus for meaning, the *logos*-principle. The *logos*-principle is the prime filter through which all phenomena must pass if they are to be recognized as phenomena *as* such. From the *logos*-principle extends one's personal horizon for intuition and understanding—"a maximum field of vision from a determined viewpoint."[26] Though the personal field of the horizon maintains the possibility of being expanded, it remains a limited field of cognitive vision for the individual person. In other words, the *logos*-principle is not an unlimited capacity for cognition in the individual person, but operates through a particular set of strictures—for example, age, life circumstances, genetic makeup, culture, language, etc.—differing from person to person. This fact does not undermine the universality of the *logos*-principle, but simply demonstrates its concrete application in the individual life of the person. Ricoeur says as much in his book *History and Truth*, from which this illuminating passage is worth quoting at length:

> The search for truth, it seems, is characterized by being stretched, so to speak, between two poles: a personal situation, and a certain intention with respect to being. On the one hand, I have something to discover personally, something that no other except myself has the task of discovering. If my existence has a meaning, if it is not empty, I have a place within being which invites me to raise a question that no one else can raise in my place. The narrowness of my condition, my information, my encounters, my reading, already outline the finished perspectives of my calling to truth. And yet, on the other hand, to search for truth means that I aspire to express something that is valid for all, that stands out on the background of my situation as something universal. I do not want to invent or to say whatever I like, but what *is*. From the very roots of my situation I aspire to be bound by being. Let being be thought in me—such is my wish for truth. And so the search for truth is itself torn between the "finitude" of my questioning and the "openness" of being.[27]

26. Tracy, *Achievement of Bernard Lonergan*, 14.

27. Ricoeur, *History and Truth*, 50–51. Cf. Ricoeur, *Rule of Metaphor*, 355–57: "Even if one does not recognize that it can be articulated in a distinct discourse, this power of the speculative supplies the horizon or, as it has been called, the logical space on the basis of which the clarification of the signifying aim of concepts is distinguished radically from any genetic explanation based on perception or images . . . If a sense that is 'one and the same' can be discerned in a meaning, it is not just because one sees it that way but because one can connect it to a network of meanings of the same order in

In these words, Ricoeur sums up the paradoxical nature of, what we are calling, the *logos*-principle: its simultaneous universality and particularity—a paradox that some Western Enlightenment thinkers were not able to swallow. For example, recall the aporia of the so-called "theological ditch" of Gotthold Lessing, himself a self-professed inquirer after truth.[28] In Ricoeur's conception, truth bears the dual character of finitude and openness, best thought in terms of conversation and intersubjectivity mediated by language and testimony.

Further, in Lonerganian terms, "beyond intelligent consciousness there is rational consciousness," that is, "beyond the intelligible emanation of concept from insight there lies the second intelligible emanation of judgment from reflective understanding."[29] It is from the latter activity of judgment where "the notions of truth and falsity, of certitude and probability, of yes or no" emerge.[30] It is this act of decision where "there arises personal commitment that makes one responsible for one's judgments," and this personal commitment we have designated as "testimony" and "original affirmation."[31] Thus judgment, and thereby testimony, can be rendered as "virtually unconditioned."[32] To recall in Lonergan's terms, "the intrinsic relation of human knowing to reality is the intelligently and rationally conscious drive of all genuine intellectual activity as it moves beyond data to intelligibility, beyond intelligibility to truth and through and in truth to being as real; beyond every known truth and being to all the truth and being still to be known."[33] Such is the progression of the logical and intellectual enterprise, wherein one moves from perceptual data to intelligible and meaningful articulations of this data, accessible through phenomenological description, to truth—the realm of the "Yes" and "No"—according to the mode of transcendental reflection. This entire process is worked out through the method of question and answer in the course of conversation. Interlocutors testify, one to the other, making claims to knowledge and truth, yet all claims mediated by testimony. In short, to know is to testify; to testify is to believe. In this sense, truth is never finished but is always in

accordance with the constitutive laws of the logical space itself . . . The signifying aim of the concept works free of interpretations, schematizations, and imaginative illustrations only if a horizon of constitution is given in advance, the horizon of speculative *logos*."

28. Cf. Lessing, *Theological Writings*, especially 51–56.

29. Tracy, *Achievement of Bernard Lonergan*, 70.

30. Ibid., 125.

31. Ibid.

32. Ibid., 128.

33. Ibid., 150.

the making. Herein is revealed the paradoxical nature of the *logos*-principle: on one hand, one can be assured of discovering truth; on the other hand, one should not be carried away by the false pretension to having the truth as in a relationship of possession.[34] This leads us back to the notion of the intentionality of faith within the context of communication.

"Intentionality of faith" signifies the mode by which anything is supposedly known or told as being the case. Stretching further beyond empirics alone, an intentionality of faith is operative in every person's claims to knowledge and meaning-making. An intentionality of faith does not imply religious belief per se on a first-level reflection, but simply the act of cognition that adheres to a particular testimony that claims such and such to be the case through the operation of conscious judgment.[35] To judge is to deem something true or false, to agree or to disagree, to respond affirmatively or negatively. Even in the case of the paradox, judgment is still confronted with a dual opposition: either the paradox itself is true or it is false; in other words, either I submit to the truth status of the paradox or I decline. In this case, judgment is an ultimate. For what can be claimed to be known *as* such without having passed through the tribunal of judgment, without being carried to judgment by attestation? It is the intentionality of faith—itself led by attestation—that leads judgment, by the hand as it were (*manuductio*), to the threshing floor of decision where the wheat of truth is separated from the chaff of falsehood. The intentionality of faith, first of all, believes in the *logos*-principle, believes that meaning and intelligibility can be achieved, that all discourse is grounded in a rationality that ensures its stability and coherence. Without this fundamental belief, nothing could be trusted as being true; nothing could warrant that such and such is the case. Everything not only would be held in utmost suspicion, but all would be floundering in a non-gravitational space of nonsensicality that, for that matter, could not even be recognized as being nonsensical because nothing

34. Ricoeur, *History and Truth*, 54–55: "I am thinking of an expression such as 'I hope I am within the bounds of Truth' . . . Plurality is therefore not the final reality, nor is misunderstanding the ultimate possibility of communication. The being of every question originally opens everyone to everyone else and grounds the historic and polemic truth of communication. But here we must be on our guard against separating the 'within' ('within the bounds of truth') from the 'I hope' ('I hope I am within the bounds of truth'). I cannot express, articulate, or enunciate the unity of this rationally, for there is no Logos within this unity. I cannot compress within a coherent discourse the 'openness' that founds the unity of all questions. Otherwise I should not say 'I hope I *am within* the bounds of truth' but 'I *have* the truth' . . . That is why [truth] is rather of the nature of Promise or of Reminiscence (which should be the same thing) . . . I maintain that the unity of truth is a timeless task only because it is first an eschatological hope."

35. Recall the "Knowledge of Truth Schema" from chapter 1.

could be recognized, not even nothing itself. In a word, nihilism. This concludes our exposition of the first dimension of the *logos*-principle: the fundamental belief and trust in the coherence and intelligibility of meaning; the principle according to which phenomena can be recognized *as* such.

Yet there is a second dimension of the *logos*-principle that must not be overlooked: its ethical dimension.[36] The first dimension of the *logos*-principle also may be called ethical insofar as truth-telling is an ethical task. However, this second dimension is called ethical more properly, for it is given in the form of action as testimony. This is the aspect of *logos* that cannot be reduced to an abstract, esoteric non-phenomenon alone, but that which also "entails corporality: sound, voice, gesture, dance, and all our senses."[37] Human action is revelatory of the *logos*-principle and grounds the possibility of phenomenological encounter and description. Ricoeur refers to this *logos*-recognition as the "I believe that I can" self-reassurance in the face of radical self-suspicion.[38] Fundamental trust in oneself as self-determining actor and overcomeer of radical suspicion and self-doubt reflectively surfaces as an integral dimension of the *logos*-principle. This could be called the will to act whereby one sets out on a course of action that is not arbitrary but authentic. Even the Greek etymology of the word "authentic" suggests a tethering of action to an a priori source that is not originally one's own: *aut -hentes* ("master; one who accomplishes"). Authentic action thus bespeaks a kind of action that is disclosive of right-ways-of-being-in-the-world. The phenomenology of law attests not only to a prototype, but to an archetype as well. For every *nomos,* there is a prefigured *logos,* for *logos* is the order of order. My personal will to act exhibits the fundamental trust in myself as actor that is given to me by my proximity and passivity vis-à-vis others. Without such proximity and passivity, I would not be able to recognize myself *as* such or *as* an actor on the world-stage of existence. My will to act—and act rightly—attests to the ordered righteousness that precedes my acting. Beyond a mere hodgepodge of cultural taboos and norms for behavior, one's will to act is configured according to a teleology of uprightness, inasmuch as the teleo-*logy* is the selfsame archeo-*logy* for human action. In other words, the end is the beginning, the beginning is the end.

In summary, we have identified two complementary dimensions of a *logos*-principle, which itself has been demonstrated to be the necessary condition for the possibilities of coherence, intelligibility and recognition.

36. Cf. Levinas, *Humanism of the Other*, 36: "Morality does not belong to Culture; it allows us to judge culture, to evaluate the dimension of its elevation. Elevation ordains being."

37. Panikkar, *Rhythm of Being*, 337.

38. Cf. Ricoeur, *Course of Recognition*, 91.

Without such a logical impetus, no phenomena would be recognizable *as* such, and no claims to meaning, meaningfulness or truth could be posited. To recall, the two dimensions of the *logos*-principle are (1) its limit-concept dimension, and (2) its ethical dimension. The former is evinced in the basic processes of communication, meaning-making and truth-telling, while the latter is evinced in the self-affirmation of "I believe that I can" in spite of an atmosphere of radical ambiguity and suspicion. By naming the overriding limit-of category (in Tracy's terminology) as "*logos*-principle," we are able to hone in on the prospect of rendering a judgment as to the status of the truth-claims of the Eucharist, recalling its phenomenological description.[39] In other words, transcendental reflection provides the necessary justification for aiming at a claim to truth, that is, truth in a universal and objective sense of the term. Transcendental reflection is not a hoax that will automatically allow the Eucharist to ascend to the status of true. Rather, transcendental reflection is that method that brings all phenomena to the threshing floor of judgment, whereupon the testimonies in which a particular phenomenon is enmeshed are brought before the jury of decision, pressing the jurors to pass a verdict as to not only the interpreted meaning of the given phenomenon, but also as to its objective and universal veracity. Perhaps this language is still too poetic and metaphorical. To try to express this in other words: by identifying the *logos*-principle underlying every phenomenological interpretation, a case is made for asking the question of truth; in asking the question of truth, competing and contradicting testimonies are articulated and at least partially understood; one who understands and therein interprets the competing and contradicting testimonies must sort out those testimonies and hazard a decision, that is, a judgment or verdict, as to the truthfulness of each testimony and, in the end, forge a new personal testimony configured according to one's judgment of those prior testimonies of others. The imperative character of the decision of judgment is due to the *logos*-principle, demanding that the truth be told and that doubt and suspicion be overcome through fundamental self-affirmation as the basis of any and all personal action.

## IV. From Metaphysics to Phenomenology and Back Again: To Risk a Judgment of Truth

Having demonstrated the a priori necessity of a so-called *logos*-principle for meaning-making and truth-telling, it is now time to demonstrate (1) how the *logos*-principle justifies and legitimates judgments of truth, and (2) how

39. Cf. Tracy, *Blessed Rage for Order*, 92–94, on the notion of "limit-of" category.

objective and universal truth-claims of the Eucharist can be posited in light of the *logos*-principle.

By virtue of its dual dimensions, specifically its limit-concept dimension and its ethical dimension, the *logos*-principle demands that truth be judged *as* such and decided upon by the individual person-in-community. This is not equivalent to the phenomenon of voting or consensus, wherein a group of persons tally their personal judgments (in a thoroughgoing context of bias) to arrive at an approximated group decision that could be revised later on by another group. Rather, the *logos*-principle calls each and every individual person to the witness stand to give an account, to testify before the world. This is to say that the *logos*-principle, according to its absolute exigencies, confronts each and every individual person at the level of personal decision: one must decide for oneself; "no one testifies for the witness." The *logos*-principle operates according to the measure of hope for meaning and truth in an ineradicable context of perennial ambiguity, but it nevertheless operates and somehow finds a clearing for truth to which to tether one's life and death. Without the exigencies of the *logos*-principle—calling the witness to testify, to speak and to give an account of one's deepest convictions writ large on the tablet of personal action—life would remain meaningless and void of truth. Absence of a *logos*-principle would render life not only anarchic, but aneschato*logical* as well. Therefore, personal decision is the sine qua non for meaningful, truthful and authentic living. Yet personal decision must be given something upon which to decide—a content that can be said to be true *as such*.[40] Without content for decision, decision decides not. If this is the case, truth-content cannot be absolutely relative—that is, exhibiting varying degrees or interchangeable properties—but must both appear and speak in an advent of ultimacy. Obviously this ultimacy will take on diverse visages in the diversity of cultures of the world, but nonetheless this ultimacy will come as a sui generis content, objective and universal in character, ripe for decision. Without such ripeness and clarity in the midst of ambiguity, decision could not be made—especially decision concerning that which is ultimate—concerning the irrevocable claim of something on which to stake one's life. To decide is to risk, without doubt; but in the end, to risk is to live. It must be admitted that all live insofar as all risk a personal life testimony—a way-of-being-in-the-world that is only possible by the anterior decision to live authentically, overcoming the threat of suicidal forfeiture. To the contrary, I believe that I can.

40. The significance of the italicization of both "as" and "such" is to connote both the interpretation and givenness/saying of truth. Truth simultaneously gives/says itself and is appropriated *as such* by the personal witness. I understand "such" to refer to the thing itself and "as" to refer to its interpretation and attestation.

Moreover, it must be clarified that this personal decision of testimony is not a solipsistic, or purely autonomous, task. Rather, it takes place in the context of a particular community, though both the community and the self remain ambiguous.[41] Even though the decision is a personal one, it nonetheless relies on those personal decisions of others that inform and inspire it. In such an inter-in-dependent situation, one decides for oneself, but not only for oneself.[42] My decision becomes a possible content for your decision; my life becomes a definitive testimony for your life-becoming-testimony, and vice versa. In this sense, no person is an island, but neither can one person's decision count for another's decision. Each person's personal decision is unique and unrepeatable, just as each person's person is *incommunicabilis*, nontransferable. Yet how is one to decide definitively and irrevocably? In a world of radical plurality, cultural diversity, and nauseating ambiguity, one can decide only according to the paradigmatic. The quest for truth as the quest for the paradigmatic asks the question, "What is that to which I can say Amen and Halleluiah?" In other words, "What is that to which I can ascribe the utmost affirmation of my life and being, and that to which I am compelled to offer the gift of praise I have to give to one alone, the one to whom it is due?" These are the fundamental life questions that shape one's personal identity and destiny. It is important to note that this move, which begins with a criterion of truthfulness in the form of a question employing notions from the Judeo-Christian tradition, is not legerdemain or a stacking of the deck in favor of an objective and universal Judeo-Christian truth outcome. I employ the notions of Amen and Halleluiah because, for me, these best indicate the personal response of decision toward ultimate truth. I readily admit that there can be, and even are, equally plausible words and notions that could convey the same meaning. However, I am arguing that truth can claim an objective and universal ultimacy according to the a priori *logos*-principle to which all meaning-making and truth-telling are bound.

41. Cf. Tracy, *Analogical Imagination*, 53: "That the self of any one of us is *both* essentially good and actually an uneasy, ambiguous combination of goodness and corruption is a lesson taught by both the Christian tradition and the most radical secular masters of suspicion in our period, Freud and Nietzsche. That lesson is available to anyone still able to believe in either the pure goodness or the unrelieved corruption of the human spirit. The truth is that the reality of the private self is as ambiguous as the realities of society, academy and church. Indeed the latter are but the self writ large"; cf. ibid., 105.

42. Panikkar, *Rhythm of Being*, 53: "Reality has an inter-in-dependent order. This is the sphere of *ontonomy*. If Being is rhythmic, each entity will enjoy a real freedom according to its nature in relation to the Whole . . . The order is an *ontonomous* order in which every being (*on*) discovers its proper *nomos* within the Whole: *ontonomy*."

If the *logos*-principle be true for all people, it follows that an instance of truth as paradigmatic not only may be truthful for all people, but is truthful for all people. Indeed, this is a risky and dangerous claim that smacks of intellectual imperialism. However, in spite of its audacity, such a claim is demanded by the exigencies of the *logos*-principle. For the *logos*-principle self-attests to its unity, both in its limit-concept dimension and in its ethical dimension. Its oneness is mediated to consciousness by the unity in plurality inter-in-dependent act of attestation. In other words, the oneness of my decision of witness itself attests to the unity of the content of truth upon which it decides. The freedom of personal decision is my own—granted that it is dependent upon the personal decisions of others—a freedom that is free to decide personally insofar as it is provided with an absolute content upon which to decide absolutely. This freedom indicates not the arbitrary, incidental decisions of everyday life, for example, what clothes to wear or what to eat today, but indicates that for which I live today—precisely the truth-content to which I choose to bind my life. To deny that one's life is bound by some so-called truth-content would be a fallacious denial. For each and every person's life manifests and proclaims a testimony that reveals the very truth-content for which one lives insofar as one acts. Our lives—our thoughts, words, and deeds—are tablets of testimony that attest to the truth that each of us has chosen as ultimate. This is not to say that there is a monadic version of truth-content that can be discerned among the host of tablets of testimony—a truth-content of certainty into which everyone should have been initiated through Gnostic rites of exclusion, in effect setting apart the enlightened from the ignorant. Rather, to maintain the notion of truth-content as truth-as-paradigmatic is to suggest that, given the project of human living, insofar as "human" refers to an inclusive understanding of personhood, that which is paradigmatic appears and proclaims itself as a pattern, a model, and exemplary for all. The paradigmatic as the real, truth as paradigmatic, self-attests to its status as the true one in the midst of its counterfeit competitors. In the fairy tale of Cinderella, the glass slipper fits the foot of only one maiden in the land. Truth as paradigmatic does not only proclaim a message to be trusted, but invites the respondent to see for oneself (manifestation). Yet "to see for oneself" would not matter were it not for its mode of proclamation with its various modes of attestation. What good is seeing for oneself without the prospect of sharing one's conviction and joy with others, in turn to receive reciprocal validation that such and such is indeed the case? And so it is that the decision of personal testimony is ultimately one's own, but made in the world of those decisions of personal testimony of others who one trusts and finds to be icons themselves of the paradigmatic. In the end, phenomenological description is led to the kiln of transcendental reflection, to the fires that test the truth-claims of all phenomena that give themselves *as such*.[43]

The first step of transcendental reflection on the Eucharist is to tally the primary meanings gleaned from the phenomenological description carried out in chapters 4 and 5, and to render explicit the necessary conditions of possibility involved in the cognitive claims that raise the meaning and meaningfulness of the Eucharist to the status of the true. As chapters 4 and 5 appropriated the phenomenological insights of Marion, Ricoeur and Levinas to the question of the phenomenality of the Eucharist, the following reflections will attempt to apply these former insights to the question of the truth status of the Eucharist by asking, is the Eucharist true *as such*? So far in chapter 6, we have made explicit the *logos*-principle as that which opens the possibility for any meaning-making and truth-telling whatsoever. We also have made the case for a necessary truth-content that claims objective and universal status insofar as it appears and speaks *the* paradigmatic. Finally, by these proposals, we have set the stage to answer the crucial question: How is the Eucharist an instance of truth as paradigmatic par excellence, that is, the paradigmatic of the paradigmatic?

To answer this question, first we must tally the primary meanings of the Eucharist gleaned through phenomenological description in chapters 4 and 5. These meanings we propose to be:

1. Phenomenologically interpreting the Eucharist as manifestation-proclamation-attestation demonstrates its trilectical form and structure of operation. The ultimately trilectical structure of eucharistic phenomenality exhibits a tripartite form of fecundity, as well as the phenomenality of paradoxical unity in difference.
2. By phenomenologically interpreting the Eucharist as manifestation-proclamation-attestation, a peculiar logic becomes evident: the logic of the cross.[44] This is none other than the logic of inversion, subversion and double negation, in a word, the logic of paradox.
3. Phenomenologically interpreting the Eucharist as manifestation-proclamation-attestation reveals its prosopic character: an inclusive phenomenon of personal and iconic intercourse wherein gift is construed as conversation.

43. Cf. 1 Cor 3:12–13: "If anyone builds on this foundation with gold, silver, precious stones, wood, hay or straw, the work of each will come to light, for the Day will disclose it. It will be revealed with fire, and the fire [itself] will test the quality of each one's work" (NAB).

44. Cf. Chauvet, *Symbol and Sacrament*, 527; Lacoste, *Experience and the Absolute*, 190–91.

Each of these three meanings was explicated in chapters 4 and 5. The task ahead is to assess the truth-claims of these meanings through the mode of transcendental reflection wherein the paradigmatic is the real and objective and universal truth is truth as paradigmatic, manifest and proclaimed in the various forms of attestation, disclosed and announced in the form of personal attestation. The following method of transcendental reflection will begin with the third meaning above, followed by the second, followed by the first.

## A. The Truth of Prosopic Intercourse

The prosopic character of the Eucharist, wherein gift is understood as conversation, attains to the status of the paradigmatic, thereby attaining to the objective and universal status of the true. Insofar as the *logos*-principle is an explicit naming of that limit-concept that allows for, and holds together, any meaning-making and truth-making whatsoever, conversation is that gifted phenomenon between persons that is the very process of meaning-making. Meanings are formulated via attestation and the iconicity of personhood, and then submitted to judgment and decision for a verdict as to their veracity. The Eucharist makes many truth-claims that call for responsive judgments, for example, that bread and wine become Christ's true body and blood; that Christ's passion, death, and resurrection are extended and offered to humanity in the eucharistic liturgy; that divine grace is conferred through the eucharistic species, met by receptive faith and contrite dispositions; that one's participation in, and reception of, the Eucharist configures one as an *alter Christus* and assimilates one anew into the mystical Body of Christ, which is the Church. In response to each truth-claim, the human subject must answer the question, is it true?

Face to face with such truth-claims, the human subject must decide, must profess a *credo*. To describe the Eucharist as essentially a phenomenon of prosopic intercourse, wherein gift is to be understood as conversation—a conversation between persons divine and human—is to say that the Eucharist exhibits the paradigmatic instance of the gift as conversation insofar as the gift is given in absolute fashion, unleashing the antiphonal possibility of erotic-agapic nuptial communion. This communion proves generative in its many fruits of conversion, reconciliation, justice making, healing, and assuming responsibility as one-for-the-other. The gift of mutual giving on display in the Eucharist demonstrates the reciprocity of gift-giving between the divine and humanity, even if in a relationship that is fundamentally asymmetrical. The Eucharist is not merely an indifferent and utterly gratuitous giving in the direction from the divine to the human alone. Rather, it is a divine invitation to commune, entering the incarnate pneumatical space of prosopic intercourse wherein every person is accorded the status of unique and unrepeatable—an inclusive banquet of love in which the dignity and uniqueness of each person is promoted inasmuch as each person bears the potential to give and to receive.

Reciprocity and graciousness function as partners in the law of the gift. In this way, the personhood of each person is promoted, prohibiting the tragedy in which a person is assumed to have nothing to offer at this table of the world. In other words, the Eucharist recognizes that each person has a gift to bring to the table of the world, and further, invites each and every person to bring their irreplaceable gifts to the altar of iconic intercourse. No person is reduced to a mere receptacle for the presumptive onslaught of the utterly gratuitous gift, but instead each person receives to the measure that she gives. It is the promotion of universal gift giving and gift receiving that constitutes the work of justice, raising all persons to their rightful status as persons and not merely objects without personality under the domination of the gift that emasculates. Justice is paradigmatic, and so is universal human dignity. The utopian vision of a world in which all persons bear the potency of gift-giving, as well as gift-receiving, not only constitutes an eschatological vision of the reign of God, but remains a real possibility for the *hic et nunc*.[45] The genius of the Eucharist aims at realizing this possibility of justice for all insofar as the Eucharist provokes the radical play of the gift as conversation in which each person gives without measure (graciousness) and receives with gratitude.[46] The Eucharist attains to the status of the true because it ascends to the status of the paradigmatic: in the Eucharist, Jesus, through his life, death and resurrection, appears, proclaims and attests to the paradigmatic form of the gift as conversation through his relationship with God the Father, in the Holy Spirit, and through his relationship with every human person, manifest, proclaimed and attested in the eucharistic locus of prosopic intercourse.[47]

45. Cf. Gutiérrez, *Theology of Liberation*, 137: "Because of its relationship to reality, its implications for praxis, and its rational character, utopia is a factor of historical dynamism and radical transformation. Utopia, indeed, is on the level of the cultural revolution which attempts to forge a new kind of humanity."

46. Cf. Gschwandtner, *Degrees of Givenness*, 176: "The Eucharist becomes, in fact, the supreme instance of the gift and the paradigm for all truly given gifts. Just as God's love is the paradigm for all human love, the eucharistic gift is the supreme instance of all human gifts . . . an overwhelmingly saturated phenomenon, which proceeds from God alone and whose sole content is Christ as God's supreme gift."

47. See Sokolowski, *Christian Faith and Human Understanding*, 71: "The Eucharist, together with the Church that is built up around it and provides the context for it, is

## B. The Truth of the Logic of the Cross

Secondly, the logic of the cross exhibited in the Eucharist, wherein the logic of paradox overturns the logic of henodox, attains to the status of the paradigmatic, thereby attaining to the objective and universal status of the true. Paul writes in his first epistle to the church in Corinth:

> For Christ did not send me to baptize but to preach the gospel, and not with eloquent wisdom, lest the cross of Christ be emptied of its power. For the word of the cross is folly to those who are perishing, but to us who are being saved it is the power of God . . . Has not God made foolish the wisdom of the world? For since, in the wisdom of God, the world did not know God through wisdom, it pleased God through the folly of what we preach to save those who believe. For Jews demand signs and Greeks seek wisdom, but we preach Christ crucified, a stumbling block to Jews and folly to Gentiles, but to those who are called, both Jews and Greeks, Christ the power of God and the wisdom of God. For the foolishness of God is wiser than men, and the weakness of God is stronger than men.[48]

For Christian faith, the cross signifies the inversive and subversive character of salvation: the last is first, the least is the greatest, the humble one is exalted. Jesus of Nazareth, in the estimation of messianic expectation and Hellenistic philosophy, is simply a poor carpenter from a small town of insignificance. Jesus is not recognized as divine progeny or as universal savior because his visage is ordinary, even more, among the least of the ordinary. Yet here is exactly the locus of divine revelation. The logic of the cross explicates the way in which divine logic perplexes and overturns the typical logic of the world. For in the world, kings live in castles, sit on thrones, wear crowns of gold and jewels, and sentence the guilty to death. The king from Nazareth, in starkest contrast, has no place to lay his head, washes the feet of all, wears a crown woven of thorns, and comes not to condemn the world but to save the world. The king from Nazareth suffers for his people in his passion and death, and serves and heals his people throughout his lifetime. In every passage of the Christian Gospels, Jesus is found subverting the

---

the prolongation of the Incarnation. The Word of God, the eternal Son of the Father, became man; God became part of what he created. But this work of God was not an event that occurred once and then receded into the past; the Incarnation was meant to change creation and to change history, and to do so in such a way that the change remained palpably present."

48. 1 Cor 1:17–18, 20–25 (RSV); cf. Phil 2:1–11.

dominant worldview at the crossroads of cultures (for example, Greek, Jewish, and Roman) in which he lived. Jesus overturns common expectations as he overturned the tables in the temple area, awakening slumbering people from their complacent apathy toward the humdrum banality of daily living and unjust structures of power and presumption. The logic of the cross is manifest, proclaimed and attested in the Eucharist, begun on the night before Jesus was handed over to death, and perpetuated by the ministry of the Church that arose in the wake of Jesus's resurrection and ascension.

In the Eucharist, Jesus, once again, surpasses even the wonder of his incarnation—that preposterous notion of the divine becoming human. In the Eucharist, the divine-human Jesus becomes for us the most humble edible and drinkable elements of bread and wine. Yet this notion, too, must be inverted to render in full the logic of the cross at work in the Eucharist: the bread and wine become Jesus's body and blood, soul and divinity. This double becoming is the very soteriological movement of the gift as conversation and as prosopic intercourse. The greatest is made the least in order for the least to be made the greatest. Is this not the very process of justice—a double movement that results in mutual equality and accord? If love is not the promotion of justice, in which the hubris of the haughty is razed and the humility of the lowly is raised, love is a demon—a perpetuation of "us/them" dichotomies and "I-am-better-than-you" worldviews. The logic of the cross, however, promotes justice through self-donative love—a love that loves for no reward other than the good of the other. At work in the logic of the cross is the mode of paradox. It was demonstrated above that a double phenomenality obtains in the Eucharist through the heuristics of metaphor and symbol. This doubling also can be named paradox—a unified phenomenon that exhibits two complementary modes of phenomenality. Paradox overturns rigid henodox worldviews in the name of procreativity. Paradox is procreative—it generates, it moves, it breathes life into creatures. Paradox stirs up the inertia of probability in the name of possibility, disclosing new ways-of-being-in-the-world. Not only this, paradox also is the core principle of the logic of the cross wherein a hypostatic transubstantiation occurs in two directions, from above and from below, converting this vertical paradigm of inequality into a horizontal paradigm of equality, resulting in a cruciform pattern depicting the justice of conversation:

Logic of Prosopic Kenosis

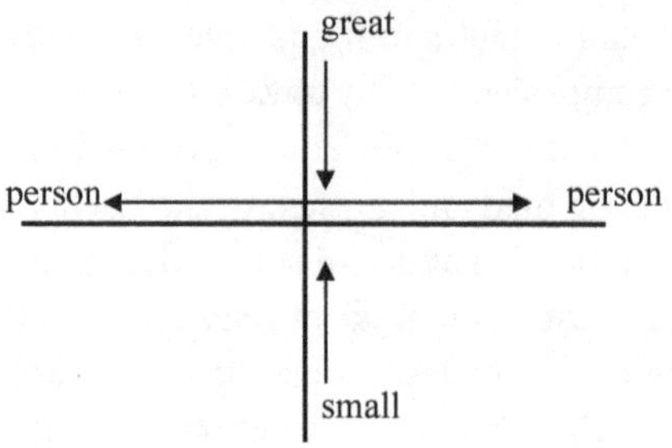


In this paradigmatic pattern, the great becomes small so that the small can become great, not by assuming the former place of dominance occupied by the great, but by an achievement of mutual greatness that is precisely the achievement of justice and equality. This horizontal achievement of justice does not remove the possibility of transcendence, but is the very realization of transcendence itself: where persons attain the status of mutual personhood without reducing one another to an object, even in the name of the gift. The Eucharist attains to the status of the true because it ascends to the status of the paradigmatic: in the Eucharist, Jesus, through his life, death and resurrection, appears, proclaims and attests to the paradigmatic form of the gift as conversation through his relationship with God the Father, in the Holy Spirit, and through his relationship with every human person, manifest, proclaimed and attested in the eucharistic locus of the logic of the cross.

## C. The Truth of Unity in Difference Revealed in the Trilectic of Testimony

Thirdly, the trilectic structure of the Eucharist, wherein fecundity is achieved through unity in difference, attains to the status of the paradigmatic, thereby attaining to the objective and universal status of the true. The fecund form of the trilectic of testimony is made possible by the unity in diversity dynamic initiated in the dialectic between manifestation and proclamation. Moreover, the pattern of unity in difference engenders extended dimensions of dynamism and fecundity, beginning with the third party witness to the integrity of the dialectic, followed by the attractive force of the trilectic to more and more witnesses. If the two parties of the dialectic are diverse but not unified, no authentic dialectic obtains; if one of the two parties of the dialectic collapses into the other (or is reduced by the other to the same) for the sake of unity, no authentic dialectic obtains. Genuine and lasting dialectic is formed when two diverse parties, through conversation, enter into a relationship of complementary and unified diversity. Each party allows the other to remain other, without threatening to reduce the other to the same. The structure of unity in difference underlies the procreativity exhibited in life. Without procreativity, life is not perpetuated but eventually becomes extinct. Procreativity is the life-principle that perpetuates the very pulse of life, the very rhythm of being.[49] Life ceases when all is reduced to the same, for the destiny of same, alone with itself, is death, as the tale of Narcissus clearly demonstrates.

The Eucharist operates by virtue of unity in difference inasmuch as it does not reduce anyone to the same but rather promotes a diversified Body of many members. It professes to be one Body but does not thereby reduce all members to any single part. Instead, this Body, the Church, exemplifies the genius of personhood that bears the iconic potential necessary for the operation of the gift as conversation. For life, the paradigmatic is fecundity in and through the structure of unity in difference. The eschatological vision of the Church depicts a glorious unity in diversity of angels and saints in beatific communion with the triune God: "After this I had a vision of a great multitude, which no one could count, from every nation, race, people, and tongue. They stood before the throne and before the Lamb, wearing white robes and holding palm branches in their hands . . . All the angels stood around the throne and around the elders and the four living creatures. They prostrated themselves before the throne [and] worshipped God."[50] The Lamb is Christ, who in turn gives and speaks himself totally in the Eucharist: "Behold the Lamb of God, behold him who takes away the sins of the world. Blessed are those called to the supper of the Lamb."[51] Since the Eucharist is an instance of unity in diversity par excellence, with its poignant nuptial form, it thereby attains to the paradigmatic of life. In the end, the Eucharist attains to the status of the true because it ascends to the status of the paradigmatic: in the Eucharist, Jesus, through his life, death and resurrection, appears, proclaims and attests to the paradigmatic form of the gift as conversation through his relationship with God the Father, in the Holy Spirit, and through his relationship with every human person, manifest, proclaimed and attested in the eucharistic locus of the principle

49. Cf. Panikkar, *Rhythm of Being*.

50. Rev 7:9, 11 (NAB).

51. See Rev 19:9: "Then the angel said to me, 'Write this: Blessed are those who have been called to the wedding feast of the Lamb.' And he said to me, 'These words are true; they come from God'" (NAB).

of unity in difference, evident in the phenomenological structure termed trilectic of testimony.

## D. The Truth of the Ultimate and Absolute Revealed in Personal Life-Testimony

Finally, the Eucharist attains to the status of truth as paradigmatic because it manifests, proclaims and attests an instance of ultimacy. In the Eucharist, Jesus gives himself as the just one who substitutes himself one-for-the-other by living a life of service and, in the end, offering his life for his beloved. In Jesus's life and death, he reveals the ultimacy of testimony; in Jesus's resurrection from the dead, he reveals the fruits of a testimony of ultimacy. Jesus lives as a servant, giving himself up to the point of abandonment and God-forsakenness so as to become one with his beloved. In complete solidarity with his beloved, he initiates relational oneness that does not reduce the other to the same, but calls the other by a personal name. In a similar way, all who dare partake of the Eucharist are summoned to the call of responsibility to substitute themselves, one-for-the-other. If one partakes of such a dangerous meal without responding affirmatively and radically to this summons, such a person makes a mockery of the meaning and truth of the Eucharist. But if one partakes fully in responding affirmatively and radically to this summons to responsibility and substitution, then one likewise partakes and participates in, proclaims and testifies to, the paradigmatic. For the paradigmatic is the real, and, in the end, the Eucharist attains to the status of the true because it ascends to the status of the paradigmatic: in the Eucharist, Jesus, through his life, death and resurrection, appears, proclaims and attests to the paradigmatic form of the gift as conversation through his relationship with God the Father, in the Holy Spirit, and through his relationship with every human person, manifest, proclaimed and attested in the eucharistic locus of personal life-testimony. Indeed, Jesus is the protagonist of this soteriological drama, but protagonist inasmuch as he breathes life into the cast of characters destined to become one with him in life, truth and body.

To conclude this section on transcendental reflection, a second attempt at a poetic construal of the Eucharist will be offered, this time with the moment of transcendental reflection in mind. It is fitting to end this chapter with a poetic rendition of personal testimony in the form of admiration of the Eucharist as the paradigmatic of the paradigmatic.[52] It is safe to say

52. See Ricoeur, *Freedom and Nature*, 477–78: "Admiration becomes a help because it is beyond willing; it is the incantation of poetry which delivers me from myself and

that people are convinced that such and such is the case—is the truth—not so much by grandiose and sophisticated arguments, but by paradigmatic instances of authentic testimony. And so this discourse will conclude, or rather begin, with a humble poetic account of my personal testimony to the Eucharist as true. May my life align with the pattern of these words.

*My Testament Made Explicit: Amen*

Halleluiah.
Lord, open my mouth and my lips will proclaim your
Praise. Wonder you are wonderful you
Beautiful in your ugliness nothing ugly you
Breathe into life *kadōsh kadōsh kadōsh* you
Are holy were holy will be holy in your
Unity diversity diverse unity communion you
Halleluiah.

Halleluiah.
Sixteen years ago sixteen years past me
A youth walking along Reeperbahn darkness me
Ambiguous turmoil sinking deep help me
Lacking condition life-decision dawn arisen in me
Do not go in living death of sin save cash for another me
*Arrivage* of witnesses thank you listened to me
Halleluiah.

purifies me . . . This then is how incantation aids the will. It delivers it in the first place from its own refusal by humbling it. At the core of refusal is defiance and defiance is the fault. To refuse necessity from below is to defy Transcendence. I have to discover the Wholly Other which at first repels me. Here lies the most fundamental choice of philosophy: either God or I. Either philosophy begins with the fundamental contrast between the Cogito and being in itself, or it begins with the self-positing of consciousness whose corollary is scorn of empirical being . . . But poetry never humbles except to heal: its hymn provokes a conversion as consciousness, renouncing the attempt at self-positing, receives being with wonder and seeks in the world and in the involuntary a manifestation of Transcendence which is given to me as the mighty companion of my freedom!"

Halleluiah.
Butterflies stomach feast word-flesh consummation she
Late nights strains of notes wrote a tune she
Hand-in-hand sunlit glance laboring she
Nursed at breast milk of finest wheat succulent she
Offspring wonder I.V. applied holy yearning she
Homeward bound fields of gold hand-in-hand she
Halleluiah.

Halleluiah.
Limit arisen injury tragedy have to be? he
Unconsoled panting for breath where is he?
Cannot tell pain befell mourning crying he
Eucharist word of promise only sense he
Eucharist only way I can touch he
Jesus come to us sacrament life together he
Halleluiah.

Amen.

Amen.

# Coda

THE PURPOSE OF A concluding word to this study is not to add anticlimactically to the resonance of the poetic discourse on the preceding page. Rather, it may be helpful to retrace the paths forged throughout the book in order to see once again the forest from the trees. Chapter 1 began with seeking a warrant for employing phenomenology as a helpful method to examine the Eucharist. A short review of the nuances of the phenomenological reduction was supplied in order to calibrate the methodological compass of the study. An introductory comparison between manifestation and proclamation was submitted to orient the project around this dialectical pairing. Chapter 2 presented Jean-Luc Marion as a thinker of manifestation and adoration, summarizing his revisions to Husserlian and Heideggerian phenomenology, while also teasing out an application of the saturated phenomenon to the Eucharist. In chapter 3, the main phenomenological contributions of Paul Ricoeur and Emmanuel Levinas were tallied in postulating them as thinkers of proclamation and attestation. The ethical dimensions of phenomenality especially came to surface in this chapter. Following the descriptions of the respective proposals of Marion, Ricoeur, and Levinas, chapter 4 averred to harness the potencies of the manifestation ↔ proclamation ↔ attestation trilectic of testimony in its application to the Eucharist. Chapter 5 extended the phenomenological description to a concentrated analysis of the prosopic and conversational attributes of eucharistic phenomenality. This interpersonal and nuptial description crescendoed to its highest pitch with a poetic text in praise of the Eucharist. Finally, chapter 6 found it necessary to shift methodology from phenomenological description to transcendental reflection in order to fashion a meaningful claim to truth regarding the Eucharist. The *logos*-principle was posited as the warrant for asserting an objective claim to truth that is universal in scope. Further, the Eucharist was argued to be true inasmuch as it gives and says the paradigmatic phenomenon—a phenomenon laced with authentic love, justice, rectitude, sacrifice and sanctity. Through transcendental reflection, the Eucharist was brought to the threshing floor of judgment, issued as an ultimatum for its respondent: Yes or No? Chapter 6 ended with yet another flourish of poetic discourse to incarnate verbally the trilectic of testimony in its triplex configuration of manifestation ↔ proclamation ↔ attestation.

In this book, the Eucharist has been described as a sexual and sacramental phenomenon as it consists of an intimate, complementary, fruitful and truthful intercourse between incarnate persons. The Eucharist is an interpersonal conversation between friends and lovers. It is an inclusive and hospitable phenomenon inasmuch as it welcomes all and simultaneously demands the uprightness of a unified profession of faith, a commitment to its given veracity, and an unobstructed communion with the host of angels and saints who gather around this cosmic table of sacrifice. The Eucharist gives and says itself as the paradigmatic instance of unity in diversity, of union in difference. It involves disclosure and concealment, as well as call and response. It is the privileged venue of gifted communion in which the gift of love is actualized through the course of conversation. Rather than a display of destructive pornographic orgy and lust, the Eucharist exhibits the truth and meaning of human sexuality through its covenantal demands of uprightness, fidelity and responsibility, one-for-the-other, wherein "*chastity* (is) the erotic virtue par excellence."[53] Not only chastity, but the remainder of the evangelical counsels—poverty and obedience—prevent the collapse of the dialectic and the reduction of the other to more of the same. According to the paradigmatic form of the evangelical counsels, one lives as a total gift of self to others to the highest degree. To become an authentic gift of self is to live in the fullness of freedom as a child of God.[54] The Eucharist extends this invitation to become a sincere gift of self, and also to receive the wondrous gifts given by others. The dialectical anatomy given and said in the Eucharist provides the emblematic pattern for just living between human sexual beings. It is, indeed, the universal vocation to the wedding feast of the sacrificial Lamb.

Has this book achieved the purpose for which it set out in its opening pages? That is for you, the reader, to decide. As far as the author is concerned, the book at least arose off the ground toward that at which it was taking aim. Much is left to be unpacked and challenged concerning the proposals of this book. Is something like a trilectic reduction possible in phenomenology? Is

53. Marion, *Erotic Phenomenon*, 183.

54. See Rom 8:18–21: "I consider that the sufferings of this present time are as nothing compared with the glory to be revealed for us. For creation awaits with eager expectation the revelation of the children of God; for creation was made subject to futility, not of its own accord but because of the one who subjected it, in hope that creation itself would be set free from slavery to corruption and share in the glorious freedom of the children of God" (NAB); and Gal 5:1: "For freedom Christ set us free; so stand firm and do not submit again to the yoke of slavery" (NAB).

the trilectic of testimony an advantageous heuristic for describing religious phenomena? Is testimony a category that must be probed more extensively in the realms of philosophy and theology alike? Is the trilectic of testimony a helpful hermeneutic device to be applied in the field of comparative theology and interreligious dialogue? Certainly the ethical must be taken much more seriously in all fields of study today. Without doubt philosophy and theology will continue to awaken the demands of responsibility in living souls that otherwise would continue to feed on the poison of a half-baked movement toward salvation, namely, enjoyment and self-gratification without concern for the other, without concern for the stranger. For, as Levinas recognizes, salvation is a matter of living immaterially for the other, in a word, spiritual life. The life of heroic virtue is characterized by a divestment of self, given up to the point of abandonment. This is the form of the paradigmatic, the eternal form of love—that same love which goes by the name of *actus purus*, pure act. It is my conjecture that Edith Stein will rise to be a prominent figure in future studies in phenomenology and theology. Stein's project of maintaining a rapprochement between Husserlian phenomenology and Thomistic *sacra scientia* may prove propitious for the unresolved dialectics submitted in this book.

In closing, may we share a fragment of poetry composed by Stein, the beginning of her ode to the Holy Spirit, "And I Remain with You: From a Pentecost Novena," revealing once again (and not for the last time) that the beginning is the end, the end is the beginning.

*Wer bist du süßes Licht, das mich erfüllt*
*und meines Herzens Dunkelheit erleuchtet?*
*Du leitest mich gleich einer Mutter Hand,*
*und ließest du mich los,*
*so wüßte keinen Schritt ich mehr zu gehen.*
*Du bist der Raum,*
*der rund mein Sein umschließt und in sich birgt.*
*Aus dir entlassen entsänk' es in den Abgrund*
*des Nichts, aus dem du es zum Licht erhobst.*
*Du, näher mir als ich mir selbst*
*und innerlicher als mein Innerstes*
*und doch untastbar und unfaßbar*
*und jeden Namen sprengend:*
*Heiliger Geist—ewige Liebe!*[55]

55. First stanza of "Und ich bleibe bei euch: Aus einer Pfingstnovene," by Edith Stein. See Stein, *Hidden Life*, 140–41. Modified translation my own.

Who are you sweet Light, that fills me
and illuminates the darkness of my heart?
You who likewise lead me with a Mother's Hand,
and were you to leave me,
no further step would I go.
You are the Space,
which encompasses round my being and holds it within itself.
Dismissed from you, it sinks into the abyss
of nothing, from which you raised it to the Light.
You, nearer to me than I am to myself
and more inward than my innermost heart
and yet impalpable and incomprehensible
and have burst asunder every name:
Holy Spirit—eternal Love!

# Appendix

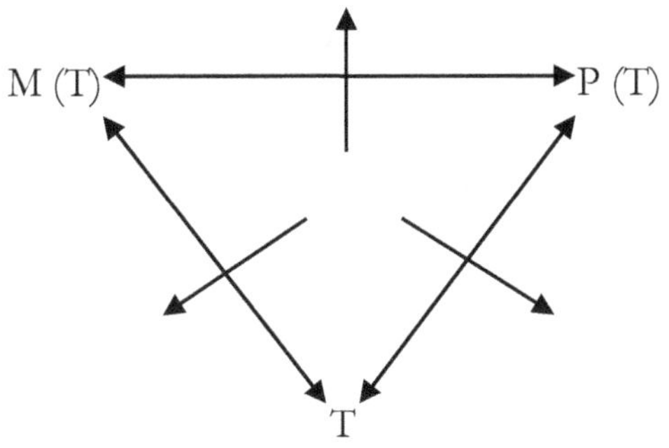


**Where M = Manifestation, P = Proclamation, and T = Testimony. The arrows that proceed from the center of the figure represent the fecundity of the trilectic.**

The manifestation ↔ proclamation dialectic is signified by the spatial relationship between M and P. Testimony (T) is a dynamic ground at work in both M and P, figuring so prominently that it appears as its own category, moving the one-dimensional figure of the dialectic to a two-dimensional figure of the trilectic. Testimony (T), as a third term, appears only to the extent that the dialectic is kept alive. If the dialectic is shattered or collapsed to one side or the other, testimony (T) will not appear as a third party to render the schema fecund. For testimony (T) is that which is generated latently in both manifestation (M) and proclamation (P) but is generated explicitly in the productive dialectical relationship between manifestation (M) and proclamation (P). Neither manifestation (M) nor proclamation (P) can be sustained adequately without the self-recognition that each is rooted in a particular testimony. Testimony (T) functions as the element which brings depth to the interaction between M and P and also serves as the condition for the possibility of their complementary and fruitful relationship. This triadic structure is evident at the heart of fecundity.

Fecundity refers to the generative power, capacity and offspring of the communion of two distinct, diverse and complementary parties or, more precisely, polarities. One need only call to mind basic life-phenomena to demonstrate this dictum, for example: lightning; electromagnetism; the reproductive workings of flowers, human beings and a host of other species; and the form of discourse itself (namely, a word spoken by someone to someone about something). Think of atomic theory in which polarity functions as the rule of chemical bonding and the condition of possibility for potential and kinetic energy, or of magnetic fields in which object attraction and repulsion function according to polar lines of force. In these examples, a kind of fruitfulness obtains—a fruitfulness that depends upon the polarity of two contrasting yet complementary parties. The contrast becomes a complementarity through the acts of intercourse between the two dialectical parties, in turn generating a third party that, in its appearing, attests to the genius and logic of the fecundity from which it arose into existence. Likewise, this third party serves as the raison d'être of, and witness to, the fecundity itself, thereby provoking the perpetual play of fecundity. The erotic interplay of the two dialectical parties finds its meaning, telos and fruit in the appearance of the nonpartisan and neutral third—neutral insofar as it cannot be identified directly with party M or party P, but stands apart as its own distinct entity, thereby promoting the respective geniuses of party M and party P. The third party attests to the equality and difference of parties M and P. To demonstrate the ensuing three-dimensional depth of the trilectic, an augmented heuristic diagram is in order:

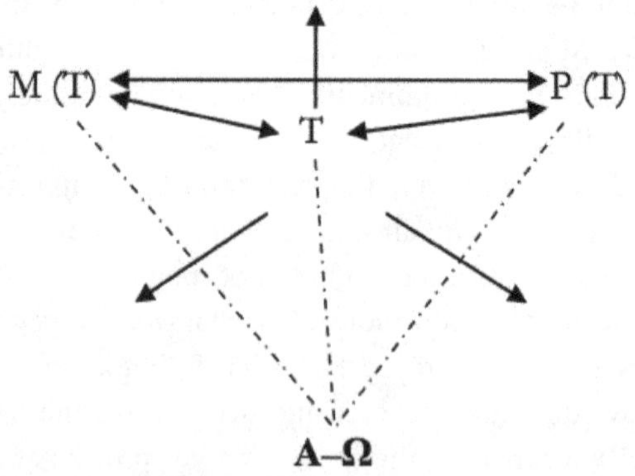


**Where M = Manifestation, P = Proclamation, and T = Testimony. The arrows that proceed from the center of the figure represent the fecundity of the trilectic. A–Ω represents the invisible Alpha-Omega point generated by the emergence of T as a neutral third position in contradistinction from A and B. A–Ω allows for the three-dimensionality and depth of the trilectic to obtain.**

The above progression demonstrates how each new dimension is generated as fruit of the former: the developing linear dialectic between M and P generates T in triangular fashion, opening a second dimension, namely, that of verticality; and the evolving two-dimensional relationality between M, P and T generates A–Ω as a third dimension of depth. A–Ω more specifically denotes the "always-already, not-yet"/"historical-proleptic, eschatological" identity of depth. The A–Ω point is neither observable nor locatable, but stretches depth into an abyss. A–Ω signifies the infinite, appearing only as a trace on the surface of the M ↔ P ↔ T matrix. Depth is not generated by self-subsisting presence or by "more of the same," but only by the sustained trialogue of M, P and T. Depth itself is a generative form that in turn engenders and promotes the fecundity of the trilectic. "Depth" not only signifies the question of being as such, but the questions of meaning and truth, origin and destiny, where beginning is end and end is beginning.[1]

The trilectic of testimony purports to be a heuristic that functions according to the principle of fecundity. The triadic structure formed by the trilectic is not accidental, but bears the imprint of creativity itself. The logic of fecundity presupposes such a threefold structure. Hans Urs von Balthasar attests to such a structure on display in the created order: "the triadic structure of creaturely logic . . . the law of life . . . (in which) fecundity is the law . . . [is attested] in the fact that every I-Thou relationship between spirits can be fulfilled only in an objective third (as Hegel never tires of stressing) or in the fact that genuine *paideia* (according to Plato) is a 'begetting in the beautiful' and thus the generation of a fruit."[2] Von Balthasar makes this claim after his analysis of Hegel, the "dialectician," and three prominent "dialogicians": Franz Rosenzweig, Martin Buber, and Ferdinand Ebner. Von Balthasar critiques "the axiom of the excluded middle" for its failure to recognize that "difference, the 'other than myself,' is always already overtaken by *a third* within which I am able to apprehend its otherness in the first place."[3] The trilectic of testimony considers testimony (T), with its simultaneous opening into depth (A–Ω), to be the *third* which allows one pole of the dialectic to apprehend appreciatively and respectfully the otherness of the opposite pole.

1. The use of the terms "depth" and "abyss" in this context is indebted to the thought of Paul Tillich. See Tillich, *Systematic Theology*, 1:79–81.

2. Balthasar, *Theo-logic*, 2:62; cf. the discourse of Diotima in Plato, *Symposium* 206–212c.

3. Balthasar, *Theo-logic*, 2:35, 62 (emphasis added).

# Bibliography


Aikin, William Carter. "Narrative Icon and Linguistic Idol: Reexamining the Narrative Turn in Theological Ethics." *Journal of the Society of Christian Ethics* 28 (2008) 87–108.

Allen, Sarah. *The Philosophical Sense of Transcendence: Levinas and Plato on Loving Beyond Being*. Pittsburgh: Duquesne University Press, 2009.

Ambrose, Glenn P. *The Theology of Louis-Marie Chauvet: Overcoming Onto-theology within the Sacramental Tradition*. Burlington, VT: Ashgate, 2011.

Anderson, Pamela Sue. "Agnosticism and Attestation: An Aporia concerning the Other in Ricoeur's *Oneself as Another*." *The Journal of Religion* 74 (1994) 65–76.

Anselm of Canterbury. *The Prayers and Meditations of Saint Anselm with the Proslogion*. Translated by Benedicta Ward. New York: Penguin, 1973.

———. *Proslogion with the Replies of Gaunilo and Anselm*. Translated by Thomas Williams. Indianapolis: Hackett, 2001.

Aristotle. *The Complete Works of Aristotle: The Revised Oxford Translation*. Edited by Jonathan Barnes. 2 vols. Princeton: Princeton University Press, 1984.

Augustine of Hippo. *Confessions*. Translated by Henry Chadwick. New York: Oxford University Press, 1991.

Balthasar, Hans Urs von. *Epilogue*. Translated by Edward T. Oakes. San Francisco: Ignatius, 2004.

———. *The Glory of the Lord*. Vol. 6, *Theology: The Old Covenant*. Translated by Brian McNeil and Erasmo Leiva-Merikakis. Edited by John Riches. San Francisco: Ignatius, 1991.

———. *The Glory of the Lord*. Vol. 7, *Theology: The New Covenant*. Translated by Brian McNeil. Edited by John Riches. San Francisco: Ignatius, 1989.

———. *Mysterium Paschale: The Mystery of Easter*. Translated by Aidan Nichols. San Francisco: Ignatius, 2005.

———. *Theo-logic*. Vol. 2, *Truth of God*. Translated by Adrian J. Walker. San Francisco: Ignatius, 2004.

Barth, Karl. *Church Dogmatics*. Edited by G. W. Bromiley and T. F. Torrance. Edinburgh: T. & T. Clark, 1960–61.

———. *The Epistle to the Romans*. Translated by Edwyn C. Hoskyns. London: Oxford University Press, 1965.

———. *On Religion: The Revelation of God as the Sublimation of Religion*. Translated by Garrett Green. New York: T. & T. Clark, 2006.

———. *Witness to the Word: A Commentary on John 1; Lectures at Münster in 1925 and at Bonn in 1933*. Edited by Walther Fürst. Translated by Geoffrey W. Bromiley. Grand Rapids: Eerdmans, 1986.

———. *The Word of God and the Word of Man*. Translated by Douglas Horton. New York: Harper & Row, 1957.

Beals, Corey. *Levinas and the Wisdom of Love: The Question of Invisibility*. Waco, TX: Baylor University Press, 2007.

Beane, Wendell C., and William G. Doty, eds. *Myths, Rites, Symbols: A Mircea Eliade Reader*. 2 vols. New York: Harper & Row, 1976.

Beckwith, Francis J. *Defending Life: A Moral and Legal Case against Abortion Choice*. New York: Cambridge University Press, 2008.

Benedict XVI, Pope. *Deus caritas est*. 2006. http://w2.vatican.va/content/benedict-xvi/en/encyclicals/documents/hf_ben-xvi_enc_20051225_deus-caritas-est.html.

Benson, Bruce Ellis. *Graven Ideologies: Nietzsche, Derrida and Marion on Modern Idolatry*. Downers Grove, IL: InterVarsity, 2002.

———. *The Improvisation of Musical Dialogue: A Phenomenology of Music*. Cambridge: Cambridge University Press, 2003.

———. *Liturgy as a Way of Life: Embodying the Arts in Christian Worship*. Grand Rapids: Baker, 2013.

Benson, Bruce Ellis, and Norman Wirzba, eds. *The Phenomenology of Prayer*. New York: Fordham University Press, 2005.

———, eds. *Words of Life: New Theological Turns in French Phenomenology*. New York: Fordham University Press, 2010.

Blankenhorn, Bernhard. "The Instrumental Causality of the Sacraments: Thomas Aquinas and Louis-Marie Chauvet." *Nova et Vetera* 4 (2006) 255–94.

Bloechl, Jeffrey, ed. *Christianity and Secular Reason: Classical Themes and Modern Developments*. Notre Dame: University of Notre Dame Press, 2012.

———, ed. *The Face of the Other and the Trace of God: Essays on the Philosophy of Emmanuel Levinas*. New York: Fordham University Press, 2000.

———. *Liturgy of the Neighbor: Emmanuel Levinas and the Religion of Responsibility*. Pittsburgh: Duquesne University Press, 2000.

———, ed. *Religious Experience and the End of Metaphysics*. Bloomington: Indiana University Press, 2003.

Bocheński, J. M. *The Methods of Contemporary Thought*. Translated by Peter Caws. Dordrecht: D. Reidel, 1965.

Boeve, Lieven. *The Interruption of Tradition: An Essay on Christian Faith in a Postmodern Context*. Leuven: Peeters, 2003.

Boeve, Lieven, and Kurt Feyaerts, eds. *Metaphor and God-Talk*. Bern: P. Lang, 1999.

Boeve, Lieven, Hans Geybels, and Stijn van den Bossche, eds. *Encountering Transcendence: Contributions to a Theology of Christian Religious Experience*. Leuven: Peeters, 2005.

Boeve, Lieven, and Lambert Leijssen, eds. *Sacramental Presence in a Postmodern Context*. Leuven: Peeters, 2001.

Boeve, Lieven, Yves de Maeseneer, and Stijn van den Bossche, eds. *Religious Experience and Contemporary Theological Epistemology*. Leuven: Peeters, 2005.

Boguslawski, Steven, and Robert Fastiggi, eds. *Called to Holiness and Communion: Vatican II on the Church*. Scranton: University of Scranton Press, 2009.

Bordeyne, Philippe, and Bruce T. Morrill, eds. *Sacraments: Revelation of the Humanity of God; Engaging the Fundamental Theology of Louis-Marie Chauvet*. Collegeville, MN: Liturgical Press, 2008.
Bouyer, Louis. *Eucharist: Theology and Spirituality of the Eucharistic Prayer*. Translated by Charles Underhill Quinn. Notre Dame: University of Notre Dame Press, 1968.
Bracken, Joseph A. "Toward a New Philosophical Theology Based on Intersubjectivity." *Theological Studies* 59 (1998) 703–19.
Bråkenhielm, Carl Reinhold. "A Response to Jean Greisch." *Svensk Teologisk Kvartalskrift* 79 (2003) 78–80.
Buber, Martin. *I and Thou*. Translated by Ronald Gregor Smith. New York: Scribner's, 1958.
Burch, Matthew I. "Blurred Vision: Marion on the 'Possibility' of Revelation." *International Journal for Philosophy of Religion* 67 (2010) 157–71.
Burggraeve, Roger, ed. *The Awakening to the Other: A Provocative Dialogue with Emmanuel Levinas*. Leuven: Peeters, 2008.
Burnham, Douglas, and Enrico Giaccherini, eds. *The Poetics of Transubstantiation: From Theology to Metaphor*. Aldershot, UK: Ashgate, 2005.
Calvin, John. *Institutes of the Christian Religion*. Translated by Henry Beveridge. Grand Rapids: Eerdmans, 1989.
Candler, Peter M., and Conor Cunningham. *The Grandeur of Reason: Religion, Tradition and Universalism*. London: SCM, 2010.
Caputo, John D. *Deconstruction in a Nutshell: A Conversation with Jacques Derrida*. New York: Fordham University Press, 1997.
———. *The Prayers and Tears of Jacques Derrida: Religion without Religion*. Bloomington: Indiana University Press, 1997.
Caputo, John D., and Michael J. Scanlon, eds. *God, the Gift, and Postmodernism*. Bloomington: Indiana University Press, 1999.
Carlson, Bruce M. *Human Embryology and Developmental Biology*. 3rd ed. Philadelphia: Mosby, 2004.
Carlson, Thomas A. *Indiscretion: Finitude and the Naming of God*. Chicago: University of Chicago Press, 1999.
Cavadini, John C. "The Church as the Sacrament of Creation: A Reading of Origen's *Commentary on the Song of Songs*." *Communio* 42 (2015) 89–118.
Cavanaugh, William T. *Torture and Eucharist: Theology, Politics, and the Body of Christ*. Malden, MA: Blackwell, 1998.
Chauvet, Louis-Marie. *The Sacraments: The Word of God at the Mercy of the Body*. Translated by Madeleine Beaumont. Collegeville, MN: Liturgical Press, 2001.
———. *Symbol and Sacrament: A Sacramental Interpretation of Christian Existence*. Translated by Patrick Madigan and Madeleine Beaumont. Collegeville, MN: Liturgical Press, 1995.
———. *Symbole et sacrement: Une relecture sacramentelle de l'existence chrétienne*. Paris: Cerf, 1987.
Chrétien, Jean-Louis. *The Ark of Speech*. Translated by Andrew Brown. New York: Routledge, 2004.
———. *The Call and the Response*. Translated by Anne A. Davenport. New York: Fordham University Press, 2004.
———. *Hand to Hand: Listening to the Work of Art*. Translated by Stephen E. Lewis. New York: Fordham University Press, 2003.

———. *Loin des premiers fleuves: poèmes*. Paris: Editions de la Différence, 1990.

———. *The Unforgettable and the Unhoped For*. Translated by Jeffrey Bloechl. New York: Fordham University Press, 2002.

Chrudzimski, Arkadiusz. *Gegenstandstheorie und Theorie der Intentionalität bei Alexius Meinong*. Dordrecht: Springer, 2007.

Ciocan, Cristian, ed. *Philosophical Concepts and Religious Metaphors: New Perspectives on Phenomenology and Theology*. Bucharest: Zeta, 2009.

Coady, C. A. J. *Testimony: A Philosophical Study*. Oxford: Clarendon, 1992.

Coakley, Sarah. *God, Sexuality and the Self: An Essay "On the Trinity"*. Cambridge: Cambridge University Press, 2013.

———. *The New Asceticism: Sexuality, Gender and the Quest for God*. London: Bloomsbury, 2016.

Cohen, Richard A., ed. *Face to Face with Levinas*. Albany: State University of New York Press, 1986.

Comstock, Gary L. "Two Types of Narrative Theology." *Journal of the American Academy of Religion* 55 (1987) 687–717.

Coward, Harold, and Toby Foshay, eds. *Derrida and Negative Theology*. Albany: State University of New York Press, 1992.

Cunningham, Conor. *Darwin's Pious Idea: Why the Ultra-Darwinists and Creationists Both Get It Wrong*. Grand Rapids: Eerdmans, 2010.

———. "The Difference of Theology and Some Philosophies of Nothing." *Modern Theology* 17 (2001) 289–312.

———. *A Genealogy of Nihilism: Philosophies of Nothing and the Difference of Theology*. London: Routledge, 2002.

———. "*Natura Pura*, the Invention of the Anti-Christ: A Week with No Sabbath." *Communio* 37 (2010) 243–54.

Cunningham, Conor, and Peter M. Candler, eds. *Transcendence and Phenomenology*. London: SCM, 2007.

Cunningham, Lawrence S. *An Introduction to Catholicism*. New York: Cambridge University Press, 2009.

Cunningham, Lawrence S., and Keith J. Egan. *Christian Spirituality: Themes from the Tradition*. New York: Paulist, 1996.

Dalton, Drew M. *Longing for the Other: Levinas and Metaphysical Desire*. Pittsburgh: Duquesne University Press, 2009.

Deleuze, Gilles. *Difference and Repetition*. Translated by Paul Patton. New York: Columbia University Press, 1994.

Denzinger, Heinrich, and Adolf Schönmetzer, eds. *Enchiridion symbolorum: definitionum et declarationum de rebus fidei et morum*. Freiburg: Herder, 1963.

DeRoo, Neal, and John Panteleimon Manoussakis, eds. *Phenomenology and Eschatology: Not Yet in the Now*. Burlington, VT: Ashgate, 2009.

Derrida, Jacques. *Adieu to Emmanuel Levinas*. Translated by Pascale-Anne Brault and Michael Naas. Stanford: Stanford University Press, 1999.

———. *Edmund Husserl's "Origin of Geometry": An Introduction*. Translated by John P. Leavey Jr. Lincoln: University of Nebraska Press, 1989.

———. *Monolinguism of the Other; or, The Prosthesis of Origin*. Translated by Patrick Mensah. Stanford: Stanford University Press, 1998.

———. *Of Grammatology*. Translated by Gayatri Chakravorty Spivak. Baltimore: Johns Hopkins University Press, 1997.

———. *Of Spirit: Heidegger and the Question*. Translated by Geoffrey Bennington and Rachel Bowlby. Chicago: University of Chicago Press, 1989.

———. *On the Name*. Translated by David Wood. Stanford: Stanford University Press, 1995.

———. *Speech and Phenomena: And Other Essays on Husserl's Theory of Signs*. Translated by David B. Allison and Newton Garver. Evanston: Northwestern University Press, 1973.

———. *The Truth in Painting*. Translated by Geoffrey Bennington and Ian McLeod. Chicago: University of Chicago Press, 1987.

———. *Writing and Difference*. Translated by Alan Bass. Chicago: University of Chicago Press, 1993.

Derrida, Jacques, and Gianni Vattimo, eds. *Religion*. Translated by David Webb. Cambridge: Polity, 1998.

Devries, Dawn. "Toward a Theology of Childhood." *Interpretation* 55 (2001) 161–73.

Dillenberger, John, ed. *Martin Luther: Selections from His Writings*. Garden City, NY: Doubleday, 1962.

Diller, Jeanine, and Asa Kasher, eds. *Models of God and Other Ultimate Realities*. Dordrecht: Springer, 2013.

Dolejšová, Ivana. "The Symbolic Nature of Christian Existence according to Ricoeur and Chauvet." *Communio Viatorum* 43 (2001) 39–59.

Dornisch, Loretta. "Symbolic Systems and the Interpretation of Scripture: An Introduction to the Work of Paul Ricoeur." *Semeia* 4 (1975) 1–21.

Downey, Michael, and Richard Fragomeni, eds. *A Promise of Presence*. Washington, DC: Pastoral Press, 1992.

Drummond, J. J., and J. G. Hart, eds. *The Truthful and the Good: Essays in Honor of Robert Sokolowski*. Dordrecht: Springer, 1996.

Dufort, Jean-Marc. *Le symbolism eucharistique aux origines de l'église*. Brussels: Desclée de Brouwer, 1969.

Dunn, Rose Ellen. *Finding Grace with God: A Phenomenological Reading of the Annunciation*. Eugene, OR: Pickwick, 2014.

Eisland, Nancy L. *The Disabled God: Towards a Liberatory Theology of Disability*. Nashville: Abingdon, 1994.

Eliade, Mircea. *Cosmos and History: The Myth of the Eternal Return*. Translated by Philip R. Trask. New York: Harper, 1959.

———. *Essential Sacred Writings from around the World*. San Francisco: HarperSanFrancisco, 1992.

———. *From Primitives to Zen: A Thematic Sourcebook of the History of Religions*. New York: Harper & Row, 1967.

———. *A History of Religious Ideas*. Translated by Willard R. Trask. 3 vols. Chicago: University of Chicago Press, 1985.

———. *Images and Symbols: Studies in Religious Symbolism*. Translated by Philip Mairet. New York: Sheed & Ward, 1961.

———. *Man and the Sacred: A Thematic Source Book of the History of Religions*. New York: Harper & Row, 1974.

———. *Mephistopheles and the Androgyne: Studies in Religious Myth and Symbol*. New York: Sheed & Ward, 1965.

———. *Myths, Dreams, and Mysteries: The Encounter between Contemporary Faiths and Archaic Realities*. Translated by Philip Mairet. New York: Harper & Row, 1967.

———. *Patterns in Comparative Religion*. Translated by Rosemary Sheed. Cleveland: World Publishing, 1963.

———. *The Quest: History and Meaning in Religion*. Chicago: University of Chicago Press, 1969.

———. *Rites and Symbols of Initiation: The Mysteries of Birth and Rebirth*. New York: Harper & Row, 1965.

———. *The Sacred and the Profane: The Nature of Religion*. Translated by Willard R. Trask. New York: Harper & Row, 1987.

———. *Symbolism, the Sacred, and the Arts*. Edited by Diane Apostolos-Cappadona. New York: Crossroad, 1985.

———. *The Two and the One*. Chicago: University of Chicago Press, 1979.

Eliade, Mircea, and Joseph M. Kitagawa, eds. *The History of Religions: Essays in Methodology*. Chicago: University of Chicago Press, 1959.

Eliot, T. S. *The Complete Poems and Plays*. New York: Harcourt Brace, 1934.

Falque, Emmanuel. *Crossing the Rubicon: The Borderlands of Philosophy and Theology*. Translated by Reuben Shank. New York: Fordham University Press, 2016.

———. *God, the Flesh, and the Other: From Irenaeus to Duns Scotus*. Translated by William Christian Hackett. Evanston: Northwestern University Press, 2015.

———. *The Metamorphosis of Finitude: An Essay on Birth and Resurrection*. Translated by George Hughes. New York: Fordham University Press, 2012.

———. *Les noces de l'agneau: Essai philosophique sur le corps et l'eucharistie*. Paris: Cerf, 2011.

———. *Passer le Rubicon: Philosophie et théologie; essai sur les frontières*. Brussels: Lessius, 2013.

———. *Le passeur de Gethsémani: Angoisse souffrance et mort; Lecture existentielle et phénoménologique*. Paris: Cerf, 1999.

Farber, Marvin. *The Aims of Phenomenology: The Motives, Methods, and Impact of Husserl's Thought*. New York: Harper & Row, 1966.

Farley, Matthew David. "Jean-Yves Lacoste on John of the Cross: Theological Thinker *Par Excellence*." *Modern Theology* 32 (2016) 3–19.

Feuerbach, Ludwig. *The Essence of Christianity*. Translated by George Eliot. Buffalo, NY: Prometheus, 1989.

———. *The Essence of Religion*. Translated by Alexander Loos. Amherst, NY: Prometheus, 2004.

———. *Lectures on the Essence of Religion*. Translated by Ralph Manheim. New York: Harper & Row, 1967.

———. *Principles of the Philosophy of the Future*. Translated by Manfred Vogel. Indianapolis: Hackett, 1986.

———. *Thoughts on Death and Immortality*. Translated by James A. Massey. Berkeley: University of California Press, 1980.

Flannery, Austin, ed. *Vatican Council II: The Sixteen Basic Documents*. Northport, NY: Costello, 1996.

Francis, Pope. *Evangelii gaudium*. 2013. http://w2.vatican.va/content/francesco/en/apost_exhortations/documents/papa-francesco_esortazione-ap_20131124_evangelii-gaudium.html.

———. *Laudato si'*. 2015. http://w2.vatican.va/content/francesco/en/encyclicals/documents/papa-francesco_20150524_enciclica-laudato-si.html.

———. *Lumen fidei*. 2013. http://w2.vatican.va/content/francesco/en/encyclicals/documents/papa-francesco_20130629_enciclica-lumen-fidei.html.

Gadamer, Hans-Georg. *Truth and Method*. Translated by Joel Weinsheimer and Donald G. Marshall. New York: Continuum, 2004.

Gibbs, Robert. "Enigmatic Authority: Levinas and the Personal Effacement." *Modern Theology* 16 (2000) 325–34.

Gilbert, Paul. "Écriture phénoménologique et méthode patristique: Les frontières de la philosophie et de la théologie selon Emmanuel Falque." *Gregorianum* 95:3 (2014) 559–75.

Gilkey, Langdon. *Naming the Whirlwind: The Renewal of God-Language*. New York: Bobbs-Merrill, 1969.

———. "Problems and Possibilities of Theological Models: Responding to David Klemm and William Klink." *Zygon* 38 (2003) 529–34.

Gosetti-Ferencei, Jennifer Anna. *Heidegger, Hölderlin, and the Subject of Poetic Language*. New York: Fordham University Press, 2004.

Green, Clifford. *Karl Barth: Theologian of Freedom*. San Francisco: Collins, 1989.

Greisch, Jean. "Is Phenomenology the Promised Land of the Philosophy of Religion?" *Svensk Teologisk Kvartalskrift* 79 (2003) 66–77.

———. "Testimony and Attestation." *Philosophy and Social Criticism* 21:5–6 (1995) 81–98.

Grondin, Jean. *Introduction to Metaphysics: From Parmenides to Levinas*. Translated by Lukas Soderstrom. New York: Columbia University Press, 2012.

Gschwandtner, Christina M. "*À Dieu* or From the Logos? Emmanuel Levinas and Jean-Luc Marion—Prophets of the Infinite." *Philosophy and Theology* 22:1–2 (2010) 177–203.

———. "Corporeality, Animality, Bestiality: Emmanuel Falque on Incarnate Flesh." *Analecta Hermeneutica* 4 (2012) 1–16.

———. *Degrees of Givenness: On Saturation in Jean-Luc Marion*. Bloomington: Indiana University Press, 2014.

———. "Ethics, Eros, or Caritas? Levinas and Marion on Individuation of the Other." *Philosophy Today* 49 (2005) 70–87.

———. "Marion and Negative Certainty." *Philosophy Today* 56 (2012) 363–70.

———. "The Neighbor and the Infinite: Marion and Levinas on the Encounter between Self, Human Other, and God." *Continental Philosophy Review* 40 (2007) 231–49.

———. "A New 'Apologia': The Relationship between Theology and Philosophy in the Work of Jean-Luc Marion." *Heythrop Journal* 46 (2005) 299–313.

———. "Paul Ricoeur and the Relationship between Philosophy and Religion in Contemporary French Phenomenology." *Ricoeur Studies* 3 (2012) 7–25.

———. *Postmodern Apologetics? Arguments for God in Contemporary Philosophy*. New York: Fordham University Press, 2013.

———. *Reading Jean-Luc Marion: Exceeding Metaphysics*. Bloomington: Indiana University Press, 2007.

———. "The Vigil as Exemplary Liturgical Experience: On Jean-Yves Lacoste's Phenomenology of Liturgy." *Modern Theology* 31 (2015) 648–57.

Gutiérrez, Gustavo. *A Theology of Liberation: History, Politics, and Salvation*. Translated and edited by Sister Caridad Inda and John Eagleson. Maryknoll, NY: Orbis, 1988.

Hahn, Lewis Edwin. *The Philosophy of Hans-Georg Gadamer*. Chicago: Open Court, 1997.

Hand, Seán. *Emmanuel Lévinas*. New York: Routledge, 2009.

Hardy, Edward R., ed. *Christology of the Later Fathers*. Louisville: Westminster John Knox, 1954.

Hart, Kevin, ed. *Counter-Experiences: Reading Jean-Luc Marion*. Notre Dame: University of Notre Dame Press, 2007.

———. *Kingdoms of God*. Bloomington: Indiana University Press, 2014.

———. *Postmodernism: A Beginner's Guide*. Oxford: Oneworld, 2004.

———. *The Trespass of the Sign: Deconstruction, Theology and Philosophy*. Cambridge: Cambridge University Press, 1989.

Hart, Kevin, and Michael A. Signer, eds. *The Exorbitant: Emmanuel Levinas between Jews and Christians*. New York: Fordham University Press, 2010.

Hart, Kevin, and Barbara Wall, eds. *The Experience of God: A Postmodern Response*. New York: Fordham University Press, 2005.

Hegel, G. W. F. *The Christian Religion*. Translated by Peter C. Hodgson. Missoula, MT: Scholars Press, 1979.

———. *Phenomenology of Spirit*. Translated by A. V. Miller. Oxford: Clarendon, 1977.

Heidegger, Martin. *Basic Writings from "Being and Time" (1927) to "The Task of Thinking" (1964)*. Edited by David Farrell Krell. Translated by Frank A. Capuzzi and J. Glenn Gray. New York: Harper & Row, 1977.

———. *Being and Time*. Translated by John Macquarrie and Edward Robinson. New York: Harper, 1962.

———. *Identity and Difference*. Translated by Joan Stambaugh. Chicago: University of Chicago Press, 2002.

———. *Mindfulness*. Translated by Parvis Emad and Thomas Kalary. New York: Continuum, 2006.

———. *On the Way to Language*. Translated by Peter D. Hertz. New York: Harper & Row, 1971.

———. *On Time and Being*. Translated by Joan Stambaugh. Chicago: University of Chicago Press, 2002.

———. *Pathmarks*. Translated by William McNeil. Cambridge: Cambridge University Press, 1998.

———. *The Phenomenology of Religious Life*. Translated by Matthias Fritsch and Jennifer Anna Gosetti-Ferencei. Bloomington: Indiana University Press, 2004.

———. *Sein und Zeit*. Tübingen: M. Niemeyer, 2006.

———. *Towards the Definition of Philosophy*. Translated by Ted Sadler. New York: Continuum, 2008.

———. *What Is Called Thinking?* Translated by J. Glenn Gray. New York: Harper & Row, 1968.

———. *Zur Sache des Denkens*. Tübingen: M. Niemeyer, 2000.

Henry, Michel. *C'est moi la vérité: Pour une philosophie du christianisme*. Paris: Seuil, 1996.

———. *L'essence de la manifestation*. Paris: Presses universitaires de France, 1963.

———. *The Essence of Manifestation*. Translated by G. J. Etzkorn. The Hague: M. Nijhoff, 1973.

———. *I Am the Truth: Toward a Philosophy of Christianity*. Translated by Susan Emanuel. Stanford: Stanford University Press, 2003.

———. *Incarnation: Une philosophie de la chair*. Paris: Seuil, 2000.

———. *Material Phenomenology*. Translated by Scott Davidson. New York: Fordham University Press, 2008.

———. *Phénoménologie matérielle*. Paris: Presses universitaires de France, 1990.

———. *Philosophie et phénoménologie du corps: Essai sur l'ontologie biranienne*. Paris: Presses universitaires de France, 1965.

———. *Philosophy and Phenomenology of the Body*. Translated by G. J. Etzkorn The Hague: M. Nijhoff, 1975.

———. *Seeing the Invisible: On Kandinsky*. Translated by Scott Davidson. New York: Continuum, 2009.

———. *Voir l'invisible: Sur Kandinsky*. Paris: F. Bourin, 1988.

———. *Words of Christ*. Translated by Christina M. Gschwandtner. Grand Rapids: Eerdmans, 2012.

Horner, Robyn. *Jean-Luc Marion: A Theological Introduction*. Burlington, VT: Ashgate, 2005.

———. *Rethinking God as Gift: Marion, Derrida, and the Limits of Phenomenology*. New York: Fordham University Press, 2001.

Hughes, Graham. *Worship as Meaning: A Liturgical Theology for Late Modernity*. Cambridge: Cambridge University Press, 2003.

Hume, David. *Dialogues Concerning Natural Religion*. Rockville, MD: Arc Manor, 2008.

———. *An Enquiry Concerning Human Understanding and Other Writings*. Edited by Stephen Buckle. Cambridge: Cambridge University Press, 2007.

Husserl, Edmund. *Analyses Concerning Passive and Active Synthesis: Lectures on Transcendental Logic*. Translated by A. J. Steinbock. Boston: Kluwer Academic, 2001.

———. *The Basic Problems of Phenomenology: From the Lectures, Winter Semester, 1910–1911*. Translated by Ingo Farin and James Hart. Dordrecht: Springer, 2006.

———. *Cartesian Meditations: An Introduction to Phenomenology*. Translated by Dorion Cairns. The Hague: M. Nijhoff, 1960.

———. *The Crisis of European Sciences and Transcendental Phenomenology: An Introduction to Phenomenological Philosophy*. Translated by David Carr. Evanston: Northwestern University Press, 1970.

———. *Experience and Judgment: Investigations in a Genealogy of Logic*. Revised and edited by Ludwig Landgrebe. Translated by James S. Churchill and Karl Ameriks. Evanston: Northwestern University Press, 1973.

———. *Formal and Transcendental Logic*. Translated by Dorion Cairns. The Hague: M. Nijhoff, 1978.

———. *The Idea of Phenomenology*. Translated by Lee Hardy. Boston: Kluwer Academic, 1990.

———. *Ideas Pertaining to a Pure Phenomenology and to a Phenomenological Philosophy: First Book*. Translated by F. Kersten. The Hague: M. Nijhoff, 1982.

———. *Ideen zu einer reinen Phänomenologie und phänomenologischen Philosophie*. Tübingen: M. Niemeyer, 2002.

———. *Introduction to the Logical Investigations*. Translated by Philip Bossert and C. H. Peters. The Hague: M. Nijhoff, 1975.

———. *Logical Investigations*. Translated by J. N. Findlay. 2 vols. New York: Routledge, 2001.

———. *The Paris Lectures*. Translated by P. Koestenbaum and Steven James Bartlett. The Hague: M. Nijhoff, 1970.

———. *Phenomenological Psychology: Lectures, Summer Semester, 1925*. Translated by John Scanlon. The Hague: M. Nijhoff, 1977.

Ignatius of Loyola. *Ignatius of Loyola: Spiritual Exercises and Selected Works*. Edited by George E. Ganss. New York: Paulist, 1991.

Irwin, Kevin W. *Models of the Eucharist*. Mahwah, NJ: Paulist, 2005.

Jager, Bernd. "Eating as Natural Event and as Intersubjective Phenomenon: Towards a Phenomenology of Eating." *Journal of Phenomenological Psychology* 30 (1999) 66–116.

Janicaud, Dominique, ed. *Phenomenology and the "Theological Turn": The French Debate*. New York: Fordham University Press, 2000.

———. *Phenomenology "Wide Open": After the French Debate*. Translated by Charles N. Cabral. New York: Fordham University Press, 2005.

John of the Cross. *The Collected Works of St. John of the Cross*. Translated by Kieran Kavanaugh and Otilio Rodriguez. Washington, DC: ICS, 1991.

John Paul II, Pope. *Dies Domini*. 1998. https://w2.vatican.va/content/john-paul-ii/en/apost_letters/1998/documents/hf_jp-ii_apl_05071998_dies-domini.html.

———. *Evangelium vitae*. 1995. http://w2.vatican.va/content/john-paul-ii/en/encyclicals/documents/hf_jp-ii_enc_25031995_evangelium-vitae.html.

———. *Fides et ratio*. 1998. http://w2.vatican.va/content/john-paul-ii/en/encyclicals/documents/hf_jp-ii_enc_14091998_fides-et-ratio.html.

———. *Man and Woman He Created Them: A Theology of the Body*. Translated by Michael Waldstein. Boston: Pauline Books & Media, 2006.

———. *Mulieris dignitatem*. In *The Theology of the Body: Human Love in the Divine Plan*, 443–92. Boston: Pauline Books & Media, 1997.

———. *Pope John Paul II on the Genius of Women*. Washington, DC: U. S. Catholic Conference, 2001.

———. *Veritatis splendor*. 1993. http://w2.vatican.va/content/john-paul-ii/en/encyclicals/documents/hf_jp-ii_enc_06081993_veritatis-splendor.html.

Jones, Tamsin. *A Genealogy of Jean-Luc Marion's Philosophy of Religion: Apparent Darkness*. Bloomington: Indiana University Press, 2011.

Jonkers, Peter, and Ruud Welten, eds. *God in France: Eight Contemporary French Thinkers on God*. Leuven: Peeters, 2005.

Joy, Morny, ed. *Paul Ricoeur and Narrative: Context and Contestation*. Calgary: University of Calgary Press, 1997.

Jurgens, William A., trans. *Faith of the Early Fathers*. Vol. 1. Collegeville, MN: Liturgical Press, 1970.

Kamuf, Peggy, ed. *A Derrida Reader: Between the Blinds*. New York: Columbia University Press, 1991.

Kant, Immanuel. *Critique of Judgment*. Translated by Werner S. Pluhar. Indianapolis: Hackett, 1987.

———. *Critique of Practical Reason*. Translated by Werner S. Pluhar. Indianapolis: Hackett, 2002.

———. *Critique of Pure Reason*. Translated by Werner S. Pluhar. Indianapolis: Hackett, 1996.

———. *The Metaphysics of Morals*. Translated and edited by Mary Gregor. Cambridge: Cambridge University Press, 1996.

———. *Prolegomena to Any Future Metaphysics That Will Be Able to Come Forward as Science: The Paul Carus Translation*. Revised by James W. Ellington. Indianapolis: Hackett, 1977.
———. *Religion Within the Boundaries of Mere Reason and Other Writings*. Translated and edited by Allen Wood and George Di Giovanni. Cambridge: Cambridge University Press, 1998.
Kaplan, David M., ed. *Reading Ricoeur*. Albany: State University of New York Press, 2008.
Kearney, Richard. *Debates in Continental Philosophy: Conversations with Contemporary Thinkers*. New York: Fordham University Press, 2004.
———. *The God Who May Be: A Hermeneutics of Religion*. Bloomington: Indiana University Press, 2001.
———. *Modern Movements in European Philosophy*. 2nd ed. Manchester: Manchester University Press, 1994.
———. *On Paul Ricoeur: The Owl of Minerva*. Burlington, VT: Ashgate, 2004.
———. *Paul Ricoeur: The Hermeneutics of Action*. London: Sage, 1996.
———. *The Wake of Imagination: Toward a Postmodern Culture*. Minneapolis: University of Minnesota Press, 1988.
Kearney, Richard, and Brian Treanor, eds. *Carnal Hermeneutics from Head to Foot*. New York: Fordham University Press, 2015.
Keenan, Dennis King. *Death and Responsibility: The "Work" of Levinas*. Albany: State University of New York Press, 1999.
Kessler, Michael, and Christian Sheppard, eds. *Mystics: Presence and Aporia*. Chicago: University of Chicago Press, 2003.
Kirchhoffer, David G., Robyn Horner, and Patrick McArdle, eds. *Being Human: Groundwork for a Theological Anthropology for the 21st Century*. Eugene, OR: Wipf & Stock, 2013.
Kitagawa, Joseph M., and Charles H. Long, eds. *Myths and Symbols: Studies in Honor of Mircea Eliade*. Chicago: University of Chicago Press, 1969.
Klemm, David E. *The Hermeneutical Theory of Paul Ricoeur: A Constructive Analysis*. London: Associated University Presses, 1983.
———. "'This Is My Body': Hermeneutics and Eucharistic Language." *Anglican Theological Review* 64 (1982) 293–310.
———. "Toward a Rhetoric of Postmodern Theology: Through Barth and Heidegger." *Journal of the American Academy of Religion* 55 (1987) 443–69.
Klemm, David E., and William H. Klink. "Consciousness and Quantum Mechanics: Opting from Alternatives." *Zygon* 43 (2008) 307–27.
———. "Dialogue on Theological Models: Constructing and Testing Theological Models." *Zygon* 38 (2003) 495–528.
———. "Models Clarified: Responding to Langdon Gilkey." *Zygon* 38 (2003) 535–41.
Knowles, Tom, ed. *Eucharist: Experience and Testimony*. Melbourne: D. Lovell, 2001.
Kosky, Jeffrey L. *Levinas and the Philosophy of Religion*. Bloomington: Indiana University Press, 2001.
LaCocque, André. *The Captivity of Innocence: Babel and the Yahwist*. Eugene, OR: Cascade, 2010.
———. *Onslaught against Innocence: Cain, Abel, and the Yahwist*. Eugene, OR: Cascade, 2008.

———. *Romance She Wrote: A Hermeneutical Essay on the Song of Songs*. Harrisburg, PA: Trinity, 1998.

———. *The Trial of Innocence: Adam, Eve, and the Yahwist*. Eugene, OR: Cascade, 2006.

LaCocque, André, and Paul Ricoeur. *Thinking Biblically: Exegetical and Hermeneutical Studies*. Translated by David Pellauer. Chicago: University of Chicago Press, 1998.

Lacoste, Jean-Yves. *Experience and the Absolute: Disputed Questions on the Humanity of Man*. Translated by Mark Raftery-Skehan. New York: Fordham University Press, 2004.

———. *From Theology to Theological Thinking*. Translated by W. Chris Hackett. Charlottesville: University of Virginia Press, 2014.

———. *La phénoménalité de Dieu*. Paris: Cerf, 2008.

———. "More Haste, Less Speed in Theology." *International Journal of Systematic Theology* 9 (2007) 263–82.

———. *Note sur le temps: Essai sur le raisons de la mémoire et de l'espérance*. Paris: Presses universitaires de France, 1990.

———. "Phénoménologie de l'Esprit à la Montée du Carmel." *Revue thomiste: revue doctrinale de théologie et de philosophie* 89 (1989) 569–98.

Lam, Jason T. "Toward a Theological Hermeneutic of Testimony." *Jian Dao* 22 (2004) 99–135.

Lawler, Michael G. *Symbol and Sacrament: A Contemporary Sacramental Theology*. Omaha, NE: Creighton University Press, 1995.

Leask, Ian, and Eoin Cassidy, eds. *Givenness and God: Questions of Jean-Luc Marion*. New York: Fordham University Press, 2005.

Lee, Jung H. "Neither Totality nor Infinity: Suffering the Other." *The Journal of Religion* 79 (1999) 250–79.

Leijssen, Lambert J. *With the Silent Glimmer of God's Spirit: A Postmodern Look at the Sacraments*. Translated by Marie Baird. New York: Paulist, 2006.

Lessing, Gotthold. *Lessing's Theological Writings: Selections in Translation*. Edited by Henry Chadwick. London: A. & C. Black, 1956.

Levinas, Emmanuel. *Alterity and Transcendence*. Translated by Michael B. Smith. New York: Columbia University Press, 1999.

———. *Beyond the Verse: Talmudic Readings and Lectures*. Translated by Gary D. Mole. Bloomington: Indiana University Press, 1994.

———. *Collected Philosophical Papers*. Translated by Alphonso Lingis. Dordrecht: M. Nijhoff, 1987.

———. *Difficult Freedom*. Translated by Seán Hand. Baltimore: Johns Hopkins University Press, 1990.

———. *Discovering Existence with Husserl*. Translated by Richard A. Cohen and Michael B. Smith. Evanston: Northwestern University Press, 1998.

———. *Emmanuel Levinas: Basic Philosophical Writings*. Edited by Adriaan T. Peperzak, Simon Critchley, and Robert Bernasconi. Bloomington: Indiana University Press, 1996.

———. *Entre Nous: On Thinking-of-the-Other*. Translated by Michael B. Smith and Barbara Harshav. New York: Columbia University Press, 1998.

———. *Ethics and Infinity: Conversations with Philippe Nemo*. Translated by Richard A. Cohen. Pittsburgh: Duquesne University Press, 1985.

———. *Existence and Existents*. Translated by Alphonso Lingis. Pittsburgh: Dusquesne University Press, 2001.

———. *God, Death, and Time*. Translated by Bettina Bergo. Stanford: Stanford University Press, 2000.
———. *Humanism of the Other*. Translated by Nidra Poller. Urbana: University of Illinois Press, 2003.
———. *In the Time of the Nations*. Translated by Michael B. Smith. Bloomington: Indiana University Press, 1994.
———. *The Levinas Reader*. Edited by Seán Hand. Cambridge, MA: Blackwell, 1989.
———. *New Talmudic Readings*. Translated by Richard A. Cohen. Pittsburgh: Duquesne University Press, 1999.
———. *Nine Talmudic Readings*. Translated by Annette Aronowicz. Bloomington: Indiana University Press, 1990.
———. *Of God Who Comes to Mind*. Translated by Bettina Bergo. Stanford: Stanford University Press, 1998.
———. *On Escape*. Translated by Bettina Bergo. Stanford: Stanford University Press, 2003.
———. *Otherwise than Being: or, Beyond Essence*. Translated by Alphonso Lingis. Pittsburgh: Dusquesne University Press, 1981.
———. *Outside the Subject*. Translated by Michael B. Smith. London: Athlone, 1993.
———. *Positivité et transcendance*. Paris: Presses universitaires de France, 2000.
———. *Proper Names*. Translated by Michael B. Smith. Stanford: Stanford University Press, 1996.
———. *The Theory of Intuition in Husserl's Phenomenology*. Translated by André Orianne. 2nd ed. Evanston: Northwestern University Press, 1995.
———. *Time and the Other*. Translated by Richard A. Cohen. Pittsburgh: Dusquesne University Press, 1987.
———. *Totality and Infinity: An Essay on Exteriority*. Translated by Alphonso Lingis. Pittsburgh: Duquesne University Press, 1969.
———. *Unforeseen History*. Translated by Nidra Poller. Chicago: University of Illinois Press, 2004.
Liguori, Alphonsus. *The Holy Eucharist*. New York: Alba House, 1994.
Lindbeck, George A. *The Nature of Doctrine: Religion and Theology in a Postliberal Age*. Louisville: Westminster John Knox, 1984.
Lonergan, Bernard. *Method in Theology*. Toronto: University of Toronto Press, 1971.
López, Antonio. *Gift and the Unity of Being*. Eugene, OR: Cascade, 2014.
Louth, Andrew. *The Origins of the Christian Mystical Tradition from Plato to Denys*. 2nd ed. New York: Oxford University Press, 2007.
Lubac, Henri de. *Corpus Mysticum: The Eucharist and the Church in the Middle Ages*. Translated by Gemma Simmonds. London: SCM, 2006.
Lukken, Gerard. *Per visibilia ad invisibilia: Anthropological, Theological and Semiotic Studies on the Liturgy and the Sacraments*. Kampen: Kok Pharos, 1994.
Mackinlay, Shane. *Interpreting Excess: Jean-Luc Marion, Saturated Phenomena, and Hermeneutics*. New York: Fordham University Press, 2010.
Madathummuriyil, Sebastian. *Sacrament as Gift: A Pneumatological and Phenomenological Approach*. Leuven: Peeters, 2012.
Makabe, Sayoko, et al. *Atlas of Human Female Reproductive Function: Ovarian Development to Early Embryogenesis after In Vitro Fertilization*. London: Taylor & Francis, 2006.

Malka, Salomon. *Emmanuel Levinas: His Life and Legacy*. Translated by Michael Kigel and Sonja M. Embree. Pittsburgh: Duquesne University Press, 2006.

Manoussakis, John Panteleimon, ed. *After God: Richard Kearney and the Religious Turn in Continental Philosophy*. New York: Fordham University Press, 2006.

———. "*Khora*: The Hermeneutics of Hyphenation." *Revista Portuguesa Filosofia* 58 (2002) 93–100.

Mansini, Guy, and James G. Hart, eds. *Ethics and Theological Disclosures: The Thought of Robert Sokolowski*. Washington, DC: Catholic University of America Press, 2003.

Marcel, Gabriel. *Tragic Wisdom and Beyond*. Evanston: Northwestern University Press, 1973.

Marion, Jean-Luc. *Being Given: Toward a Phenomenology of Givenness*. Translated by Jeffrey L. Kosky. Stanford: Stanford University Press, 2002.

———. *Cartesian Questions: Method and Metaphysics*. Translated by Jeffrey L. Kosky et al. Chicago: University of Chicago Press, 1999.

———. *Certitudes négatives*. Paris: Grasset, 2010.

———. *Le croire pour le voir: Réflections diverses sur la rationalité de la révélation et l'irrationalité de quelques croyants*. Paris: Parole et Silence, 2010.

———. *The Crossing of the Visible*. Translated by James K. A. Smith. Stanford: Stanford University Press, 2004.

———. *Dieu sans l'être*. 2nd ed. Paris: Quadrige/PUF, 2002.

———. *The Erotic Phenomenon*. Translated by Stephen E. Lewis. Chicago: University of Chicago Press, 2007.

———. *The Essential Writings*. Edited by Kevin Hart. New York: Fordham University Press, 2013.

———. *Givenness and Hermeneutics*. Translated by Jean-Pierre Lafouge. Milwaukee: Marquette University Press, 2013.

———. *Givenness and Revelation*. Translated by Stephen E. Lewis. New York: Oxford University Press, 2016.

———. *God without Being: Hors-Texte*. Translated by Thomas A. Carlson. Chicago: University of Chicago Press, 1991.

———. *The Idol and Distance: Five Studies*. Translated by Thomas A. Carlson. New York: Fordham University Press, 2001.

———. *L'idole et la distance: Cinq études*. Paris: Grasset, 1977.

———. *In Excess: Studies of Saturated Phenomena*. Translated by Robyn Horner and Vincent Berraud. New York: Fordham University Press, 2002.

———. *In the Self's Place: The Approach of Saint Augustine*. Translated by Jeffrey L. Kosky. Stanford: Stanford University Press, 2012.

———. "The Invisibility of the Saint." Translated by Christina M. Gschwandtner. *Critical Inquiry* 35 (2009) 703–10.

———. *Negative Certainties*. Translated by Stephen E. Lewis. Chicago: University of Chicago Press, 2015.

———. *On Descartes' Metaphysical Prism: The Constitution and the Limits of Onto-theology in Cartesian Thought*. Translated by Jeffrey L. Kosky. Chicago: University of Chicago Press, 1999.

———. *On the Ego and on God: Further Cartesian Questions*. Translated by Christina M. Gschwandtner. New York: Fordham University Press, 2007.

———. "La phénoménalité du sacrement: être et donation." *Communio* 26 (2001) 59–75.

———. *Prolegomena to Charity*. Translated by Stephen E. Lewis. New York: Fordham University Press, 2002.

———. "The Question of the Unconditioned." Translated by Christina M. Gschwandtner. *The Journal of Religion* 93 (2013) 1–24.

———. *The Reason of the Gift*. Translated by Stephen E. Lewis. Charlottesville: University of Virginia Press, 2011.

———. *Reduction and Givenness: Investigations of Husserl, Heidegger, and Phenomenology*. Translated by Thomas A. Carlson. Evanston: Northwestern University Press, 1998.

———. *Réduction et donation: Recherches sur Husserl, Heidegger et la phenomenologie*. Paris: Presses universitaires de France, 1989.

———. *The Visible and the Revealed*. Translated by Christina M. Gschwandtner et al. New York: Fordham University Press, 2008.

Marsh, James L., John D. Caputo, and Merold Westphal, eds. *Modernity and Its Discontents*. New York: Fordham University Press, 1992.

McFague, Sallie. *Metaphorical Theology: Models of God in Religious Language*. Philadelphia: Fortress, 1982.

McGinn, Bernard. *The Foundations of Mysticism: Origins to the Fifth Century*. New York: Crossroad, 1991.

McGowan, Andrew. *Ascetic Eucharists: Food and Drink in Early Christian Ritual Meals*. Oxford: Clarendon, 1999.

McPartlan, Paul. *Sacrament of Salvation: An Introduction to Eucharistic Ecclesiology*. Edinburgh: T. & T. Clark, 2000.

———. *A Service of Love: Papal Primacy, the Eucharist, and Church Unity*. Washington, DC: Catholic University of America Press, 2013.

Meinong, Alexius. "Über Gegenstandstheorie." In *Über Gegenstandstheorie; Selbstdarstellung*, edited by Josef M. Werle. 1–51. Hamburg: F. Meiner, 1988.

Merleau-Ponty, Maurice. *The Merleau-Ponty Reader*. Edited by Ted Toadvine and Leonard Lawlor. Evanston: Northwestern University Press, 2007.

———. *The Primacy of Perception and Other Essays on Phenomenological Psychology, the Philosophy of Art, History and Politics*. Edited by James M. Edie. Evanston: Northwestern University Press, 1964.

———. *The Visible and the Invisible: Followed by Working Notes*. Edited by Claude Lefort. Translated by Alphonso Lingis. Evanston: Northwestern University Press, 1968.

———. *The World of Perception*. Translated by Oliver Davis. New York: Routledge, 2004.

Migne, Jacques-Paul, ed. *Patrologia graeca, Vols. 1–161*. Paris: Migne, 1857–66.

———, ed. *Patrologia latina, Vols. 1–217*. Paris: Migne, 1844–55.

Milbank, John. *Being Reconciled: Ontology and Pardon*. London: Routledge, 2003.

———. *The Suspended Middle: Henri de Lubac and the Renewed Split in Modern Catholic Theology*. 2nd ed. Grand Rapids: Eerdmans, 2014.

———. *The Word Made Strange: Theology, Language, Culture*. Oxford: Wiley-Blackwell, 1997.

Milbank, John, and Catherine Pickstock. *Truth in Aquinas*. London: Routledge, 2000.

Milbank, John, Catherine Pickstock, and Graham Ward, eds. *Radical Orthodoxy: A New Theology*. London: Routledge, 1999.

Mitchell, Nathan D. "Mystery and Manners: Eucharist in Post-modern Theology." *Worship* 67 (1993) 164–73.

Molnar, Paul D. *Karl Barth and the Theology of the Lord's Supper: A Systematic Investigation*. New York: P. Lang, 1996.

Moran, Dermot. *Introduction to Phenomenology*. New York: Routledge, 2000.

Morgan, Michael L. *Discovering Levinas*. New York: Cambridge University Press, 2007.

Morris, Thomas V. *God and the Philosophers: The Reconciliation between Faith and Reason*. New York: Oxford University Press, 1994.

Nabert, Jean. *Elements for an Ethic*. Translated by William J. Petrek. Evanston: Northwestern University Press, 1969.

———. *Le désir de Dieu*. Paris: Cerf, 1996.

Nancy, Jean-Luc. *Listening*. Translated by Charlotte Mandell. New York: Fordham University Press, 2007.

———. *Noli me tangere: On the Raising of the Body*. Translated by Sarah Clift, Pascale-Anne Brault, and Michael Naas. New York: Fordham University Press, 2008.

Nicholas of Cusa. *The Vision of God*. Translated by Emma Gurney Salter. New York: Cosimo, 2007.

Ochs, Peter. "From Phenomenology to Scripture: A General Response." *Modern Theology* 16 (2000) 341–45.

Ó Murchadha, Felix. *A Phenomenology of Christian Life: Glory and Night*. Bloomington: Indiana University Press, 2013.

O'Rourke, Fran. *Pseudo-Dionysius and the Metaphysics of Aquinas*. Notre Dame: University of Notre Dame Press, 2005.

Osborne, Kenan B. "Contemporary Understandings of the Eucharist: A Survey of Catholic Thinking." *Journal of Ecumenical Studies* 13 (1976) 192–201.

Otto, Rudolf. *The Idea of the Holy: An Inquiry into the Non-rational Factor in the Idea of the Divine and Its Relation to the Rational*. Translated by John W. Harvey. 2nd ed. New York: Oxford University Press, 1958.

———. *Mysticism East and West: A Comparative Analysis of the Nature of Mysticism*. Translated by Bertha L. Bracey and Richenda C. Payne. New York: Macmillan, 1932.

Paden, William E. *Interpreting the Sacred: Ways of Viewing Religion*. Rev. and updated ed. Boston: Beacon, 2003.

Palsey, Malcomb, ed. *Nietzsche: Imagery and Thought*. Berkeley: University of California Press, 1978.

Panikkar, Raimon. *The Rhythm of Being: The Gifford Lectures*. Maryknoll, NY: Orbis, 2010.

Pascal, Blaise. *Pensées*. Paris: Éditions Garnier Frères, 1964.

Patterson, Colin, and Conor Sweeney, eds. *God and Eros: The Ethos of the Nuptial Mystery*. Eugene, OR: Cascade, 2015.

Peperzak, Adriaan Theodoor. *Beyond: The Philosophy of Emmanuel Levinas*. Evanston: Northwestern University Press, 1997.

———, ed. *Ethics as First Philosophy: The Significance of Emmanuel Levinas for Philosophy, Literature and Religion*. New York: Routledge, 1995.

———. *To the Other: An Introduction to the Philosophy of Emmanuel Levinas*. West Lafayette, IN: Purdue University Press, 1993.

Pickstock, Catherine. *After Writing: On the Liturgical Consummation of Philosophy*. Oxford: Blackwell, 1998.

Pinckaers, Servais. *The Sources of Christian Ethics*. Translated by Mary Thomas Noble. Washington, DC: Catholic University of America Press, 1995.

Plato. *Complete Works*. Edited by John M. Cooper. Indianapolis: Hackett, 1997.

Power, David N. *The Eucharistic Mystery: Revitalizing the Tradition*. New York: Crossroad, 1992.

———. *Love without Calculation: A Reflection on Divine Kenosis*. New York: Crossroad, 2005.

———. *Sacrament: The Language of God's Giving*. New York: Crossroad, 1999.

Powers, Joseph M. *Eucharistic Theology*. New York: Herder and Herder, 1967.

Pseudo-Dionysius. *Pseudo-Dionysius: The Complete Works*. Translated by Colm Luibheid. New York: Paulist, 1987.

Purcell, Michael. "An *Agape* of Eating: The Eucharist as Substitution (Levinas)." *Bijdragen* 57 (1996) 318–36.

Rahner, Karl. *The Church and the Sacraments*. Translated by W. J. O'Hara. New York: Herder & Herder, 1963.

———. *The Eucharist: The Mystery of Our Christ*. Translated by Salvator Attanasio. Denville, NJ: Dimension Books, 1970.

———. *Foundations of Christian Faith*. Translated by William V. Dych. New York: Seabury, 1978.

———. *Grundkurs des Glaubens: Einführung in den Begriff des Christentums*. Freiburg: Herder, 1976.

———. *Hearers of the Word*. Translated by Michael Richards. New York: Herder and Herder, 1969.

———. *Theological Investigations*. Vol. 13, *Theology, Anthropology, Christology*. Translated by David Bourke. New York: Seabury, 1975.

———. *Theological Investigations*. Vol. 14, *Ecclesiology, Questions in the Church, the Church in the World*. Translated by David Bourke. New York: Seabury, 1976.

Ratzinger, Joseph. *Introduction to Christianity*. San Francisco: Ignatius, 2004.

———. *Truth and Tolerance: Christian Belief and World Religions*. San Francisco: Ignatius, 2004.

Reali, Nicola, ed. *Il mondo del sacramento: Teologia e filosophia a confronto*. Milan: Paoline, 2001.

Reynolds, Thomas E. *Vulnerable Communion: A Theology of Disability and Hospitality*. Grand Rapids: Brazos, 2008.

Richardson, Cyril C., ed. *Early Christian Fathers*. New York: Touchstone, 1996.

Ricoeur, Paul. "Biblical Hermeneutics." *Semeia* 4 (1975) 29–148.

———. *The Conflict of Interpretations: Essays in Hermeneutics*. Edited by Don Ihde. Evanston: Northwestern University Press, 1974.

———. *The Course of Recognition*. Translated by David Pellauer. Cambridge, MA: Harvard University Press, 2005.

———. *Essays on Biblical Interpretation*. Edited by Lewis S. Mudge. Philadelphia: Fortress, 1980.

———. *Fallible Man*. Revised translation by Charles A. Kelbley. Rev. ed. New York: Fordham University Press, 1986.

———. *Figuring the Sacred: Religion, Narrative, and Imagination*. Translated by David Pellauer. Edited by Mark I. Wallace. Minneapolis: Fortress, 1995.

———. *Freedom and Nature: The Voluntary and the Involuntary*. Translated by Erazim V. Kohák. Evanston: Northwestern University Press, 2007.

———. *Freud and Philosophy: An Essay on Interpretation*. Translated by Denis Savage. New Haven: Yale University Press, 1970.
———. *From Text to Action*. Translated by Kathleen Blamey and John B. Thompson. Essays in Hermeneutics 2. Evanston, IL: Northwestern University Press, 1991.
———. *Hermeneutics and the Human Sciences: Essays on Language, Action and Interpretation*. Translated by John B. Thompson. New York: Cambridge University Press, 1993.
———. *History and Truth*. Translated by Charles A. Kelbley. Evanston: Northwestern University Press, 1965.
———. *Husserl: An Analysis of His Phenomenology*. Translated by Edward G. Ballard and Lester E. Embree. Evanston: Northwestern University Press, 1967.
———. *Interpretation Theory: Discourse and the Surplus of Meaning*. Fort Worth: Texas Christian University Press, 1976.
———. *The Just*. Translated by David Pellauer. Chicago: University of Chicago Press, 2000.
———. *A Key to Husserl's "Ideas I"*. Translated by Bond Harris and Jacqueline Bouchard. Milwaukee: Marquette University Press, 1996.
———. *Main Trends in Philosophy*. New York: Holmes & Meier, 1979.
———. "Manifestation and Proclamation." *The Journal of the Blaisdell Institute* 12 (1978) 13–35.
———. *Memory, History, Forgetting*. Translated by David Pellauer and Kathleen Blamey. Chicago: University of Chicago Press, 2004.
———. *Oneself as Another*. Translated by Kathleen Blamey. Chicago: University of Chicago Press, 1994.
———. "Philosophy and Religious Language." *The Journal of Religion* 54 (1974) 71–85.
———. *Reflections on the Just*. Translated by David Pellauer. Chicago: University of Chicago Press, 2007.
———. *The Rule of Metaphor: The Creation of Meaning in Language*. Translated by Robert Czerny, Kathleen McLaughlin, and John Costello. New York: Routledge, 2003.
———. *The Symbolism of Evil*. Translated by Emerson Buchanan. New York: Harper & Row, 1967.
———. *Time and Narrative*. Translated by Kathleen McLaughlin and David Pellauer. 3 vols. Chicago: University of Chicago Press, 1984.
Rivera, Joseph. "Corpus Mysticum and Religious Experience: Henry, Lacoste and Marion." *International Journal of Systematic Theology* 14 (2012) 327–49.
———. "Toward a Liturgical Existentialism." *New Blackfriars* 94:1049 (2013) 79–96.
Robbins, Jill, ed. *Is It Righteous to Be? Interviews with Emmanuel Levinas*. Stanford: Stanford University Press, 2001.
Rocha, Samuel D. *Folk Phenomenology: Education, Study, and the Human Person*. Eugene, OR: Pickwick, 2015.
Rolnick, Philip A. *Person, Grace, and God*. Grand Rapids: Eerdmans, 2007.
Romano, Claude. *Event and World*. Translated by Shane Mackinlay. New York: Fordham University Press, 2009.
———. *There Is: The Event and the Finitude of Appearing*. Translated by Michael B. Smith. New York: Fordham University Press, 2015.
Rosenzweig, Franz. *The Star of Redemption*. Translated by William W. Hallo. Notre Dame: University of Notre Dame Press, 1985.

Ross, Susan A. *Extravagant Affections: A Feminist Sacramental Theology*. New York: Continuum, 2001.
Sarot, Marcel, and Wessel Stoker, eds. *Religion and the Good Life*. Assen: Royal Van Gorcum, 2004.
Schalow, Frank. *Heidegger and the Quest for the Sacred: From Thought to the Sanctuary of Faith*. Boston: Kluwer Academic, 2001.
Schillebeeckx, Edward. *The Eucharist*. Translated by N. S. Smith. New York: Sheed & Ward, 1968.
Schleiermacher, Friedrich. *The Christian Faith*. Edited by H. R. Mackintosh and J. S. Stewart. New York: T. & T. Clark, 1999.
———. *On Religion: Speeches to Its Cultured Despisers*. Translated by Richard Crouter. Cambridge: Cambridge University Press, 1988.
Schoenwolf, Gary C., et al. *Larsen's Human Embryology*. 4th ed. Philadelphia: Elsevier/ Churchill Livingstone, 2009.
Schönborn, Christoph. *God's Human Face: The Christ-Icon*. Translated by Lothar Krauth. San Francisco: Ignatius, 1994.
Schrijvers, Joeri. "God and/in Phenomenology: Jean-Yves Lacoste's *Phenomenality of God*." *Bijdragen* 71 (2010) 85–93.
———. *An Introduction to Jean-Yves Lacoste*. Burlington, VT: Ashgate, 2012.
———. "Jean-Yves Lacoste: A Phenomenology of Liturgy." *Heythrop Journal* 46 (2005) 314–33.
———. *Ontotheological Turnings? The Decentering of the Modern Subject in Recent French Phenomenology*. Albany: State University of New York Press, 2011.
———. "Ontotheological Turnings? Marion, Lacoste and Levinas on the Decentering of Modern Subjectivity." *Modern Theology* 22 (2006) 221–53.
———. "Phenomenology, Liturgy, and Metaphysics: The Thought of Jean-Yves Lacoste." In *God in France: Eight Contemporary French Thinkers on God*, edited by Peter Jonkers and Ruud Welten, 207–25. Leuven: Peeters, 2005.
Schwartz, Regina. *Sacramental Poetics at the Dawn of Secularism: When God Left the World*. Stanford: Stanford University Press, 2008.
———, ed. *Transcendence: Philosophy, Literature, and Theology Approach the Beyond*. New York: Routledge, 2004.
Shanley, Brian J. *One Hundred Years of Philosophy*. Washington, DC: Catholic University of America Press, 2001.
Shenton, Andrew, ed. *Messiaen the Theologian*. Burlington, VT: Ashgate, 2010.
Sholl, Robert, ed. *Messiaen Studies*. New York: Cambridge University Press, 2007.
Simmons, J. Aaron, and Bruce Ellis Benson. *The New Phenomenology: A Philosophical Introduction*. New York: Bloomsbury, 2013.
Simms, Eva-Maria. "Milk and Flesh: A Phenomenological Reflection on Infancy and Coexistence." *Journal of Phenomenological Psychology* 32 (2001) 22–40.
Siniscalchi, Glenn B. *Retrieving Apologetics*. Eugene, OR: Pickwick, 2016.
Smart, Ninian. *The Phenomenon of Religion*. New York: Herder & Herder, 1973.
———. *The Science of Religion and the Sociology of Knowledge: Some Methodological Questions*. Princeton: Princeton University Press, 1973.
Smith, James K. A. *Who's Afraid of Postmodernism? Taking Derrida, Lyotard, and Foucault to Church*. Grand Rapids: Baker, 2006.
Smith, Michael B. *Toward the Outside: Concepts and Themes in Emmanuel Levinas*. Pittsburgh: Duquesne University Press, 2005.

Sokolowski, Robert. *Christian Faith and Human Understanding: Studies on the Eucharist, Trinity, and the Human Person*. Washington, DC: Catholic University of America Press, 2006.

———, ed. *Edmund Husserl and the Phenomenological Tradition: Essays in Phenomenology*. Washington, DC: Catholic University of America Press, 1988.

———. *Eucharistic Presence: A Study in the Theology of Disclosure*. Washington, DC: Catholic University of America Press, 1994.

———. *The God of Faith and Reason: Foundations of Christian Theology*. Washington, DC: Catholic University of America Press, 1995.

———. *Husserlian Meditations: How Words Present Things*. Evanston: Northwestern University Press, 1974.

———. *Introduction to Phenomenology*. New York: Cambridge University Press, 2000.

———. *Phenomenology of the Human Person*. New York: Cambridge University Press, 2008.

———. *Pictures, Quotations, and Distinctions*. Notre Dame: University of Notre Dame Press, 1992.

———. *Presence and Absence: A Philosophical Investigation of Language and Being*. Bloomington: Indiana University Press, 1978.

Spaemann, Robert. *Persons: The Difference between "Someone" and "Something"*. New York: Oxford University Press, 2006.

Stein, Edith. *Der Aufbau der Menschlichen Person*. Freiburg: Herder, 1994.

———. *Essays on Woman*. Edited by L. Gelber and Romaeus Leuven. Translated by Freda Mary Oben. 2nd ed. Washington, DC: ICS, 1996.

———. *La estructura de la persona humana*. Translated by José Mardomingo. Madrid: Biblioteca de Autores Cristianos, 1998.

———. *Finite and Eternal Being: An Attempt at an Ascent to the Meaning of Being*. Translated by Kurt F. Reinhardt. Washington, DC: ICS, 2002.

———. *The Hidden Life: Hagiographic Essays, Meditations, Spiritual Texts*. Translated by Waltraut Stein. Washington, DC: ICS, 1992.

———. *Knowledge and Faith*. Translated by Walter Redmond. Washington, DC: ICS, 2000.

———. *Life in a Jewish Family*. Translated by Josephine Koeppel. Washington, DC: ICS, 1986.

———. *On the Problem of Empathy*. Translated by Waltraut Stein. Washington, DC: ICS, 1989.

———. *Philosophy of Psychology and the Humanities*. Translated by Mary Catherine Baseheart and Marianne Sawicki. Washington, DC: ICS, 2000.

———. *Potency and Act: Studies Toward a Philosophy of Being*. Translated by Walter Redmond. Washington, DC: ICS, 2009.

———. *The Science of the Cross*. Translated by Josephine Koeppel. Washington, DC: ICS, 2002.

———. *The Science of the Cross: A Study of St. John of the Cross*. Edited by L. Gelber and Romaeus Leuven. Translated by Hilda Graef. London: Burns & Oates, 1960.

———. *Self-Portrait in Letters: 1916–1942*. Edited by L. Gelber and Romaeus Leuven. Translated by Josephine Koeppel. Washington, DC: ICS, 1993.

———. *Self-Portrait in Letters: Letters to Roman Ingarden*. Translated by Hugh Candler Hunt. Washington, DC: ICS, 2014.

———. *Was ist der Mensch? Theologische Anthropologie*. Freiburg: Herder, 2005.

———. *Welt und Person: Beitrag zum Christlichen Wahrheitsstreben*. Freiburg: Herder, 1962.

Sweeney, Conor. *Sacramental Presence after Heidegger: Onto-theology, Sacraments, and the Mother's Smile*. Eugene, OR: Cascade, 2015.

Tanner, Norman P., ed. *Decrees of the Ecumenical* Councils. 2 vols. Washington, DC: Georgetown University Press, 1990.

Teresa of Avila. *The Interior Castle*. Translated by Kieran Kavanaugh and Otilio Rodriguez. Washington, DC: ICS, 2010.

———. *Obras de Santa Teresa de Jesus*. Burgos: El Monte Carmelo, 1915.

Thérèse of Lisieux. *Story of a Soul*. Translated by John Clarke. 3rd ed. Washington, DC: ICS, 1996.

Third Council of Baltimore. *The Baltimore Catechism of 1891*. The Catholic Primer, 2005. http://www.pcpbooks.net/docs/baltimore_catechism.pdf.

Thomas Aquinas. *Devoutly I Adore Thee: The Prayers and Hymns of St. Thomas Aquinas*. Translated by Robert Anderson and Johann Moser. Manchester, NH: Sophia Institute Press, 1993.

———. *Summa theologiae*. http://www.corpusthomisticum.org/sth0000.html.

———. *Summa Theologica*. Translated by the Fathers of the English Dominican Province. 5 vols. Notre Dame: Ave Maria Press, 1981.

Tillich, Paul. *Systematic Theology*. 3 vols. Chicago: University of Chicago Press, 1951–63.

Titus, Craig Steven, ed. *On Wings of Faith and Reason: The Christian Difference in Culture and Science*. Arlington, VA: Institute for the Psychological Sciences, 2008.

Toyohiko, Kagawa. *Cosmic Purpose*. Edited by Thomas John Hastings. Eugene, OR: Cascade, 2014.

Tracy, David. *The Achievement of Bernard Lonergan*. New York: Herder & Herder, 1970.

———. *The Analogical Imagination: Christian Theology and the Culture of Pluralism*. New York: Crossroad, 1981.

———. *Blessed Rage for Order: The New Pluralism in Theology*. Chicago: University of Chicago Press, 1996.

———. *Dialogue with the Other: The Inter-religious Dialogue*. Leuven: Peeters, 1990.

———. *On Naming the Present: God, Hermeneutics, and Church*. Maryknoll, NY: Orbis, 1994.

———. *Plurality and Ambiguity: Hermeneutics, Religion, Hope*. Chicago: University of Chicago Press, 1987.

Van Inwagen, Peter, and Dean Zimmerman, eds. *Persons: Human and Divine*. New York: Oxford University Press, 2007.

Van Maas, Sander. *The Reinvention of Religious Music: Olivier Messiaen's Breakthrough Toward the Beyond*. New York: Fordham University Press, 2012.

Vattimo, Gianni. *Beyond Interpretation: The Meaning of Hermeneutics for Philosophy*. Translated by David Webb. Stanford: Stanford University Press, 1997.

Vedder, Ben. *Heidegger's Philosophy of Religion: From God to the Gods*. Pittsburgh: Duquesne University Press, 2007.

Veeck, Lucinda L., and Nikica Zaninović, eds. *An Atlas of Human Blastocysts*. New York: Parthenon, 2003.

Vorgrimler, Herbert. *Sacramental Theology*. Collegeville, MN: Liturgical Press, 1992.

Wachterhauser, Brice R., ed. *Hermeneutics and Truth*. Evanston: Northwestern University Press, 1994.

Wall, John. "Childhood Studies, Hermeneutics, and Theological Ethics." *Journal of Religion* 86 (2006) 523–48.

Wallace, Mark I. "From Phenomenology to Scripture? Paul Ricoeur's Hermeneutical Philosophy of Religion." *Modern Theology* 16 (2000) 301–13.

Wallenfang, Donald. "Aperture of Absence: Jean-Luc Marion on the God Who 'Is Not.'" In *Models of God and Alternative Ultimate Realities*, edited by Jeanine Diller and Asa Kasher, 861–73. New York: Springer, 2013.

———. "Face Off for Interreligious Dialogue: A *Theo*logy of Childhood in Jean-Luc Marion versus a Theology of Adulthood in Emmanuel Levinas." *Listening: Journal of Communication Ethics, Religion, and Culture* 50 (2015) 106–16.

———. "Figures and Forms of Ultimacy: Manifestation and Proclamation as Paradigms of the Sacred." *The International Journal of Religion in Spirituality and Society* 1 (2011) 109–14.

———. *Human and Divine Being: A Study on the Theological Anthropology of Edith Stein*. Eugene, OR: Cascade, 2017.

———. "Levinas and Marion on Law and Freedom: Toward a New Dialectical Theology of Justice." *Pacifica* 29:1 (2016) 71–98.

———. "Sacramental Givenness: The Notion of Givenness in Husserl, Heidegger, and Marion, and Its Import for Interpreting the Phenomenality of the Eucharist." *Philosophy and Theology* 22:1–2 (2010) 131–54.

———. "Trilectic of Testimony: A Phenomenological Construal of the Eucharist as Manifestation-Proclamation-Attestation." PhD, Loyola University Chicago, 2011.

Ward, Graham, ed. *The Blackwell Companion to Postmodern Theology*. Oxford: Blackwell, 2001.

———. *Cities of God*. London: Routledge, 2000.

———, ed. *The Postmodern God: A Theological Reader*. Oxford: Blackwell, 1997.

Wardley, Kenneth Jason. *Praying to a French God: The Theology of Jean-Yves Lacoste*. Burlington, VT: Ashgate, 2014.

Welz, Claudia. "God—a Phenomenon? Theology as Semiotic Phenomenology of the Invisible." *Studia Theologica* 62 (2008) 4–24.

Westphal, Merold. *God, Guilt, and Death: An Existential Phenomenology of Religion*. Bloomington: Indiana University Press, 1984.

———. *History and Truth in Hegel's Phenomenology*. Atlantic Highlands, NJ: Humanities, 1979.

———. "The Importance of Overcoming Metaphysics for the Life of Faith." *Modern Theology* 23 (2007) 253–78.

———. *Levinas and Kierkegaard in Dialogue*. Bloomington: Indiana University Press, 2008.

———. *Overcoming Onto-theology: Toward a Postmodern Christian Faith*. New York: Fordham University Press, 2001.

———. *Suspicion and Faith: The Religious Uses of Modern Atheism*. Grand Rapids: Eerdmans, 1993.

———. *Transcendence and Self-Transcendence: On God and the Soul*. Bloomington: Indiana University Press, 2004.

———. "Vision and Voice: Phenomenology and Theology in the Work of Jean-Luc Marion." *International Journal for Philosophy of Religion* 60 (2006) 117–37.

Whitehouse, Glenn. "Ricoeur on Religious Selfhood: A Response to Mark Wallace." *Modern Theology* 16 (2000) 315–23.

Willis, Megan L. "Language as the Sanctuary of Being: A Theological Exploration with Louis-Marie Chauvet." *Heythrop Journal* 51 (2010) 872–80.

Wittgenstein, Ludwig. *Culture and Value: A Selection from the Posthumous Remains*. Edited by Georg Henrik von Wright and Heikki Nyman. Rev. 2nd ed. Oxford: Blackwell, 1998.

———. *On Certainty*. Edited by G. E. M. Anscombe and G. H. von Wright. Translated by Denis Paul and G. E. M. Anscombe. Oxford: Blackwell, 1969.

———. *Tractatus Logico-Philosophicus*. Translated by D. F. Pears and B. F. McGuinness. London: Routledge & Kegan Paul, 1966.

Wojtyła, Karol. *Love and Responsibility*. Translated by H. T. Willetts. San Francisco: Ignatius, 1981.

———. *Über die Möglichkeit, eine christliche Ethik in Anlehnung an Max Scheler zu schaffen* [Evaluation of the possibility of constructing a christian ethics on the assumptions of Max Scheler's system of philosophy]. In *Primat des Geistes: Philosophische Schriften*, edited by Juliusz Stroynowski, 35–197. Stuttgart-Degerloch: Seewald, 1980.

Worgul, George S., Jr. *From Magic to Metaphor: A Validation of the Christian Sacraments*. New York: Paulist, 1980.

Yannaras, Christos. *On the Absence and Unknowability of God: Heidegger and the Areopagite*. Edited by Andrew Louth. Translated by Haralambos Ventis. New York: T. & T. Clark, 2005.

———. *Person and Eros*. Translated by Norman Russell. Brookline, MA: Holy Cross Orthodox Press, 2007.

Young, William. *Hegel's Dialectical Method: Its Origins and Religious Significance*. Nutley, NJ: Craig, 1972.

———. "Ritual as First Phenomenology: A Response to Robert Gibbs." *Modern Theology* 16 (2000) 335–39.

Zimmerman, Joyce Ann. *Liturgy and Hermeneutics*. Collegeville, MN: Liturgical Press, 1999.

———. *Liturgy as Language of Faith: A Liturgical Methodology in the Mode of Paul Ricoeur's Textual Hermeneutics*. Lanham, MD: University Press of America, 1988.

Zimmermann, Nigel. *Facing the Other: John Paul II, Levinas, and the Body*. Eugene, OR: Cascade, 2015.

Žižek, Slavoj, and John Milbank. *The Monstrosity of Christ: Paradox or Dialectic?* Edited by Creston Davis. Cambridge, MA: MIT Press, 2011.

Zizioulas, John D. *Being as Communion: Studies in Personhood and the Church*. Crestwood, NY: St. Vladimir's Seminary Press, 1985.

———. *Communion and Otherness: Further Studies in Personhood and the Church*. Edited by Paul McPartlan. London: T. & T. Clark, 2006.

# INDEX

CPSIA information can be obtained
at www.ICGtesting.com
Printed in the USA
BVHW071813211122
652433BV00002B/95

9 781498 293396